Lecture Notes in Artificial Intelligence 2650

Edited by J. G. Carbonell and J. Siekmann

Subseries of Lecture Notes in Computer Science

Springer

Berlin
Heidelberg
New York
Barcelona
Hong Kong
London
Milan
Paris
Tokyo

Marc-Philippe Huget (Ed.)

Communication in Multiagent Systems

Agent Communication Languages and Conversation Policies

 Springer

Series Editors

Jaime G. Carbonell, Carnegie Mellon University, Pittsburgh, PA, USA
Jörg Siekmann, University of Saarland, Saarbrücken, Germany

Volume Editor

Marc-Philippe Huget
University of Liverpool, Department of Computer Science
Agent Applications, Research and Technology Group
Chadwick Building, Peach Street, L69 7ZF Liverpool, UK
E-mail: M.P.Huget@csc.liv.ac.uk

Cataloging-in-Publication Data applied for

A catalog record for this book is available from the Library of Congress.

Bibliographic information published by Die Deutsche Bibliothek.
Die Deutsche Bibliothek lists this publication in the Deutsche Nationalbibliografie;
detailed bibliographic data is available in the Internet at <http://dnb.ddb.de>.

CR Subject Classification (1998): I.2.11, I.2, C.2.4, C.2, D.2, F.3

ISSN 0302-9743
ISBN 3-540-40385-X Springer-Verlag Berlin Heidelberg New York

Springer-Verlag Berlin Heidelberg New York
a member of BertelsmannSpringer Science+Business Media GmbH

http://www.springer.de

© Springer-Verlag Berlin Heidelberg 2003
Printed in Germany

Typesetting: Camera-ready by author, data conversion by Markus Richter, Heidelberg
Printed on acid-free paper   SPIN: 10937761   06/3142   5 4 3 2 1 0

Preface

Agents in multiagent systems are concurrent autonomous entities that need to coordinate and to cooperate so as to perform their tasks (buying items on the Internet or retrieving information, for instance). These coordination and cooperation tasks might be achieved through communication. Communication (also called 'interaction' by some authors) represents one of the main elements in multiagent systems. Without communication, agents will not be able to exchange information or coordinate with each other. Research on communication has been an established field for at least 20 years and moved from early work on protocols to direct agent communication, to communication that encompasses some human conversation patterns. Between these two points, several areas are considered in agent communication: agent communication languages, coordination, argumentation, negotiation and dialogue games, to name a few.

The first idea when editing this book was to bring together several papers on different areas of agent communication, thus offering a snapshot of the domain to newcomers. As a consequence, the book is divided into three parts.

As background, we present three seminal papers in the agent communication domain: the paper written by Cohen and Perrault about the theory of speech acts, which roots the work in FIPA ACL semantics; the paper written by Singh on different agent communication languages; and, finally, the paper written by Davis and Smith describing the Contract Net protocol which is certainly the *Escherichia coli* in the domain of communication, and is the most well-known protocol and the one most used in the literature.

The second part of this book is the main one, and depicts current work in agent communication. The chapters are classified in clusters. The first cluster is about agent communication. The second cluster presents several uses of communication such as coordination and argumentation. The third cluster focuses on protocols. As stated above, protocols are no longer the only approach to represent agent communication; the remaining cluster describes dialogue games and conversational agents.

Finally, the last part of the book considers the future of agent communication.

Some chapters were accepted papers at the AAMAS 2002 Workshop on Agent Communication Languages and Conversation Policies (ACL 2002) that I co-chaired with Frank Dignum and Jean-Luc Koning.

My hope is that this book will be useful for newcomers and students in learning agent communication.

February 2003

Marc-Philippe Huget

Agent ART Group
Department of Computer Science
University of Liverpool
UK

Table of Contents

Elements of a Plan-Based
Theory of Speech Acts*

Philip R. Cohen

Bolt Beranek and Newman Inc.

AND

C. Raymond Perrault

University of Toronto

This paper explores the truism that people think about what they say. It proposes that, to satisfy their own goals, people often *plan* their speech acts to affect their listeners' beliefs, goals, and emotional states. Such language use can be modelled by viewing speech acts as operators in a planning system, thus allowing both physical and speech acts to be integrated into plans.

Methodological issues of how speech acts should be defined in a plan-based theory are illustrated by defining operators for requesting and informing. Plans containing those operators are presented and comparisons are drawn with Searle's formulation. The operators are shown to be inadequate since they cannot be composed to form questions (requests to inform) and multiparty requests (requests to request). By refining the operator definitions and by identifying some of the side effects of requesting, compositional adequacy is achieved. The solution leads to a metatheoretical principle for modelling speech acts as planning operators.

1. INTRODUCTION

The Sphinx once challenged a particularly tasty-looking student of language to solve the riddle: "How is saying 'My toe is turning blue,' as a request to get off my toe, similar to slamming a door in someone's face?" The poor student stammered that in both cases, when the agents are trying to communicate something, they have analogous intentions. "Yes indeed" countered the Sphinx, "but what are those intentions?" Hearing no reply, the monster promptly devoured the poor student and sat back smugly to wait for the next oral exam.

*The research described herein was supported primarily by the National Research Council of Canada, and also by the National Institute of Education under Contract US-NIE-C-400-76-0116, the Department of Computer Science of the University of Toronto, and by a summer graduate student associateship (1975) to Cohen from the International Business Machines Corporation.

M.-P. Huget (Ed.): Communications in Multiagent Systems, LNAI 2650, pp. 1-36, 2003.
© Cognitive Science, 1979, 177-212, 3(1)

Contemporary philosophers have been girding up for the next trek to Giza. According to Grice (1957)[1], the slamming of a door communicates the slammer's anger only when the intended observer of that act realizes that the slammer wanted both to slam the door in his face and for the observer to believe that to be his intention. That is, the slammer intended the observer to recognize his intentions. Slamming caused by an accidental shove or by natural means is not a communicative act. Similarly, saying "My toe is turning blue" only communicates that the hearer is to get off the speaker's toe when the hearer has understood the speaker's intention to use that utterance to produce that effect.

Austin (1962) has claimed that speakers do not simply produce sentences that are true or false, but rather perform speech actions such as requests, assertions, suggestions, warnings, etc. Searle (1969) has adapted Grice's (1957) recognition of intention analysis to his effort to specify the necessary and sufficient conditions on the successful performance of speech acts. Though Searle's landmark work has led to a resurgence of interest in the study of the pragmatics of language, the intentional basis of communicative acts requires further elaboration and formalization; one must state for any communicative act, precisely which intentions are involved and on what basis a speaker expects and intends those intentions to be recognized.

The Sphinx demands a competence theory of speech act communication—a theory that formally models the possible intentions underlying speech acts. This paper presents the beginnings of such a theory by treating intentions as plans and by showing how plans can link speech acts with nonlinguistic behavior. In addition, an adequacy test for plan-based speech act theories is proposed and applied.

1.1 A Plan-based Theory of Speech Acts

Problem solving involves pursuing a goal state by performing a sequence of actions from an initial state. A human problem-solver can be regarded as "executing" a *plan* that prespecifies the sequence of actions to be taken. People can construct, execute, simulate, and debug plans, and in addition, can sometimes infer the plans of other agents from their behavior. Such plans often involve the communication of beliefs, desires and emotional states for the purpose of influencing the mental states and actions of others. Furthermore, when trying to communicate, people expect and want others to recognize their plans and may attempt to facilitate that recognition.

Formal descriptions of plans typically treat actions as *operators*, which are defined in terms of applicability conditions, called *preconditions*, *effects* that will be obtained when the corresponding actions are executed, and *bodies* that describe the means by which the effects are achieved. Since operators are repre-

---

[1] See also (Strawson, 1964; Schiffer, 1972)

sentations, their preconditions, effects, and bodies are evaluated relative to the problem-solver's model of the world. We hypothesize that people maintain, as part of their models of the world, symbolic descriptions of the world models of other people. Our plan-based approach will regard speech acts as operators whose effects are primarily on the models that speakers and hearers maintain of each other.[2]

Any account of speech acts should answer questions such as:

—Under what circumstances can an observer believe that a speaker has sincerely and successfully performed a particular speech act in producing an utterance for a hearer? (The observer could also be the hearer or speaker.)

—What changes does the successful performance of a speech act make to the speaker's model of the hearer, and to the hearer's model of the speaker?

—How is the meaning (sense/reference) of an utterance x related to the acts that can be performed in uttering x?

To achieve these ends, a theory of speech acts based on plans should specify at least the following:

—A planning system: a formal language for describing states of the world, a language for describing operators, a set of plan construction inferences, a specification of legal plan structures. Semantics for the formal languages should also be given.

—Definitions of speech acts as operators in the planning system. What are their effects? When are they applicable? How can they be realized in words?

As an illustration of this approach, this paper presents a simple planning system, defines the speech acts of requesting and informing as operators within that system, and develops plans containing direct requests, informs and questions (which are requests to inform). We do not, however, discuss how those speech acts can be realized in words.

We argue that a plan-based theory, unlike other proposed theories of speech acts, provides formal adequacy criteria for speech act definitions: given an initial set of beliefs and goals, the speech act operator definitions and plan construction inferences should lead to the generation of plans for those speech acts that a person could issue appropriately under the same circumstances.[3] This adequacy criterion should be used in judging whether speech act definitions pass certain tests, in particular, the test of compositionality. For instance, since a speaker can request that a hearer do some arbitrary action, the operator definitions should show how a speaker can request a hearer to perform a speech act. Similarly, since one can inform a hearer that an action was done, the definitions should capture a speaker's informing a hearer that a speech act was performed. We show how a number of previous formulations of requesting and informing are

---

[2]This approach was inspired by Bruce and Schmidt (1974) and Bruce (1975). This paper can be viewed as supplying methodological foundations for the analyses of speech acts and their patterned use that they present.

[3]Though this could perhaps be an empirical criterion, it will be used intuitively here.

compositionally inadequate, and then develop definitions of informing that can be composed into questions.

Another goal of this research is to develop metatheoretical principles that state how to formulate speech act definitions to pass these adequacy tests. This paper proposes such a principle and shows how its application leads to compositionally adequate definitions for multiparty requests (as in "Ask Tom to open the door").

To simplify our problems in the early stages of theory construction, several restrictions on the communication situation that we are trying to model have been imposed:

—Any agent's model of another will be defined in terms of "facts" that the first believes the second believes, and goals that the first believes the second is attempting to achieve. We are not attempting to model obligations, feelings, etc.

—The only speech acts we try to model are requests, informs, and questions since they appear to be definable solely in terms of beliefs and goals. Requesting and informing are prototypical members of Searle's (1976) "directive" and "representative" classes, respectively, and are interesting since they have a wide range of syntactic realizations, and account for a large proportion of everyday utterances.

—We have limited ourselves to studying "instrumental dialogues"—conversations in which it is reasonable to assume that the utterances are planned and that the topic of discourse remains fixed. Typically, such dialogues arise in situations in which the conversants are cooperating to achieve some task-related goal (Deutsch, 1974), for example, the purchasing of some item. The value of studying such conversations relative to the structure of a task is that the conversants' plans can be more easily formalized.

1.2   A Competence Theory of Speech Acts

At least two interdependent aspects of a plan-based theory should be examined—the plans themselves, and the methods by which a person could construct or recognize those plans. This paper will be concerned with theories of the first aspect, which we shall term *competence* theories, analogous to competence theories of grammar (Chomsky, 1965). A plan-based competence theory of speech acts describes the *set of possible plans* underlying the use of particular kinds of speech acts, and thus states the conditions under which speech acts of those types are appropriate. Such descriptions are presented here in the form of a set of operator definitions (akin to grammatical "productions") and a specification of the ways in which plans are created from those operators.

The study of the second aspect aims for a *process* theory, which concerns *how* an ideal speaker/hearer chooses one (or perhaps more than one) plan out of the set of possible plans. Such a theory would characterize how a speaker decides what speech act to perform and how a hearer identifies what speech act was performed by recognizing the plan(s) in which that utterance was to play a part.

By separating out these two kinds of theoretical endeavors we are not claiming that one can study speech act competence totally divorced from issues of processing. On the contrary, we believe that for a (careful) speaker to issue a particular speech act appropriately, she must determine that the hearer's speech act recognition process(es) will correctly classify her utterance. Thus, a competence theory would state the conditions under which a speaker can make that determination—conditions that involve the speaker's beliefs about the hearer's beliefs, goals, and inferential processes.

Our initial competence theory has been embodied in a computer program (Cohen, 1978) that can construct most of the plans presented here. Programs often point out weaknesses, inconsistencies, and incorrect assumptions in the statement of the competence theory, and can provide an operational base from which to propose process theories. However, we make no claims that computational models of plan construction and recognition are cognitive process theories; such claims would require empirical validation. Moreover, it is unclear whether there could be just one process theory of intentional behavior since each individual might use a different method. A more reasonable goal, then, is to construct computational models of speech act use for which one could argue that a person could employ such methods and converse successfully.

1.3 Outline of the Paper

The thread of the paper is the successive refinement of speech act definitions to meet the adequacy criteria. First, we introduce in sections 2 and 3 the tools needed to construct plans: the formal language for describing beliefs and goals, the form of operator definitions, and a set of plan construction inferences.

As background material, section 4 summarizes Austin's and Searle's accounts of speech acts. Then, Searle's definitions of the speech acts of requesting and informing are reformulated as planning operators in section 5 and plans linking those speech acts to beliefs and goals are given. These initial operator definitions are shown to be compositionally inadequate and hence are recast in section 6 to allow for the planning of questions. Section 7 shows how the definitions are again inadequate for modelling plans for composed requests. After both revising the preconditions of requests and identifying their side effects, compositional adequacy for multiparty requests is achieved. The solution leads to a metatheoretical ''point of view'' principle for use in formulating future speech act definitions within this planning system. Finally, section 8 discusses the limitations of the formalism and ways in which the approach might be extended to handle indirect speech acts.

2. ON MODELS OF OTHERS

In this section, we present criteria that an account of one agent's (AGT1) model of another's (AGT2's) beliefs and goals ought to satisfy.[4] A theory of speech acts need not be concerned with what is actually true in the real world; it should

---

[4]The representations used by Meehan (1976), and Schank and Abelson (1977) do not, in a principled way, maintain the distinctions mentioned here for belief or want.

describe language use in terms of a person's beliefs about the world. Accordingly, AGT1's model of AGT2 should be based on "believe" as described, for example, in Hintikka (1962; 1969). Various versions of the concept "know" can then be defined to be agreements between one person's beliefs and another's.

2.1 Belief

Apart from simply distinguishing AGT1's beliefs from his beliefs about AGT2's beliefs, AGT1's belief representation ought to allow him to represent the fact that AGT2 knows *whether* some proposition P is true, without AGT1's having to know which of P or ~ P it is that AGT2 believes. A belief representation should also distinguish between situations like the following:

1. AGT2 believes that the train leaves from gate 8.
2. AGT2 believes that the train has a departure gate.
3. AGT2 knows what the departure gate is for the train.

Thus, case 3 allows AGT1 to believe *that* AGT2 knows what the departure gate is without AGT1's actually knowing which gate AGT2 thinks that is. This distinction will be useful for the planning of questions and will be discussed further in section 6.

Following Hintikka (1969), belief is interpreted as a model operator A BELIEVE(P), where A is the believing agent, and P the believed proposition.[5] This allows for an elegant, albeit too strong, axiomatization and semantics for BELIEVE. We shall point out uses of various formal properties of BELIEVE as the need arises.

A natural question to ask is how many levels of belief embedding are needed by an agent capable of participating in a dialogue? Obviously, to be able to deal with a disagreement, AGT1 needs two levels (AGT1 BELIEVE and

[5]The following axiom schemata will be assumed:

  B.1 aBELIEVE(all axioms of the predicate calculus)
  B.2 aBELIEVE(P) => aBELIEVE(aBELIEVE(P))
  B.3 aBELIEVE(P) OR aBELIEVE (Q) => aBELIEVE(P OR Q)
  B.4 aBELIEVE(P&Q) <=>aBELIEVE(P) & aBELIEVE(Q)
  B.5 aBELIEVE(P) => ~ aBELIEVE(~ P)
  B.6 aBELIEVE(P => Q) => (aBELIEVE(P) => aBELIEVE(Q))
  B.7 ∃x aBELIEVE(P(x)) => aBELIEVE(∃x P(x))
  B.8 all agents believe that all agents believe B.1 to B.7.

These axioms unfortunately characterize an idealized "believer" who can make all possible deductions from his beliefs, and doesn't maintain contradictory beliefs. Clearly, the logic should be weakened. However, we shall assume the usual possible worlds semantics of BELIEVE in which the axioms are satisfied in a model consisting of a *universe* U, a subset A of U of *agents*, a set of *possible worlds* W, and *initial world* WO in W, a *relation* R on the cross-product A × W × W, and for each world w and predicate P, a subset Pw of U called the *extension* of P in w. The truth functional connectives *and*, *or*, *not*, and => have their usual interpretations in all possible worlds. aBELIEVE(P) is true in world w if P is true in all worlds w1 such that R(a', w,w1), where a' is the interpretation of a in w. ∃x P(x) is true in world w if there is some individual i in U such that P(x) is true in w when all free occurrences of x in P are interpreted as i.

AGT1 BELIEVE AGT2 BELIEVE). If AGT1 successfully lied to AGT2, he would have to be able to believe some proposition P, while believing that AGT2 believes that AGT1 believes P is false (i.e., AGT1 BELIEVE AGT2 BELIEVE AGT1 BELIEVE ($\sim$ P)). Hence, AGT1 would need at least three levels. However, there does not seem to be any bound on the possible embeddings of BELIEVE. If AGT2 believes AGT1 has lied, he would need four levels. Furthermore, Lewis (1969) and Schiffer (1972) have shown the ubiquity of *mutual belief* in communication and face-to-face situations—a concept that requires an infinite conjunction of beliefs.[6] Cohen (1978) shows how a computer program that plans speech acts can represent beliefs about mutual beliefs finitely.

2.2 Want

Any representation of AGT2's goals (wants) must distinguish such information from: AGT2's beliefs, AGT1's beliefs and goals, and (recursively) from AGT2's model of someone else's beliefs and goals. The representation for WANT must also allow for different scopes of quantifiers. For example, it should distinguish between the readings of "AGT2 wants to take a train" as "There is a specific train that AGT2 wants to take" or as "AGT2 wants to take any train." Finally, it should allow arbitrary embeddings with BELIEVE. Wants of beliefs (as in "AGT1 WANTS AGT2 BELIEVE P") become the reasons for AGT1's telling P to AGT2, while beliefs of wants (i.e., AGT1 BELIEVES AGT1 WANTS P) will be the way to represent AGT1's goals P.[7] In modelling planning behavior, we are not concerned with goals that the agent does not think he has, nor are we concerned with the subtleties of "wish," "hope," "desire," and "intend" as these words are used in English. The formal semantics of WANT, however, are problematic.

3. MODELS OF PLANS

In most models of planning (e.g., Fikes & Nilsson, 1971; Newell & Simon, 1963), real world actions are represented by *operators* that are organized into plans.[8] To execute a plan, one performs the actions corresponding to the

---

[6]Lewis (1969) and Schiffer (1972) talk only about mutual or common knowledge, but the extension to mutual belief is obvious.

[7]This also allows a third place to vary quantifier scope, namely:

$$\exists x \text{ aBELIEVE aWANT } P(x)$$
$$\text{aBELIEVE } \exists x \text{ aWANT } P(x),$$
$$\text{aBELIEVE aWANT } \exists x P(x)$$

[8]One usually generalizes operators to *operator schemata* in correspondence with *types* of actions; operator instances are then formed by giving values to the parameters of an operator schema. Since only operator instances are contained in plans we will not distinguish between the operator schema and its instances unless necessary. The same schema/instance, type/token distinction applies as well to speech acts modelled as planning operators.

operators in that plan. An operator will be regarded as transforming the planner's model of the world, the *propositions* that the planner believes, in correspondence with the changes to the real world made by the operator's associated action.[9] An operator is *applicable* to a model of the world in which that operator's *preconditions* hold. Operators can be defined in terms of others, as stated in their *bodies* (Sacerdoti, 1975). The changes that an operator makes to the world model in which it is evaluated to produce a new world model are called that operator's *effects*.

We shall view plans for an arbitrary agent S to be constructed using (at least) the following heuristic principles of purposeful behavior:

At the time of S's planning:

1. S should not introduce in the plan actions whose effects S believes are (or will be) true at the time the action is initiated.

2. If E is a goal, an operator A that achieves E can be inserted into the plan.

3. If an operator is not applicable in the planner's belief model, all the preconditions of that operator that are not already true can be added to the plan.

   The previous two inferences reflect an agent's reasoning "in order to do this I must achieve that."

4. If the planner needs to know the truth-value of some proposition, and does not, the planner can create a goal that it know whether that proposition is true or false.

5. If the planner needs to know the value of some description before planning can continue, the planner can create a goal that it find out what the value is.

   The previous two inferences imply that the planner does not have to create an entire plan before executing part of it.

6. Everyone expects everyone else to act this way.

   Since agents can sometimes recognize the plans and goals of others, and can adopt others' goals (or their negations) as their own, those agents can plan to facilitate or block someone else's plans. Bruce and Newman (1978) and Carbonell (1978) discuss these issues at length.

The process of planning to achieve a goal is essentially a search through this space of inferences to find a temporal sequence of operators such that the first operator in the sequence is applicable in the planner's current world model and the last produces a world model in which the goal is true. A new world model is obtained by the execution of each operator.

3.1 The Form of Operators

Early approaches to problem-solving based on first order logic (Green, 1969; McCarthy & Hayes, 1969) have emphasized the construction of provably correct

---

[9]We are bypassing the fact that people need to observe the success or failure of their actions before being able to accurately update their beliefs. The formalism thus only deals with operators and models of the world rather than actions and the real world. Operators names will be capitalized while their corresponding actions will be referred to in lower case.

plans. Such approaches formalize the changes an action makes to the state of the world model by treating an operator as a predicate of one whose arguments is a *state variable*, which ranges over states of the world model. Unfortunately, to be able to reason about what is true in the world after an action is executed, one must give axiom schemata that describe which aspects of the state of the world are *not* changed by each operator. For instance, calling someone on the telephone does not change the height of the Eiffel Tower. This thorny "frame problem" (McCarthy & Hayes, 1969) occurs because individual states of the world are not related to one another *a priori*.

To overcome this problem, Fikes and Nilsson (1971) in their STRIPS planning system assume that all aspects of the world stay constant except as described by the operator's effects and logical entailments of those effects. Such an assumption is not formalized in the reasoning system, making it difficult to prove the correctness of the resulting plans. Nevertheless, it has become the standard assumption upon which to build problem-solvers. We too will make it and thus shall describe an operator's effects by the propositions that are to be added to the model of the world.[10]

All operator schemata will have two kinds of preconditions—"cando" and "want" preconditions. The former, referred to as CANDO.PRs, indicate proposition schemata that, when instantiated with the parameter values of an operator instance, yield propositions that must be true in the world model for that operator instance to be applicable. We do not discuss how they can be proven true. The "want" precondition, henceforth WANT.PR, formalizes a principle of intentional behavior—the agent of an action has to want to do that action.

The following example serves to illustrate the form of such definitions.

MOVE(AGT,SOURCE,DESTINATION)

CANDO.PR:	LOC(AGT,SOURCE)
WANT.PR:	AGT BELIEVE AGT WANT move-instance
EFFECT:	LOC(AGT, DESTINATION)

The parameters of an operator scheme are stated in the first line of the definitions and it is assumed that values of these parameters satisfy the appropriate selectional restrictions, (here, a person, and two locations, respectively). The WANT.PR uses a parameter "move-instance" that will be filled by any instance of the MOVE operator schema that is currently being planned, executed, or recognized. The CANDO.PR states that before an agent can move from the SOURCE location, he must be located there. The EFFECT of the MOVE indicates that the agent's new location is the DESTINATION.

S's plan to achieve goal G is pictured schematically in Figure 1 (P and Q are arbitrary agents, A1 and A2 are arbitrary actions). Instead of indicating the entire state of the planner's beliefs after each operator, those propositions that are effects of an operator and are preconditions of some other operator in the plan are presented.

[10]Those propositions that need to be deleted (or somehow made "invisible" in the *current* worlmodel) will not be discussed here.

S BELIEVE S WANT:

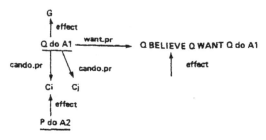

Figure 1.   A schematic of S's plan to achieve G.

This diagram illustrates the building block of plans—given goal G, S applies an inference of type 2 and selects operator A1, whose agent is Q as a producer of that effect. That operator is applicable when preconditions Ci and Cj hold and when agent Q wants to perform A1. Type 3 inferences allow each of the preconditions to be achieved by other actions (e.g., A2), which may be performed by another agent (e.g., P). This chaining of operators continues until all preconditions are satisfied. Plan diagrams are thus read from ''top'' to ''bottom''.

To indicate that this schematic is part of agent S's plan, the plan components are ''embedded'' in what S BELIEVE S WANTs. The truth or falsity of preconditions is evaluated with respect to S's beliefs. For example, verifying the WANT.PR of operator A1 (i.e., Q BELIEVE Q WANT Q do A1) would involve establishing that S BELIEVE Q BELIEVE Q WANT Q do A1. If Q is the same person as S (i.e., S is planning her own action A1) then this condition is trivially true since A1 is already part of S's plan, and since for all agents R, we assume that if R BELIEVE (P) then R BELIEVE R BELIEVE (P). However, if Q is not the same as S, the WANT.PR also needs to be achieved, leading, as we shall see, to S's planning a speech act.

4.   SPEECH ACTS

4.1   Austin's Performatives

Austin (1962) notes a peculiar class of declarative utterances, which he termed *performatives*, that do not state facts but rather constitute the performance of an action. For instance saying, ''I hereby suggest you leave'' is an act of suggesting. Unlike the usual declaratives, such sentences are not true or false, but rather are subject to the same kinds of failures (''infelicities'') as nonlinguistic actions—such as being applied in the wrong circumstances or being performed insincerely.

Generalizing further, Austin claims that in uttering any sentence, one performs three types of speech acts: the *locutionary*, *illocutionary*, and *perlocution-*

ary acts. A speaker performs a *locutionary* act by making noises that are the uttering of words in language satisfying its vocabulary and grammar, and by the uttering of sentences with definite meaning (though perhaps having more than one). Such acts are used in the performance of *illocutionary acts* which are those acts performed *in* making utterances. For instance, stating, requesting, warning, ordering, apologizing, are claimed to be different types of illocutionary acts, each of which is said to have a unique *illocutionary force* that somehow characterizes the nature of the act. Each illocutionary act contains *propositional content* that specifies what is being requested, warned about, ordered, etc.

New distinctions, however, bring new problems. Frequently, when performative verbs are not used, the utterance's illocutionary force is not directly interpretable from its content. For example, to understand the force of the utterance "The door," the hearer may need to use his beliefs that the door is currently closed, that the speaker has two arm-loads of groceries, and that he wants to be on the other side of the door in determining that the speaker has requested that the door be opened. Furthermore, a speaker may appear to be performing one illocutionary act, and actually may be trying to use it to do something else. Thus, "We have to get up early tomorrow" may simply be an assertion but when said at a party, may be intended as an excuse to the host for leaving, *and* may be intended as a request that the hearer leave. Such *indirect speech acts* (Gordon & Lakoff, 1971; Searle, 1975) are the touchstone of any theory of speech acts.

The last major kind of act identified by Austin is the *perlocutionary* act—the act performed *by* making an utterance. For instance, with the illocutionary act of asserting something, I may *convince* my audience of the truth of the corresponding proposition (or *insult* or *frighten* them). Perlocutionary acts produce *perlocutionary effects*: convincing produces belief and frightening produces fear. While a speaker often has performed illocutionary acts with the goal of achieving certain perlocutionary effects, the actual securing of those effects is beyond his control. Thus, it is entirely possible for a speaker to make an assertion, and for the audience to recognize the force of the utterance as an assertion and yet not be convinced.

4.2   Speech Acts a la Searle

Searle (1969) presents a formulation of the structure of illocutionary acts (henceforth referred to simply as speech acts) by suggesting a number of necessary and sufficient conditions on their successful performance. He goes on to state rules corresponding to these conditions, for a speaker's using any "indicator of illocutionary force" to perform a particular speech act.

As an example, let us consider Searle's conditions for a speaker S, in uttering T, to request that some hearer H do action A. The conditions are grouped as follows:

Normal Input/Output Conditions. These include such conditions as: H is not deaf and S is not mute, joking, or acting.

Propositional Content Conditions. Literal speech acts only use propositions of certain forms. The restrictions on these forms are stated in the *propositional content conditions*. For a request, the proposition must predicate a future act of H.

Preparatory Condition. A preparatory condition states what must be true in the world for a speaker to felicitously issue the speech act. For a request, the preparatory conditions include:

— H is able to do A.
— S believes H is able to do A.
— It is not obvious to S and H that H will do A in the normal course of events (the "non-obviousness" condition).

Searle claims the non-obviousness condition is not peculiar to illocutionary acts. This paper will support his claim by showing how the condition can be applied more generally to rational, intentional behavior.

Sincerity Condition. A *sincerity condition* distinguishes a sincere performance of the speech act from an insincere one. In the case of a request, S must want H to do A; for a promise, S must intend to do the promised action; for an assertion, S must believe what he is asserting.

Essential Condition. An *essential condition* specifies what S was trying to do. For a request, the act is an attempt to get H to do A.

Force Condition (our terminology). The purpose of the *force condition* is to require that the speaker utter a speech act only if he intends to communicate that he is performing that act. "Intending to communicate" involves having certain intentions regarding how the hearer will recognize the force of the utterance. The basic idea is that it is intended that the hearer recognize that the speaker is trying to bring about the satisfaction of the essential condition. For a request this amounts to the speaker's wanting the hearer to realize the speaker intends for him to do A.

5. A FIRST REFORMULATION OF SEARLE'S CONDITIONS

Searle (1969) unfortunately does not supply justifications for the adequacy of his definitions for various kinds of speech acts. A primary goal of this paper is to show how a plan-based theory provides the basis for such adequacy criteria by allowing one to see clearly how changes in speech act definitions affect the plans that can be generated.

A second, more specific point of this formulation exercise is to show which of Searle's conditions are better regarded as pertaining to more general aspects of intentional behavior than to particular speech acts. In this spirit, we show how the sincerity condition, which we shall argue is a misnomer, and the propositional content and "non-obviousness" conditions arise during the course of planning. Concerning the remaining conditions, we assume the "normal input/output conditions," but have chosen not to deal with the force condition until we have a better understanding of the plans for speech acts and how they can be recognized. The remaining conditions, the preparatory and essential conditions, will be mapped into the formalism as the preconditions and effects of speech act operators.

5.1 First Definition of REQUEST

Searle claims the preparatory conditions are required for the "happy" performance of the speech act—where "happy" is taken to be synonymous with Austin's use of "felicitous." Austin was careful to distinguish among infelicities, in particular, misapplications (performing the act in the wrong circumstances), and flaws (incorrectly performing the act). We take Searle's preparatory conditions as conditions guaranteeing applicability rather than successful performance, allowing them to be formalized as preconditions. Thus if an operator's preconditions are not satisfied when it is performed, then the operator was "misapplied." Before expressing preconditions in a formalism, a systematic "point of view" must be adopted. Since the applicability conditions affect the planning of that speech act, the preconditions are stated as conditions on the speaker's beliefs and goals. Correspondingly, the effects describe changes to the hearer's mental state.[11] We establish a *point-of-view principle*, that is intended to be a guideline for constructing speech act definitions in *this* planning system—namely: preconditions begin with "speaker believe" and effects with "hearer believe."

Let us consider Searle's preparatory conditions for a request: H is able to do ACT, and S believes H is able to do ACT. From our discussion of "belief," it should be clear what H can *in fact* do, i.e., what the real world is like is not essential to the success of a request. What may be relevant is that S and/or H thinks H can do ACT. To formalize "is able to do A," we propose a predicate CANDO (Q,ACT) that is true if the CANDO.PR's of ACT are true (with person Q bound to the agent role of ACT).[12]

The essential condition, which is modeled as the EFFECT of a REQUEST,

---

[11]This does not violate our modelling just one person's view since a speaker, after having issued a speech act, will update his beliefs to include the effects of that speech act, which are defined in terms of the hearer's beliefs.

[12]This should be weakened to " . . . are true or are easily achievable"—i.e. if Q can plan to make them true.

is based on a separation of the illocutionary act from its perlocutionary effect. Speakers, we claim, cannot influence their hearers' beliefs and goals directly. The EFFECTs of REQUEST are modeled so that the hearer's actually wanting to do ACT is not essential to the successful completion of the speech act. Thus, the EFFECT is stated as the hearer's believing the speaker wants him to do the act. For important reasons, to be discussed in section 5.7, this formulation of the essential condition will prove to be a major stumbling block.

The operator REQUEST from SPEAKER to HEARER to do action ACT, which represents a literal request, can now be defined as:

```
REQUEST(SPEAKER,HEARER,ACT)

CANDO.PR:       SPEAKER BELIEVE HEARER CANDO ACT
                    AND
                SPEAKER BELIEVE
                    HEARER BELIEVE HEARER CANDO ACT
WANT.PR:        SPEAKER BELIEVE SPEAKER WANT request-instance
EFFECT:         HEARER BELIEVE
                    SPEAKER BELIEVE SPEAKER WANT ACT
```

5.2 Mediating Acts and Perlocutionary Effects

To bridge the gap between REQUESTs and the perlocutionary effect for which they are planned, a mediating step named CAUSE-TO-WANT is posited, that models what it takes to get someone to want to do something. Our current analysis of this "act" trivializes the process it is intended to model by proposing that to get someone to want to do something, one need only get that person to know that you want them to do it.

The definition of an agent's (AGT1) causing another agent (AGT) to want to do ACT is:

```
CAUSE-TO-WANT (AGT1,AGT,ACT)

CANDO.PR:       AGT BELIEVE
                    AGT1 BELIEVE AGT 1 WANT ACT
EFFECT:         AGT BELIEVE AGT WANT ACT
```

The plan for a REQUEST is now straightforward. REQUEST supplies the necessary precondition for CAUSE-TO-WANT (as will other act combinations). When the WANT.PR of some action that the speaker is planning for someone else to perform, is not believed to be true, the speaker plans a REQUEST. For example, assume a situation in which there are two agents, SYSTEM[13](S) and JOHN, who are located inside a room (i.e., they are at location INROOM). Schematically, to get JOHN to leave the room by moving himself to location

---

[13]The agent who creates plans will often be referred to as "SYSTEM," which should be read as "planning system."

OUTROOM, the plan would be as in Figure 2. Notice that the WANT.PR of the REQUEST itself, namely

> S BELIEVE
> S WANT
> REQUEST(S,JOHN,MOVE(JOHN,INROOM,OUTROOM))

is trivially true since that particular REQUEST is already part of S's plan. The CANDO.PR's of the REQUEST are true if S believes JOHN is located INROOM and if it believes JOHN thinks so too. Thus, once the planner chooses someone else, say H, to do some action that it believes H does not yet want to do, a directive act (REQUEST) may be planned.

5.3   Comparison with Searle's Conditions for a REQUEST

Searle's "non-obviousness" condition for the successful performance of a request stated that it should not be obvious to the speaker that the hearer is about to

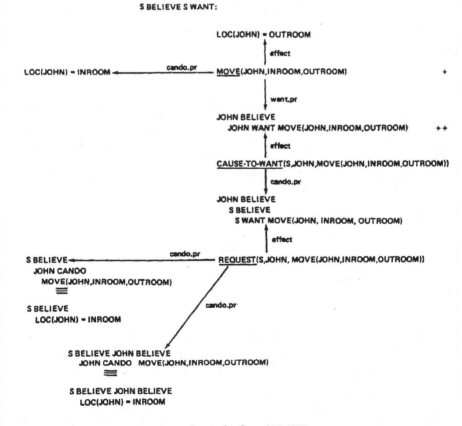

Figure 2.   A plan for a REQUEST.

do the action being requested, independently of the request. If that were obvious to the speaker, the request would be pointless. However, as Searle noted, the non-obviousness condition applies more generally to rational, intentional behavior than to speech acts alone. In our formalism, it is the WANT.PR of the act being requested (goal "++" in Figure 2). If the planning system believed the WANT.PR were already true, i.e., if it believed that John already wanted to leave the room, then the plan would proceed no further; no REQUEST would take place.

Searle's "sincerity" condition, stated that the speaker had to want the requested act to be performed. The sincerity condition in the plan of Figure 2 is the goal labeled "+." The speaker's wanting the hearer to move is the reason for planning a REQUEST.

Notice also that the propositional content of the REQUEST, a future act to be performed by the hearer, is determined by prior planning—i.e., by a combination of that act's WANT.PR, the mediating act CAUSE-TO-WANT, and by the EFFECT of a REQUEST. Searle's propositional content condition thus seems to be a function of the essential condition (which is approximated by the EFFECTs of the speech act operator), as Searle claimed. So far, we have factored out those aspects of a request that Searle suggested were eliminable. Future revisions will depart more significantly.

5.4   Definition of INFORM

The speech act of informing is represented by the operator INFORM, which is defined as a speaker's stating a proposition to a hearer for the purpose of getting the hearer to believe that the speaker believes that proposition to be true. Such acts will usually be planned on the basis of wanting the hearer to believe that proposition. For a SPEAKER to INFORM a HEARER that proposition PROP is true, we have:

INFORM(SPEAKER, HEARER, PROP)

CANDO.PR:	SPEAKER BELIEVE PROP
WANT.PR:	SPEAKER BELIEVE
	SPEAKER WANT inform-instance
EFFECT:	HEARER BELIEVE
	SPEAKER BELIEVE PROP

The CANDO.PR simply states that the only applicability condition to INFORMing someone that proposition PROP is true is that the speaker believes PROP.[14] The EFFECT of an INFORM is to communicate what the speaker believes. This allows for the hearer to refuse to believe the proposition without

---

[14]Other preconditions to the INFORM act could be added—for instance, to talk to someone one must have a communication link (Schank & Abelson, 1977); which may require telephoning or going to that person's location, etc. However, such preconditions would apply to *any* speech act, and hence probably belong on the locutionary act of making noises to someone.

invalidating the speaker's action as an INFORM. Therefore, an intermediate "act," termed CONVINCE, is necessary to get the hearer to believe the proposition.

For a person AGT 1 to CONVINCE another person AGT that proposition PROP is true, we define:

CONVINCE(AGT1, AGT, PROP)

CANDO.PR:	AGT BELIEVE
	AGT1 BELIEVE PROP
EFFECT:	AGT BELIEVE PROP

This operator says that for AGT 1 to convince AGT of the truth of PROP AGT need only believe that AGT1 thinks PROP is true. Though this may be a necessary prerequisite to getting someone to believe something, it is clearly not sufficient. For a more sophisticated precondition of CONVINCE, one might state that before AGT will be convinced, she needs to know the justifications for AGT1's belief, which may require that AGT believe (or be CONVINCE of) the justifications for believing those justifications, etc. Such a chain of reasons for believing might be terminated by mutual beliefs that people are expected to have or by a belief AGT believes AGT1 already has. Ideally, a good model of CONVINCE would allow one to plan persuasive arguments.[15]

5.5 Planning INFORM Speech Acts

The planning of INFORM speech acts now becomes a simple matter. For any proposition PROP, S's plan to achieve the goal H BELIEVE PROP would be that of Figure 3. Notice that it is unnecessary to state as a precondition to inform, that the hearer H does not already believe PROP. Again, this non-obviousness condition that can be eliminated by viewing speech acts in a planning context.

What would be Searle's sincerity condition for the INFORM above (S BELIEVE PROP) turns out to be a precondition for the speech act rather than a reason for planning the act as we had for REQUEST's sincerity condition, (i.e., SPEAKER BELIEVE SPEAKER WANT HEARER do ACT). If we were to use REQUEST as a model, the sincerity condition for an INFORM would be SPEAKER BELIEVE SPEAKER WANT HEARER BELIEVE PROP. One may then question whether Searle's sincerity condition is a consistent naming of distinctive features of various kinds of speech acts. Insincerity is a matter of falsely claiming to be in a psychological state, which for this model is either belief or want. By this definition, both conditions, SPEAKER BELIEVE PROP

---

[15]Without a specification of the justifications for a belief, this operator allows one to become convinced of the truth of one's own lie. That is, after speaker S lies to hearer H that P is true, and receives H's acknowledgment indicating H has been convinced, S can decide to believe P because he thinks H thinks so. Further research needs to be done on CONVINCE and BELIEVE to eliminate such bizarre behavior.

S BELIEVE S WANT:
H BELIEVE PROP
effect
CONVINCE (S,H,PROP)
cando.pr
H BELIEVE S BELIEVE PROP
effect
INFORM (S,H,PROP)
cando.pr
S BELIEVE PROP

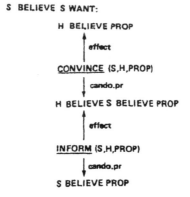

Figure 3. A plan for an INFORM.

and SPEAKER BELIEVE SPEAKER WANT HEARER BELIEVE PROP, are subject to insincerity.

5.6 Planning an INFORM of a WANT

As stated earlier, there are other ways to satisfy the precondition to CAUSE-TO-WANT. Since REQUEST was taken as a prototypical directive act, all members of that class share the same EFFECT (Searle's (1976) "illocutionary point"). However, issuing an INFORM of a WANT, as in "I want you to do X," also achieves it. Another plan to get John to move appears in Figure 4.

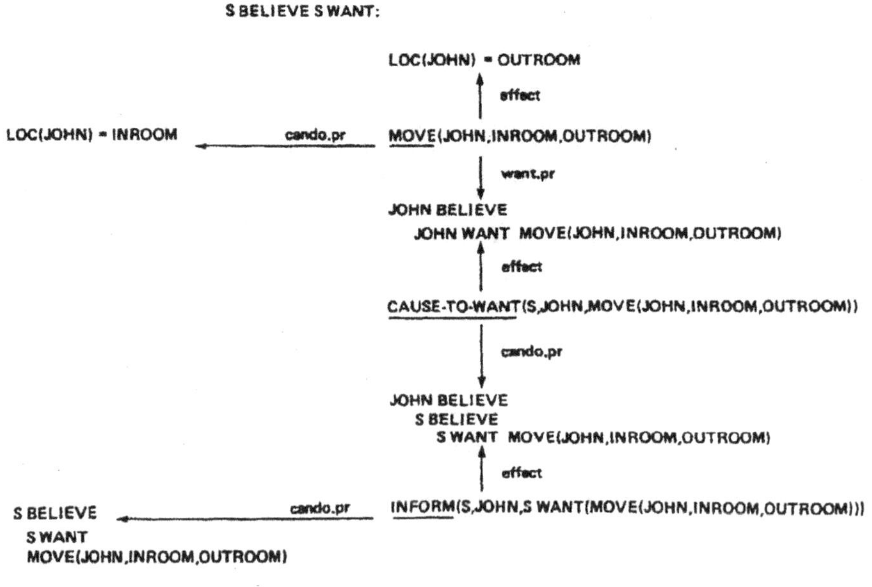

S BELIEVE S WANT:
LOC(JOHN) = OUTROOM
effect
LOC(JOHN) = INROOM
cando.pr
MOVE(JOHN,INROOM,OUTROOM)
want.pr
JOHN BELIEVE
JOHN WANT MOVE(JOHN,INROOM,OUTROOM)
effect
CAUSE-TO-WANT(S,JOHN,MOVE(JOHN,INROOM,OUTROOM))
cando.pr
JOHN BELIEVE
S BELIEVE
S WANT MOVE(JOHN,INROOM,OUTROOM)
effect
S BELIEVE
S WANT
MOVE(JOHN,INROOM,OUTROOM)
cando.pr
INFORM(S,JOHN,S WANT(MOVE(JOHN,INROOM,OUTROOM)))

Figure 4. A plan for an INFORM of a WANT.

The initial stages of this plan are identical to that of Figure 2 through the CANDO.PR of CAUSE-TO-WANT. This precondition is achieved by an IN-FORM whose propositional content is S WANT MOVE (JOHN, INROOM, OUTROOM). In this instance, the planning system does not need to proceed through CONVINCE since an INFORM of a WANT produces the necessary effects. Testing the CANDO.PR of INFORM determines if the system believes this proposition, which it does since the MOVE by John is already one of its goals. The WANT.PR of INFORM is trivially true, as before, and thus the plan is complete.

5.7   REQUEST vs. INFORM of WANT

Searle claimed that the conditions he provided were necessary and jointly suffi-cient for the successful and nondefective performance of various illocutionary acts. Any behavior satisfying such a set of conditions was then said to be a particular illocutionary act. Thus, if two utterances have the same illocutionary force, they should be equivalent in terms of the conditions on their use. We believe that the two utterances "please open the door" and "I want you to open the door (please)" *can* have the same force as directives, differing only in their politeness. That is, they both *can be* planned for the same reasons. However, our treatment does not equate the literal speech acts that could realize them when they should be equated. The condition on REQUEST that distinguishes the two cases is the precondition SPEAKER BELIEVE HEARER BELIEVE HEARER CANDO ACT. Since there is no corresponding precondition in the plan for the INFORM of a WANT, there is no reason to check the hearer's beliefs.

In order to force an equivalence between a REQUEST and an INFORM of a WANT, various actions need to be redefined. We shall remove the above condition as a CANDO.PR from REQUEST and add it as a new CANDO.PR to CAUSE-TO-WANT. In other words, the new definition of CAUSE-TO-WANT would say that you can get a person to decide to want to do some action if she believes you want her to do it and if she believes she can do it. With these changes, both ways of getting someone to want to do some action would involve her believing she is able to do it. More formally, we now define:

REQUEST (SPEAKER, HEARER, ACT)

CANDO.PR:	SPEAKER BELIEVE HEARER CANDO ACT
WANT.PR:	SPEAKER BELIEVE SPEAKER WANT request-instance
EFFECT:	HEARER BELIEVE
	SPEAKER BELIEVE SPEAKER WANT ACT

CAUSE-TO-WANT (AGT1, AGT, ACT)

CANDO.PR:	AGT BELIEVE
	AGT1 BELIEVE AGT1 WANT ACT
	AND
	AGT BELIEVE AGT CANDO ACT
EFFECT:	AGT BELIEVE AGT WANT ACT

Though REQUEST and INFORM of a WANT can achieve the same effect, they are not interchangeable. A speaker (S), having previously said to a hearer (H) ''I want you to do X,'' can deny having the intention to get H to want to do X by saying ''I simply told you what I wanted, that's all.'' It appears to be much more difficult, however, after having requested H to do X, to deny the intention of H's wanting to do X by saying ''I simply requested you to do X, that's all.'' S usually plans a request for the purpose of getting H to want to do some act X by means of getting H to believe that S wants H to do it. While maintaining the distinction between illocutionary acts and perlocutionary effects, thus allowing for the possibility that H could refuse to do X, we need to capture this distinction between REQUEST and INFORM of WANT. The solution (Allen, 1979; Perrault & Allen, forthcoming) lies in formulating speech act bodies as plans achieving the perlocutionary effect—plans that a hearer is intended to recognize.

In the next two sections, we investigate the compositional adequacy of these operator definitions via the planning of REQUESTs that a hearer perform REQUEST or INFORM speech acts.

6. COMPOSITIONAL ADEQUACY: QUESTIONS

We are in agreement with many others, in proposing that questions be treated as requests for information. In terms of speech act operators, the questioner is performing a REQUEST that the hearer perform an INFORM. That is, the REQUEST leads to the satisfaction of INFORM's "want precondition." However, for a wh-question, the INFORM operator as defined earlier cannot be used since the questioner does not know the full proposition of which he is to be informed. If he did know what the proposition was there would be no need to ask; he need only decide to believe it.

Intuitively, one plans a wh-question to find out the value of some expression and a yes/no question to find out whether some proposition is true. Such questions are planned, respectively, on the basis of believing *that* the hearer knows what the value of that expression is or *that* the hearer knows whether the proposition is true, without the speaker's having to know what the hearer believes.

Earlier we stated that a person's (AGT1) belief representation should represent cases like the following distinctly:

1. AGT2 believes the Cannonball Express departs at 8 p.m.
2. AGT2 believes the Cannonball Express has a departure time.
3. AGT2 knows what the departure time for the Cannonball Express is.

Case 1 can be represented by a proposition that contains no variables. Case 2 can be represented by a belief of a quantified proposition—i.e.,

> **AGT2 BELIEVE**
>
> ∃x (the y : DEPARTURE-TIME(CANNONBALL-EXPRESS,y)) = x)

However, Case 3 can be approximated by a *quantified belief*, namely,

> ∃x AGT2 BELIEVE
>
> (the y : DEPARTURE-TIME(CANNONBALL-EXPRESS,y)) = x),

where "the y : P(y)," often written "ɿy P(y)," is the logical description operator read "the y which is P." This formula is best paraphrased as "there is something which AGT2 believes to be the departure time for the Cannonball Express."[16] Typical circumstances in which AGT1 might acquire such quantified beliefs are by understanding a definite description uttered by AGT2 referentially (Donnellan, 1966). Thus, if AGT2 says "the pilot of TWA 461 on July 4," AGT1 might infer that AGT2 knows who that pilot is.

Quantified beliefs often become goals when a planner needs to know the values of the parameters of an operator and when these parameters occur in that operator's preconditions.[17] We show how, when a quantified belief is a goal for AGT, AGT can plan a wh-question.

6.1 Planning Wh-Questions

First, a new operator, INFORMREF, and its associated mediating act CONVINCEREF, are needed.[18]

> <u>INFORMREF(SPEAKER,HEARER, λxDx) (i.e., D is a predicate of one argument)</u>
>
> CANDO.PR: ∃y SPEAKER BELIEVE (ɿxDx) = y
>
> WANT.PR: SPEAKER BELIEVE SPEAKER WANT informref-instance
>
> EFFECT: ∃y HEARER BELIEVE SPEAKER BELIEVE (ɿxDx) = y

---

[16]Another conjunction can be added to the representation of (3) as suggested by Allen (1979) to refine our representations of "AGT2's knowing what the value of the description is," namely:

$$∃x \left[(\text{the } y: D(y) = x \ \& \ \text{AGT2 BELIEVE } ((\text{the } y: D(y)) = x) \right]$$

We shall, however, use the simpler quantified belief formulation.

[17]We would prefer to formalize declaratively that "the agent of an action must know the values of the parameters of the action." One way of doing this is suggested by Moore (1979).

[18]In Cohen (1978) we achieved the same effect by parameterizing INFORM and CONVINCE so that different sets of preconditions and effects were used if the original goal was a quantified belief. In addition, Cohen (1978) did not use descriptions. We believe the formulation that follows, due to J. Allen, is clearer. The actual names for these acts were suggested by W. Woods.

Thus, before a speaker will inform a hearer of the value of some description, there must be some individual that the speaker believes is the value of the description, and the speaker must want to say what it is. The effect of performing this act is that there is then some individual that the hearer thinks the speaker believes to be the value of the description. As usual, we need a mediating act to model the hearer's then believing that individual to be the value of the description. To this end, we define AGT1's convincing AGT of the referent of the description as:

CONVINCEREF(AGT1,AGT, λxDx)

CANDO.PR: ∃y AGT BELIEVE AGT1 BELIEVE (ixDx) = y

EFFECT: ∃y AGT BELIEVE (ixDx) = y

Using these operators, if the planning system wants to know where Mary is and believes that Joe knows where she is, it can create the plan underlying the question "Where is Mary?" as is shown in Figure 5. After the system plans for Joe to tell it Mary's location, on the basis of believing that he knows where she is, it must get Joe to want to perform this act. In the usual fashion, this leads to a REQUEST and hence the construction of a question. The precondition to

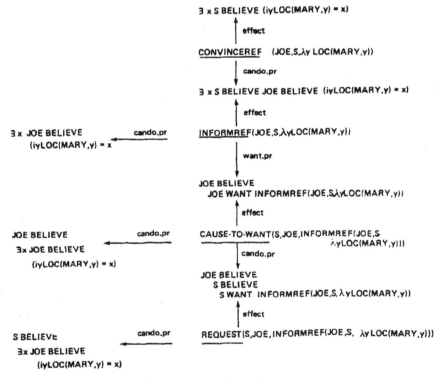

Figure 5.   A plan for a wh-question.

CAUSE-TO-WANT, namely, JOE BELIEVE JOE CANDO the INFORMREF is actually:

$$\text{JOE BELIEVE}$$
$$\exists y \text{ JOE BELIEVE}$$
$$ixLOC(MARY,x) = y$$

which is implied by

$$\exists y \text{ JOE BELIEVE } ixLOC(MARY,x) = y$$

that was asserted, for this example, to be one of the planning system's beliefs. Notice, that the planning of this question depends upon the system's having chosen Joe to tell it the answer, and upon its having chosen itself to get Joe to want to perform the INFORM. Section 7 discusses what happens when different decisions are made.

6.2 Plans for Yes/No Questions

To plan a yes/no question about some proposition P, one should think that the hearer knows whether P is true or false (or, at least "might know"). An approximate representation of AGT2's knowing whether P is true or false is OR (AGT2 BELIEVE P, AGT2 BELIEVE ~ P)).[19] Such goals are often created, as modelled by our type 4 inference, when a planner does not know the truth-value of P. Typical circumstances in which an agent may acquire such disjunctive beliefs about another are telephone conversations, in which AGT1 believes that there are certain objects in AGT2's view. AGT1 then probably believes that AGT2 knows whether certain visually derivable (or easily computable) properties of those objects are true, such as whether object A is on top of object B.

   To accommodate yes/no questions into the planning system, a third INFORM, called INFORMIF, and its associated mediating act CONVINCEIF are defined as follows:

INFORMIF(SPEAKER,HEARER,P)

CANDO.PR:	OR(SPEAKER BELIEVE P, SPEAKER BELIEVE ~ P)
EFFECT:	OR(HEARER BELIEVE SPEAKER BELIEVE P,
	HEARER BELIEVE SPEAKER BELIEVE ~ P)
WANT.PR:	SPEAKER BELIEVE SPEAKER WANT informif-instance

CONVINCEIF(AGT,AGT1,P)

CANDO.PR:	OR(AGT BELIEVE AGT1 BELIEVE P,
	AGT BELIEVE AGT1 BELIEVE ~ P)
EFFECT:	OR(AGT BELIEVE P, AGT BELIEVE ~ P)

[19]Allen (1979) also points out that another conjunct can be added to the representation of "knowing whether" as a disjunctive belief, to obtain (P & AGT2 BELIEVE (P)) OR (~ P & AGT2 BELIEVE (~ P)).

The plan for a yes/no question to Joe is now parallel to that of a wh-question.[20] That is, in the course of planning some other act, if the system wants proposition P to be true or to be false, and if the truth-value of proposition P is unknown to it, it can create the goal OR(SYSTEM BELIEVE P, SYSTEM BELIEVE ~ P). For instance if P were LOC(MARY,INROOM), the illocutionary acts underlying the question to Joe "Is Mary in the room?" can be planned provided the planning system believes that Joe either believes P is true or he believes P is false. That disjunctive belief could be stated directly or could be inferred from a belief like $\exists y$ JOE BELIEVE(ixLOC(MARY,x)) = y—i.e., there is something Joe believes is Mary's location. But if it had some idea where Joe thought Mary was, say OUTROOM, then it would not need to ask.

6.3 Summary

A plan for a question required the composition of REQUEST and INFORM and led to the development of two new kinds of informing speech acts, INFORMREF and INFORMIF, and their mediating acts. The INFORMREF acts lead to "what," "when," and "where" questions while INFORMIF results in a yes/no question.[21] The reason for these new acts is that, in planning a REQUEST that someone else perform an INFORM act, one only has incomplete knowledge of their beliefs and goals; but an INFORM, as originally defined can only be planned when one knows what is to be said.

7. COMPOSITIONAL ADEQUACY AND THE POINT OF VIEW PRINCIPLE

Earlier, a guiding "Point of View Principle" (POVP) for defining speech acts as planning operators was proposed: the preconditions of the operator should be stated from the speaker's point of view, i.e., in terms of the speaker beliefs; the effects should be stated from the hearer's point of view. We now wish to judge the adequacy of speech act definitions formulated along these lines. The test case

---

[20]Searle (1969) suggested there were different speech acts for real and teacher-student (or exam) questions, where in the latter case, the questioner just wants to know what the student thinks is the answer. Since teacher-student questions seem to have similar conditions on their appropriateness as real questions, save the questioner's intention to be convinced, we have good reason for factoring the mediating acts out of each of the three INFORM act types. This leaves the INFORM acts neutral with respect to what kind of question they are contained in. In general, if the perlocutionary effects of an INFORM were incorporated into the act's definition, then we would need two new primitive teacher-student question speech acts. For now, we opt for the former.

[21]The language for stating operators needs to be extended to account for "which," "how," and "why" questions. For instance, "why" and "how" questions involve quantifying over actions and/or plans.

will be the composing of REQUESTs, i.e., the planning of a REQUEST that some third party himself perform a REQUEST. For instance, the utterance "Ask Tom to tell you where the key is" is an example of such a third party request.

The current definitions of speech acts will be shown to be compositionally inadequate since they force speakers to have unnecessary knowledge about intermediaries' beliefs. Achieving compositional adequacy, however, requires more than a simple restatement of the point of view principle; the side effects of speech act operators also must be considered.

Our scrutiny will be focused upon the seemingly innocent precondition to REQUEST, SPEAKER BELIEVER HEARER CANDO ACT whose form depended on the POVP. The goal is to show how the POVP leads us astray and how a formulation of that precondition according to a new POVP that suggests a more neutral point of view for speech act definitions sets us back on course. From here on, the two versions of the precondition will be referred to as the "speaker-based" and "neutral" versions.

7.1 Plans for Multiparty Speech Acts

Multiparty speech acts can arise in conversations where communication is somehow restricted so as to pass through intermediaries.[22] The planning system, since it is recursive, can generate plans for such speech acts using any number of intermediaries provided that appropriate decisions are made as to who will perform what action.

Let us suppose that the planning system wants to know where a particular key is and that it must communicate through John. We shall use the speaker-based precondition on REQUEST for this example, and for readibility, the following abbreviations:

SYSTEM—S	TOM—T	JOHN—J
BELIEVE—B	WANT—W	LOC(KEY23,y)—D(y)

Figure 6 shows the plan for the specific three-party speech act underlying "Ask Tom to tell me where the key is."

S develops the plan in the following fashion: T is chosen to tell S the key's location since, we shall assume, he is believed to know where it is. Since T is not believed to already want to tell, and since S cannot communicate directly with T (but T can communicate with S), J is chosen to be the one to talk T into telling. Since J is not believed to already want to do that, S plans a REQUEST that J perform a REQUEST, namely REQUEST(S,J,REQUEST (J,T,INFORMREF (T,S,λyLOC (KEY23,y)))). J, then, is an intermediary who is just expected to do what he is asked; his status will be discussed soon.

---

[22]For instance, in the Stanford Research Institute Computer-based Consultant research (Deutsch, 1974) communication between an expert and an apprentice was constrained in this way. The apprentice typically issued such speech acts, while the expert did not.

The preconditions that need to be satisfied in this plan are:

S BELIEVE:

(P1) $\exists y$ T BELIEVE $\left[ixLOC(KEY23,x)=y \right]$

(P2) T BELIEVE (P1) (implied by P1)

(P3) J BELIEVE (P1)

(P4) J BELIEVE J BELIEVE (P1) (implied by P3)

(P5) S BELIEVE J BELIEVE (P1) (implied by P3)

S BELIEVE S WANT:

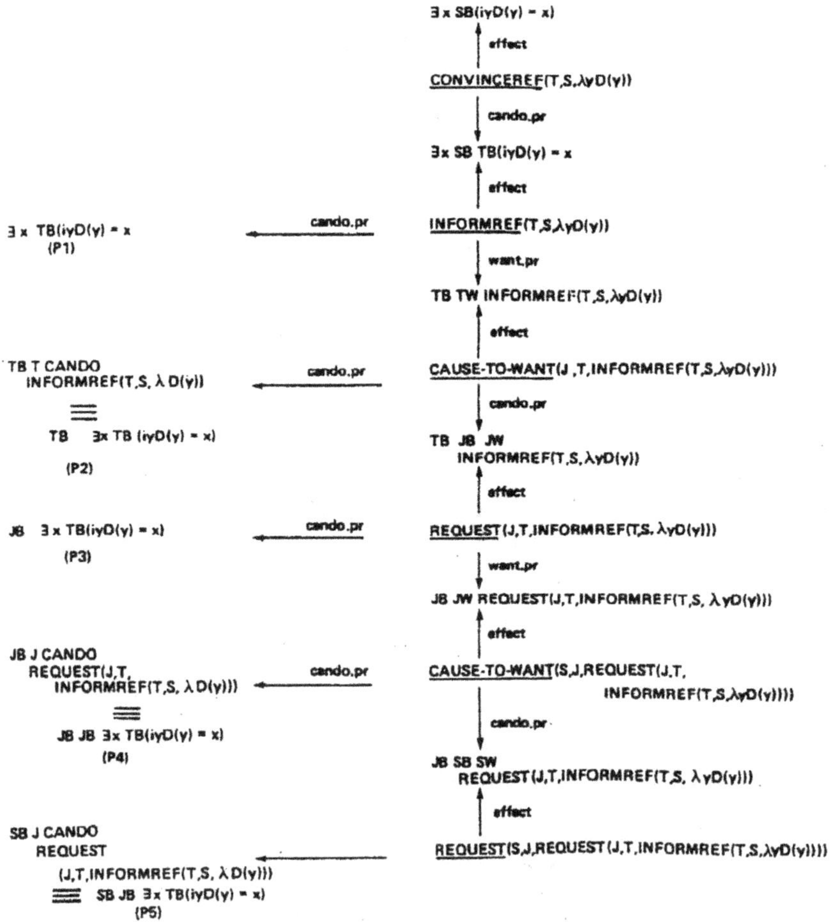

Figure 6.   A plan for a third party REQUEST.

While the plan appears to be straightforward, precondition P3 is clearly unnecessary—S ought to be able to plan this particular speech act without having any *prior* knowledge of the intermediary's beliefs. This prior knowledge requirement comes about because precondition P5 is constructed by composing

REQUEST's precondition schema with precondition P3, and P3 is similarly constructed from P1.

The problem can be eliminated by reformulating REQUEST's precondition as HEARER CANDO ACT. Consider a general plan for three-party REQUESTs, as in Figure 7. T's INFORMREF has been generalized to "ACT(T)" whose precondition is "P."

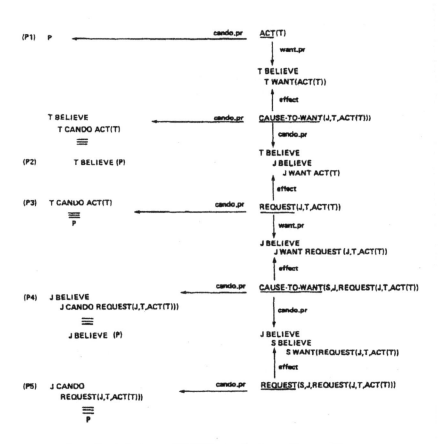

Figure 7.   A third party REQUEST using the "neutral" precondition.

The preconditions that have to be satisfied in S's plan are:

S BELIEVE:

(P1) P (also P3 and P5)

(P2) T BELIEVE (P)

(P4) J BELIEVE (P)

Conditions P3 and P5 are the same as P1, and thus the preconditions to the REQUESTs in the plan, are independent of the speaker's beliefs; they depend only on *the planner's* beliefs. While the use of the neutral precondition eliminates prior knowledge requirements for REQUESTs *per se*, condition P4 still requires, as a precondition to CAUSE-TO-WANT, that the planner have some knowledge of the intermediary's beliefs. The next section shows why the planner need not have such beliefs at the time of plan construction.

7.2   Side Effects

The performance of a speech act has thus far been modeled as resulting in an EFFECT that is specific to each speech act type. But, by the very fact that a speaker has attempted to perform a particular speech act, a hearer learns more—on identifying which speech act was performed, a hearer learns that the speaker believed the various preconditions in the *plan* that led to that speech act held. The term *side effect* will be used to refer to the hearer's acquisition of such beliefs by way of the performance of a speech act. Since the plan the hearer infers for the

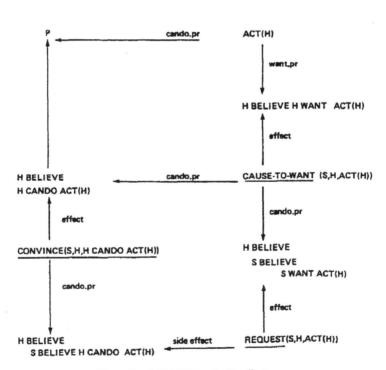

Figure 8.   A REQUEST with side effects.

speaker depends upon his beliefs about the speaker's beliefs and goals, the side effects of a speech act cannot be specified in advance. However, the hearer is minimally entitled to believe the speaker thought her speech act's preconditions held (Bruce, 1975; Bruce & Schmidt, 1974).[23] Furthermore, not only do hearers make such assumptions about speakers' beliefs, but speakers know that and often depend on those assumptions for the success of their plans. Figure 8 is a schematic of a simple plan by S to REQUEST H to do action ACT that illustrates this situation.

The minimal side effect is that the hearer believes the speaker believes the precondition of the REQUEST holds, i.e., that HEARER BELIEVE SPEAKER BELIEVE HEARER CANDO ACT. This goal satisfies, via a CONVINCE, the CANDO.PR of CAUSE-TO-WANT, and hence the REQUEST achieves two goals in the plan.[24] The schematic can be applied twice in Figure 7 to obtain Figure 9.

After the side effects of J's REQUEST to T take hold, T would think J believes the preconditions to J's REQUEST (P) obtain. We claim that it is because T thinks that J believes P that T comes to believe P. In this way, precondition (P2) is satisfied as a result of J's REQUEST. Naturally, the side effect argument applies equally to J as the hearer of S's REQUEST. That is, J comes to believe P (precondition (P4)) because he thinks S believes P. S's belief that the preconditions to action A hold thus gets "passed" down the line of intermediaries, whatever its length, to the final agent of A. In this way S can issue the third party REQUEST without having any prior knowledge of J's beliefs about P; S's REQUEST provides all the necessary information!

An interesting aspect of this transmission is that, while J may come to believe P and, by making a REQUEST to T, transmit this belief, T's belief *that* P may be of little use to T. Consider Figure 9 again. Suppose P were

$$\exists y \; T \; BELIEVE \; (ixLOC(KEY23,x)) = y$$

which we are loosely paraphrasing as T knows where the key is. S's REQUEST conveys S's belief *that* T knows where the key is. Though J, to decide to perform his REQUEST, need only think *that* T knows where the key is, T actually has to know where it is before he can do A.[25] J's conveying his belief does no good

---

[23]The hearer may in fact believe those preconditions are false.

[24]The simple backward-chaining planning algorithm described in Cohen (1978) could not easily construct this plan since it ignores intermediate states of the world model that would be created after each operator's execution (i.e., after S's, and J's, REQUESTs).

[25]T cannot obtain that information from believing P since

$$\exists y \; T \; BELIEVE \; ixLOC(KEY23,x) = y \; \text{cannot be inferred from}$$
$$T \; BELIEVE \; \exists y \; T \; BELIEVE \; ixLOC(KEY23,x) = y, \; \text{by B.2 and B.7 (footnote 5).}$$

If CONVINCE can be defined so that AGT1 cannot be convinced by AGT2 that AGT1 believes something, then J could not CONVINCE T that $\exists y \; T \; BELIEVE \; ixLOC(KEY23,x) = y$ on the basis of T's thinking that J believes it.

S BELIEVE S WANT:

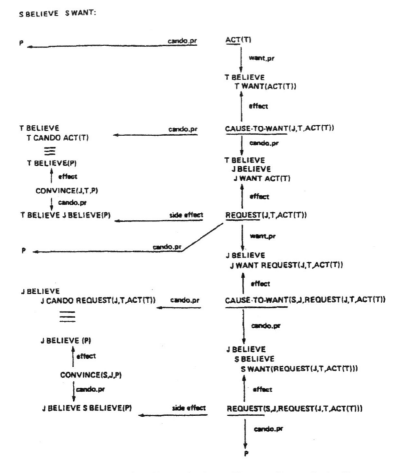

Figure 9.   A third party REQUEST using the "neutral" precondition and side effects.

since he has supplied information for a CONVINCE; but T needs information sufficient for a CONVINCEWH. A planning system has to be able to realize this and to plan, by making the same choices as before, the additional REQUEST that John perform an INFORM, e.g., "Tell Tom that the key is in the closet."[26]

7.3   A New Point-of-View Principle

In addition to considering side effects for speech acts, we are led to propose a new point-of-view principle:

> The "Cando" preconditions and effects of speech acts should be defined in a way that does not depend on who the speaker of that speech act is. That is, no CANDO.OR or EFFECT should be stated as a proposition beginning with "SPEAKER BELIEVE."

[26]The side effects again figure in this additional three-party REQUEST—John comes to believe that the key is in the closet by believing that S thinks so.

The CANDO.PRs of speech acts defined according to this principle not only resolve our difficulties with composite speech acts, but they also behave as desired for the usual noncomposite cases since preconditions now depend only on the *planner's* beliefs, and the planner is often the speaker. Thus speech act operator definitions are intimately bound to the form of the planning system.

The only result the new principle has on the form of the EFFECTs of speech acts is to make clear whose beliefs should be updated with those EFFECTs. After successfully executing a speech act to H, the speaker can update his model of H with the speech act's EFFECTs. But, for a composite speech act *ultimately* directed to H, the initial planner must observe or assume the success of the rest of the multiparty plan in order to conclude that the EFFECTs of the final speech act to H hold.

While the new principle guarantees that the EFFECTs of speech acts are independent of the use of intermediaries, hearers have every right to believe that the speakers of those speech acts believe that the preconditions hold. Because side effects are stated in terms of the hearer's beliefs about the speaker's beliefs, intermediaries are vulnerable to a charge of insincerity if they brazenly execute the speech acts they were requested to perform. It is to avoid such a charge, and thus make intermediaries "responsible for" the speech acts they execute, that we place the condition on CAUSE-TO-WANT stating that AGT BELIEVE AGT CANDO ACT.

Finally, to complete the reexamination of speech act definitions we point out that the WANT.PR also has a SPEAKER BELIEVE on it. One cannot, in the spirit of "housecleaning," remove the SPEAKER BELIEVE SPEAKER WANT from the WANT.PR of speech acts since a speaker's goal cannot be characterized independently of the speaker's beliefs, unless one is willing to model someone's "unconscious" goals. We are not.[27]

7.4   New Definitions of REQUEST and INFORM

Using this principle, REQUEST is redefined as:

REQUEST(SPEAKER,HEARER,ACT)

CANDO.PR:	HEARER CANDO ACT
WANT.PR:	SPEAKER BELIEVE
	SPEAKER WANT *request-instance*
EFFECT:	HEARER BELIEVE
	SPEAKER BELIEVE SPEAKER WANT ACT

The principle applied to the definition of the operator INFORM results in a CANDO.PR stated as PROP rather than as SPEAKER BELIEVE PROP.[28] Such a change allows one to plan to request an intermediary, say a child, to tell

---

[27]The fact that a WANT.PR is found on *every* intentional act makes us suspect that it belongs on some single "element" that is present for every act.

[28]Of course, what must be satisfied in any plan for INFORM is that the planner believe PROP.

someone else that the key is in the closet without the planner's having to believe, at the time of planning, that the child thinks so. The new definition of INFORM then becomes:

INFORM(SPEAKER,HEARER,PROP)

CANDO.PR:	PROP
WANT.PR:	SPEAKER BELIEVE
	SPEAKER WANT inform-instance
EFFECT:	HEARER BELIEVE
	SPEAKER BELIEVE PROP

Regarding the other informing speech acts, the principle cannot be used to justify the deleting of the SPEAKER BELIEVE from the CANDO.PR of IN-FORMREF and INFORMIF since the highest elements of those conditions are "∃" and "OR", respectively. Intuitively speaking, this is a sensible result since a speaker SP cannot plan for an intermediary, INT, to tell H whether P is true, or what the value of description D is unless INT is believed to have that information.

7.5 Summary

The appropriate planning of composite speech acts has turned out to be a powerful test of the adequacy of speech act definitions. To meet its demands on the planning of questions and multiparty speech acts, two new speech acts, IN-FORMREF and INFORMIF have been defined, and the preconditions to RE-QUEST and INFORM have been reformulated according to a point-of-view principle. Since these last two speech acts were taken to be prototypes of Searle's (1976) "directive" and "representative" classes, the principle will find wide application.

A side effect of direct requests was identified and used in planning multiparty speech acts. Side effects, however, cannot be calculated until the hearer has recognized the speaker's plan and thus has classified the observed utterance as a particular speech act type. Thus the minimal side effect formulation given here should be further justified on the basis of what a hearer needs to assume about the speaker's beliefs in order to identify an utterances's illocutionary force.

There may be other ways to meet compositional adequacy. For instance, one could state explicitly that an action's preconditions should be true at the time the action is to be done (Bruce, 1975). For our multiparty REQUESTS, such an approach (using a speaker-based precondition) produces preconditions like: S believes J will believe P will be true when ACT is to be done, which seems reasonable. However, the minimal side effect of S's REQUEST then becomes: J now believes that (before that REQUEST) S *expected* J to believe that P would be true when ACT is done (where "now" is just after the REQUEST was made). As yet, we do not have an analogue of CONVINCE that would allow J to then come to believe that P would be true. Again, if REQUEST is defined using the neutral precondition, this problem does not arise.

8.   CONCLUDING REMARKS

It has been argued that a theory of speech acts can be obtained by modelling them in a planning system as operators defined, at least, in terms of the speakers' and hearers' beliefs, and goals. Thus, speech acts are treated in the same way as physical acts, allowing both to be integrated into plans. Such an approach suggests new areas for application. It may provide a more systematic basis for studying real dialogues arising in the course of a task—a basis that would facilitate the tracking of conversants' beliefs and intentions as dialogue and task proceed. A similar analysis of characters' plans has also been shown (Bruce & Newman, 1978) to be essential to a satisfactory description of narrative. Finally, Allen (1979) and Cohen (1978) have suggested how computer conversants might plan their speech acts and recognize those of their users.

Given this range of application, the methodological issues of how speech acts should be modelled in a planning system become important. Specifically, a plan-based competence theory, given configurations of beliefs and goals, speech act operators, and plan construction inferences should generate plans for all and only those speech acts that are appropriate in those configurations. This paper developed tests that showed how various definitions of the speech acts of requesting and informing were inadequate, especially to the demand that they generate appropriate plans when composed with other speech acts to form questions and multiparty requests.

To resolve the difficulties, two "views" of INFORM to be used in constructing questions were defined, allowing the questioner to have incomplete knowledge of the hearer's beliefs. After revising both the form of speech act preconditions and identifying some speech act side effects, compositional adequacy for multiparty REQUESTS was achieved. The solution led to a metatheoretical "point-of-view" principle for use in defining future speech acts as operators within this planning system.

Our approach has both assumed certain idealized properties of speaker/ hearers, and has been restricted in its scope. The preconditions and effects of our operators are stated in the language of logic, not because of any desire to perform logically valid inferences, but because the conditions in the plans should have well-defined semantics. While this has been partially realized through the adoption of the possible-worlds semantics for belief, the semantics is too strong to be a faithful model of human beliefs. For instance, it leads here to requiring a questioner to have very strong, though incomplete, knowledge of the hearer's beliefs. To reflect human beliefs more accurately, one needs to model (at least): degrees of belief, justifications, the failure to make deductions, inductive leaps, and knowing what/who/where something is. These refinements, though needed by a theory of speech acts, are outside its scope. Finally, the semantics for WANT and for actions are lacking (but see Moore (1979) for an interesting approach to the latter).

Only two kinds of speech acts, prototypes of Searle's (1976) directive and representative classes, have been examined here, but the approach can be extended to other members of those classes (Bruce, 1975) and perhaps to the commissive class that includes promises. However, in order to model promises and warnings, a better understanding of the concepts of benefit and obligation is necessary.

Finally, we have so far discussed how a planning system can select illocutionary force and propositional content of a speech act, but not how utterances realizing it can be constructed nor how illocutionary acts can be identified from utterances. Extending the plan-based approach to the first area means investigating the extent of "pragmatic influence" of linguistic processing. An important subproblem here is the planning of referring expressions involved in performing illocutionary acts (Perrault & Cohen, forthcoming; Searle, 1969). Regarding speech act identification, the acid-test of a plan-based approach is its treatment of indirect speech acts (Searle, 1975). Gordon and Lakoff (1971) proposed "conversational postulates" to account for the relation between the direct or literal and the indirect illocutionary forces of an utterance. But, as Morgan (1977) notes, by calling them "postulates," one implies they cannot be explained by some other independently motivated analysis.

We suggest that the relation between direct and indirect readings can be largely accounted for by considering the relationship between actions, their preconditions, effects, and bodies, and by modelling how language users can recognize plans, which may include speech acts, being executed by others. The ability to recognize plans is seemingly required in order to be *helpful*, independent of the use of indirect speech acts. For instance, hearers often understand a speaker's utterance literally but go beyond it, inferring the speaker's plans and then performing acts that would enable the speaker's higher level goals to be fulfilled. Indirect speech acts arise because speakers can intend hearers to perform helpful inferential processing and they intend for hearers to know this. Allen (1979) and Perrault and Allen (forthcoming) formalize this process of intended plan-recognition (and thus Searle's force condition) extending our plan-based approach to the interpretation of indirect speech acts.

ACKNOWLEDGMENTS

We would like to thank Marilyn Adams, James Allen, Ron Brachman, Chip Bruce, Sharon Oviatt, Bill Woods and the referees for their comments, and Brenda Starr, Jill O'Brien, and Beverly Tobiason for their tireless assistance in the paper's preparation. Special thanks are extended to Brenda Starr for her invaluable editorial help.

REFERENCES

Allen, J. A plan-based approach to speech act recognition. Ph.D. Thesis, Technical Report No. 131/79, Dept. of Computer Science, University of Toronto, January, 1979.

Austin, J. L. *How to do things with words*. J. O. Urmson (Ed.), Oxford University Press, 1962.

Bruce, B. Belief systems and language understanding. Report No. 2973, Bolt Beranek and Newman, Inc. January, 1975.

Bruce, B., & Newman, D. Interacting plans. *Cognitive Science*, 1978, *2*, 195–233.

Bruce, B., & Schmidt, C. F. Episode understanding and belief guided parsing. Presented at the Association for Computational Linguistics Meeting at Amherst, Massachusetts (July 26–27, 1974).

Carbonell, J. G. Jr. POLITICS: Automated idealogical reasoning. *Cognitive Science*, 1978, *2*, 27–51.

Chomsky, N. *Aspects of the theory of syntax*. Cambridge, Mass. MIT Press, 1965.

Cohen, P. R. On knowing what to say: Planning speech acts. Ph.D. Thesis, Technical Report No. 118, Department of Computer Science, University of Toronto, January 1978.

Deutsch, B. G. The structure of task-oriented dialogues. In L. D. Erman (Ed.), *Proceedings of the IEEE symposium on speech recognition*. Pittsburgh, PA: Carnegie-Mellon University, 1974.

Donnellan, K. Reference and definite description. In *The Philosophical Review*, v. 75, 1960, 281–304. Reprinted in Steinberg & Jacobovits (Eds.), *Semantics*, Cambridge University Press, 1966.

Fikes, R., & Nilsson, N. J. STRIPS: A new approach to the application of theorem proving to problem solving. *Artificial Intelligence*, 1971, *2*, 189–208.

Gordon, D., & Lakoff, G. Conversational postulates. *Papers from the Seventh Regional Meeting*, Chicago Linguistic Society, 1971, 63–84.

Green, C. Application of theorem-proving techniques to problem-solving. In D. E. Walker & L. M. Norton (Eds.), *Proceedings of the international joint conference on artificial intelligence*. Washington, D.C., May 1969.

Grice, H. P. Meaning. In *The Philosophical Review*, 1957, *66*, 377–388. Reprinted in D. A. Steinberg & L. A. Jacobovits (Eds.), *Semantics: An interdisciplinary reader in philosophy, linguistics, and psychology*. New York: Cambridge University Press, 1971.

Hintikka, J. *Knowledge and belief*. Ithaca: Cornell University Press, 1962.

Hintikka, J. Semantics for propositional attitudes. In J. W. Davis et al. (Eds.), *Philosophical logic*. Dordrecht-Holland: D. Reidel Publishing Co., 1969. Reprinted in L. Linsky (Ed.), *Reference and modality*. New York: Oxford University Press, 1971.

Lewis, D. K. *Convention: A philosophical study*. Cambridge, Mass: Harvard University Press, 1969.

McCarthy, J., & Hayes, P. J. Some Philosophical Problems from the Standpoint of Artificial Intelligence. In B. Meltzer & D. Michie (Eds.) *Machine intelligence 4*, New York: American Elsevier, 1969.

Meehan, J. R. Tale-spin, an interactive program that writes stories. In *Proceedings of the fifth international joint conference on artificial intelligence*, Cambridge, Mass., 91–98.

Moore, R. C. Reasoning about knowledge and action. Ph.D. Thesis, Artificial Intelligence Laboratory, Department of Electrical Engineering and Computer Science, Massachusetts Institute of Technology, February, 1979.

Morgan, J. Conversational postulates revisited. *Language*, 1977, 277–284.

Newell, A., & Simon, H. A. GPS, A program that simulates human thought. In E. A. Feigenbaum & J. Feldman (Eds.), *Computers and thought*. New York: McGraw Hill, 1963.

Perrault, C. R., & Allen, J. F. A plan-based analysis of indirect speech acts. Forthcoming.

Perrault, C. R., & Cohen, P. R. Inaccurate Reference, *Proceedings of the workshop on computational aspects of linguistic structure and discourse setting*, Joshi, A. K., Sag, I. A., & Webber, B. L. (Eds.), Cambridge University Press, forthcoming.

Sacerdoti, E. D. A structure for plans and behavior. Ph.D. Thesis, Technical Note 109, Artificial Intelligence Center, Stanford Research Institute, Menlo Park, California, August 1975.

Schank, R., & Abelson, R. *Scripts, plans, goals, and understanding*. Hillsdale, N.J.: Lawrence Erlbaum Associates, 1977.

Schiffer, S. *Meaning*. Oxford: Oxford University Press, 1972.

Searle, J. R. A taxonomy of illocutionary acts. In K. Gunderson (Ed.), *Language mind and knowledge*, University of Minnesota Press, 1976.

Searle, J. R. Indirect speech acts. In P. Cole & J. L. Morgan (Eds.), *Syntax and semantics*, (Vol. 3), *Speech acts*. New York: Academic Press, 1975.

Searle, J. R. *Speech acts: An essay in the philosophy of language*. Cambridge: Cambridge University Press, 1969.

Strawson, P. F. Intention and convention in speech acts. In *The Philosophical Review*, v: lxxiii, 1964. Reprinted in *Logico-linguistic papers*, London: Methuen & Co., 1971.

Agent Communication Languages:
Rethinking the Principles

Munindar P. Singh

Department of Computer Science
North Carolina State University
Raleigh, NC 27695-7535, USA

singh@ncsu.edu

Abstract. Agent communication languages have been used for years in proprietary multiagent systems. Yet agents from different vendors—or even different research projects—cannot communicate with each other. The author looks at the underlying reasons and proposes a conceptual shift from individual agent representations to social interaction.

Introduction

Agents are important because they let software components interoperate within modern applications like electronic commerce and information retrieval. Most of these applications assume that components will be added dynamically and that they will be autonomous (serve different users or providers and fulfill different goals) and heterogeneous (be built in different ways). Agents can also be components themselves, which is characteristic of some promising modern systems.

Some entities are misrepresented as agents. The "agents" that marketing groups sometimes refer to, for example, are typically no more than glorified search engines or user interfaces. Such entities for the most part neither are aware of nor can communicate with other entities like them [1]. In the true sense of the word, an agent is a persistent computation that can perceive its environment and reason and act both alone and with other agents. The key concepts in this definition are *interoperability* and *autonomy*.

These concepts set agents apart from conventional objects, which always fulfill any methods invoked on them. Agents, in contrast, should be able to refuse an action. Thus, agents must be able to talk to each other to decide what information to retrieve or what physical action to take, such as shutting down an assembly line or avoiding a collision with another robot. The mechanism for this exchange is the *agent communication language.*

Theoretically, an ACL should let heterogeneous agents communicate. However, none currently do: Although ACLs are being used in proprietary multiagent applications, nonproprietary agents cannot interoperate. Many believe the fault lies in the lack of formal semantics. Past efforts to standardize on the Knowledge Query Management Language, for example, failed because many dialects arose.

M.-P. Huget (Ed.): Communications in Multiagent Systems, LNAI 2650, pp. 37–50, 2003.

The sidebar "Dialects and Idiolects" later explains in more detail how this can occur.

To provide agent interoperability, the Foundation for Intelligent Physical Agents is proposing a standard ACL based on France Télécom's Arcol. The hope is that Arcol's formal semantics will offer a rigorous basis for interoperability and prevent the proliferation of dialects. The sidebar "How Agent Communication Languages Evolved" describes how ACLs have attempted to realize these goals.

I believe this move toward a formal semantics is essential if ACLs are to unlock the full potential of agents. I am not convinced, however, that the existing work on ACLs, especially on the semantics, is heading in the right direction. It appears to be repeating the past mistake of emphasizing *mental agency*— the supposition that agents should be understood primarily in terms of mental concepts, such as beliefs and intentions. It is impossible to make such a semantics work for agents that must be autonomous and heterogeneous: This approach supposes, in essence, that agents can read each other's minds. This supposition has never held for people, and for the same reason, it will not hold for agents.

In this article, I show why an ACL's formal semantics should emphasize *social agency*. This approach recognizes that communication is inherently public, and thus depends on the agent's social context. I believe such an emphasis will help ease the fundamental tension between standardizing ACLs and allowing dialects. Both are desirable, but have thus far been mutually exclusive. A standard is needed to ensure that an ACL complies with a particular protocol: dialects are needed to address the different scenarios that can arise with heterogeneous, autonomous agents.

In making the case for social agency, I look at the demands on an ACL and examine how KQML and Arcol are handling features along two critical dimensions: meaning and agent construction.

Sidebar: How Agent Communication Languages Have Evolved

Figure A shows the progression of ACLs since the early days of agents, when there was little agent autonomy, and each project would invent its own ACL. The first significant interproject ACL was Knowledge Query Management Language, proposed as part of the US Defense Advanced Research Projects Agency's Knowledge Sharing Effort [2] in the late 1980s. Several KQML dialects are still being used.

KQML includes many primitives, all assertives or directives, which agents use to tell facts, ask queries, subscribe to services, or find other agents. A sample KQML message is (`tell :sender A :receiver B :content ''raining''`). The semantics of KQML presupposes a virtual knowledge base for each agent. Telling a fact corresponds to reporting on that knowledge base: querying corresponds to the sending agent's attempts to extract something from the receiving agent's knowledge base.

In the early 1980s, France Télécom developed Arcol [6], which includes a smaller set of primitives than KQML. Again, the primitives are all assertives or directives, but unlike KQML they can be composed. Arcol has a formal semantics, which presupposes that agents have beliefs and intentions, and can represent their uncertainty about various facts. Arcol gives performance conditions, which define when an agent may perform a specific communication. For example, in Arcol, agent Avi can tell agent Bob something only if Avi believes it also and can establish that Bob does not believe it. Arcol's performance conditions thus require the agents to reason about each other's beliefs and intentions and behave cooperatively and sincerely.

The most recent evolution of ACLs is the draft standard proposed by the Foundation for Intelligent Physical Agents (http://www.fipa.org/). The standard is heavily influenced by Arcol, adopting the Arcol model and semantics, although it softens a few of Arcol's performance conditions. The newer versions of the standard also discuss interaction protocols—a more promising line of thought. The FIPA standard also uses Lisp-like syntactic conventions similar to KQML's. For most purposes, however, the current FIPA standard can be treated the same as Arcol.

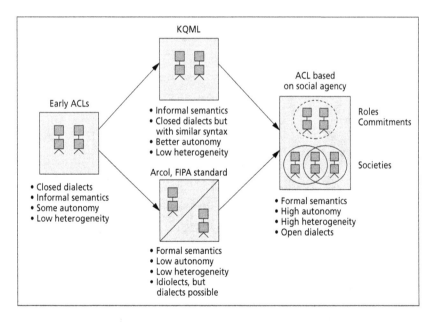

Fig. A. ACL progression since the early days of agents

Elements of Meaning

When agents function together, whether to cooperate or compete, they form a *multiagent system*. Multiagent systems provide higher-level abstractions than traditional distributed programming. These abstractions are closer to users' expectations, and allow the designer more flexibility in determining behavior. For example, instead of hardwiring a specific behavior into the agents, multiagent systems designers might have the agents negotiate with one another to determine the best course of action for that situation. Thus, ACLs must be flexible enough to accommodate abstractions such as negotiation. However, the same flexibility makes it harder to nail down their semantics.

For this reason, to arrive at the meaning of a communication you must examine many elements, including perspective, type of meaning, basis (semantics or pragmatics), context, and coverage (the number of communicative acts included).

Figure 1 shows the elements in this dimension. The region in the lower left characterizes existing ACLs such as KQML and Arcol.

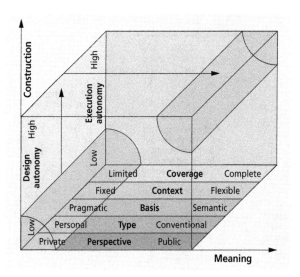

Fig. 1. The design space of agent communication languages: The region in the lower left represents existing ACLs, which follow a mental agency model. This region in the upper right represents the desired goals, which dictate a social agency model: high design and execution autonomy, high coverage (includes all significant categories of communicative acts), flexible context, semantic basis for meaning, conventional meaning type, and a public perspective.

Perspective

Each communication has potentially three perspectives: the sender's, the receiver's and the society's (that of other observers). The first two represent a *private* perspective. The third is a *public* perspective—the perspective of the multiagent system—available to all—as opposed to that of the individual agents.

Whose meaning should a language primarily reflect? As Figure 1 shows, both Arcol and KQML emphasize the private perspective. In fact, they are concerned only with the sender's perspective. This goes against the literature on human discourse (the very model that mental agency supposedly follows), which advocates treating the sender and the receiver as equal partners.

For an ACL to be a true lingua franca, it must be *normative*—correctly designed agents must comply with the ACL so that agents from different design environments can understand each other. A normative ACL, in turn, must rely on some standard to ensure that different implementations preserve that ACL's meaning. To be effective, such a standard must provide some way to test for compliance. If an interaction breaks down, you should be able to determine what component failed (is not complying). If you cannot determine compliance, the standard is useless.

Furthermore, for compliance to be testable the ACL's semantics must have a public perspective. That is, it must emphasize social agency.

In fact, private perspectives are simply approximations of the public perspective. They merely have a role in determining how the agents decide what to communicate and how it is to be interpreted. An agent's designer may use the private perspectives, but only to set up the agent's beliefs and intentions so that its public behavior will comply with the standard.

Type of Meaning

The formal study of language has three aspects. *Syntax* deals with how the symbols are structured, *semantics* with what they denote, and *pragmatics* with how they are interpreted and used. Meaning is a combination of semantics and pragmatics.

Pragmatics includes considerations external to the language proper, such as the mental states of the communicating agents and the environment in which they exist. Consequently, pragmatics can constrain how agents relate to one another and how they process the messages they send and receive. When the agents are not fully cooperative or cannot determine implications as well as humans, they cannot meet the pragmatic requirements. If these requirements are an essential part of the ACL, no one can correctly apply it.

As Figure 1 shows, both Arcol and KQML emphasize pragmatics. In Arcol, an agent must make only *sincere contributions* (assertives that are believed true, requests that it intends should succeed) and may assume that other agents also make sincere contributions. Consequently, you cannot use Arcol in settings where sincerity cannot be taken for granted—for example, in electronic commerce or, broadly, in negotiation of any kind.

Semantics versus Pragmatics

A perspective can be combined with a type of meaning, either personal or conventional. In *personal* meaning, the meaning of communicative acts (described later) is based on the *intent* or interpretation of either the receiver or the sender. For example, the receiver may understand an act as a directive (purge this file) when it is syntactically an assertion (this is an old file) because the receiver is able to infer something from what the sender is saying.

Both Arcol and KQML emphasize a personal meaning, which can lead to problems. Even the recently proposed formalization of KQML [2] remains focused on personal meaning, although it considers the effect of a message on the receiver.

Consider Arcol's `inform` construct, which is supposed to merely give information. However, suppose an agent is to inform another agent that it is raining, but lacks either a beliefs in this statement or an intention to convey the belief to the receiving agent. Does an `inform` action take place? Traditional approaches offer no clear answer.

In *conventional* meaning, the meaning of communicative acts is based on usage conventions. The very idea of a lingua franca presupposes a well-defined conventional meaning. Indeed, language is nothing *but* a system of conventions, and they have proved to have considerable force. If you bid for an expensive item at Sotheby's, for example, you are liable for the price even if you didn't intend to pay.

By violating the idea of conventions, traditional approaches go against the wisdom of having different labels for communicative acts. KQML-based agents are notorious for replacing all their communicative acts with variants of the `tell` construct—KQML's version of Arcol's `inform`. Likewise, in Arcol, `requests` corresponds to `informs` of a certain kind. That is, if Agent Avi is informed that agent Bob needs some information, Avi would supply that information as if Bob had requested it.

Thus, although traditional ACLs have different communicative acts, they are not capturing different conventions, but rather providing convenient abbreviations.

Context

In general, you cannot understand a communication without looking at the context—the agent's physical or simulated environment. Social context is central to the goals of an ACL. For agents, the social context need not be quite as subtle as it is for humans; it must determine only what agents expect of one another in their range of response, sincerity, and so on.

As Figure 1 shows, both Arcol and KQML have a fixed context, partly because both languages have too many constraints and partly because they are inflexible. For example, by imposing the pragmatic requirement to be cooperative; Arcol requires the informing agent to believe the proposition being asserted is true: the informed agent to not already believe it; and the informer to intend that the informed agent come to believe it.

These requirements may not be acceptable in certain contexts. For example, suppose agent Avi wishes to repeat the conclusion of its negotiations with Bob with the phrase: "Okay, so the price is $5." Avi may communicate this only to formally conclude the negotiations even though it believes Bob already agrees. In Arcol, Avi would be unable to make this communication because it would violate a key prerequisite—that Avi believes Bob does not believe the price is $5.

Coverage of Communicative Acts

When heterogeneous, autonomous agents exchange information, the meaning of the exchange is characterized by *communicative acts*. For most computing scenarios, these acts fall into one of seven categories:

- *Assertives*, which inform: The door is shut.
- *Directives*, which request: Shut the door—or query: Can pelicans fly?
- *Commissives*, which promise something: I will shut the door.
- *Permissives*, which give permission for an act: You may shut the door.
- *Prohibitives*, which ban some act: You may not shut the door.
- *Declaratives*, which cause events in themselves: I name this door the Golden Gate.
- *Expressives*, which express emotions and evaluations: I wish this door were the Golden Gate.

Communicative acts can be put into a stylized form like "I hereby request ..." or "I hereby declare ...". This grammatical form emphasizes that through language you not only make statements but also perform actions. Acting by speaking becomes the essence of communication. For example, when a justice of the peace declares a couple man and wife, she is not only reporting their marital status, but also changing it. (For that reason, communicative acts are sometimes called *performatives*.)

As Figure 1 shows Arcol and KQML have limited coverage: all primitives are either assertives or directives. In Arcol, you can simulate commissives using other acts. You can also reduce all acts to assertives, but using only the restricted meanings Arcol has for these categories. For example, a request in Arcol is the same as conveying to the receiver that the sender intends for it to perform the given action.

Although ACL designers should not try to anticipate all possible applications, they should be able to include acts from all seven categories because agents need them to enter into and manage more complex social relationships. Interacting with the underlying information system, for example, is important in many applications. This requires some way to initiate and maintain sessions, and authorize and commit to actions [3]. Commissives are essential for the agents to promise. Permissives and prohibitives let agents create or deny authority. Declaratives aid in appointing an agent as a representative or a group leader. And expressives let an agent convey evaluations and approvals. (This last category, although now rarely used, is likely to become more important when emotional agents become more common.)

Agent Construction

Every ACL semantics must implicitly or explicitly embody some agent model. However, ACLs vary in what they emphasize (an individual agent's mental state or the social aspects of communication) and in how much design and execution autonomy they give an agent. Figure 1 shows how existing ACLs like KQML and Arcol handle the elements of agent construction.

Mental versus Social Agency

Mental agency emphasizes an agent's mental state, typically described as beliefs and intentions. Social agency regards agents as social creatures that interact with one another. As Figure 1 shows, both Arcol and KQML promote mental agency.

Mental states include:

- *beliefs*, which characterize what an agent imagines its world state to be;
- *goals*, which describe what states the agent would prefer;
- *desires*, which describe the agent's preferences, sometimes with motivational aspects; and
- *intentions*, which characterize the goals or desires the agent has selected to work on.

Mental agency presupposes the *intentional stance*, which is the doctrine that you can describe any system using terms such as beliefs and intentions [4]. This is a compelling view because it says that modelers can create an agent using intentional terms. However, it does not solve the practical problems of how to determine the unique beliefs and intentions of an arbitrary agent just from its design and environment.

Consider the snippets of code for Agent Avi in Figure 2. How can you say whether or not Avi believes it is raining? Suppose you say that only agents with an explicit string `raining` in the data structure `beliefs` believe that it is raining. With that criterion, you eliminate a large subset of practical agents, because most agents do not carry a `beliefs` data structure. Moreover, if two agents did have a `beliefs` data structure and the structures were the same, the agents could act differently enough—because of differences in their programs or other data structures—that you couldn't say for sure whether they have the same beliefs.

On the other hand, without an explicit representation, anyone can claim anything about an agent's beliefs. For this reason, mental agency alone cannot provide the normative basis for an ACL semantics.

Each communicative act in Figure 2 poses a challenge for languages that promote mental agency. Traditional approaches also ignore whether Bob can really make it rain (when requested or permitted) or stop the rain (when prohibited); whether Avi can make it rain (when he promises); whether Avi has has the authority to permit or prohibit any of Bob's actions or to name weather conditions.

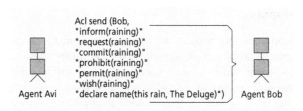

Acl send (Bob,
 "inform(raining)"
 "request(raining)"
 "commit(raining)"
 "prohibit(raining)"
 "permit(raining)"
 "wish(raining)"
Agent Avi   "declare name(this rain, The Deluge)")   Agent Bob

Fig. 2. Why you cannot determine compliance under the mental agency model. You cannot determine whether agent Avi is compliant in sending the inform message, because there is no way to determine whether Avi believes it is raining. Similarly, the request is problematic, because there is no way to determine whether Avi believes Bob can make it rain. The same is true for the wish message. The other messages have a similar fate, although most wouldn't fit in traditional ACL syntax anyway.

Ultimately, traditional ACL approaches conclude that if Avi's designer wants it to comply, it does. This is profoundly unsatisfactory, because it means that compliance depends on neither the agent's behavior nor its design, but on how the design is documented. This position is conceptually and practically incoherent, because it means that any designer who cares to insert a comment saying "This program is correct" is freed from establishing its compliance.

A more promising approach is to consider communicative acts as part of an ongoing social interaction. Even if you can't determine whether agents have a specific mental state, you can be sure that communicating agents are able to interact socially. This is analogous to the distinction between an object's behavior (external) and state (internal). Interfaces in traditional software design are based on behavior, although state representations may be used to realize the desired behavior.

Practically and even philosophically, the compliance of an agent's communication depends on whether it is obeying the conventions in its society, for example, by keeping promises and being sincere.

Design Autonomy

Design autonomy minimizes requirements on agent builders, thus promoting heterogeneity (the freedom to have agents of different design and construction). This, in turn leads to a wider range of practical systems. For example, in a traditional setting, a Web browser can be implemented in any way as long as it follows the standard protocols.

Traditional approaches such as Arcol and KQML require agents to be implemented using representations of the mental concepts. As Figure 1 shows, this requirement reduces design autonomy. Agents may have to have beliefs and intentions, be able to plan and perform some logical inferences, or be rational. These constraints also preclude many practical agent designs because you cannot uniquely determine an agent's mental state.

Execution Autonomy

Execution autonomy corresponds to an agent's freedom to choose its own actions. An ACL can limit execution autonomy by requiring agents to be sincere, cooperative, benevolent, and so on. Execution autonomy is orthogonal to design autonomy because agents of a fixed design can have actions their designers cannot control; likewise, agents of diverse designs can have controllable actions. For example, two users with the same Web browser can still act differently, and those with different browsers can act the same if the browsers have similar functionality.

As Figure 1, shows execution autonomy is low in Arcol; indeed, the language constrains agents to behave in ways many people could not emulate: Arcol agents must always speak the truth, believe each other, and help each other. This is appropriate for user interfaces—Arcol's original application domain—because the computational agent deals only with one other agent, the user. However, in other applications, this low autonomy means that Arcol can be applied only if the agent designers themselves subvert its semantics.

KQML, on the other hand, does not demand any specific form of sincerity or helpfulness and therefore better preserves execution autonomy. The historical reason for this difference is that KQML was designed for interoperation (although it failed), whereas Arcol was designed as a proprietary language for a specific system. Arcol designers reduced autonomy to suit that system, which simplified that system's design.

Toward Social Principles

If, as Figure 1 shows, you assume that the ideal ACL would take a public perspective, emphasize conventional meaning, avoid pragmatics, consider context, and include all major communicative acts, you would be advocating a model that endorses *social agency*.

In an effort to move ACLs more closely toward that ideal, my colleagues and I at North Carolina State University are developing an approach based on societies of agents.

Protocols and Societies

In our approach, agents play different roles within a society. The roles define the associated social commitments or obligations to other roles. When agents join a group, they join in one or more roles, thereby acquiring the commitments that go with those roles. The commitments of a role are restrictions on how agents playing that role must act and, in particular, communicate. In general, agents can operate on their commitments by manipulating or even cancelling them.

These operations enable flexible behavior, but are themselves constrained by metacommitments to ensure that arbitrary behaviors do not result. Consequently, we specify protocols as sets of commitments rather than as finite state machines. Such protocol specifications can accommodate the kinds of exceptions that arise in multiagent systems.

Suppose that agent Avi is a seller and agent Bob is a buyer. Our protocol could include the following actions:

- Avi must respond to requests for price quotes (a form of cooperative behavior).
- Avi's price quotes issued to different agents within a specified period must be the same (sincerity).
- If Bob agrees to buy at a price, its check won't bounce (keeping promises).
- Avi will honor a price quote, provided Bob responds within a specified period (keeping promises).

Designers can create specific protocols, and hence societies, for different applications such as electronic commerce, travel applications, industrial control, logistics, and student registration. As societies are designed, we envision that their specifications would be published.

Different vendors could supply agents to play different roles in these societies. Each vendor's agent would have to comply with the protocols in which it participates. Because protocol requirements would be expressed solely in terms of commitments, agents could be tested for compliance on the basis of their communications. This means the implementation need not be revealed, which is an important practical consideration (for example, to protect trade secrets). Also, because agents participate in a society, the society supplies the social context in which the communications occur. Thus, communicative acts can be more expressive and powerful because designers who agree on a standard society can assume a lot more about each other's agents.

Our framework presupposes a richer infrastructure for agent management, which we term *society management*. This infrastructure supports the definition of commitments, roles, and groups, as well as operations for agents to join a society in specific roles, to change roles, and to exit the society. Our framework also promotes execution autonomy. For example, Avi might only make assertions that it believes others don't already believe, whereas Bob may not restrict itself in such a manner. In general, the agents can act as they please provided they obey the restrictions of the societies they belong to and the protocols they follow.

Sidebar: Dialects and Idiolects

When agents from different vendors—or event different research projects—attempt to parse each other's messages, they cannot understand them correctly. This happens for two reasons. First, the receiving agent may not recognize the application-specific terms the sending agent is using to communicate. Second—and perhaps more important—even basic communication components are not uniformly understood. Both these problems stem from differing interpretations of key concepts, and the result is the evolution of multiple dialects within a language.

Idiolects—a variant of a language specific to one agent—result when the language emphasizes private perspective and personal meaning, as described in the main text. When only the private perspective is considered, an agent can produce or interpret messages as it unilaterally sees fit. Such an agent follows the philosophy of Lewis Carroll's Humpty Dumpty: Words mean exactly what I want them to. And communicating agents suffer the same problem as Alice, who failed to understand much of what Humpty Dumpty said.

Challenges

Our society-based approach avoids the problem of idiolects described in the sidebar "Dialects and Idiolects" because the essential semantic components act as normatives for agent behavior. Designers can create and popularize specialized societies—those that support more restrictive protocols for specific applications. When a protocol explicitly involves mental concepts (for example, by requiring a role to be sincere), it must also give some criteria to evaluate an agent's beliefs.

As such, our approach actually encourages dialects. The difference from the dialect problem described in the sidebar is that dialects in our approach have a social semantics and are not proprietary. Designers can define societies of their liking and implement agents to play appropriate roles in them. However, designers also know ahead of time the precise differences among dialects, and can expect their agents to communicate successfully with agents from other societies only to the extent that their dialects agree. Dialects of this variety enable the context sensitivity that is essential to building significant applications. Such dialects are good. The problem with traditional approaches is not the use of dialects per se, but that the dialects are arbitrary and cannot be adequately formalized in the chosen framework.

We envision the design and establishment of societies as essentially a community effort, much like Internet evolution. Protocols will spread much like the proliferation of network protocols, markup languages, and e-mail data formats: When enough vendors support a protocol, it will become a worthwhile target for other vendors.

The challenges thus becomes finding an approach that is normative at the society level and preserves some of the intuitions behind the high-level abstractions such as beliefs and intentions. Such an approach would provide a canonical form of protocols and a canonical definition for the different communicative acts. There are two obvious solutions. The first is to have a purely behavior-based approach, but this may limit the ability to describe complex agent states. The second is to have a purely mentalist approach, which as I have described, reduces design autonomy and is inherently noncanonical.

A third, less obvious, approach is to combine social commitments with a public perspective on the mental states. This approach, which I originated and am currently investigating [5], defines when an agent's communicative act would be wholeheartedly satisfied. For example, assertives are satisfied if the world matches what they describe. Directives are satisfied when the receiver acts to ensure their success—and has the required intentions and know-how. Commissives are satisfied when the sender acts to ensure their success. This approach is thus a hybrid: Although it takes some steps toward a coarse canonical set of objective definitions, it does not uniquely ascribe beliefs and intentions to agents. However, designers can use it to construct agents that would keep their public commitments.

Conclusion

Although all the fundamental issues in agent communication are far from resolved, my advice to people attempting to build multiagent systems is not to lose heart. Only through experience can some of these key questions be resolved. I have two recommendations. First, reflect on the issues this article raises as they affect a particular ACL or its implementation:

- What model of agency does the ACL require?
- How much does an ACL constrain an agent's design?
- Which perspective does the ACL embody?
- How can I determine what an agent believes or intends? You might need to make additional assumptions, essentially killing interoperation, to determine beliefs and intentions unambiguously. Alternatively, you might use beliefs and intentions only to design your own agents and not expect to know the details of other designs.

If, after answering these questions, you decide to use a specific ACL, understand that you have accepted its limitations as well. If the answers are unacceptable, you know to explore alternatives. A reasonable option is to reject the official semantics and use a commitment-based semantics instead.

My second recommendation is to start building systems. Always keep in mind that protocols are more important than individual communicative acts, and the best semantics is what you negotiate with other designers. For this reason, I believe that the strongest standards will develop in applications and markets that use agents heavily. As often happens in computing, the challenge will then be for the theoreticians to catch up.

Acknowledgements. This is an extended and revised version of a position paper presented at the Fifth Meeting of the Foundation for Intelligent Physical Agents (FIPA) held in Reston, Virginia in April 1997. I thank Manny Aparicio, Michael Huhns, Yannis Labrou, Abe Mamdani, David Sadek, and Donald Steiner for discussions, the anonymous *Computer* reviewers for comments, and Nancy Talbert for careful editing.

This work is supported by the NCSU College of Engineering, the National Science Foundation under grants IIS-9529179 and IIS-9624425 (Career Award), and IBM Corp.

References

1. M. Huhns and M. Singh. Agents and multiagent systems: Themes, approaches, challenges. In M. Huhns and M. Singh, editors, *Readings in Agents*, pages 1–23. Morgan Kaufmann, San Mateo, Calif., 1998. 37
2. Y. Labrou and T. Finin. Semantics and conversations for an agent communication language. In M. Huhns and M. Singh, editors, *Readings in Agents*, pages 235–242. Morgan Kaufmann, San Mateo, Calif., 1998. 38, 42
3. M. Singh, J. Barnett, and M. Singh. Enhancing conversational moves for portable dialogue systems. In *Working Notes of the AAAI Fall Symposium Communicative Action in Humans and Machines*, Menlo Park, Calif., 1997. 43
4. J. McCarthy. Ascribing mental qualities to machines. In V. Lifschitz, editor, *Formalizing Common Sense: Papers by John McCarthy*, pages 93–118. Ablex Publishing, Norwood, N.J., 1990. 44
5. M. Singh. *Multiagent Systems: A Theoretical Framework for Intentions, Know-How, and Communications*. Springer-Verlag, Heidelberg, 1994. 48
6. P. Breiter and D. M. Sadek. A rational agent as a kernel of a cooperative dialogue system: Implementing a logical theory of interaction. In *Proceedings of ECAI 96 Workshop on Agent Theories, Architectures and Languages*. Springer-Verlag, Berlin, 1996. 38

Negotiation as a Metaphor for Distributed Problem Solving

Randall Davis
Artificial Intelligence Laboratory, Massachusetts Institute of Technology, Cambridge, MA 02139, U.S.A.

Reid G. Smith*
Defence Research Establishment Atlantic, Dartmouth, Nova Scotia B2Y 3Z7, Canada

Recommended by Lee Erman

ABSTRACT

We describe the concept of distributed problem solving and define it as the cooperative solution of problems by a decentralized and loosely coupled collection of problem solvers. This approach to problem solving offers the promise of increased performance and provides a useful medium for exploring and developing new problem-solving techniques.

We present a framework called the contract net *that specifies communication and control in a distributed problem solver. Task distribution is viewed as an interactive process, a discussion carried on between a node with a task to be executed and a group of nodes that may be able to execute the task. We describe the kinds of information that must be passed between nodes during the discussion in order to obtain effective problem-solving behavior. This discussion is the origin of the negotiation metaphor: Task distribution is viewed as a form of contract negotiation.*

We emphasize that protocols for distributed problem solving should help determine the content of the information transmitted, rather than simply provide a means of sending bits from one node to another.

The use of the contract net framework is demonstrated in the solution of a simulated problem in area surveillance, of the sort encountered in ship or air traffic control. We discuss the mode of operation of a distributed sensing system, a network of nodes extending throughout a relatively large geographic area, whose primary aim is the formation of a dynamic map of traffic in the area.

From the results of this preliminary study we abstract features of the framework applicable to problem solving in general, examining in particular transfer of control. Comparisons with PLANNER, CONNIVER, HEARSAY-II, *and* PUP6 *are used to demonstrate that negotiation—the two-way transfer of information—is a natural extension to the transfer of control mechanisms used in earlier problem-solving systems.*

* The author's current address is: Schlumberger–Doll Research, Ridgefield, CT 06877, U.S.A.

Artificial Intelligence **20** (1983) 63–109
0004-3702/83/0000–0000/$03.00 © 1983 North-Holland

1. Introduction

Traditional work in problem solving has, for the most part, been set in the context of a single processor. Recent advances in processor fabrication techniques, however, combined with developments in communication technology, offer the chance to explore new ideas about problem solving employing multiple processors.

In this paper we describe the concept of *distributed problem solving*, characterizing it as the cooperative solution of problems by a decentralized, loosely coupled collection of problem solvers. We find it useful to view the process as occurring in four phases: problem decomposition, sub-problem distribution, sub-problem solution, and answer synthesis. We focus in this paper primarily on the second phase, exploring how negotiation can help in matching problem solvers to tasks.

We find three issues central to constructing frameworks for distributed problem solving: (i) the fundamental conflict between the complete knowledge needed to ensure coherence and the incomplete knowledge inherent in any distribution of problem solving effort, (ii) the need for a problem solving protocol, and (iii) the utility of negotiation as an organizing principle. We illustrate our approach to those issues in a framework called the contract net.

Section 2 describes our concept of distributed problem solving in more detail, contrasting it with the more widely known topic of distributed processing. Section 3 explores motivations, suggesting what we hope to gain from this work. In Section 4 we consider the three issues listed above, describing what we mean by each and documenting the importance of each to the problems at hand.

Section 5 describes how a group of human experts might cooperate in solving a problem and illustrates how this metaphor has proved useful in guiding our work. Section 6 then considers how a group of computers might cooperate to solve a problem and illustrates how this has contributed to our work.

Section 7 describes the contract net. We focus on its use as a framework for orchestrating the efforts of a number of loosely coupled problem solvers. More detailed issues of its implementation, as well the tradeoffs involved in its design, are covered elsewhere (see, e.g., [26, 27, 28]). Section 8 describes an application of the contract net. We consider a problem in distributed sensing and show how our approach permits a useful degree of self-organization.

Section 9 then takes a step back to consider the issue of transfer of control. We show how the perspective we have developed—notably the issue of negotiation—offers useful insights about the concept of control transfer. We review invocation techniques from a number of programming languages and illustrate that the whole range of them can be viewed as a progression from simple to increasingly more sophisticated information exchange. In these terms the negotiation technique used in the contract net becomes a natural next step.

Sections 10 and 11 consider the sorts of problems for which our approach is well suited and describe the limitations and open problems in our work to date.

2. Distributed Problem Solving: Overview

In our view, some of the defining characteristics of distributed problem solving are that it is a *cooperative* activity of a group of *decentralized* and *loosely coupled* knowledge-sources (KSs). The KSs cooperate in the sense that no one of them has sufficient information to solve the entire problem: information must be shared to allow the group as a whole to produce an answer. By decentralized we mean that both control and data are logically and often geographically distributed; there is neither global control nor global data storage. Loosely coupled means that individual KSs spend most of their time in computation rather than communication.

Interest in such problem solvers arises from the promise of increased speed, reliability, and extensibility, as well as ability to handle applications with a natural spatial or functional distribution, and the potential for increased tolerance to uncertainty in data and knowledge.

Distributed problem solving differs in several fundamental respects from the more widely known topic of *distributed processing*. Perhaps the most important distinction arises from examining the origin of the system and the motivations for interconnecting machines.

Distributed processing systems often have their origin in the attempt to synthesize a network of machines capable of carrying out a number of widely disparate tasks. Typically, several distinct applications are envisioned, with each application concentrated at a single node of the network, as for example in a three-node system intended to do payroll, order entry, and process control. The aim is to find a way to reconcile any conflicts and disadvantages arising from the desire to carry out disparate tasks, in order to gain the benefits of using multiple machines (sharing of data bases, graceful degradation, etc.).

Unfortunately, the conflicts that arise are often not simply technical (e.g., word sizes, database formats, etc.) but include sociological and political problems as well (see, e.g., [6]). The attempt to synthesize a number of disparate tasks thus leads to a concern with issues such as access control and protection, and results in viewing cooperation as a form of *compromise* between potentially conflicting desires.

In distributed problem solving, on the other hand, there is a single task envisioned for the system and the resources to be applied have no other predefined roles to carry out. We are building up a system de novo and can as a result choose hardware, software, etc. with one aim in mind: the selection that will lead to the most effective environment for cooperative behavior. This also means we view cooperation in terms of benevolent problem solving behavior, i.e., how can systems that are perfectly willing to accommodate one another act so as to be an effective team? Our concerns are thus with developing frameworks for *cooperative behavior between willing entities*, rather than frameworks for enforcing cooperation as a form of compromise between potentially incompatible entities.

A second important distinction arises from our focus on traditional issues of problem solving. We intend, for example, that the system itself should include as part of its basic task the partitioning and decomposition of a problem. Work in distributed processing, by comparison, has not taken problem solving as a primary focus. It has generally been assumed that a well-defined and a priori partitioned problem exists. The major concerns lie in an optimal static distribution of tasks, methods for interconnecting processor nodes, resource allocation, and prevention of deadlock. Complete knowledge of the problem has also been assumed (i.e., explicit knowledge of timing and precedence relations between tasks) and the major reason for distribution has been assumed to be load-balancing (e.g., [1, 2]). Since we do not make these assumptions, we cannot take advantage of this pre-planning of resources. As will become clear, this makes for significant differences in the issues which concern us and in the design of the system.

A final distinction results from the lack of substantial cooperation in most distributed processing systems. Typically, for instance, most of the processing is done at a central site and remote processors are limited to basic data collection (e.g., credit card verification). The word *distributed* is usually taken to mean spatial distribution of data—distribution of function or control is not generally considered.

One way to view the various research efforts is in terms of the three levels indicated in Fig. 1. At the lowest level the focus is the processor architecture. The main issues here are the design of the individual nodes and the interconnection mechanism. The components of an individual node must be selected (e.g., processors and memory), and appropriate low-level interconnection methods must be chosen (e.g., a single broadcast channel, complete interconnection, a regular lattice, etc.).

The middle level focuses on systems aspects. Among the concerns here are issues of guaranteeing message delivery, guaranteeing database consistency, and techniques for database recovery.

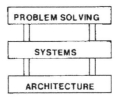

FIG. 1. A layered approach to distributed problem solving.

The focus at the top level is problem solving, where the concerns are internode control and knowledge organization; in particular how to achieve effective problem-solving behavior from a collection of asynchronous nodes. There is therefore a greater concern with the *content* of the information to be communicated between nodes than with the *form* in which the communication is effected.

All of these levels are important foci of research and each successive level depends on the ones below it for support. Our concern in this paper, however, lies primarily at the level of problem solving.

For the remainder of this paper we will assume that the hardware is a network of loosely coupled, asynchronous nodes. Each node has a local memory; no memory is shared by all nodes. Each node typically contains several distinct KSs. There is no central controller; each node makes its own choices about tasks to work on. The nodes are interconnected so that every node can communicate with every other by sending messages, perhaps over a broadcast channel. We also assume the existence of a low-level protocol to effect communication of bit streams between nodes.

3. Distributed Problem Solving: Motivation

A major motivation for this work lies in the potential it offers for making available more problem solving power, by applying a collection of processors to the solution of a single problem. It may, for example, prove much easier to coordinate the actions of twenty medium-sized machines than it is to build a single machine twenty (or even ten) times as large.

A distributed approach may also be well suited to problems that have either a spatial distribution or a large degree of functional specialization. Spatial distribution often occurs in problems involving interpretation of signal data from multiple sensors (e.g., [20]). Functional specialization may occur in problems like understanding continuous speech (e.g., [7]): information from many different knowledge-sources (e.g., signal processors, parsers, etc.) must be combined to solve the problem.

Distributed problem solving also offers a way to apply to problem solving the recent advances in both processor fabrication and communication technology. Low-cost, small-scale VLSI processors are now commonplace, with larger scale processors expected in the near future [21]. The synthesis of advanced computer and communication technology that has resulted in networks of resource-sharing computers (e.g., [13, 15]) offers a foundation for work on distributed architectures. With these two developments as foundations, work can begin focusing on techniques for effective use of networks of machines.

One reason for interest in distributed architectures in general is their capacity for reliable computation and graceful degradation. By placing problem solving in this environment, we have the chance to make it similarly reliable.

The use of an approach like the contract net, which distributes both control and data, also makes possible additional responses to component failure. In addition to the standard response of continuing to function as before (albeit more slowly), the option may exist of having the system reconfigure itself to take into account the hardware available.

Finally, and somewhat more speculatively, there is the issue of 'bounded rationality'. Some tasks appear difficult because of their size. They are 'too big' to contemplate all at once and are not easily broken into modular sub-problems (e.g., the working of the national economy, the operation of a large corporation). In such cases it may be difficult, both conceptually and practically, for a single problem solver to deal effectively with more than a small part of all of the data or knowledge required to solve the problem. Trying to scale up the hardware of a single problem solver may ease the practical problem but does not solve the conceptual difficulty. It may instead prove more effective to use multiple problem solvers, each of which handles some fraction of the total problem, and to provide techniques for dealing with the interaction between the sub-problems.

Recent work has explored a number of ideas relevant to accomplishing this goal. There is, for example, the original HEARSAY-II model of cooperating KSs ([7]), in which each KS had a sharply limited domain of expertise. It demonstrated the practicality of using a number of independent KSs to encode large amounts of knowledge about a domain. The work in [17] reports on an experiment that distributed knowledge and data, and to a limited degree, control. In Section 7 we describe an approach to distributing problem solving effort that dynamically distributes knowledge, data and control.

4. The Fundamental Issues

Our study of distributed problem solving to date has identified three issues that appear to be central to the undertaking: (i) the fundamental difficulty of ensuring global coordination of behavior when that behavior results from the aggregation of actions based on local *incomplete* knowledge, (ii) the necessity of a protocol dealing with *problem solving* rather than with *communication*, and (iii) the utility of *negotiation* as a fundamental mechanism for interaction. In this section we describe each of the issues briefly, Sections 5 and 6 then demonstrate how these issues arise from basic considerations of the task at hand.[1]

4.1. Global coherence and limited knowledge

One obvious problem that arises in employing multiple problem solvers is

---

[1]Other work on distributed problem solving is based on similar issues. Work described in [18], for example, also finds (i) and (ii) above to be central issues.

'coherence'. Any time we have more than one active agent in the system there is the possibility that their actions are in some fashion mutually interfering rather than mutually supportive. There are numerous ways in which this can happen. We may have conflict over resources, one agent may unknowingly undo the results of another, the same actions may be carried out redundantly, etc. In general terms, the collection of agents may somehow fail to act as a well-coordinated, purposeful team.

We believe that this problem is due to the fundamental difficulty of obtaining coordinated behavior when each agent has only a limited, local view. We could, of course, guarantee coordination if every agent 'knew everything', i.e., it had complete knowledge. If, for example, every problem solver had complete knowledge of the actions of all the others, it would be possible to avoid redundant or conflicting efforts.[2]

Yet any reasonable model of distribution appears to require incomplete, local views of the problem. Complete information is, for example, at least impractical. As we argue in Section 6, bandwidth limitations make it unreasonable to consider having every node constantly informed of all developments.

A limited local view also simplifies the problem conceptually. The problem becomes far more difficult to think about (and to program) if every problem solver has to keep track of everything. It also seems contrary to the basic notion of distribution: Part of the motivation is to allow a problem solver to focus on one part of the problem and ignore the rest.

For these reasons at least, then, any distribution of problem solving effort appears to imply incomplete, local knowledge.

And when we say "incomplete knowledge", we include in "knowledge" the information indicating "who needs to know what". That is, we do not assume that we start out with a map of subproblems and their interactions. Without such a map, there is the chance that necessary interactions are overlooked and hence we lose a guarantee of coordinated behavior.

As noted earlier, we consider problem decomposition—the creation of the map of subproblems—to be part of the system's task. Once the system creates its best guess at such a map, we can count on the locality of action and information to make distributed problem solving practical. By locality of action and information, we mean that the problems typically attacked in AI are generally decomposable into a set of subproblems in which the effects of actions and the relevance of information is local. The actions taken to solve one subproblem generally affect only a few other subproblems; the

---

[2]This difficulty is not limited to distributed problem solving, it is only more painfully obvious there. The standard notion of problem decomposition in centralized systems results in limited, local knowledge, and the same difficulty manifests itself as the well-known problem of interacting subgoals.

information discovered in solving one subproblem is generally relevant to only a few other subproblems.[3] As a result, each problem solver will have to interact with at most a few others, making limited bandwidth a challenging but not fatal constraint.

To summarize: the conflict arises because distribution seems by its nature to require supplying each problem solver with only a limited, local view of the problem, yet we wish to accomplish a global effect—the solution of the problem at hand. It is not obvious how we can guarantee overall coordination from aggregations of actions based on local views with incomplete information. Thus, while the locality of action and information means that distributed problem solving is feasible, the necessity of incomplete knowledge means that guaranteeing coordinated activity is difficult.

One general answer is to provide something that extends across the network of nodes, something that can be used as a foundation for cooperation and organization. As will become clear, three elements of our framework help provide that foundation: (i) the concept of negotiation as a mechanism for interaction (Section 7.1), (ii) the network of tasks that results from decomposing a problem (Section 8.2), and (iii) a common language shared by all nodes (Section 7.4). The announcement—bid—award sequence of messages (Section 7.3) also offers some support. Even though each problem solver has only a limited view of the problem, these messages offer one way for a node to find out who else has relevant information. Together, all of these mechanisms provide an initial step toward a basis for achieving coordinated behavior.

4.2. The need for a problem solving protocol

In most work on protocols for distributed computation the emphasis has been on establishing reliable and efficient communication. Some degree of success has been achieved, at levels ranging from individual packets to atomic actions (see, e.g., [29]). But these protocols are only a prerequisite for distributed problem solving. In the same sense that communication among a group of entities needs a carefully constructed communication protocol, so problem solving by a group of entities requires a problem solving protocol. Cooperation cannot be established between nodes simply by indicating how they are to communicate; we must also indicate what they should say to each other.

The issue can also be viewed in the terms suggested by Fig. 1. At each level we need to give careful consideration to the basic architecture and we need the

---

[3]The first half of this observation—the locality of the effects of actions—is typically used to justify informal solutions to the frame problem. We can, for instance, account for the effects of an action with a list of consequences, because that list tends to be short and predictable.

Similarly, the impact of information tends to be local. If I, as one member of a team, am working on one part of a problem, most of what is discovered about the rest of the problem is irrelevant to me. Keeping me up to date on every detail will only prove to be a distraction.

appropriate protocols. In the same sense that we pay attention to hardware and systems architecture, so we need to consider a 'problem solving architecture'; as we have protocols that organize the communication of bits and files, so we need protocols to organize the problem solving activity.

As discussed in Section 7, the contract net takes a first step in this direction by providing a set of message types indicating the kind of information that nodes should exchange in order to effect one form of cooperation.

4.3. The utility of negotiation

The central element in our approach to a problem solving protocol is the concept of negotiation. By negotiation, we mean a discussion in which the interested parties exchange information and come to an agreement. For our purposes negotiation has three important components: (a) there is a two-way exchange of information, (b) each party to the negotiation evaluates the information from its own perspective, and (c) final agreement is achieved by mutual selection.

Negotiation appears to have multiple applications. In Section 7, for example, we explore its application to the problem of matching idle problem solvers to outstanding tasks. This matching is carried out by the system itself, since, as noted, we do not assume that the problem has already been decomposed and distributed.

In Section 9.2 we explore a second application of negotiation by considering its utility as a basis for transfer of control and as a way of viewing invocation as the matching of KSs to tasks. This view leads to a more powerful mechanism for control transfer, since it permits a more informed choice from among the alternative KSs which might be invoked. The view also leads to a novel perspective on the outcome of the interaction. In most previous systems, the notion of selecting what to do next typically involves taking the best choice from among those currently available. As will become clear, in the contract net either party has the option of deciding that none of the currently available options is good enough, and can decide instead to await further developments.

5. A Cooperating Experts Metaphor

A familiar metaphor for a problem solver operating in a distributed environment is a group of human experts experienced at working together, trying to complete a large task.[4] Of primary interest to us in examining the operation of a group of human experts are: (a) the way in which they interact to solve the overall problem, (b) the manner in which the workload is distributed among them, and (c) how results are integrated for communication outside the group.

---

[4]This metaphor has been used as a starting point by [11], [16] and [18], but has resulted in systems that differ from ours in several ways. The different systems are compared in Section 9.

For reasons discussed above, we assume that no one expert is in total control of the others, although one expert may be ultimately responsible for communicating the solution of the top-level problem to the customer outside the group.

One possible model for the interaction involves group members cooperating in the execution of individual tasks, a mode we have called 'task-sharing' [28]. In such a situation we might see each expert spending most of his time working alone on various subtasks, pausing only occasionally to interact with other members of the group. These interactions generally involve requests for assistance on subtasks or the exchange of results.

An expert (E1) may request assistance because he encounters either a task too large to handle alone, or a task for which he has no expertise. If the task is too large, he will first attempt to partition it into manageable subtasks and then attempt to find other experts who have the appropriate skills to handle the new tasks. If the original task is beyond his expertise, he attempts right away to find another, more appropriate expert to handle it.

In either case, E1's problem is now to find experts whose skills match the tasks that he wishes to distribute. If E1 knows which other experts have the necessary expertise, he can notify them directly. If he does not know anyone in particular who may be able to assist him (or if the tasks require no special expertise), he can simply describe the tasks to the entire group.

If another, available expert (E2) believes he is capable of carrying out the task that E1 announced, he informs E1 of his availability and perhaps indicates as well any especially relevant skills he may have. E1 may wind up with several such volunteers and can choose from among them. The chosen volunteer might then request additional details from E1 and the two will engage in further direct communication for the duration of the task.

In order to distribute the workload in a group of experts, then, those with tasks to be executed must find others capable of executing those tasks. At the same time, it is the job of idle experts to find suitable tasks on which to work. Those with tasks to be executed and those capable of executing the tasks thus engage in a form of *negotiation* to distribute the workload. They become linked together by agreements or informal contracts, forming subgroups of varying sizes that are created and broken up dynamically during the course of work.[5]

6. Observations and Implications

The metaphor of a group of human experts offered several suggestions about

[5]Subgroups of this type offer two advantages. First, communication among the members does not needlessly distract the entire group. This is important, because communication itself can be a major source of distraction and difficulty in a large group (see for example [9]). Thus one of the major purposes of organization is to reduce the amount of communication that is needed. Second, the subgroup members may be able to communicate with each other in a language that is more efficient for their purpose than the language in use by the entire group (for more on this see [27]).

organizing problem solving effort. Here we consider how a group of computers might cooperate and examine what that can tell us about how to proceed. We approach this by comparing the use of multiple, distributed processors with the more traditional model of operation on a uniprocessor. We list several basic observations characterizing the fundamental differences and consider the implications that follow. While the list is not exhaustive, it deals with the differences we find most important.

Communication is slower than computation.

That is, bits can be created faster than they can be shipped over substantial distances.[6] With current technology, communication over such distances is in fact much slower than computation. Attempting to interconnect large numbers of high speed processors can easily lead to saturation of available bandwidth. Present trends indicate [23] that this imbalance in speed will not only continue, but that the disparity is likely to increase. It appears as well that the relative costs of communication and computation will follow a similar trend.

Several implications follow from this simple observation (Fig. 2). It means for example that we want problem decompositions that yield *loosely coupled* systems—systems in which processors spend the bulk of their time computing and only a small fraction of their time communicating with one another. The desire for loose coupling means in turn that we need to pay attention to the *efficiency* of the communication protocol: With a more efficient protocol, fewer bits need to be transmitted and less time is spent in communicating. It also means that we need to pay attention to both the *modularity* and *grain size* of the problems chosen. Problems should be decomposed into tasks that are both independent and large enough to be worth the overhead involved in task distribution. Non-independent tasks will require communication between processors, while for very small tasks (e.g., simple arithmetic) the effort involved in distributing them and reporting results would likely be greater than the work involved in solving the task itself.

Communication is slower than computation
→ loose-coupling
   → efficient protocol
   → modular problems
   → problems with large grain size

FIG. 2. Observations and implications.

[6]Over short distances, of course, permanent hardwired links can be very effective. Where distances are large or varying (e.g., mobile robots), bandwidth again becomes a limiting factor.

Note also that we mean communicating all the bits involved in a computation, not just the final answer. Otherwise communicating, say, one bit to indicate the primality of a 100-digit number would surely be faster than doing the computation to determine the answer.

We have argued above for loose coupling and based the argument on technological considerations. The point can be argued from two additional perspectives as well. First, the comments earlier concerning the locality of action and information suggest that, for the class of problems we wish to consider, tight coupling is unnecessary. The activities and results of any one problem solver are generally relevant to only a few others. More widespread dissemination of information will mostly likely only prove to be distracting.

A second argument, described in [18], takes a more emphatic position and argues for loose coupling even where it is known to produce temporary inconsistencies. They note that standard approaches to parallelism are typically designed to ensure that all processors always have mutually consistent views of the problem. Such complete consistency, and the tight coupling it requires, is, they claim, unnecessary. They suggest instead that distributed systems can be designed to be 'functionally accurate', i.e., the system will produce the correct answer eventually even though in an intermediate state some processors may have inconsistent views of the problem.

Thus we have arguments against tight coupling based on technological considerations (the communication/computation imbalance), pragmatic issues (the locality of action and information), and empirical results which suggest that it may be unnecessary.

Any unique node is a potential bottleneck.

Any node with unique characteristics is potentially a bottleneck that can slow down the system (Fig. 3). If those characteristics make the distinguished node useful to enough other nodes in the system, eventually those nodes may be forced to stand idle while they wait for service. This is equally true for a resource like data (for which the issue has been extensively studied) and a 'resource' like control (for which considerably less work has been done). If one node were in charge of directing the activities of all other nodes, requests for decisions about what to do next would eventually accumulate faster than they could be processed.[7]

What steps can we take to reduce the likelihood of bottlenecks due to centralized control? First, we can distribute it: Each node should have some

Any unique node is a potential bottleneck
→ distribute data
→ distribute control
→ organized behavior is hard to guarantee

FIG. 3. Further observations and implications.

[7]Such a node would also be an Achilles' heel in the system, since its failure would result in total failure of the system.

degree of autonomy in generating new tasks and in deciding which task to do next. By so dividing up and distributing the responsibility for control, we reduce the likely load on any one node. Second, we might distribute it redundantly: If more than one node is capable of making decisions about control, we further reduce the likelihood that any one node becomes saturated, and can ensure that no one node is unique. Finally, we can distribute control dynamically: We might provide a mechanism that allows dynamic redistribution in response to demands of the problem.

Organized behavior is difficult to guarantee if control is decentralized.

In a system with completely centralized control, one processor is responsible for directing the activities of all the others. It knows what all the other processors are doing at any given time, and, armed with this global view of the problem, can assign processors to tasks in a manner that assures organized behavior of the system as a whole. By 'organized', we mean that (among other things) all tasks will eventually be attended to, they will be dealt with in an order that reduces or eliminates the need for one processor to wait for results from another, processor power will be well matched to the tasks generated, etc. In more general terms, the set of processors will behave like a well-coordinated, purposeful team.

In the absence of a global overview, coordination and organization becomes much more difficult. When control is decentralized, no one node has a global view of all activities in the system; each node has a local view that includes information about only a subset of the tasks. The appropriate organization of a number of such subsets does not necessarily result in appropriate organization and behavior of the system as a whole.

In Section 4 we described the general problem of ensuring well-coordinated behavior; this is a specific instantiation of that problem with respect to control. We are trying to achieve a global effect (coherent behavior) from a collection of local decisions (nodes organizing subsets of tasks). We cannot centralize control for reasons noted above, yet it is not clear how to ensure coherent behavior when control is distributed.

7. A Framework for Distributed Problem Solving

7.1. A view of distributed problem solving

We view distributed problem solving as involving four central activities: problem decomposition, sub-problem distribution, solution of sub-problems, and synthesis of the overall solution. By decomposition we mean the standard notion of breaking a large problem into smaller, more manageable pieces; distribution involves the matching of sub-problems with problem solvers capable of handling them; the sub-problems are then solved; and finally those individual solutions may need to be synthesized into a single, overall solution.

Each of these can happen several times as a problem is decomposed into several levels of subproblems.

These four activities may occur individually and in the sequence noted, or may be combined or carried out in parallel. The point is simply that all of them can make important contributions to the problem solving process, so we need some mechanism for dealing with each.[8]

7.2. Task-sharing, negotiation and the connection problem

We have emphasized above the importance of having a protocol for organizing problem solving activity and proposed negotiation as a plausible basis for that protocol. But what shall we negotiate? Our work to date has followed the lead suggested by the cooperating experts metaphor and explored the distribution of tasks as an appropriate subject. Thus, in this paper we focus on application of the contract net to the distribution phase of distributed problem solving and show how negotiation appears to be an effective tool for accomplishing the matching of problem solvers and tasks.

To illustrate this, recall that the group of experts distributed a problem by decomposing it into ever smaller subtasks and distributing the subtasks among the group. We term this mode of operation 'task-sharing', because cooperation is based on the dynamic decomposition and distribution of subproblems.[9] But to enable distribution of the subproblems, there must be a way for experts with tasks to be executed to find idle experts capable of executing those tasks. We call this the 'connection problem'.

The contract net protocol supplies a mechanism to solve the connection problem: As we will see, nodes with tasks to be executed negotiate with idle nodes over the appropriate matching of tasks and nodes.

This approach is appropriate for a distributed problem solver because it requires neither global data storage nor global control. It also permits some degree of dynamic configuration and reconfiguration. A simple example of dynamic configuration is given in Section 8.3; reconfiguration is useful in the event of node failure or overloading. We have explored a number of simple mechanisms for detecting node failure and reconfiguring in response [26, 22], but the problem is not yet well studied.

A few words of terminology will be useful. The collection of nodes is referred to as a *contract net*. Each node in the net may take on the role of a *manager* or a *contractor*. A manager is responsible for monitoring the execu-

[8]For some problems the first or last activity may be trivial or unnecessary. Where a problem is geographically distributed, for example, the decomposition may be obvious (but see the discussion of the sensor net in Section 8). In problems of distributed control (e.g., traffic light control), there may be no need to synthesize an 'overall' answer.

[9]Task-sharing in its simplest form can be viewed as the distributed version of the traditional notion of problem decomposition. For a different approach to distribution, see [18].

tion of a task and processing the results of its execution. A contractor is responsible for the actual execution of the task.[10]

Individual nodes are not designated *a priori* as managers or contractors; these are only roles, and any node can take on either role dynamically during the course of problem solving. Typically a node will take on both roles, often simultaneously for different contracts. This has the advantage that individual nodes are not statically tied to a control hierarchy.

For the sake of exposition, we describe the protocol in successive layers of detail, describing first the *content* of the messages exchanged (Section 7.3), then their *format* (Section 7.4), and finally the details of the *language* in which they are written (Section 7.5).

7.3. Contract net protocol—message content

Message content is the heart of the issue, since it indicates what kinds of things nodes should say to one another and provides the basis for cooperation.

Negotiation is initiated by the generation of a new task. As suggested in the experts metaphor, this may occur when one problem solver decomposes a task into sub-tasks, or when it decides that it does not have the knowledge or data required to carry out the task. When this occurs, the node that generates the task advertises existence of the task with a *task announcement* message (Fig. 4). It then acts as the manager of that task for its duration. Many such announcements are made over the course of time as new tasks are generated.

Meanwhile, nodes in the net are listening to the task announcements (Fig. 5). They evaluate their own level of interest in each task with respect to their specialized resources (hardware and software), using *task evaluation procedures* specific to the problem at hand.[11]

When a task is found to be of sufficient interest, a node submits a bid (Fig. 6). A bid message indicates the capabilities of the bidder that are relevant to execution of the announced task.

A manager may receive several bids in response to a single task announcement (Fig. 7). Based on the information in the bids, it selects one or more nodes for execution of the task, using a task-specific *bid evaluation procedure*.

The selection is communicated to the successful bidders through an *award* message (Fig. 8). The selected nodes assume responsibility for execution of the task, and each is called a contractor for that task.

A contractor will typically partition a task and enter into (sub)contracts with

---

[10]The basic idea of contracting is not new. For example, a rudimentary bidding scheme was used for resource allocation in the Distributed Computing System (DCS) [8]. The contract net takes a wider perspective and allows a broader range of descriptions to be used during negotiation. For a detailed discussion see [27].

[11]It is in general up to the user to supply this and other task-specific procedures, but useful defaults are available (see [26]).

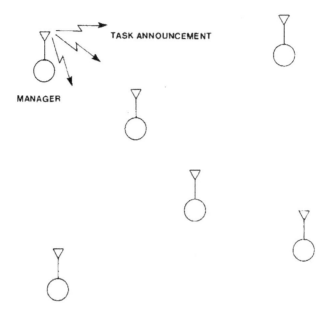

FIG. 4. Node issuing a task announcement.

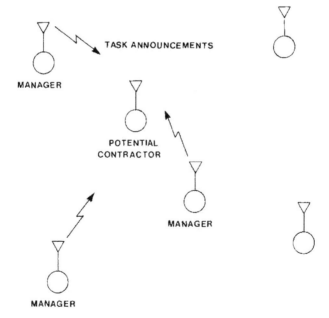

FIG. 5. Idle node listening to task announcements.

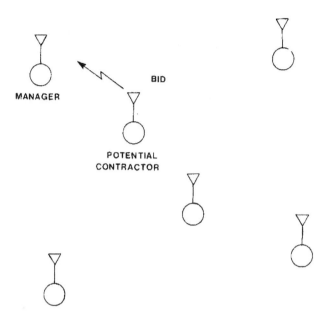

FIG. 6. Node submitting a bid.

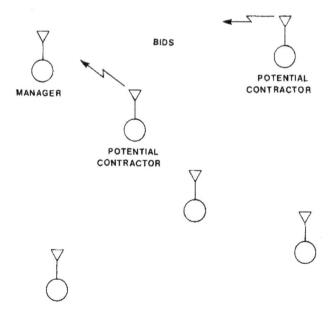

FIG. 7. Manager listening to bids coming in.

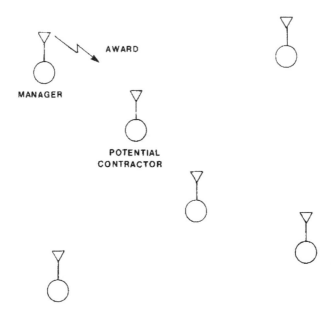

FIG. 8. Manager making an award.

other nodes. It is then the manager for those contracts. This leads to the hierarchical control structure that is typical of task-sharing.

A report is used by a contractor to inform its manager that a task has been partially executed (an *interim report*) or completed (a *final report*). The report contains a *result description* that specifies the results of the execution.[12]

The manager may terminate contracts with a *termination* message. The contractor receiving such a message terminates execution of the contract and all related outstanding subcontracts.

A contract is thus an explicit agreement between a node that generates a task (the manager) and a node that executes the task (the contractor, Fig. 9). Note that establishing a contract is a process of mutual selection. Available contractors evaluate task announcements until they find one of interest; the managers then evaluate the bids received from potential contractors and select the ones they determine to be most appropriate. Both parties to the agreement have evaluated the information supplied by the other and a mutual selection has been made.

We have dealt here with a simple example in order to focus on the issue of

[12]Interim reports are useful when generator-style control is desired. A node can be set to work on a task and instructed to issue interim reports whenever the next result is ready. It then pauses, awaiting a message that instructs it to continue and produce another result.

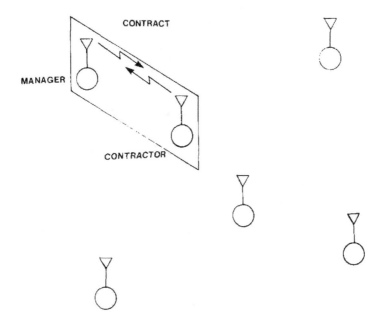

FIG. 9. A contract established.

cooperation. Additional complications which arise in implementing the protocol are discussed in detail in [26]; we note them briefly here for reference. *Focused addressing* is a more direct communication scheme used where the generality of broadcast is not required. *Directed contracts* are used when a manager knows which node is appropriate for a task. A *request-response* mechanism allows simple transfers of information without the overhead of contracting. And finally, a *node-available* message allows reversal of the normal negotiation process: When the computation load on the net is high, most task announcements will not be answered with bids because all nodes will already be busy. The node-available message allows an idle node to indicate that it is searching for a task to execute. The protocol is thus load-sensitive in response to changing demands of the task: When the load is low, the spawning of a task is the important event; when the load is high, the availability of a node is important.

7.4. Contract net protocol—message format

Each message is composed of a number of slots that specify the kind of information needed in that type of message. A task announcement message, for example, has four main slots (Fig. 10).[13] The *eligibility specification* is a list

---

[13]There are also slots that contain bookkeeping information.

Main Task Announcement Slots

Eligibility specification
Task abstraction
Bid specification
Expiration time

Fig. 10. Task announcement format.

of criteria that a node must meet to be eligible to submit a bid. The *task abstraction* is a brief description of the task to be executed. It enables a node to rank the announced task relative to other announced tasks. The *bid specification* is a description of the expected form of a bid. It gives a manager a chance to say, in effect, "Here's what I consider important about a node that wants to bid on this task." This provides a common basis for comparison of bids, and enables a node to include in a bid only the information about its capabilities that are relevant to the announced task. Finally, the *expiration time* is a deadline for receiving bids.

For any given application, the information that makes up the eligibility specification, etc., must be supplied by the user. Hence while the contract net protocol offers a framework specifying the types of information that are necessary, it remains the task of the user to supply the actual information appropriate to the domain at hand.

7.5. Contract net protocol—the common internode language

Finally, we need a language in which to specify the information in the slots of a message. For a number of reasons, it is useful to specify a single, relatively high level language in which all such information is expressed. We call this the *common internode language*. This language forms a common basis for communication among all the nodes.

As an example, consider a task announcement message that might be used in a system working on a signal processing task. Assume that one node attempting to analyze a signal determines that it would be useful to have a Fourier transform of that signal. Unwilling or unable to do the task itself (perhaps because of hardware limitations), it decides to announce the task in order to solicit assistance. It might issue a task announcement of the sort shown in Fig. 11.

The announcement is broadcast to all nodes within range ("To: *"), and indicates that there is a TASK of TYPE FOURIER-TRANSFORM to be done. In order to consider bidding on it a node must have an FFTBOX and a bid should specify estimated time to completion of the task.

The common internode language is currently built around a very simple *attribute, object, value* representation. There are a number of predefined

To: *
From: 25
Type: TASK ANNOUNCEMENT
Contract: 43-6

Eligibility Specification
    MUST-HAVE FFTBOX

Task Abstraction
    TASK TYPE FOURIER-TRANSFORM
    NUMBER-POINTS 1024
    NODE NAME 25
    POSITION LAT 64N LONG 10W

Bid Specification
    COMPLETION-TIME

Expiration Time
    29 1645Z NOV 1980

FIG. 11. Task announcement example.

(domain-independent) terms (like TYPE of TASK); these are supplemented with domain-specific terms (like FFTBOX). The domain-independent terms are part of the language offered to the user and help him organize and specify the information he has to supply. The domain-specific terms have to be added by the user as needed for the application at hand.

All of this information is stated in terms of something we here called a common internode language. The two important points here are that the information in messages is viewed as statements in a language, and that the language is common to all the nodes.

It is useful to view the messages as statements in a language because this sets the appropriate perspective on the character of the interaction we are trying to achieve. Viewing the message exchange as, say, pattern matching would lead to a much more restricted form of communication: A pattern either matches or fails; if it succeeds the only information available comes from the bindings of pattern variables. Viewing the messages as statements in a language offers the chance for a more interesting exchange of information, since the nodes are examining and responding to the messages, not simply matching patterns. In particular, we find the two-way exchange of information an important capability (see Section 9).

It is useful to identify a common 'core' language shared by all the nodes. This makes it much easier to add new nodes to the net. Any new node, preloaded with only the common internode language, can use that language to isolate the information it needs to begin to participate in solving the problem at hand. It can listen to and understand task announcements and express a request for the transfer of any required information. If there were a number of distinct internode languages, then a new node entering the net could interact with only a limited subset of the nodes, those which spoke its language.[14] This would make addition of new nodes to the net less effective.

A common language also makes possible invocation schemes that are more flexible than standard procedure invocation, and this also facilitates addition of a new node to the net. For example, a common language makes it possible to use invocation based on describing tasks to be done,[15] rather than naming specific KSs (procedures) to invoke next. When this technique is used, new nodes can simply be added to the existing collection; they will find their own place in the scheme of things by listening to task announcements, issuing bids, etc. With more traditional invocation schemes (e.g., standard procedure calling), a new node would have to be linked explicitly to others in the network.

8. Example: Distributed Sensing

The protocol described above has been implemented in INTERLISP and used to solve several problems in a simulated multi-processor environment. The problems included search (e.g., the 8-queens problem) and signal interpretation (for details see [26]). In this section we describe use of the contract net on one such problem in signal interpretation: area surveillance of the sort encountered in air or ship traffic control. We explore the operation of a network of nodes, each having either sensing or processing capabilities and all spread throughout a relatively large geographic area. We refer to such a network as a distributed sensing system (DSS).

Although an operational DSS may have several functions, ranging from passive analysis to active control over vehicle courses and speeds, we focus here on the analysis function. The task involves detection, classification, and tracking of vehicles; the solution to the problem is a dynamic map of traffic in the area. Construction and maintenance of the map requires interpretation of the large quantity of sensory information received by the collection of sensor elements.

Since we want to produce a single map of the entire area, we may choose to have one processor node—which we will call the monitor node—carry out the final integration of information and transmit it to the appropriate destination. It is also useful to assign that node the responsibility for beginning the initialization of the DSS. Its total set of responsibilities therefore includes starting the initialization as the first step in net operation, integrating the overall

---

[14]Note that the extreme case (in which every pair of nodes communicates in its own private language) is precisely standard procedure invocation. To decode a procedure call, one must know the expected order, type, and number of arguments. This is information which is shared only by the caller and procedure involved, in effect a private language used for communication between them.

[15]As is also done in PLANNER and the other pattern-directed languages.

map as the last step in analysis, and then communicating the result to the appropriate agent. We will see that this monitor node does not, by the way, correspond to a central controller.

Since the emphasis in this work has been on organizing the problem solving activities of multiple problem solvers, work on the signal interpretation aspects did not include construction of low-level signal processing facilities. Instead it assumed the existence of appropriate signal processing modules and focused on the subsequent symbolic interpretation of that information.

8.1. Hardware

All communication in the DSS is assumed to take place over a broadcast channel (using for example packet radio techniques [14]). The nodes are assumed to be in fixed positions known to themselves but not known a priori to other nodes in the net. Each node has one of two capabilities: sensing or processing. The sensing capability includes low-level signal analysis and feature extraction. We assume that a variety of sensor types exists in the DSS, that the sensors are widely spaced, and that there is some overlap in sensor area coverage. Nodes with processing capability supply the computation power necessary to effect the high-level analysis and control in the net. They are not necessarily near the sensors whose data they process.

Fig. 12 is a schematic representation of a DSS.

In the example that follows, some assumptions about such things as node locations, what one node knows about another, etc., may seem to be carefully chosen rather than typically what one would expect to find. This is entirely true. We have combined a number of plausible but carefully chosen (and occasionally atypical) assumptions about hardware and software available in order to display a number of the capabilities of the contract net in a single, brief example.

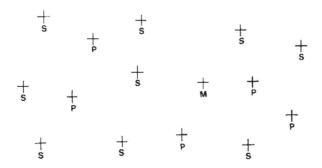

FIG. 12. A distributed sensing system. M: monitor node; P: processor node; S: sensor node.

8.2. Data and task hierarchy

The DSS must integrate a large quantity of data, reducing it and transforming it into a form meaningful to a human decision maker. We view this process as occurring in several stages, which together form a data hierarchy (Fig. 13).

As we have chosen to solve the problem for this illustration, at any given moment a particular node handles data at only one level of the data hierarchy, but may communicate with nodes at other levels. In addition, the only form of signal processing we consider is narrow band spectral analysis.[16]

At the bottom of the hierarchy we have audio *signals*, which are described in terms of several features: frequency, time of detection, strength, changes in strength, name and position of the detecting node, and name, type, and orientation of the detecting sensor.

Signals are formed into *signal groups*, collections of related signals. One common signal group is the harmonic set, a collection of signals in which the frequency of each signal is an integral multiple of the lowest frequency. In the current example, a signal group is described in terms of its fundamental frequency, time of formation, identity of the detecting node, and features of the detecting sensor.

FIG. 13. Data hierarchy.

[16]Noise radiated by a vehicle typically contains narrow band signal components caused by rotating machinery. The frequencies of such signals are correlated with the type of rotating machine and its speed of rotation; hence they are indicators of the classification of the vehicle. Narrow band signals also undergo shifts in frequency due to Doppler effect or change in the speed of rotation of the associated machine; hence they also provide speed and directional information. (Unfortunately, alterations in signal strength occur both as a result of propagation conditions and variations in the distance between the vehicle and the sensor.)

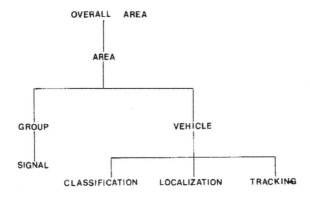

FIG. 14. Task hierarchy.

The next level of the hierarchy is the description of the *vehicle*. It has one or more signal groups associated with it and is further specified by position, speed, course, and classification. Position can be established by triangulation, using matching groups detected by several sensors with different positions and orientations. Speed and course must generally be established over time by tracking.

The *area map* forms the next level of the data hierarchy. It contains information about the vehicle traffic in a given area. There will be several such maps for the DSS—together they span the total area of coverage of the system.

The final level is the complete or *overall area map*, produced in this example by the monitor, which integrates information in the individual area maps.

The hierarchy of tasks, Fig. 14, follows directly from the data hierarchy. The monitor node manages several *area* contractors. These contractors are responsible for the formation of traffic maps in their immediate areas. Each area contractor, in turn, manages several *group* contractors that provide it with signal groups for its area. Each group contractor integrates raw signal data from *signal* contractors that have sensing capabilities.

The area contractors also manage several *vehicle* contractors that are responsible for integrating information about individual vehicles. Each of these contractors manages a *classification* contractor that determines vehicle type, a *localization* contractor that determines vehicle position, and a *tracking* contractor that tracks the vehicle.

8.3. Contract net implementation

There are two phases to this problem: initialization of the net and operation. Although there are interesting aspects to both of these phases, our concern here is primarily with initialization, since this phase most easily illustrates the states and we summarise the general framework (§ 2.7). Using this framework as a reference we describe several notions of verification and testing (§ 3). We use the framework to analyse existing ACLs to determine if they are verifiable (§ 4) and we identify the type of ACL which would be appropriate in an open system. Finally we discuss how compliance might be enforced in an open system (§ 5) and conclude (§ 6).

2   A General Agent Communication Framework

Before discussing verification and compliance testing we need to describe a general agent communication framework containing the necessary components of a multi-agent system. Our framework builds on the framework presented by Wooldridge [14]; we attempt to make the framework more general to allow ACLs with social semantics to be accommodated.

An agent communication language (ACL) typically has two functions[1]:

– To specify the meaning of messages; this is useful to an agent designer who is deciding when an agent will plan to send a message and also what way the agent will update its internal state upon receiving a message.
– To provide a normative specification for communication in the system; this is necessary to ensure that the multi-agent system does not become dysfunctional, for example to ensure that agents respond when spoken to and that they honour their commitments.

We say that the first part defines a semantics for each communicative act while the second (normative) part defines a specification which must be satisfied by the system of agents using that language. It is important to note that there is a distinction between *program semantics* for communication statements in an agent's program and *ACL semantics* (which constitute specifications) for communicative acts. If an agent is ACL-compliant then its program semantics will satisfy the semantics defined by the ACL specification. ACL semantics may be defined in different ways and each way implies different notions of verification.

Communicating agents operate in a certain context, the entire context includes the private states and programs of agents as well as the publicly observable state of the society. ACL semantics for communicative acts must specify something about the state of this context. ACLs based on mental states typically specify semantics by means of preconditions and/or postconditions [7] which must be true before or after the communicative act is performed. ACLs based on social states typically specify social facts that are created or modified by the performance of a communicative act [11]. Thus an agent communication framework will need to include a representation of the multi-agent system which captures information about the internal states of agents in the system as well as observable (social) states.

---

[1] The first agent communication languages confused these two functions (for example FIPA [3] and KQML [7]).

partition the system's span of coverage into areas based on the positions of the nodes selected. For purposes of illustration we assume that the monitor node knows the names of the nodes that are potential area contractors, but must establish their positions in order to do the partitioning.

It begins by announcing the task of area map formation. Because it knows the names of potential contractors, it can avoid using a general broadcast and instead uses focused addressing. The components of the announcement of interest here are the task abstraction, the eligibility specification, and the bid specification. The task abstraction is simply the task type. The eligibility specification is blank, since in this case the monitor node knows which nodes are potential contractors and can address them directly. The bid specification informs a prospective area contractor to respond with its position.

Recall that the purpose of a bid specification is to inform a node of how to bid so that a manager can select from all of the bidders the most appropriate one(s) to execute the task. In this case, node position is the relevant information. Potential area contractors respond with their positions, and, given that information, the monitor node can partition the overall span of coverage into approximately equal-sized areas. It then selects a subset of the bidders to be area contractors, informing each of its area of responsibility in an award message. The negotiation sequence thus makes available to the monitor node the positions of all of the potential area contractors, making possible a partitioning of the overall area of the DSS based on these positions. This in turn enables the DSS to adjust to a change in the number or position of potential area contractors.

Area contractors integrate vehicle data into area maps. They must first establish the existence of vehicles on the basis of group data. To do this, each area contractor solicits other nodes to provide that data. In the absence of any information about which nodes are suitable, each area contractor announces the task using a general broadcast. The task abstraction in this message is the type of task. The eligibility specification is the area for which the area contractor is responsible.[17] The bid specification is again node position. Potential group contractors respond with their respective positions, and based on this information the area contractors award contracts to nodes in their areas of responsibility.

The group contractors integrate signal features into groups, and start by finding a set of contractors to provide the signal features. Recall that we view node interaction as an agreement between a node with a task to be done and a node capable of performing that task. Sometimes the perspective on the ideal character of that agreement differs depending on the point of view of the

---

[17]This ensures that a node is eligible to bid on this task only if it is in the same area as the announcing area contractor and helps to prevent a case in which a group contractor is so far away from its manager that reliable communication is difficult to achieve.

participant. For example, from the perspective of the signal task *managers*, the best set of contractors would have an adequate spatial distribution about the surrounding area and an adequate distribution of sensor types. From the point of view of the signal task *contractors*, on the other hand, the ideal match involves finding managers that are closest to them (in order to minimize potential communication problems).

The ability to express and deal with such disparate viewpoints is one advantage of the contract net framework. To see how the appropriate resolution is accomplished, consider the messages exchanged between the signal managers and potential signal contractors. Each signal manager announces its own signal task, using a message of the sort shown in Fig. 16. The task abstraction is the type of task, the position of the manager making the announcement, and a specification of its area of responsibility. This enables a potential contractor to determine the manager to which it should respond. The eligibility specification indicates that the only nodes that should bid on the task are those which (a) have sensing capabilities, and (b) are located in the same area as the manager that announced the task. The bid specification indicates that a bid should contain the position of the bidder and the number of each of its sensor types, information that a manager needs to select a suitable set of sensor nodes.

The potential signal contractors listen to the task announcements made by signal managers. They respond to the nearest manager with a bid (Fig. 17) that supplies their position and a description of their sensors. The managers use this

```
To:         *
From:       25
Type:       TASK ANNOUNCEMENT
Contract:   22-3-1

Eligibility Specification
            MUST-HAVE SENSOR
            MUST-HAVE POSITION AREA A

Task Abstraction:
            TASK TYPE SIGNAL
            POSITION LAT 47N LONG 17E
            AREA NAME A SPECIFICATION (. . .)

Bid Specification
            POSITION LAT LONG
            EVERY SENSOR NAME TYPE

Expiration Time
            28 1730Z FEB 1979
```

FIG. 16. Signal task announcement.

```
To:        25
From:      42
Type:      BID
Contract:  22-3-1

Node Abstraction
   LAT 62N LONG 9W
   SENSOR NAME S1 TYPE S
   SENSOR NAME S2 TYPE S
   SENSOR NAME TI TYPE T
```

FIG. 17. Signal bid.

information to select a set of bidders that covers their area of responsibility with a suitable variety of sensors, and then award signal contracts on this basis (Fig. 18).

The signal contract is a good example of the negotiation process. It involves a mutual decision based on local processing by both the managers and the potential contractors. The potential contractors base their decision on a distance metric and respond to the closest manager. The managers use the number of sensors and distribution of sensor types observed in the bids to select a set of contractors that covers each area with a variety of sensors. Thus each party to the contract evaluates the proposals made by the other using its own distinct evaluation procedure.

To review the initialization process: we have a single monitor node that manages several area contractors. Each area contractor manages several group contractors, and each group contractor manages several signal contractors. The data initially flows from the bottom to the top of this hierarchy. The signal contractors supply signal features; each group contractor integrates the features from several signal contractors to form a signal group, and these groups are passed along to the area contractors, which eventually form area maps by integrating information based on the data from several group contractors. All

```
To:        42
From:      25
Type:      AWARD
Contract:  22-3-1

Task Specification
   SENSOR NAME S1
   SENSOR NAME S2
```

FIG. 18. Signal award.

the area maps are then passed to the monitor which forms the final traffic map.[18]

The initialization process reviewed above may appear at first glance to be somewhat more elaborate than is strictly necessary. We have purposely taken a fairly general approach to the problem to emphasize two aspects of contract net performance. First, as illustrated by the signal contract, contract negotiation is an interactive process involving (i) a *two-way transfor of information* (task announcements from managers to contractors, bids from contractors to managers), (ii) *local evaluation* (each party to the negotiation has its own local evaluation procedure), and (iii) *mutual selection* (bidders select from among task announcements, managers select from among bids).

Second, the contract negotiation process offers a useful degree of flexibility, making it well suited to AI problems whose decomposition is not known a priori and well suited to problems whose configuration is likely to change over time. To illustrate this, consider that exactly the same initialization process will work across a large variation in *the number of and position of nodes available* (indeed the description given never mentions how many nodes there are, where they are located, or how wide the total area of coverage is). There are clearly limits to this flexibility: If the area of coverage were large enough to require several thousand area contractors, it might prove useful to introduce another level of distribution in the hierarchy (Fig. 14) between the monitor node and the area contractor. But the current approach works with a wide range of available resources and needs no modification within that range. This can be useful when available hardware resources cannot be identified a priori with certainty, or when operating environments are hostile enough to make hardware failure a significant occurrence.

8.3.2. Operation

We now consider the activities of the system as it begins operation. For the sake of brevity the actions are described at the level of task announcements, bids, and contracts. For additional details and examples of messages sent, see [25].

When a signal is detected or when a change occurs in the features of a known signal, the detecting signal contractor reports this fact to its manager. This node, in turn, attempts either to integrate the information into an existing signal group or to form a new signal group (recall that the manager for the signal task is also a contractor for the task of group formation, Fig. 15).

---

[18]As noted, in this example one area contractor manages several group contractors and each group contractor in turn manages several signal contractors. It is possible, however, that a single group contractor could supply information to several area contractors, and a single signal contractor could supply information to several group contractors. It may be useful, for instance, to have a particular group contractor near an area boundary report to the area contractors on both sides of the boundary. This is easily accommodated within our framework.

Whenever a new group is detected, the contractor reports existence of the group to its manager (an area contractor). The area contractor attempts to find a node to execute a vehicle contract, which involves classifying, localizing, and tracking the vehicle. The area contractor must first determine whether the newly detected group is attributable to a known vehicle. To do this, it uses a request-response interchange to get from all current vehicle contractors an indication of their belief that the new group can in fact be attributed to one of the known vehicles.[19] Based on the responses, the area contractor either starts up a new vehicle contractor (if the group does not seem to fit an existing vehicle) or augments the current contract of the appropriate vehicle contractor, adding to it the task of making certain that the new group corresponds to a known vehicle. This may entail such things as gathering new data via the adjustment of sensors or the creation of contracts with new sensor nodes.

The vehicle contractor then makes two task announcements: vehicle classification and vehicle localization. A classification contractor may be able to classify directly, given the signal group information or it may require more data, in which case it can communicate directly with the appropriate sensor nodes.[20] The localization task is a simple triangulation which is awarded to the first bidder.

Once the vehicle has been localized, it must be tracked. This is handled by the vehicle contractor, which issues additional localization contracts from time to time and uses the results to update its vehicle description. Alternatively, the area contractor could award separate tracking contracts. The decision as to which method to use depends on loading and communication. If, for example, the area contractor is very busy with integration of data from many group contractors, it seems more appropriate to isolate it from the additional load of tracking contracts. If, on the other hand, the area contractor is not overly busy, we can let it handle updated vehicle contracts, taking advantage of the fact that it is in the best position to integrate the results and coordinate the efforts of multiple tracking contractors. In this example, we assume that the management load would be too large for the area contractor.

A variety of other issues have to be considered in the design and operation of a real distributed sensing system. Most of them, however, are quite specific to the DSS application and hence outside the main focus of this paper.

---

[19]In response to the request, the vehicle contractor has two options. It can compute the answer itself, or, if it decides that that would require more processing power than it can spare, it can issue a contract and have another node compute the answer.

[20]As this example illustrates, it is possible in the contract net for two contractors to communicate directly (i.e., horizontal communication across the hierarchy) as well as via the more traditional (vertical) communication between managers and contractors. This is accomplished with request-response exchanges. If the identity of the recipient of the request is not known by name, then the request can be sent out using the focused addressing scheme mentioned in Section 7.3.

9. A Progression in Mechanisms for Transfer of Control

9.1. The basic questions and fundamental differences

The contract net appears to offer a novel perspective on the traditional concepts of invocation and transfer of control. To illustrate this, we examine a range of invocation mechanisms that have been created since the earliest techniques were developed, and compare the perspective implicit in each to the perspective used in the contract net.

In doing this comparison, we consider the process of transfer of control from the perspective of both the caller and the respondent. We focus in particular on the issue of *selection* and consider what opportunities a calling process has for selecting an appropriate respondent and what opportunities a potential respondent has for selecting the task on which to work. In each case we consider two basic questions that either the caller or the respondent might ask:

> *What is the character of the choice available?* (i.e., at runtime, does the caller know about all potential respondents and can it choose from among them; similarly does each respondent know all the potential callers for whom it might work and can it choose from among them?)

> *On what kind of information is that choice based?* (e.g., are potential respondents given, say, a pattern to match, or some more complex form of information? What information is the caller given about the potential respondents?)

The answers to these questions will demonstrate how our view of control transfer differs from that of the earlier formalisms with respect to:

> *Information transfer*: The announcement-bid-award sequence means that there is the potential for more information, and more complex information, transferred in both directions (between caller and respondent) during the invocation process.

> *Local evaluation*: The computation devoted to the selection process, based on the information transfer noted above, is more extensive and more complex that that used in traditional approaches. It is *local* in the sense that information is evaluated in a context associated with, and specific to, an individual KS (rather than embodied in a global evaluation function).

> *Mutual selection*: The local selection process is symmetric, in the sense that the caller evaluates potential respondents from its perspective (via the bid evaluation procedure) and the respondents evaluate the available tasks from their perspective (via the task evaluation procedures).

To put it another way, in the contract net the issue of *transfer of control* is more broadly viewed as a problem of connecting managers (and their tasks) with contractors (and their KSs). This view is inherently *symmetric* in that both the caller (manager) and respondents (bidders) have a selection to make. This symmetry in turn leads to the concept of establishing connection via *negotiation* between the interested parties. Then, if we are to have a fruitful discussion, the participants need to be able to 'say' interesting things to one another (i.e., they need the ability to transfer *complex information*). As the discussion below should made clear, previous models of invocation do not share these qualities. They view transfer of control as an essentially unidirectional process (from caller to respondent), offer minimal opportunity for selection at runtime, and provide restricted channels of communication between caller and respondent.

9.2. The comparison

In discussing the various approaches to invocation we often refer to 'standard' or 'traditional' forms of these approaches. Each of them could conceivably be modified in ways that would render our comments less relevant, but our point here is to examine the techniques as conceived and as typically used.

Standard subroutine (procedure) invocation represents, by our standard, a degenerate case. All the selection of routines to be invoked is done beforehand by the programmer and is hardwired into the code. The possible respondents are thus named explicitly in the source code, leaving no opportunity for choice or nondeterminism at runtime.

In traditional production rule systems, a degree of choice for the caller (in this case the interpreter) is available, since a number of rules may be retrieved at once. A range of selection criteria have been used (called *conflict resolution* schemes—see [5]), but these have typically been implemented with a single syntactic criterion hardwired into the interpreter. One standard scheme, for instance, is to assign a fixed priority to each rule and then from among those retrieved for possible invocation, simply select the rule with the highest priority. Selection is thus determined by a single procedure applied uniformly to every set of rules.

In this approach to invocation there is some choice available in selecting a KS to be invoked (since more than one rule may be retrieved), but the mechanism provided for making that choice allows for only a single, preselected procedure that is to be applied in all cases. In addition, all of the selection is done by the 'caller'; there is no mechanism that offers the rules any ability to select how they are to be invoked (e.g., if a rule can match the database in several ways, which of the possible matches will actually be used?). Finally, only minimal information is transferred from potential respondents back to the caller (at most a specification of what items in the database have been matched, and how).

PLANNER'S [11] pattern-directed invocation provides a facility at the programming language level for nondeterministic KS retrieval, by matching goal specifications (patterns) against theorem patterns. In the simplest case, theorems are retrieved one by one and matched against the goal specification until a match is found. The order in which the theorems are tried is not defined by the language and is dependent on implementation decisions.

PLANNER does offer, in the *recommendation list*, a mechanism designed to allow the user to encode selection information. The *use* construct provides a way of specifying (by name) which theorems to try in which order. The *theorem base filter* construct offers a way of invoking a predicate function which takes one argument (the name of the next theorem whose pattern has matched the goal) and which can veto the use of that theorem.

Note that there is a degree of selection possible here, since the theorem base filter offers a way of choosing among the theorems that might possibly be used. The selection may involve a considerable amount of computation by the theorem base filter, and is local, in the sense that filters may be specific to a particular goal pattern. However, the selection is also limited in several ways. First, in the standard PLANNER invocation mechanism, the information available to the caller is at best the name of the next potential respondent. The caller does not receive any additional information (such as, for instance, exactly how the theorem matched the pattern), nor is there any easy way to provide for information transfer in that direction. Second, the choice is, as noted, a simple veto based on just that single KS. That is, since final judgment is passed on each potential KS in turn, it is not possible to make comparisons between potential KSs or to pass judgment on the whole group and choose the one that looks by some measure the best. Both of these shortcomings could be overcome if we were willing to create a superstructure on top of the existing invocation mechanism, but this would be functionally identical to the announcement-bid-award mechanism described above. The point is simply that the standard PLANNER invocation mechanism has no such facility, and the built-in depth-first search with backtracking makes it expensive to implement.

CONNIVER [19] represents a useful advance in nondeterministic invocation, since the result of a pattern-directed call is a 'possibilities list' containing *all* the KSs that match the pattern. While there is no explicit mechanism parallel to PLANNER's recommendation list, the possibilities list is accessible as a data structure and can be modified to reflect any judgments the caller might make concerning the relative utility of the KSs retrieved. Also, paired with each KS on the possibilities list is an association-list of pattern variables and bindings, which makes possible a determination of how the calling pattern was matched by each KS. This mechanism offers the caller some information about each respondent that can be useful in making the judgments noted above. CONNIVER does not, however, offer the respondent any opportunity to perform local processing to select from among callers.

The HEARSAY-II [7] system illustrates a number of similar facilities in a data-directed system. In particular, the focus of attention mechanism has a pointer to all the KSs that are ready to be invoked (i.e., those whose *stimulus frames* have been matched), as well as information (in the *response frame*) for estimating the potential contribution of each of the KSs. The system can effect some degree of selection regarding the KSs ready for invocation and has available to it a body of knowledge about each KS on which to base its selection. The response frame thus provides information transfer from respondent to caller that, while fixed in format, is more extensive than previous mechanisms. Considerable computation is also devoted to the selection process. Note, however, that the selection is not local, since there is a single, global strategy used for every selection.

The concept of meta-rules [3] offers a further advance in mechanisms to support more elaborate control schemes. It suggests that KS selection can be viewed as problem solving and can be effected using the same mechanism employed to solve problems in the task domain. It views selection as a process of pruning and reordering the applicable KSs and provides local selection by allowing meta-rules to be associated with specific goals.[21]

There are several things to note about the systems reviewed thus far. First, we see an increase in the amount and variety of information that is transferred from caller to respondent (e.g., from explicit naming in subroutines, to patterns in PLANNER) and from respondent to caller (e.g., from no response in subroutines to the response frames of HEARSAY-II). Note, however, that in no case do we have available a general information transmission mechanism. In all cases, the mechanisms have been designed to carry one particular sort of information and are not easily modified.

Second, we see a progression from the retrieval of a single KS to the retrieval of the entire set of potentially useful KSs, providing the opportunity for more complex varieties of selection.

Finally, note that all the selection so far is from one perspective; the selection of respondents by the caller. In none of these systems do the respondents have any choice in the matter.

To illustrate this last point, consider turning HEARSAY-II around and creating a system where respondents performed the selection: a 'task blackboard' system. The simplest form of such a system would have a central task blackboard that contains an unordered list of tasks that need to be performed. As a KS works on its current task, it may discover new (sub)tasks that require execution and add them to the blackboard. When a KS finishes its current task, it looks at the blackboard, evaluates the lists of tasks there, and decides which one it wants to execute.

---

[21]The concept of negotiation in the contract net grew, in part, from generalizing this perspective to make it 'bi-directional': Both managers and potential contractors can devote computational effort to selecting from the alternatives available to them.

Note that in this system the respondents would have all the selection capability. Rather than having a caller announce a task and evaluate the set of KSs that respond, we have the KSs examining the list of tasks and selecting the one they wish to work on. It is thus plausible to invert the standard situation, but we still have unidirectional selection—in this case, on the part of the respondent rather than the caller.

PUP6 [16], on the other hand, was the first system to suggest that transfer of control could be viewed as a *discussion* between the caller and potential respondents. In that system, if a KS receives more than one offer to execute a task, a special 'chooser' KS momentarily takes control and asks 'questions' of the respondents to determine which of them ought to be used. This is accomplished by querying the *parts* of the KS. Each KS is composed of a standard set of *parts*, each *part* designed to deal with a particular question about that KS. For example, the procedures in the WHEN and COMPLEXITY parts of a KS answer the questions "When should you take control?" and "How costly are you?" This interchange is highly stylized and not very flexible, but does represent an attempt to implement explicit two-way communication.

The contract net differs from these approaches in several ways. First, from the point of view of the caller (the manager), the standard task broadcast and response interchange has been improved by making possible a *more informative* response. That is, instead of the traditional tools that allow the caller to receive only a list of potential respondents, the contract net has available a mechanism that makes it possible for the caller to receive a description of potential utility from each respondent (the bidders). The caller also has available (as in other approaches) a list of respondents rather than a sequence of names presented one at a time.[22] Both of these make it possible to be more selective in making decisions about invocation.

Second, the contract net emphasizes *local evaluation*. An explicit place in the framework has been provided for mechanisms in which the caller can invest computational effort in selecting KSs for invocation (using its bid evaluation procedure) and the respondents can similarly invest effort in selecting tasks to work on (using their task evaluation procedures). These selection procedures are also local in the sense that they are associated with and written from the perspective of the individual KS (as opposed to, say, HEARSAY-II's global focus of attention procedure).

Third, while we have labeled this process *selection*, it might more appropriately be labeled *deliberation*. This would emphasize that its purpose for the caller is to decide in general *what to do* with the bids received and not merely *which of them to accept*. Note that one possible decision is that *none* of the bids is adequate and thus none of the potential respondents would be

---

[22]More precisely, the caller has available a list of all those that have responded by the expiration time of the contract.

invoked (instead, the task may be re-announced later).[23] This choice is not typically available in other problem solving systems and emphasizes the wider perspective taken by the contract net on the transfer of control issue.

Finally, there appears to be a novel symmetry in the transfer of control process. Recall that PLANNER. CONNIVER, and HEARSAY-II all offer the caller some ability to select from among the respondents, while a task blackboard system allows the respondents to select from among the tasks. The contract net (and PUP6), however, use an interactive, *mutual selection* process where task distribution is the result of a discussion between processors. As a result of the information exchanged in this discussion, the caller can select from among potential respondents while the KSs can select from among potential tasks.

10. Suitable Applications

In this section we consider the sorts of problems for which the contract net is well suited.

The framework has, for instance, been designed to provide a more powerful mechanism for transfer of control than is available in current problem-solving systems. This mechanism will be useful when we do not know in advance which KS should be invoked or do not know which node should be given the task in question. In the first of these situations—not knowing in advance which KS to invoke—we require some machinery for making the decision. The contract net's negotiation and deliberation process is one such mechanism. It will prove most useful for problems in which especially careful selection of KSs is important (i.e., problems for which we prefer the 'knowledge' end of the knowledge vs. search tradeoff).

The second situation—matching nodes and tasks—is inherent in a distributed architecture, since no one node has complete knowledge of either the capabilities of or the busy/idle state of every node in the network. We have labeled this the connection problem and have explored the negotiation and deliberation process as a way of solving it as well.

The framework is well-matched to problems that can be viewed in terms of a hierarchy of tasks (e.g., heuristic search), or levels of data abstraction (e.g.,

---

[23]Similarly the potential bidders deliberate over task announcements received and may decide that none is worth submitting a bid. Note also that receiving bids but deciding that none is good enough is distinctly different from receiving no bids at all. In a system using pattern-directed inference, receiving no bids is analogous to finding no KSs with matching patterns; receiving bids but turning down all of them after due consideration has no precise analogy in existing languages.

Agenda-based systems come close, in that KSs put on the agenda may have such a low ranking that they are effectively ignored. But this is not the same, for two reasons. First, if the queue ever does get sufficiently depleted, those KSs will in fact be run. Second, and more important, there is no explicit decision to ignore those KSs, simply an accident of the ordering, or perhaps the KS's own estimation of its individual utility. The contract net offers a mechanism for making the decision explicitly and based on an evaluation of all the candidates.

applications that deal with audio or video signals). Such problems lend themselves to decomposition into a set of relatively independent tasks with little need for global information or synchronization. Individual tasks can be assigned to separate processor nodes; these nodes can then execute the tasks with little need for communication with other nodes.

The manager-contractor structure provides a natural way to effect hierarchical control (in the distributed case, it's actually concurrent hierarchical control), and the managers at each level in the hierarchy are an appropriate place for data integration and abstraction.

Note, by the way, that these control hierarchies are not simple vertical hierarchies but are more complex generalized hierarchies. This is illustrated by the existence of communication links other than those between managers and contractors. Nodes are able to communicate horizontally with related contractors or with any other nodes in the net, as we saw in the DSS example, where classification contractors communicated directly with signal contractors using the request-response style of interaction.

The framework is also primarily applicable to domains where the subtasks are large and where it is worthwhile to expend a potentially nontrivial amount of computation and communication to invoke the best KSs for each subtask. It would, for instance, make little sense to go through an extended mutual selection process to get some simple arithmetic done or to do a simple database access. While our approach can be abbreviated to an appropriately terse degree of interchange for simple problems (e.g., directed contacts and the request-response mechanism), other systems are already capable of supporting this variety of behavior. The primary contribution of our framework lies in applications to problems where the more complex interchange provides an efficient and effective basis for problem solving.

Finally, the contract net is also useful in problems where the primary concerns are in distributing control, achieving reliability, and avoiding bottlenecks, even if, in these problems, the more complex variety of information exchange described above is unnecessary. The contract net's negotiation mechanism offers a means for distributing control; sharing responsibility for tasks between managers and contractors offers a degree of reliability; and the careful design of the message types in the protocol helps avoid saturating the communication channel and causing bottlenecks.

11. Limitations, Extensions, Open Problems

11.1. The other stages

Earlier we noted that this paper focuses on application of the contract net to the distribution stage of distributed problem solving. The other stages—decomposition, sub-problem solution, and answer synthesis—are important foci for additional work. Problem decomposition, for example, is not a well-understood process. It is easy to recognize when it is done well or badly, but there are relatively few principles that can be used prospectively to produce good decompositions. We address below the issue of sub-problem solution, noting that a more cooperative approach—one in which individual nodes share partial solutions as they work—can be useful in a variety of problems. Finally, as we have explored elsewhere [4], there are a number of approaches to synthesizing individual sub-problem results, each addressing a different anticipated level of problem interaction. In future work we intend to explore applications of the contract net and the negotiation metaphor to each of these topics.

11.2. Instantiating the framework

The framework we have proposed—the task announcement, bid, award sequence, the common internode language, etc.—offers some ideas about what kinds of information are useful for distributed problem solving and how that information can be organized. There is still a considerable problem involved in instantiating the framework in the context of a specific task domain. Our protocol provides a site for embedding particular types of information (e.g. an eligibility specification), but does not specify exactly what that information is for any specific problem.

In this sense the contract net protocol is similar to AI languages like PLANNER, CONNIVER, QLISP [24], etc., which supply a framework for problem solving (e.g., the notions of goal specifications, theorem patterns, etc.), but leave to the user the task of specifying the content of that framework for any given problem. We expect that further experience with our framework will lead to additional structure to help guide its use.

11.3. Alternate models of cooperation

We have emphasized task-sharing as a means of internode cooperation and have attempted to provide some mechanisms for the communication required to effect this mode of cooperation. We have not as yet, however, adequately studied *result-sharing* [28] as a means of cooperation. In what approach, nodes assist each other through sharing of partial results. This type of cooperation appears to be of use in dealing with several sorts of problems. For problems where erroneous data or knowledge lead to conflicting views at individual nodes, sharing results can help to resolve those inconsistencies (as for example in [17]). For some tasks, any individual subproblem is inherently ambiguous even when data and knowledge are complete and exact (e.g., the blocks world scene identification in [31]); here the sharing of intermediate results can be an effective means of reducing or removing ambiguity. It is our intention to examine the structure of communication for this mode of cooperation with a view to extending the contract net framework to incorporate it.

It would also be useful to develop a more advanced form of task-sharing. In our current formulation, task distribution results in the traditional form of "hand out a subtask and get back a result" interaction. We are currently exploring the possibility of expanding this to a more cooperative form of interaction in which "what is to be done" is negotiated as well as "who is to do it".

We are also exploring further development of the dynamic configuration capability which the contract net makes possible. As noted in Section 8.3, initialization of the DSS can take into account the resources available (number of sensors, etc.). We intend to extend this to dynamic reconfiguration: the negotiation technique should provide a mechanism that allows nodes which have become overloaded to shed some of their workload by distributing tasks to other available nodes.

11.4. Optimality of the negotiation process

As noted, a major goal of the contract net framework is to provide a mechanism for solving the connection problem—achieving an appropriate matching of tasks to processor nodes. Yet it is easily seen that the negotiation process described above does not guarantee an *optimal* matching of tasks and nodes.

There are two reasons why this may occur. First, there is the problem of timing. A node that becomes idle chooses a task to bid on from among the task announcements it has heard up to that time. Similarly, a manager chooses what to do on the basis of the bids it has received by the expiration time for its task announcement. But since the net operates asynchronously, new task announcements and new bids are made at unpredictable times. A better matching of nodes to tasks might be achieved if there were some way to know that it was appropriate for a node to wait just a little longer before bidding, or for a manager to wait a little longer before awarding a task.

Second, at any given instant in time, the complete matching of nodes and tasks results from a number of local decisions. Each idle node chooses the most interesting task to bid on, without reference to what other idle nodes may be choosing; each manager chooses the best bid(s) it has received without reference to what any other manager may be doing. The best global assignment does not necessarily result from the simple concatenation of all of the best local assignments.[24]

Consider for example a situation in which two managers (A and B) have both announced tasks, and two potential contractors (X and Y) have each responded by bidding on both tasks. Imagine further that from A's perspective, X's bid is rated 0.9 (on a 0 to 1 scale), while Y's is rated 0.8 (Fig. 19). Conversely, from B's perspective, X is rated 0.8 and Y is rated 0.2.

---

[24]This appears to be a variety of the 'prisoner's dilemma' problem (see e.g., [10, 30]).

```
        A              B
   X   0.9        X   0.8
   Y   0.8        Y   0.2
```

FIG. 19. Managers rating bids from prospective contractors.

From a purely local perspective, both of the managers want X as their contractor; from a more global perspective it may make more sense to have A 'settle' for Y, and give X to B. Yet we cannot in general create the more global perspective without exchanging what may turn out to be extensive amounts of information.

The first of the two problems (timing) appears unavoidable given that we have chosen to deal with the kinds of problems typically attacked in AI, problems whose total decomposition is not known a priori. In a speech understanding problem, for instance, we cannot set up a fixed sequence of KS invocations beforehand because the utility of any given KS is not predictable in advance. Similarly, in a DSS, we have the same inability to predict KS utility, plus the added difficulty of new signals arriving at unpredictable moments.

If we do not know in advance which subtasks will arise and when, or exactly which KSs will be useful at each point, then we clearly cannot plan the *optimal* assignment of nodes to tasks for the entire duration of the problem. Some planning may be possible, however, even if we lack complete knowledge of a problem's eventual decomposition. We are currently studying ways to make use of partial information about tasks yet to be encountered or nodes that are soon going to be idle.

The second problem (local decisions) appears inherent in any decentralization of control and decision making. As noted earlier, we want to distribute control (for reasons of speed, problem-solving power, reliability, etc.). Given distributed control, however, globally *optimal* control decisions are possible only at the cost of transmitting extensive amounts of information between managers every time an award is about to be made. With that approach, inefficiencies due to suboptimal control decisions are traded for inefficiencies arising from transmission delays and channel saturation. We are currently studying this tradeoff and exploring ways of minimizing the difficulties that arise from this problem.

It appears then, that as a result of the unpredictability of the timing of subtasks and the necessity of making local decisions, precisely optimal matching of nodes to tasks is not possible. Note, however, that our stated goal is an *appropriate* assignment of nodes to tasks. Operation of the contract net is not predicated on optimal matching. In addition, the small set of experiments we have done so far (see [27]) indicate that overall performance is not seriously degraded by suboptimal matching.

11.5. Coherent behavior

We do not yet fully understand the more general problem of achieving globally coherent behavior in a system with distributed control. The fundamental difficulty was described earlier: We require distributed control in order to effect loose coupling, yet coherent behavior usually requires a global perspective.

Some aspects of the contract net protocol were motivated by attempts to overcome this problem. First, the task abstraction supplies information which enables a node to compare announcements and select the most appropriate. In a similar fashion, information in bids (the node abstraction) enables managers to compare bids from different nodes and select the most appropriate. Second, each node in a contract net maintains a list of the best recent task announcements it has seen—a kind of window on the tasks at hand for the net as a whole. This window enables the nodes to compare announcements over time, helping to avoid mistakes associated with too brief a view of the problem at hand.

We still have the problem that good local decisions do not necessarily add up to good global behavior, as the example in the previous section showed. However, the steps noted at least contribute to local decisions that are made on the basis of an extended (not snapshot) view of system performance and decisions that are based on extensive information about tasks and bids.

In the most general terms we see our efforts aimed at developing a problem solving protocol. The protocol should contain primitives appropriate for talking about and doing problem solving, and should structure the interaction between problem solvers in ways that contribute to coordinated behavior of the group. We have thus far taken an initial step in this direction with the development of the task announcement, bid, and award sequence.

12. Summary

The preceding discussion considered the contract net in a number of different contexts. In the most specific view, it was considered a mechanism for building a distributed sensing system. More generally, it offered an approach to distributed problem solving and a view of distributed processing. In the most general view, it was considered in the context of AI problem solving techniques. In the sections that follow we consider the advantages offered by the contract net in each of these contexts, reviewing in the process the central themes of the paper.

12.1. Contributions to distributed processing

A distributed processing approach to computation offers the potential for a number of benefits, including speed and the ability to handle applications that have a natural spatial distributon. The design of the contract net framework attempts to ensure that these potential benefits are indeed realized.

In order to realize speed in distributed systems, we need to avoid bot-tlenecks. They can arise in two primary ways: by concentrating disproportionate amounts of computation or communication at central resources, and by saturating available communication channels so that nodes must remain idle while messages are transmitted.

To avoid bottlenecks we distribute control and data. In the DSS example, data is distributed dynamically as a result of the division of the net into areas during the initialization phase. Control is distributed dynamically through the use of a negotiation process to effect the connection of tasks with idle processors.

The contract net design also tries to avoid communication channel saturation by reducing the number and length of messages. The information in task announcements (like eligibility specifications), for instance, helps eliminate extra message traffic, thereby helping to minimize the amount of channel capacity consumed by communication overhead. Similarly, bid messages can be kept short and 'to the point' through the use of the bid specification mechanism.

Finally, the ability to handle applications with a natural spatial or functional distribution is facilitated by viewing task distribution as a connection problem and by having the processors themselves negotiate to solve the problem. This makes it possible for the collection of available processors to 'spread them-selves' over the set of tasks to be done, distributing the workload dynamically.

12.2. Contributions to distributed problem solving

As we noted earlier (Section 6), a central issue in distributed problem solving is organization: How can we distribute control and yet maintain coherent behavior?

One way to accomplish this is by what we have called task-sharing, the distribution around the net of tasks relevant to solving the overall problem. As we have seen, the contract net views task-sharing in terms of connecting idle nodes with tasks yet to be done. It effects this matching by structuring interaction around negotiation as an organizing principle.

Negotiation in turn is implemented by focusing on what it is that processors should say to one another. The motivation for our protocol is thus to supply one idea on *what to say* rather than *how to communicate.*

As the example in Section 8 showed, use of the contract net makes it possible for the system to be configured dynamically, taking into account (in that example) such factors as the number of sensor and processor nodes available, their location, and the ease with which communication can be extablished. Such a configuration offers a number of improvements over a static, a priori configuration. It provides, for instance, a degree of simplicity: The same software is capable of initializing and running networks with a wide variation of available hardware. If the configuration were static, each new configuration would presumably require human intervention for its basic design (e.g., assigning nodes to tasks) and might require modifications to software as well.

Dynamic configuration also means that most nodes that must cooperate are able to communicate with one another directly. This reduces the amount of communication needed, since it reduces the need for either indirect routing of messages or the use of powerful transmitters.

The contract net also offers advantages in terms of increased reliability. By distributing both control and data, for instance, we ensure that there is no one node or even a subset of nodes whose loss would totally cripple the system. In addition, recovery from failure of a node is aided by the presence of explicit links between managers and their contractors. The failure of any contractor can be detected by its manager; the contract for which it was responsible can then be re-announced and awarded to another node. There is, in addition, the possibility of reliability arising from "load-sensitive redundancy". When load on the net is low, we might take advantage of idle processors by making redundant awards of the same contract. The system thus offers the opportunity to make resource allocation decisions opportunistically, taking advantage of idle resources to provide additional reliability.

The framework also makes it reasonably easy to add new nodes to the net at any time. This is useful for replacing nodes that have failed or adding new nodes in response to increased computational load on the net. Two elements of the framework provide the foundation for this capability. First, the contract negotiation process uses a form of "anonymous invocation": the KSs to be invoked are *described* rather than *named*. Second, there is a single language "spoken" by all the nodes.

The concept of describing rather than naming KSs has its roots in the goal-directed invocation of various AI languages and the notion of pattern-directed invocation generally (see, e.g. [32]), where it was motivated by the desire for more sophisticated forms of KS retrieval. It also however, turns out to offer an interesting and useful form of "substitutability", simply because where names are unique, descriptions are not, and a wide range of KSs may satisfy a single description. As a result, in a system with invocation by name, the addition of a new KS requires modification of the existing code to ensure that the new KS is indeed invoked. When invocation is by description, adding a new KS involves simply making it available to the existing collection of KSs; it will be invoked whenever its description is matched (in our case, whenever it chooses to bid on a task announcement). The contract net thus shares with other systems using anonymous invocation the ability to add new KSs by simply "throwing them into the pot".

Second, the use of a single language 'spoken' by all the nodes simplifies communication. If we are to add a new node, it must have some way of communicating with other nodes in the net. The contract net simplifies this issue by providing a very compact language: The basic protocol (task announcement, bid, award) provides the elementary 'syntax' for communication, while the common internode language provides the vocabulary used to express message content.

Thus, anonymous invocation means that it is possible for a new node to begin participating in the operation of the net by listening to the messages being exchanged. (If invocation were by name, listening to message traffic would do no good.) The use of a single language means that the node will understand the messages, and the use of a very simple language means that the task of initializing a node is easier.

12.3. Contributions to artificial intelligence

The contract net offers a novel view on the nature of the invocation process. As we have seen, it views task distribution as a problem of connecting tasks to KSs capable of executing those tasks, and it effects this connection via negotiation.

In Section 9 we used this perspective to examine existing models of invocation and evaluate them along several dimensions. This discussion showed, first, that in previous models connection is typically effected with a transfer of information that is unidirectional; hence the connection process is asymmetric. Control resides either with the tasks (goal-driven invocation) or with the KSs (data-driven invocation). In the contract net view, by contrast, the transfer is two-way, as each participant in the negotiation offers information about itself. This in turn means that control can be shared by both; the problem becomes one of mutual selection.

We then showed that the information transferred is typically limited in content. In the contract net, on the other hand, the information is not limited to a name or pattern, but is instead expanded to include statements expressible in the common internode language.

Third, the discussion showed that information about a more complete collection of candidate KSs is available before final selection is made. This makes possible a wider range of KS and task selection strategies than are possible if KSs and tasks must be selected or rejected as they are encountered.

Finally, we noted that this expanded view of invocation effects a true deliberation process, since one possible outcome of the negotiation is that none of the bids received is judged good enough, and hence none of the potential contractors will be selected. This appears to be a useful advance that has no precise analogy in previous programming languages and applications.

12.4. Conclusion: the major themes revisited

Two of the major themes of this paper are the notion of protocols aimed at problem solving rather than communication and the concept of negotiation as a basic mechanism for interaction. The first was illustrated by the use of message types like task announcement, bid, and award. This focused the contract net protocol at the level of problem solving and provided a step toward indicating what kinds of information should be transferred between nodes.

The utility of negotiation as an interaction mechanism was demonstrated in two settings. First, our basic approach to cooperation relies on task-sharing, and negotiation is used to distribute tasks among the nodes of the net. This makes possible distribution based on mutual selection, yielding a good match of nodes and tasks. Second, negotiation was used to effect transfer of control. In that setting it offered a framework in which the matching of KSs to tasks was based on more information than is usually available (due to the transfer of information in both directions, and the transfer of more complex information). As a result, negotiation makes it possible to effect a finer degree of control and to be more selective in making decisions about invocation than is the case with previous mechanisms.

ACKNOWLEDGMENT

This work describes research done at the Artificial Intelligence Laboratory of the Massachusetts Institute of Technology and at the Defence Research Establishment Atlantic of the Department of National Defence, Research and Development Branch, Canada. Support for the Artificial Intelligence Lab is provided in part the Advanced Research Projects Agency of the Department of Defense under Office of Naval Research Contract N00014-80-C-505.

The assistance of Bruce Buchanan and Ed Feigenbaum in the original development of these ideas is greatefully acknowledged. Carmen Bright, Joe Maksym, Lee Erman, Carl Hewitt, Patrick Winston, and Judy Zinnikas provided useful comments on earlier drafts of this paper.

REFERENCES

1. Baer, J.-L., A survey of some theoretical aspects of multiprocessing, *Comput. Surveys* **5** (1) (1973) 31–80.
2. Bowdon, E.K., Sr. and Barr, W.J., Cost effective priority assignment in network computers, in: *FJCC Proceedings* **41** (AFIPS, Montvale, NJ, 1972) 755–763.
3. Davis, R., Meta-rules: reasoning about control, *Artificial Intelligence* **15** (1980) 179–222.
4. Davis, R., Models of problem solving: Why cooperate?, *SIGART Newsletter* **70** (1980) 50–51.
5. Davis, R. and King, J., An overview of production systems, in: E.W. Elcock and D. Michie (Eds.), *Machine Intelligence* **8** (Wiley, New York, 1977) 300–332.
6. D'Olivera, C.R., An analysis of computer decentralization, Rept. LCS, TM90, MIT, Cambridge, MA, 1977.
7. Erman, L.D., Hayes-Roth, F., Lesser, V.R. and Reddy, D.R., The Hearsay-II speech-understanding system: Integrating knowledge to resolve uncertainty, *Comput. Surveys* **12** (1980) 213–253.
8. Farber, D.J. and Larson, K.C., The structure of the distributed computing system—Software, in: J. Fox (Ed.), *Proceedings of the Symposium on Computer-Communications Networks And Teletraffic* (Polytechnic Press, Brooklyn, NY, 1972) 539–545.
9. Galbraith, J.R., Organizational design—an information processing view, in: Kolb (Ed.), *Organizational Psychology* (Prentice Hall, Englewood Cliffs, NJ, 2nd. ed., 1974) 313–322.
10. Hamburger, H., N-person prisoner's dilemma, *J. Math. Sociology* **3** (1973) 27–48.
11. Hewitt, C., Description and theoretical analysis (using schemata) of PLANNER: A language for proving theorems and manipulating models in a robot, MIT AI TR 258, MIT, Cambridge, MA, 1972.

12. Hewitt, C., Viewing control structures as patterns of passing messages, *Artificial Intelligence* **8** (1977) 323–364.
13. Kahn, R.E., Resource-sharing computer communications networks, *Proc. IEEE* **60** (11) (1972) 1397–1407.
14. Kahn, R.E., The organization of computer resources into a packet radio network, in: *NCC Proceedings* **44** (AFIPS, Montvale, NJ, 1975) 177–186.
15. Kimbleton, S.R. and Schneider, G.M., Computer communications networks: approaches, objectives, and performance considerations, *Comput. Surveys* **7** (3) (1975) 129–173.
16. Lenat, D.B., Beings: knowledge as interacting experts, *IJCA* **4** (1975) 126–133.
17. Lesser, V.R. and Erman, L.D., Distributed interpretation: a model and experiment, *IEEE Trans. Comput.* **29** (1980) 1144–1163.
18. Lesser, V.R. and Corkill, D.D., Functionally accurate cooperative distributed systems, *IEEE Trans. Systems Man Cybernet.* **11** (1) (1981) 81–96.
19. McDermott, D.V. and Sussman, G.J., The CONNIVER Reference Manual, AI Memo 259a, MIT, Cambridge, MA, 1974.
20. Nii, H.P. and Feigenbaum, E.A., Rule-based understanding of signals, in: D.A. Waterman and F. Hayes-Roth (Eds.), *Pattern-Directed Inference Systems* (Academic Press, New York, 1978) 483–501.
21. Noyce, R.N., From relays to MPU's, *Comput.* **9** (12) (1976) 26–29.
22. Prince, P.S., Recovery from failure in a contract net, B.S. Thesis, EECS Department, MIT, Cambridge, MA, 1980.
23. Roberts, L.G., Data by the packet, *IEEE Spectrum* **11** (2) (1974) 46–51.
24. Sacerdoti et al., QLISP—A language for the interactive development of complex systems, *Proc. NCC* **45** (1976) 349–356.
25. Smith, R.G. and Davis, R., Applications of the contract net framework: distributed sensing, *Proc. ARPA Distributed Sensor Net Symp.*, Pittsburgh, PA (1978) 12–20.
26. Smith, R.G., *A framework for distributed problem solving* (VMI Research Press, 1981); also: Stanford Memo STAN-CS-78-700, Stanford University Stanford, CA, 1978.
27. Smith, R.G., The contract net protocol: high level communication and control in a distributed problem solver, *IEEE Trans. Comput.* **29** (1980) 1104–1113.
28. Smith, R.G. and Davis, R., Frameworks for cooperation in a distributed problem solver, *IEEE Trans Systems Man Cybernet.* **11** (1981) 61–70.
29. Svodobova, L., Liskov, B. and Clark, D., Distributed computer systems: structure and semantics, MIT-LCS-TR-215, MIT, Cambridge, MA, 1979.
30. Tucker, A.W., A two-person dilemma, Mimeo, Stanford University, Stanford, CA, 1950.
31. Waltz, D., Understanding line drawings of scenes with shadows, in: Winston (Ed.), *The Psychology of Computer Vision* (McGraw-Hill, New York, 1975).
32. Waterman, D.A. and Hayes-Roth, F. (Eds.), *Pattern-Directed Inference Systems* (Academic Press, New York, 1978).

Received April 1981

Verification and Compliance Testing

Frank Guerin and Jeremy Pitt

Intelligent and Interactive Systems,
Department of Electrical & Electronic Engineering,
Imperial College of Science, Technology & Medicine,
Exhibition Road, London, SW7 2BT.
{f.guerin,j.pitt}@ic.ac.uk
Phone: +44 20 7594 6318 / Fax: 6274

Abstract. Verification and compliance testing are required if agents are
to be delegated responsibility for legally binding contracts, for example
in electronic markets. This paper describes a general agent communication framework which allows several different notions of verification
and compliance testing to be described. In particular we consider what
type of verification or testing may be possible depending on the information which may be available (agent internals, observable behaviour,
normative specifications) and the semantic definition of the communication language. We use this framework to identify the types of languages
which will permit verification and testing in open systems where agents'
internals are kept private. This analysis gives some ideas about how compliance might be enforced in an open system.

1 Introduction

Verification means checking the specifications or programs of a multi-agent system at design time to ensure that the system will behave as desired in all possible
runs. Compliance testing means checking the behaviour of the system at run time
to determine if it behaves as desired. Desired behaviour may mean compliance
with some normative specification, for example honouring contracts in an e-
commerce system. Such a normative specification must specify something about
required states of the multi-agent system, these states may be agent states or
states of the society. Before we can investigate different notions of verification
and compliance testing we must have a frame of reference: a general agent communication framework which describes the normative constraints as well as the
states of the system.

We begin by describing a general agent communication framework (§ 2). This
framework must describe the agent programs which a multi-agent system in composed of; these can be represented by a computational model for the multi-agent
system (§ 2.1). We then specify additional variables to capture observable states
of an open system through a representation of the agents' social context (§ 2.2)
and the states of this context (§ 2.3). Next we define the ACL component of the
framework (§ 2.6) which can accomodate languages based on mental or social

M.-P. Huget (Ed.): Communications in Multiagent Systems, LNAI 2650, pp. 98–112, 2003.

states and we summarise the general framework (§ 2.7). Using this framework as a reference we describe several notions of verification and testing (§ 3). We use the framework to analyse existing ACLs to determine if they are verifiable (§ 4) and we identify the type of ACL which would be appropriate in an open system. Finally we discuss how compliance might be enforced in an open system (§ 5) and conclude (§ 6).

2 A General Agent Communication Framework

Before discussing verification and compliance testing we need to describe a general agent communication framework containing the necessary components of a multi-agent system. Our framework builds on the framework presented by Wooldridge [14]; we attempt to make the framework more general to allow ACLs with social semantics to be accommodated.

An agent communication language (ACL) typically has two functions[1]:

- To specify the meaning of messages; this is useful to an agent designer who is deciding when an agent will plan to send a message and also what way the agent will update its internal state upon receiving a message.
- To provide a normative specification for communication in the system; this is necessary to ensure that the multi-agent system does not become dysfunctional, for example to ensure that agents respond when spoken to and that they honour their commitments.

We say that the first part defines a semantics for each communicative act while the second (normative) part defines a specification which must be satisfied by the system of agents using that language. It is important to note that there is a distinction between *program semantics* for communication statements in an agent's program and *ACL semantics* (which constitute specifications) for communicative acts. If an agent is ACL-compliant then its program semantics will satisfy the semantics defined by the ACL specification. ACL semantics may be defined in different ways and each way implies different notions of verification.

Communicating agents operate in a certain context, the entire context includes the private states and programs of agents as well as the publicly observable state of the society. ACL semantics for communicative acts must specify something about the state of this context. ACLs based on mental states typically specify semantics by means of preconditions and/or postconditions [7] which must be true before or after the communicative act is performed. ACLs based on social states typically specify social facts that are created or modified by the performance of a communicative act [11]. Thus an agent communication framework will need to include a representation of the multi-agent system which captures information about the internal states of agents in the system as well as observable (social) states.

---

[1] The first agent communication languages confused these two functions (for example FIPA [3] and KQML [7]).

In addition to an agent's current state, we also need a representation of the agent's program because we might need to know what the agent is going to do. The ACL specification for the semantics of communicative acts may refer to future actions and we may need to verify that an agent will do them. For example, in order to specify that an agent holds a certain intention as a precondition to sending a promise act, the specification for the act may require that the agent's program eventually executes the intention.

2.1   Computational Model

Each agent in a multi-agent system can be described as a module. An entire multi-agent system can be described by a single program P executing all these modules in parallel. Each module has a set of asynchronous buffered input channels on which it can receive messages from other agents and a set of asynchronous buffered output channels on which it sends messages to other agents. A channel is a variable whose value is a list of messages.

A computational model is a mathematical structure which can represent the behaviour of a program. The behaviour of a program can be described as a sequence of states that the program could produce, where a state gives a value to all the variables in the program including the control variable which describes the location of the next statement. In addition to the internal variables of agents we will model the social states of the system.

The computational model we choose for multi-agent systems is a fair transition system [8]. This is a system which contains variables and transitions and an initial comdition specifying initial values for the variables. Variables represent the states of the agents and transitions represent the state changes caused by statements in the agents' programs. A *state* is an interpretation of the variables, assigning each variable a value over its domain. As a program executes it passes through a sequence of states in which variables may take on different values.

2.2   Representing Social Context

A language $\mathcal{L}_F$ is introduced to describe social facts. Social facts describe role relationships, commitments to perform actions and publicly expressed attitudes. Each agent may have a differing view of the social context, since it may not have received all events (communications) occurring in the system; therefore for each agent we use a unique variable to describe the social state observable to it. The type of each social state variable is a mapping from well formed formulae of the social facts language $\mathcal{L}_F$ to true or false values. We also define an initial condition Φ for the social state variables.

Given an initial social state Φ and a certain sequence of messages, we can work out the values of the social facts in subsequent states as follows: The social state is unchanged if no communication occurs; or if a communication does occur the social state is modified according to the state change function described by the ACL. For example, if an agent i promises something to another agent, the

ACL semantics of the communicative act for *promise* may require that a new social commitment proposition becomes true in the social state.

The social state need not be explicitly represented anywhere in a real multi-agent system, parts of it may or may not be represented by the the local variables of agents in the system. Each agent should store a copy of all the information in the social state that might be relevant to its interactions so that it may correctly interpret context dependent communicative acts and keep track of its social commitments. The complete social state is then implicit. As an external observer we need to know the social state if we wish to understand the interactions taking place in the system. We need to know the social knowledge observable to each agent in a system in order to determine if it is complying with the social conventions to the best of its knowledge.

2.3   States and Computations

A state s is an interpretation of the variables, assigning each variable a value over its domain. An infinite sequence of states

$$\sigma : s^0, s^1, s^2, s^3, \ldots$$

is called a *system model*. A system model is a *computation of the program* P (which identifies our fair transition system) if s^0 satisfies the initial condition and if each state s^{j+1} is accessible from the previous state s^j via one of the transitions in the system. A computation is a sequence of states that could be produced by an execution of the program. All computations are system models but not vice versa. Thus the agent programs identify the components of a fair transition system and the fair transition system describes all the possible computations that a program could produce. This is how we say what a program means, mathematically: it is described as the set of all the sequences it could produce.

This constrains only the interpretations of variables in the agent programs. We specify additional constraints on the interpretations of the social state variables so that the social state changes in response to communicative acts between agents. We define a *computation of the multi-agent system* S with initial social fact Φ to be a system model σ which is a computation of the program P and where the social facts variables are also updated according to the ACL specification each time a communication occurs.

2.4   System for a Single Agent

If we are the designers of a single agent and only have access to that agent's internals we can construct a new fair transition system S_i where the variables, initial condition and transition sets of the system are just the same as if i was the only agent in the system [8]. The initial condition for social facts Φ will include social facts that will be true for the system we intend to allow our agent to run in. We add one extra transition τ_E, the environmental transition which represents all the things other agents could do; τ_E cannot modify any variables in agent i's program apart from the communication channels; the outbound communication channels can be modified by the removal of a message and the inbound ones can be modified by addition of a message. Other variables may be modified arbitrarily. S_i represents all the possible behaviours of agent i in any multi-agent system.

2.5 External System

If we do not have access to the internals of any agent, but can detect each message being sent, we can construct a fair transition system S_E which represents all possible observable sequences. The variables of S_E are simply the communication channels we can observe and there are only two transitions, the idling transition τ_I (preserves all variables and does nothing) and the environmental transition τ_E. The environmental transition allows arbitrary modification of any variable outside of the observable channels and allows a channel to be modified by adding a message to the end or removing one from the front. In order to complete the social states in computations of the multi-agent system S_E we must also know the initial social facts for the initial condition Φ. A computation of the multi-agent system S_E does not care about how its states interpret variables which are not observable, it only cares about channels and social facts variables.

2.6 Agent Communication Language

When agents communicate they exchange messages which are well-formed formulae of a language $\mathcal{L}_C$. Agents pass messages in order to perform communicative acts and these acts must have a well defined semantics which is a part of the ACL specification. The specification for the semantics of communicative acts is a function $[\![-]\!]_C$ which varies depending on whether the ACL is based on mental or social states.

Mental: The function $[\![-]\!]_C$ returns a formula in temporal logic $\mathcal{L}_T$. The formula specifies properties of the system, for example, it may describe pre and/or postconditions which must be true of sender or receiver or some other element of the fair transition system. Preconditions should be true when the message is sent, postconditions should be applied after i.e. they define things that should become true after the message is passed. For example, a precondition might require that a certain mental state exist in the sender or that the receiver has performed some action before a message can be sent. A postcondition might assert that the receiver is obliged to adopt a certain mental state upon receiving the message. The formula is given a semantics $[\![-]\!]_T$ in terms of the set of models where the formula is satisfied.

Social: The function $[\![-]\!]_C$ returns a function from social state to social state. The function describes the change to the social state caused by the message transmitted. Since the ACL is responsible for defining the changes that messages cause in the social state, the ACL must also define the language $\mathcal{L}_F$ for social facts whose semantics $[\![-]\!]_F$ returns a temporal formula in $\mathcal{L}_T$ which is interpreted over an observable model (i.e. a model where we are concerned only with how states interpret observable variables). Thus $[\![a, i]\!]_F$, the semantics of a social facts assertion a for agent i describes the set of models where the formula a is satisfied by agent i. Many social facts may be simply satisfied in all situations, but some such as a commitment to do an action may be satisfied only in those models where the action is eventually done by the agent. The social facts semantics function $[\![-]\!]_F$ is allowed to make use of channel variables and any of the observable state variables but it cannot place constraints on agent internals.

Therefore a complete ACL for our general framework is a 3-tuple:

$$\mathcal{ACL} = \langle \mathcal{L}_C, \mathcal{L}_F, \mathcal{L}_T \rangle$$

Each of these languages can by specified by a tuple;
for example $\mathcal{L}_C = \langle \mathit{wff}(\mathcal{L}_C), [\![-]\!]_C \rangle$, where the first part of the tuple gives the set of well formed formulae of the languages and the second part gives the semantics.

2.7   Agent Communication Framework

An agent communication framework is a 4-tuple:

$$\langle \mathit{Ag}, \mathit{Compmodel}, \mathcal{ACL}, \Phi \rangle$$

- Ag is a set of agent names, $\mathit{Ag} = \{1, \ldots, n\}$;
- $\mathit{Compmodel}$ is the fair transition system representing all the programs of all the agents in the multi-agent system;
- $\mathcal{ACL} = \langle \mathcal{L}_C, \mathcal{L}_F, \mathcal{L}_T \rangle$ is an ACL including mental and social components;
- Φ is the initial assertion for social states.

Using this framework we can define a few notions of verification and compliance testing.

3   Types of Verification and Testing

Several different types of verification and compliance testing are possible depending on the *type of ACL* used, the *information available* and whether we wish to verify at *design time* or test at *run time*. Design time verification is important when we want to prove some properties (of an agent or the entire system) to guarantee certain behaviours or outcomes in a system. Run time testing is used to determine if agents are misbehaving in a certain run of the system. Run time compliance testing is important in an open system because it may be the only way to identify rogue agents. We must be able to identify misbehaving agents if we are to take action against them and hence guarantee that they will not prevent the society from functioning in the desired way.

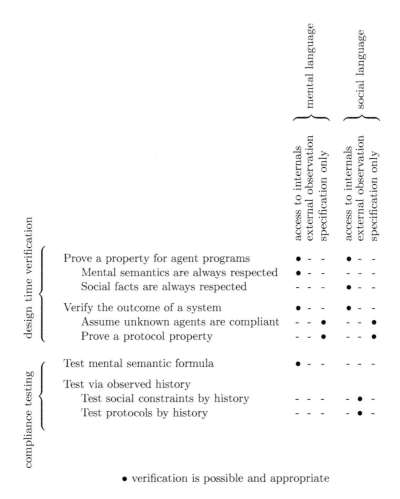

• verification is possible and appropriate

Table 1. Types of Verification and Compliance Testing

Type of ACL: Our general framework allows the semantics of an act to include both a formula which must be satisfied in the system and a social state change function (see § 2.6), in which case both would need to be verified. In practise there exist no ACLs which include both parts and ACLs can partitioned into *mental languages* and *social languages.*

Information available: There are three relevant types of information that might be available for verification and testing.

1. *Internal States*: The agent designer or system designer will typically have access to internal states. By internal states we mean the agents' program code as well as their state during execution. Knowledge of the agents' code permits verification of future behaviour. This type of knowledge is usually necessary to verify compliance with mental languages. When a social language is used, the agent designer who has access to internal states of the agents may still wish to verify at design time that the agent will always respect the semantics. We may use information about internal states for both design time verification and run time testing.

2. *External States*: In an e-commerce scenario different vendors contribute their own agents to the system; these vendors might not desire to publicise the internal code of their agents. Even if the code is publicised, the agents might be based on very different architectures making it too difficult to verify their behaviour by analysis of the code. In such cases the system administrator has to perform some type of compliance testing which works with observable social states. If we assume that the communications occurring in a run of the system can be observed then testing based on external states is possible at run time for languages based on social states.

3. *Language specification*: With only the language specification available we can still prove certain properties. For example by assuming that all agents respect the language's semantics during the execution of a protocol we can verify that certain outcomes will result. In this case we have no information about runs of the system so only design time verification is possible.

Table 1 shows the types of verification and testing that are possible and appropriate based the information available. Note how the only hope for run time compliance testing in an open system (where agent internals are inaccessible) is with a social language. We now give a more detailed explanation in terms of our general framework.

3.1   Prove a Property for Agent Programs

This entails ensuring that some property holds for the system at design time. In relation to communicating agents this verification has been used by van Eijk [2] where a certain property is specified and proven to hold for a certain system of communicating agents; this does not necessarily imply the use of any communication language. In our framework we have a communication language which may be social or mental, corresponding to these possibilities there are two special cases of proving properties that are of particular interest to us.

Verify Mental Semantics are Always Respected: Given a mental language we can verify at design time that the semantics of the communication language are always respected by the agents in all possible computations of the system. This means that for any computation, we verify that for each state which involves message passing, the semantics of that message are satisfied. The semantic property may be a precondition in the case of the FIPA ACL or a conjunction of a precondition and postcondition in the case of KQML.

Verify Social Facts are Always Respected: With social languages acts create or modify social facts and we may discuss whether or not agents respect the social facts. If we have access to an agent's internals, we can verify at design time that the agent will always respect its social facts regardless of what other agents in a system do. From the agent's code we construct the transition system S_i as described in § 2.4; to verify that agent i always respects its social commitments we need to prove that in all computations of the multi-agent system S_i, whenever a social fact x is true for agent i, the semantic formula corresponding to x holds in the model.

In practice we will not need to check all possible well formed formulae of the social facts language, inspection of the ACL specification can allow us to identify the set of social facts that may arise. This is provided that our ACL satisfies certain reasonable requirements, for example an agent should not be able to create commitments for another agent without notifying the other. If an agent is implemented by a finite state program[2] then we can use a model checking algorithm to perform the verification, it is less complex than proof theoretic verification.

3.2   Verify the Outcome of a System

The designer of a multi-agent system may want to verify that a certain outcome will occur given a certain initial state. If the internals of all agents are known this is simply a matter of proving that a property holds eventually in all computations of the system. This is independent of any communication language. If we don't know the internals of all the agents in the system, we cannot say much about the outcome unless we make some assumptions about unknown agents.

Verify Outcome for Compliant Agents: Supposing we have designed an agent (whose internals are known to us) and we wish to verify at design time that a certain outcome is guaranteed when we let our agent run in a system of agents whose internals we do not have access to. We construct a fair transition system which represents all the possible behaviours of our agent in any environment as described in § 2.4. Then we prove that our desired outcome is guaranteed if all external transitions in the environment are compliant with the normative constraints of the ACL. This type of verification is possible both with mental and social languages.

Prove a Protocol Property: Proving properties of protocols at design time is possible for both mental and social languages even when the internals of agents are not accessible. If a property p holds for any system of compliant agents executing a protocol *prot*, then we say that protocol *prot* has property p. With a social language, the proof is carried out as follows

---

[2] A finite state program is one where each system variable assumes only finitely many values in all computations.

- Let p be an assertion characterising the desired property to be proved for protocol *prot*.
- Set the initial condition Φ to an assertion characterising a social state where protocol *prot* has started.
- Construct a fair transition system S_E which represents all possible observable sequences of states (see § 2.5).
- Prove the following over all computations of the multi-agent system S_E:
  if all agents are compliant then property p will hold.

The antecedant "all agents are compliant" requires that all social facts are respected by all agents; in practice and we need only consider social facts that can arise in the protocol under consideration; likewise we need only consider agents that are involved in the protocol and these agents must be specified in the initial condition Φ as they will occupy certain roles in the protocol. For a worked example of this type of verification see [5].

3.3   Test Mental Semantic Formula at Run Time

This type of compliance testing is performed at run time with a mental language. Given that the system is in a certain state s where a communication has just taken place (by passing a message m), we wish to check if the semantics of the communication language are satisfied for that communication. We check that the mental semantic formula is satisfied on all possible paths from this point. This type of testing allows for the possibility that the semantics are respected in this instance but may not always be respected by the agents of the system. We set the initial assertion to an assertion characterising the state s. Then we check for this system that the mental semantic formula for message m holds. The type of verification discussed by Wooldridge [14] falls in this category.

3.4   Testing Using an Observable History

This is used to determine if an agent is compliant by observing its external behaviour at run time. We assume that we have access to the ACL specification, an initial description of social facts and an observable history which takes the form of a history of messages exchanged by one agent or by the entire system. With this information it may be possible to determine if agents have complied with the ACL thus far, but not to determine if they will comply in future. However, this is probably the only kind of testing possible in open systems.

Test social constraints by history: This is the type of compliance testing discussed by Singh, where "agents could be tested for compliance on the basis of their communications"[11]. Recall that a history of messages and an initial social state description Φ can uniquely describe a sequence of observable states. From information of sending events we construct social states which are consistent with the sequence of sending events. We then construct a fair transition system

S_E which represents all possible observable sequences of states. Φ is the initial condition of S_E; the variables are the channels of agents present in Φ and the social state variables; the transitions are τ_I and τ_E as described in § 2.5. We then find the set of all models which match the observed finite sequence up to its final state and thereafter take all possible paths by taking the idling or environmental transitions. Note that the models constructed here do not coincide with models of the entire system where the transitions of agent programs are considered and many transitions do not involve message passing; however, the semantics of social facts will never refer to an absolute number of states, so this model is sufficient for testing.

Now we can interpret the semantics of each of our observed agent's social facts over these *observed* models. Certain social facts in states of an observed model may already have their semantics satisfied before the state where the last observed message was passed (i.e. satisfied in the sequence which proceeds after that state by infinite applications of the idling transition) for example obligations which have been fulfilled. Certain other facts may not have their semantics satisfied yet, though it may be possible that they will be satisfied after and do not yet constitute a violation.

Thus we wish to check if there exists an observed model in which the semantic formulae for all social facts in all states are satisfied; i.e. it is possible that the observed sequence is part of a model where the observed agent is compliant.

Test Protocols by History: With a protocol based language it may be possible to test compliance with a protocol by observing a history of communications if the semantics of acts define obligations to perform observable actions. This is the case with sACL [9] which defines the semantics of an act as a postcondition which is an intention for the receiver to reply, given a predefined possible set of replies. Given an observable history as described above (§ 3.4), we can see if each agent respects the protocol by checking that an agent does send the message he is obliged to send after receiving a message. This approach is effectively giving a social semantics to the intention to reply by interpreting it as an observable obligation, hence we are really creating a new language which is no longer entirely mental. This is why table 1 states that protocols cannot be tested for a mental language by observing a history.

4   Verifiability

Table 1 has shown what types of verification are possible for mental and social languages; however, some languages may not be verifiable at all if certain components of the communication framework are missing. Typically we describe this in terms of missing language components; recall that we had three languages as part of our ACL: A communication language, a social facts language and temporal logic. In the more general case the temporal logic language $\mathcal{L}_T$ can be replaced by any semantic language $\mathcal{L}_s$ which will provide a relationship between the semantics of communication (either mental states or social facts) and a grounded computational model. Table 3 shows what language components are present in several different languages. For mental languages both $wff(\mathcal{L}_s)$ and $[\![-]\!]_s$ must be present to allow any type of verification at all. While FIPA has specified a semantic language $wff(\mathcal{L}_s)$, it has given it a semantics using modal operators;[3] it has not attempted to give it a grounded semantics in terms of a computational model, and this is what we require of the component $[\![-]\!]_s$ in our framework. In contrast, the QUETL language of Wooldridge [13] includes all four components necessary for a mental language to be verifiable. Although it defines the semantics of an *inform* in terms of an agent's knowledge, this knowledge operator is grounded in terms of states of the agent program.

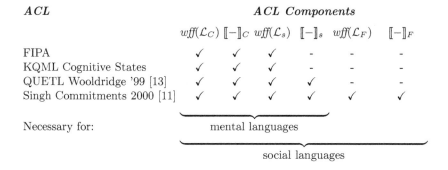

| *ACL* | *ACL Components* | | | | | |
	$wff(\mathcal{L}_C)$	$[\![-]\!]_C$	$wff(\mathcal{L}_s)$	$[\![-]\!]_s$	$wff(\mathcal{L}_F)$	$[\![-]\!]_F$
FIPA	✓	✓	✓	-	-	-
KQML Cognitive States	✓	✓	✓	-	-	-
QUETL Wooldridge '99 [13]	✓	✓	✓	✓	-	-
Singh Commitments 2000 [11]	✓	✓	✓	✓	✓	✓

Necessary for: mental languages

social languages

Table 2. Some ACLs and their Constituent Language Components.

A social language must specify all six components if it is to be verifiable: messages are written in $\mathcal{L}_C$ and $[\![-]\!]_F$ defines how they create or modify social facts; both $wff(\mathcal{L}_F)$ and $[\![-]\!]_F$ are necessary to provide a mapping from social facts to social facts semantics; both $wff(\mathcal{L}_s)$ and $[\![-]\!]_s$ are necessary to give that semantics a grounding in the computational model. We see that the language of Singh [11] does have all six components, let us look at a *request* and its objective meaning as an example:

- $\mathcal{L}_C$ is the language in which messages are written, such as $request(x, y, p)$; this is given a semantics $[\![-]\!]_C$ which maps it to $C(x, y, G, RFp)$, an expression in a social language $\mathcal{L}_F$ (this is the objective meaning, there is also a subjective and practical meaning for each act).
- $\mathcal{L}_F$ is a language of commitments, the expression $C(x, y, G, RFp)$ means that x commits that he expects y to make p true. This expression is in turn given a semantics $[\![-]\!]_F$ as an expression in $\mathcal{L}_s$.

---

[3] The semantics of these operators is not given in any of the FIPA documents, see also [10].

– $\mathcal{L}_s$ is a variant of Computation Tree Logic (CTL), CTL formulas have a semantics $[\![-]\!]_s$ in terms of the system models where they are satisfied.

Singh has in fact put together the languages $\mathcal{L}_s$ and $\mathcal{L}_F$ by extending the syntax and semantics of CTL so that commitments can be specified within it, and their semantics given in terms of the other CTL primitives. The semantics of the objective and practical meanings are grounded in observable social states of the system.

As mentioned earlier, in an open system it may only be possible to make external observations and if so, as shown in table 1, the only verification possible will be by observing a history with a social language. The only language in our table which could be verifiable in an open system is Singh's language; this is because the semantics of communication is grounded in *social states* (which are observable in an open system), in contrast the semantics of a mental language is grounded in *program states* (which might not be accessible in an open system).

5   Verification, Testing and Enforcement in an Open System

The following are the most important types of verification in an open system.

1. Verify that an agent always satisfies its social facts.
2. Prove a property of a protocol.
3. Determine if an agent is not respecting its social facts at run time.

These types support each other, for example, proving properties of open systems requires three verification types: agent designers must be able to prove that individual agents are compliant (type 1); the protocol designer must be able to prove properties for a system of compliant agents using the protocol (type 2); and the system itself needs to determine if agents do comply with social commitments at run time (type 3) in order to police the society and guarantee that rogue agents cannot damage the system's properties.

5.1   Policing an Open Society

With reference to the enumerated verification types for an open system above, type 2 requires that all agents comply. To be able to use this in an open system there must be some way to enforce compliance. The issue of policing a society can be tackled in one of the following three ways.

Sentinel agents may monitor the observable behaviour of agents and have the capability to place sanctions or to evict or terminate offending agents. If we guarantee that all violators are evicted then the system progresses as if all agents complied; however, we must design protocols in such a way that an eviction cannot destroy the desirable properties of the system.

If the society has to police itself we may introduce notions like trust and politeness, whereby agents violating certain commitments or conventions of the society are branded as untrustworthy or antisocial and are ostracised by the rest of the society. Prisoner's dilemma experiments [1] have shown that a strategy of reciprocating (rewarding good behaviour and punishing bad behaviour) has the effect of policing the society because agents will not tend to misbehave if they cannot thereby gain an advantage. If we want self policing we must consider this in the design of protocols so that all agents participating can observe enough information to determine if an agent complies.

Yet another possibility is that agent owners will be legally responsible for the behaviour of their agents. Agents will not be allowed to participate in a system unless their owner guarantees that they are compliant. Then if such an agent misbehaves at run time some sanction (such as a fine) can be placed on the agent owner. This approach has the drawbacks that it requires some centralised authority and the practicality of policing a system as distributed as the internet might be questionable [12]. However, if the exchange of real money is to be carried out by agents, there will inevitably be some human or institution who is liable.

6   Conclusions and Future Work

We have described a general agent communication framework which includes a computational model and an agent communication language component which can accomodate an ACL based on mental or social states. This allowed us to investigate different types of verification and to identify which components must be present in the framework to facilitate each type of verification. We have identified the need for a language based on social conventions for applications with open systems of agents, such as e-commerce applications. We have also described the types of verification that are possible in such systems and the types of policing which could be used to enforce compliance. This theoretical framework could be used to implement useful tools for such systems. For example, an agent platform could automatically monitor the messages exchanged and identify (and take action against) rogue agents. A tool could aid a designer by automatically checking if an agent's code is compliant and checking if protocols give the expected outcomes.

The use of temporal logic for the specification of social facts allows many properties to be specified but does not allow an absolute time frame to be referenced; this could be achieved by moving to a clocked transition system [6].

Current and future work involves applying a model checking algorithm to each type of verification; this will use protocol diagrams as state transition diagrams for observable systems, much of this is described in [4].

References

[1] R. Axelrod. *The evolution of cooperation.* Basic Books, New York, 1984. 111

[2] R. M. v. Eijk. *Programming Languages for Agent Communication.* PhD thesis, Department of Information and Computing Sciences, Utrecht University, 2000. 105

[3] FIPA. [FIPA OC00003] FIPA 97 Part 2 Version 2.0: Agent Communication Language Specification. In *Website of the Foundation for Intelligent Physical Agents. http://www.fipa.org/specs/fipa2000.tar.gz*, 1997. 99

[4] F. Guerin. *Specifying Agent Communication Languages.* PhD thesis, Department of Electrical and Electronic Engineering, Imperial College, UK, 2002. 111

[5] F. Guerin and J. Pitt. Guaranteeing properties for e-commerce systems. In *Autonomous Agents 2002 Workshop on Agent Mediated Electronic Commerce IV: Designing Mechanisms and Systems, Bologna*, 2002. 107

[6] Y. Kesten, Z. Manna, and A. Pnueli. Verifying clocked transition systems. In *Hybrid Systems III, LNCS vol. 1066*, pages 13–40. Springer-Verlag, Berlin, 1996. 111

[7] Y. Labrou and T. Finin. A semantics approach for kqml – a general purpose communication language for software agents. In *Third International Conference on Information and Knowledge Management (CIKM'94)*, pages 447–455, 1994. 99, 99

[8] Z. Manna and A. Pnueli. *Temporal Verification of Reactive Systems (Safety), vol. 2.* Springer-Verlag, New York, Inc., 1995. 100, 101

[9] J. Pitt and A. Mamdani. A protocol-based semantics for an agent communication language. In *Proceedings 16th International Joint Conference on Artificial Intelligence IJCAI'99, Stockholm*, pages 486–491. Morgan-Kaufmann Publishers, 1999. 108

[10] J. Pitt and A. Mamdani. Some remarks on the semantics of FIPA's agent communication language. *Autonomous Agents and Multi-Agent Systems*, 4:333–356, 1999. 109

[11] M. Singh. A social semantics for agent communication languages. In *IJCAI Workshop on Agent Communication Languages, Springer-Verlag, Berlin.*, 2000. 99, 107, 109, 109

[12] M. Wooldridge. Verifiable semantics for agent communication languages. In *IC-MAS'98*, 1998. 111

[13] M. Wooldridge. Verifying that agents implement a communication language. In *Sixteenth National Conference on Artificial Intelligence (AAAI-99), Orlando, FL, (July 1999)*, 1999. 109, 109

[14] M. Wooldridge. Semantic issues in the verification of agent communication languages. *Journal of Autonomous Agents and Multi-Agent Systems*, 3(1):9–31, 2000. 99, 107

Process Algebra for Agent Communication: A General Semantic Approach

Rogier M. van Eijk[1], Frank S. de Boer[1],
Wiebe van der Hoek[2], and John-Jules Ch. Meyer[1]

[1] Institute of Information and Computing Sciences
Utrecht University, P.O. Box 80.089,
3508 TB Utrecht, The Netherlands
{rogier,frankb,jj}@cs.uu.nl

[2] Department of Computer Science
University of Liverpool,
Liverpool L69 7ZF, United Kingdom
wiebe@csc.liv.ac.uk

Abstract. In this paper, we consider the process algebra ACPL, which models the basics of agent communication. This algebra combines the information-processing aspects of Concurrent Constraint Programming (CCP) with a generalisation of the synchronous handshaking communication mechanism of Communicating Sequential Processes (CSP). The operational semantics of ACPL is given in terms of a transition system that consists of local and global transition rules. The local rules describe the operational behaviour of agents, like the local effects of communication actions. The global rules define the operational behaviour of multi-agent systems including the matching of communication actions. We show how ACPL provides a general basis to address the semantics of agent communication languages such as KQML and FIPA-ACL. Finally, we address several extensions of the basic algebra.

1 Introduction

One of the topics of current research on multi-agent systems is the development of standard *agent communication languages* that enable agents from different platforms to interact with each other on a high level of abstraction [21,30]. The most prominent communication languages are the language KQML [13] and the language FIPA-ACL [14,24]. In essence, an agent communication language provides a set of communication acts that agents in a multi-agent system can perform. The purpose of these acts is to convey information about an agent's own mental state with the objective to effect the mental state of the communication partner.

Communication actions of agent communication languages are comprised of a number of distinct layers. Figure 1 depicts the three-layer model of KQML. The first layer of KQML consists of the informational content of the communication action. This content is expressed in some agreed-upon language, like a propositional, first-order or other knowledge representation language. The second layer of the communication action expresses a particular attitude towards the informational content in the form of a *speech*

M.-P. Huget (Ed.): Communications in Multiagent Systems, LNAI 2650, pp. 113–128, 2003.
© Springer-Verlag Berlin Heidelberg 2003

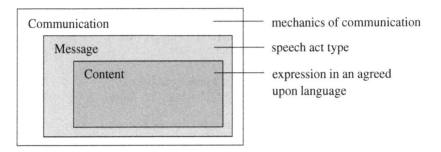

Fig. 1. Layers of the agent communication language KQML

act [1,29]. Examples of speech acts are `tell` to express that the content is believed to hold, `untell` to express that the content is not believed to hold or `ask` to ask whether the content is believed to hold. Finally, the third layer deals with the mechanics of communication, involving aspects like the channel along which the communication takes place and the direction of the communication (that is, sent or received).

An example of a communication action is: $c \ ! \ ask(p)$. The content layer of the action consists of the proposition p, the message layer of the speech act `ask` and the communication layer of the communication channel c and the operator "!". The operator "!" indicates that the message is sent along the communication channel (the anticipated receipt of messages will be indicated by the operator "?").

For a clear understanding of agent communication we find it important not to consider communication actions in isolation, but to study them in the larger context of the multi-agent system in which they are performed. In this larger context, we can study aspects of conversations and dialogues, such as the specific order in which communication actions are executed, the conditions under which they take place and the effects they have on the (mental) states of the agents that are involved (see also [17]). Therefore, we add one extra level to the three-layer model of KQML, namely the layer of the *multi-agent system*. We consider multi-agent systems that are defined in terms of a particular programming language. We assume the programming language to contain basic programming concepts, such as actions to examine and manipulate an agent's mental state, the aforementioned communication actions for interaction between agents, operators to make complex agent programs and operators to combine individual agent programs to form multi-agent programs.

Process Algebra

The main principle of structured programming, as originally advocated by Dijkstra, is that under all circumstances a programmer must keep the program within his or her intellectual grasp [7,8]. During the last decades many formalisms have been developed to obtain a thorough understanding of the different aspects of programming. *Process Algebra* is the common name of a family of abstract programming notations for reasoning about concurrently executing, communicating computer systems. These frameworks concentrate on the essential features of programming and thereby abstract from all implementation details.

In a process algebra, a process is defined in terms of a set of basic operators, like sequential composition, choice, parallelism and looping. These operators are typically given semantics through a *structural operational semantics*, originally developed by Plotkin [25]. An example is one of the rules that governs parallel composition:

$$\frac{P \stackrel{l}{\longrightarrow} P'}{P \parallel Q \stackrel{l}{\longrightarrow} P' \parallel Q}$$

The rule states that if it is possible for a process P to perform a computation step l, yielding process P', then it is also possible for the parallel composition of P and Q, to perform the computation step l, yielding the parallel composition of P' and Q. This reflects the interleaving model of parallel execution.

Usually, processes are considered with respect to a particular sort of observational behaviour. Two processes are considered equivalent if they exhibit the same observational behaviour. Equivalences can be formally proven by means of rewriting systems that consist of axioms and inference rules in the form of algebraic equivalences. An example of an algebraic equivalence is:

$$P \parallel Q = Q \parallel P$$

expressing that parallel composition is a commutative operator.

The main algebraic approaches to concurrency are Hoare's Communicating Sequential Processes (CSP) [19,6], Milner's Calculus of Communicating Systems (CCS) [22], and Bergstra & Klop's Algebra of Communicating Processes (ACP) [3]. Over the last years, many extensions and refinements of these algebras have been developed, like extensions with time [2], channel-passing (e.g., π-calculus [23]), constraints [5], and higher-order communication [32] in which processes themselves can be passed in a communication step.

In [4,9,10,11,12], a process algebra for agent communication has been developed. The computational model of this algebra, which is called Agent Communication Programming Language (ACPL), consists of an integration of the declarative paradigm of Concurrent Constraint Programming (CCP) [27] and the imperative programming paradigm of CSP. The constraint programming techniques are used to represent and process information, whereas the communication mechanism of ACPL is based upon a generalisation of the synchronous handshaking mechanism of CSP. The generalisation consists of the exchange of *information*, i.e., constraints, instead of the communication of simple *values*. In essence, a communication step consists of a handshake between an agent that sends information φ and an agent that anticipates the receipt of information ψ, where for successful communication it is required that φ contains at least as much information as ψ.

The paper is organised as follows. In Section 2, we define the syntax of the multi-agent language ACPL. The structural operational semantics of this language is described in Section 3. The subject of Section 4 is the application of the framework to agent communication languages as FIPA-ACL and KQML. Finally, in Section 5, we wrap up and provide some pointers to extensions of the basic algebra.

2 Syntax

In this section, we introduce the syntax of ACPL, which like Concurrent Constraint Programming is parameterised by a constraint system that is used to represent information.

Definition 1 (Constraint systems)
A *constraint system* C is a tuple $(C, \sqsubseteq, \wedge, true, false)$, where C (the set of constraints, with typical element φ) is a set ordered with respect to $\sqsubseteq$, $\wedge$ is the least upperbound operation, and *true*, *false* are the least and greatest elements of C, respectively.

A constraint system is an abstract model of information. It consists of a set of basic pieces of information, which can be combined to form more complex constraints by means of a conjunction operator "$\wedge$". For instance, constraints can be formulas from propositional logic, like p and $p \rightarrow q$. Constraints are ordered by means of an information-ordering. That is, $\varphi \sqsubseteq \psi$ denotes that φ contains less information than ψ. For instance, q contains less information than $p \wedge (p \rightarrow q)$. Usually, the reverse of the information-ordering is used, which is called the entailment relation (e.g., a PROLOG interpreter, a theorem-prover and so on), denoted as "$\vdash$". For instance, we have $p \wedge (p \rightarrow q) \vdash q$. The entailment relation for instance indicates how the agent deals with negations; i.e., whether it employs a negation-as-failure strategy, a finite-failure strategy, and so on. Moreover, it can be thought of representing the agent's decision-making capabilities.

In order to model *hiding* of local variables and *parameter passing* in constraint programming, in [28] the notion of a constraint system is enriched with a hiding operator $\exists_x$ (which in the CCP literature is called a cylindrification operator, following [18]). This operator satisfies the usual properties of existential quantification, such as $\varphi \vdash \exists_x \varphi$, $\varphi \vdash \psi$ implies $\exists_x \varphi \vdash \exists_x \psi$, $\exists_x \exists_y \varphi \equiv \exists_y \exists_x \varphi$ and $\exists_x (\varphi \wedge \exists_x \psi) \equiv \exists_x \varphi \wedge \exists_x \psi$, where $\equiv$ denotes logical equivalence. We use the notation $\varphi[y/x]$ to denote the formula $\exists_x (d_{xy} \sqcup \varphi)$, which can be intepreted as the formula obtained from φ by replacing all the free occurrences of x by y. We also assume the generalisation $\varphi[\bar{y}/\bar{x}]$ to sequences of variables.

Aditionally, in order to model the dynamics of belief bases, we assume a particular *belief update operator* [15]. We use the notation $\varphi \circ \psi$ to denote an agent's belief base φ that has been updated with the information ψ. A constraint system together with existential quantification $\exists_x$ and an update operator $\circ$ constitute a *belief system*.

The main objective of the programming language defined below is to provide a generic framework for the exchange of information in multi-agent systems, which abstracts from the specific nature of the underlying belief system.

In the following definition, we assume a given set $Chan$ of (unidirectional) communication channels, with typical element c.

In the remainder of this paper, we assume a particular belief system $\mathcal{B}$ to be given.

Definition 2 (Basic actions)
The *basic actions* of the programming language are defined as follows:

$$a ::= c!\varphi \mid c?\varphi \mid \mathsf{query}(\varphi) \mid \mathsf{update}(\varphi).$$

The execution of the output action $c!\varphi$ consists of sending the information φ along the channel c, which has to synchronise with a corresponding input $c?\psi$, for some ψ with $\varphi \vdash \psi$. In other words, the information φ can be sent along a channel c only if some information entailed by φ is anticipated to be received. The execution of an input action $c?\psi$, which consists of anticipating the receipt of the information ψ along the channel c, also has to synchronise with a corresponding output action $c!\varphi$, for some φ with $\varphi \vdash \psi$. The execution of a basic action $\mathsf{query}(\varphi)$ by an agent consists of checking whether the private store of the agent entails φ. On the other hand, the execution of $\mathsf{update}(\varphi)$ consists of updating the belief base with φ.

In the following definition, we assume a given set $Proc$ of procedure identifiers, with typical element p.

Definition 3 (Statements)
The behaviour of an agent is then described by a *statement* S:

$$S ::= a \cdot S \mid S_1 + S_2 \mid S_1 \,\&\, S_2 \mid \mathsf{loc}_x S \mid p(\bar{x}) \mid \mathsf{skip}.$$

Statements are thus built up from the basic actions using the following standard programming constructs: action prefixing, denoted by "$\cdot$"; non-deterministic choice, denoted by "$+$"; internal parallelism, denoted by "$\&$"; local variables, denoted by $\exists_x S$, which indicates that x is a local variable in S; and (recursive) procedure calls of the form $p(\bar{x})$, where $p \in Proc$ constitutes the name of the procedure and $\bar{x}$ denotes a sequence of variables which constitute the actual parameters of the call. We assume that no information on a local variable x can be communicated. Hence, we additionally require that in $\exists_x S$ the variable x does not occur free in a communication of S; that is, for every communication action $c?\varphi$ or $c!\varphi$ of S we have $\exists_x \varphi \equiv \varphi$. Finally, skip denotes the empty statement.

Definition 4 (Multi-agent systems)
A *multi-agent system* A is defined as follows:

$$A ::= \langle D, S, \varphi \rangle \mid A_1 \parallel A_2 \mid \delta_H(A).$$

A *basic agent* in a multi-agent system is represented by a tuple $\langle D, S, \varphi \rangle$. The set D consists of procedure declarations of the form $p(\bar{x}) :\!- S$, where $\bar{x}$ denote the formal parameters of p and S denotes its body. In order to facilitate the operational description of procedure calls, we assume that D satisfies the following property:

$$\text{if } p(\bar{x}) :\!- S \in D \text{ then } p(\bar{y}) :\!- S[\bar{y}/\bar{x}] \in D$$

for all $\bar{x}$ and $\bar{y}$, where $S[\bar{y}/\bar{x}]$ denotes the statement S in which each constraint φ is replaced by $\varphi[\bar{y}/\bar{x}]$. The statement S in $\langle D, S, \varphi \rangle$ describes the behaviour of the agent with respect to its *private* store φ. The threads of S, i.e. the concurrently executing substatements of S, interact with each other via the private store of the basic agent by means of the actions $\mathsf{query}(\psi)$ and $\mathsf{update}(\psi)$. As in the operational semantics below the set D of procedure declarations will not change, we usually omit it from notation and simply write $\langle S, \varphi \rangle$ instead of $\langle D, S, \varphi \rangle$.

Additionally, a multi-agent system itself consists of a collection of concurrently operating agents that interact with each other only via a synchronous information-passing mechanism by means of the communication actions $c!\psi$ and $c?\psi$. Our choice for synchronous communication is motivated by the fact it can be used to model asynchronous communication as well, as we will see in Section 4. Note that we restrict to the parallel composition of agent systems, and leave sequential composition, non-deterministic choice and recursion at the level of multi-agent systems out of consideration.

Finally, the encapsulation operator δ_H with $H \subseteq Chan$, which stems from the process algebra ACP, is used to define local communication channels [3]. That is, $\delta_H(A)$ denotes a multi-agent system in which the communication channels in H are for internal use only and hence, cannot be used for communication with agents outside the system.

3   Operational Semantics

In this section, we consider the structural operational semantics of ACPL.

3.1   Transition Systems

The central idea of structural operational semantics is to define the meaning of a program directly in terms of the behaviour that it exhibits. More specifically, the behaviour of a program can be modelled as a sequence of *transitions* between consecutive *configurations*. A configuration denotes the state of the program at a particular point in its execution. A transition corresponds to an individual computation step of the program, reflecting the effects on the current configuration.

A simple and elegant formalism to define structural operational semantics is via the well-known technique of *transition systems*, originally developed in [25]. In short, a transition system collects a set of rules that are used for the formal derivation of computation steps of a program. These rules define the effects that the different programming constructs have on the current configuration of the program. Such a configuration not only contains a description of the state of the program, but also the part of the program that still needs to be executed after the transition. In its most general form, a *transition* looks as follows:

$$\langle P, \sigma \rangle \longrightarrow \langle P', \sigma' \rangle.$$

It denotes a computation step of the program P which changes the current state of the system σ to the state σ', where P' is identified to be the part of the program P that still needs to be executed. Assuming that programs have been defined *inductively*, we can define the transitions of a program in terms of the transitions of its components. For example, the transitions of a sequential composition of two programs P_1 and P_2 can be derived from the transitions of P_1 and the transitions of P_2. That is, the compound program performs the computation steps that the program P_1 executes, and upon termination of P_1, the computation steps that P_2 performs.

In general, transitions are formally derived by means of *transition rules*, which are of the following format:

$$\langle P_1, \sigma_1 \rangle \longrightarrow \langle P_1', \sigma_1' \rangle$$

$$\vdots$$

$$\frac{\langle P_n, \sigma_n \rangle \longrightarrow \langle P_n', \sigma_n' \rangle}{\langle P, \sigma \rangle \longrightarrow \langle P', \sigma' \rangle} \quad \text{if } cond$$

Such a rule denotes that the transition below the line can be derived if the transitions above the line are derivable, provided that the condition *cond* holds. Sometimes, we write transition rules with several transitions below the line. They are used to abbreviate a collection of rules each having one of these transitions as its conclusion. A rule with no transitions above the line is called an *axiom*, and is simply written as $\langle P, \sigma \rangle \longrightarrow \langle P', \sigma' \rangle$. A *transition system* is then a set of of transition rules.

In order to be able to describe communication, we can make use of *labelled transition systems* in which the transitions are of the following form:

$$\langle P, \sigma \rangle \xrightarrow{l} \langle P', \sigma' \rangle.$$

The label l in this transition is used to denote the *mode* of the computation step. In our case, we distinguish between three different modes; viz., internal computation steps, input actions and output actions.

The advantage of using transitions systems is that they allow the operational semantics to closely follow the syntactic structure of the language. As an effect, if we view the configurations of the form $\langle P, \sigma \rangle$ as states of an abstract machine then the transitions specify the actions that this machine should perform. In fact, this machine could act as an *interpreter* for the language.

3.2 Local Transitions of ACPL

The structural operational semantics of ACPL is defined by means of a *local* and a *global* transition system. Given a set of declarations D, a local transition is of the form

$$\langle S, \varphi \rangle \xrightarrow{l} \langle S', \psi \rangle$$

where either l equals τ in case of an *internal* computation step, that is, a computation step which consists of the execution of skip or a basic action of the form query(φ) or update(φ), or l is of the form $c!\varphi$ or $c?\varphi$, in case of a communication step. We employ the symbol E to denote successful termination.

Definition 5 *(Transitions for basic actions)*

$$\langle \text{query}(\varphi), \psi \rangle \xrightarrow{\tau} \langle E, \psi \rangle \qquad \text{if } \psi \vdash \varphi$$
$$\langle \text{update}(\varphi), \psi \rangle \xrightarrow{\tau} \langle E, \psi \circ \varphi \rangle$$
$$\langle c!\varphi, \psi \rangle \xrightarrow{c!\varphi} \langle E, \psi \rangle$$
$$\langle c?\varphi, \psi \rangle \xrightarrow{c?\varphi} \langle E, \psi \rangle$$

The actions query(φ) and update(φ) are the familiar operations from CCP which allow an agent to inspect and update its private store. The semantics of the basic action update is defined in terms of the belief update operator $\circ$ from the belief system $\mathcal{B}$. By adding new information the store can become inconsistent, such as for instance if the action update$(x = 1)$ is performed in a situation where the store contains the information $x = 0$. We assume that such conflicts are resolved by the belief update operator $\circ$.

In the third transition, the information φ to be sent does not necessarily follow from the agent's belief base ψ. The programmer can try to accomplish sincerity by letting the output action precede by a test that φ follows indeed from the information store:

$$\text{query}(\varphi) \cdot c!\varphi$$

In this case, the communication action will only be executed in case the test query(φ) has been successfully executed first. However, in the case of multiple concurrently operating threads in an agent, it is possible that the consecutive execution of these two actions is interleaved by another action that updates the private store. Due to this intermediate update it is possible that the information φ will not be entailed by the store at the moment of communication. Thus, sincerity assumes either that an agent has one single thread or that its belief base shows monotonically increasing behaviour; i.e., information is only added to the store and not removed from it.

In the fourth transition, the information φ that is anticipated to be received is not automatically added to the agent's belief state. The addition of this information can be controlled by the programmer through a subsequent execution of the update operator:

$$c?\varphi \cdot \text{update}(\varphi).$$

Furthermore, we have the following rules for action prefixing, procedure calls and the programming constructs for non-deterministic choice and parallel composition.

Definition 6 *(Transition for prefixing)*

$$\frac{\langle a, \psi \rangle \xrightarrow{l} \langle E, \psi' \rangle}{\langle a \cdot S, \psi \rangle \xrightarrow{l} \langle S, \psi' \rangle}$$

The computation step of a prefixed statement $a \cdot S$ corresponds to the execution of its prefix a. That is, the transition of the prefixed statement $a \cdot S$ is inferred from the transition of the action a, in which the label l is propagated together with the change of the private store from ψ to ψ'. Finally, the statement S is identified to be the part of $a \cdot S$ that needs to be executed next.

Definition 7 *(Transition for internal parallelism)*

$$\frac{\langle S_1, \psi \rangle \xrightarrow{l} \langle S_1', \psi' \rangle}{\begin{array}{c} \langle S_1 \mathbin{\&} S_2, \psi \rangle \xrightarrow{l} \langle S_1' \mathbin{\&} S_2, \psi' \rangle \\ \langle S_2 \mathbin{\&} S_1, \psi \rangle \xrightarrow{l} \langle S_2 \mathbin{\&} S_1', \psi' \rangle \end{array}}$$

A derivation rule that has two transitions below the line, is a shorthand notation for two derivation rules that each have one of these two transitions as its conclusion. The execution of a parallel statement $S \,\&\, T$ is modelled as an interleaving of the computation steps of S and T. That is, an execution step of the composed statement $S \,\&\, T$ is given by a computation step of one the statements S and T. Therefore in the above transition rule, the transition of the statement S_1 induces a transition of the compound statement $S_1 \,\&\, S_2$ in which it acts as the left operand, as well a transition of the compound statement $S_2 \,\&\, S_1$ in which it acts as the right operand. The statements $S_1' \,\&\, S_2$ and $S_2 \,\&\, S_1'$ then denote the part of the composed statements that remains to be executed, respectively.

Definition 8 *(Transition for non-deterministic choice)*

$$\frac{\langle S_1, \psi \rangle \stackrel{l}{\longrightarrow} \langle S_1', \psi' \rangle}{\begin{array}{c}\langle S_1 + S_2, \psi \rangle \stackrel{l}{\longrightarrow} \langle S_1', \psi' \rangle \\ \langle S_2 + S_1, \psi \rangle \stackrel{l}{\longrightarrow} \langle S_1', \psi' \rangle\end{array}}$$

The computation steps of a non-deterministic choice $S + T$ are given by the transitions of either of the statements S and T. Hence, in the transition rule above, the transition of S_1 yields a transition for the compound statement $S_1 + S_2$ as well as for the compound statement $S_2 + S_1$. The part of the non-deterministic choice that remains to be executed is given by S_1'. The rule reflects that "+" is a commutative operator. Due to non-deterministic choice the execution of a multi-agent system can lead to different ending states. Note the difference with the rule for internal parallelism in which the statement S_2 remains to be executed as well.

Definition 9 *(Transition for local variables)*

$$\frac{\langle S, \varphi \circ \exists_x \psi \rangle \stackrel{l}{\longrightarrow} \langle S', \psi' \rangle}{\langle \mathsf{loc}_x^\varphi S, \psi \rangle \stackrel{l}{\longrightarrow} \langle \mathsf{loc}_x^{\varphi'} S', \psi \circ \exists_x \varphi' \rangle}$$

The syntax of the language is extended with a construct of the form $\mathsf{loc}_x^\varphi S$ denoting that in the statement S the variable x is a local variable, where the constraint φ collects the information on the local variable x. In this notation, the statement $\mathsf{loc}_x S$ is written as $\mathsf{loc}_x^{true} S$, denoting that the local constraints on x are initially empty.

The idea of the transition rule is that the transition of the construct $\mathsf{loc}_x^\varphi S$ is derived from the transition of the statement S. In order to achieve this, we need to replace the constraints on the global variable x in the state ψ (if present) by the constraints φ on the local variable x. This yields the state $\varphi \circ \exists_x \psi$. The statement S is then executed relative to this state. After one computation step, φ' denotes the new state and S' represents the part of S that still remains to be executed. In order to obtain from ψ' the resulting store, we remove the constraints on the local variable x from it and add the remainder to the old private store ψ, yielding the new state $\psi \circ \exists_x \varphi'$. Finally, the constraints on the local variable x need to be stored for later use; hence, the statement $\mathsf{loc}_x^{\varphi'} S'$ denotes the part of the program that needs to be executed next.

Note that no information on the local variable x can be communicated, because by definition x does not occur free in φ in case l is of the form $c?\varphi$ or $c!\varphi$.

Definition 10 *(Transition for procedure calls)*

$$\langle p(\bar{y}), \psi \rangle \xrightarrow{\ \tau\ } \langle S, \psi \rangle \ \text{ where } p(\bar{y}) :- S \in D$$

The transition of a procedure call is given by the replacement of the call by the body of the procedure.

Definition 11 *(Transition for skip)*

$$\langle \mathsf{skip}, \psi \rangle \xrightarrow{\ \tau\ } \langle E, \psi \rangle$$

The rule shows that the statement skip always succeeds and has no effects on the information store ψ.

3.3   Global Transitions of ACPL

A *global* transition is of the form $A \xrightarrow{\ l\ } A'$, where l indicates whether the transition involves an internal computation step, that is, $l = \tau$, or a communication, that is, $l = c!\varphi$ or $l = c?\varphi$.

Definition 12 *(Transitions for multi-agent systems)*
The following rule describes parallel composition by interleaving of the basic actions:

$$\frac{A_1 \xrightarrow{\ l\ } A_1'}{\begin{array}{c} A_1 \parallel A_2 \xrightarrow{\ l\ } A_1' \parallel A_2 \\ A_2 \parallel A_1 \xrightarrow{\ l\ } A_2 \parallel A_1' \end{array}}$$

In order to describe the synchronisation between agents we introduce a synchronisation predicate $|$, which is defined as follows. For all $c \in Chan$ and $\varphi, \psi \in \mathcal{B}$, if $\varphi \vdash \psi$ then

$$(c!\varphi \mid c?\psi) \text{ and } (c?\psi \mid c!\varphi).$$

In all other cases, the predicate $|$ yields the boolean value false. We then have the following synchronisation rule:

$$\frac{A_1 \xrightarrow{\ l_1\ } A_1' \quad A_2 \xrightarrow{\ l_2\ } A_2'}{A_1 \parallel A_2 \xrightarrow{\ \tau\ } A_1' \parallel A_2'} \ \text{ if } l_1 \mid l_2$$

This rule shows that an action of the form $c?\psi$ only matches with an action of the form $c!\varphi$ in case ψ is entailed by φ. In all other cases, the predicate $|$ yields false and therefore no communication can take place.

Finally, *encapsulation* of communications along a set of channels H is described by the rule:

$$\frac{A \xrightarrow{\ l\ } A'}{\delta_H(A) \xrightarrow{\ l\ } \delta_H(A')} \ \text{ if } chan(l) \cap H = \emptyset$$

where $chan$ is defined by $chan(c!\varphi) = chan(c?\varphi) = \{c\}$ and $chan(\tau) = \emptyset$.

4   Agent Communication Languages

The framework ACPL provides a general basis for the semantics of agent communication languages. Consider the different layers of the agent communication language KQML in Figure 1. Constraint systems can be used to represent the content layer. With respect to the second layer we assume an extension of the entailment relation of the constraint system that includes speech acts. For example, a KQML expression consisting of a content expression φ that is encapsulated in a message wrapper containing the speech act untell, which allows to derive negative information in terms of the closed world assumption [26], is represented by the expression $\text{untell}(\varphi)$. This operator can be defined by an extension of the information ordering of the constraint system. For instance, given the constraints ψ and φ, we define:

$$\psi \nvdash \varphi \;\;\Leftrightarrow\;\; \psi \vdash \text{untell}(\varphi).$$

Assuming that ψ represents the belief base of an agent, this rule formalises the closed world assumption. Assuming $\neg p \nvdash p$, we can for instance derive: $\neg p \vdash \text{untell}(p)$. Note that we cannot derive $\text{untell}(p) \vdash \neg p$.

The anti-monotonicity property of the untell operator is expressed by:

$$\text{untell}(\psi) \vdash \text{untell}(\varphi) \;\;\Leftrightarrow\;\; \varphi \vdash \psi.$$

So, for instance, we have $\text{untell}(p) \vdash \text{untell}(p \wedge q)$, or in other words $\text{untell}(p \wedge q)$ contains less information than $\text{untell}(p)$.

The general use of the entailment relation in the semantics of communication actions allows us to abstract from among others the following :

- the particular *syntax* of information, for instance, $\text{untell}(p \wedge q)$ entails $\text{untell}(q \wedge p)$ and vice versa.
- redundant logical strength, e.g., $\text{untell}(p)$ entails $\text{untell}(p \wedge q)$.
- the *kind* of communicated information, e.g., simple constraints on the domain of discourse or information containing speech acts.

The third layer involves the communication channel and the direction of communication. At this level, we consider the interplay between sending and anticipating the receipt of information. In ACPL, the basic communication mechanism is synchronous. A synchronous communication step consists of a handshake between an agent that performs a communication action of the form $c\,!\,\text{speech\_act}_1(\varphi_1)$ and an agent that performs a matching communication act of the form $c\,?\,\text{speech\_act}_2(\varphi_2)$ along the same channel c. For them to match it is required that the sent message $\text{speech\_act}_1(\varphi_1)$ contains at least as much information as the message that is anticipated to be received, or in terms of the entailment relation:

$$\text{speech\_act}_1(\varphi_1) \vdash \text{speech\_act}_2(\varphi_2).$$

For instance, employing the above stipulations, we have that $c\,!\,\neg p$ matches with $c\,?\,\text{untell}(p)$, but $c\,!\,\text{untell}(p)$ does not match with $c\,?\,\neg p$.

Thus, the basic communication mechanism of ACPL is *synchronous*, i.e., the receipt of information takes place at the same time at which it is sent. Our choice for synchronous communication is motivated by the fact that in the field of concurrency theory, asynchronous communication can be modelled in terms of synchronous communication [20]. In particular, asynchronous communication can be modelled in our agent framework by means of communication facilitators. This is illustrated in the next example.

Example 13 Sending a question $\text{ask}(\varphi)$ along a channel c without waiting for its answer (to be received along a channel d) can be described by the following code:

$$c!\text{ask}(\varphi) \cdot (S_1 \ \& \ (d?\varphi \cdot S_2 + d?\text{untell}(\varphi) \cdot S_3)),$$

where S_1 represents the remaining activities of the agent and S_2 and S_3 represent the agent's subsequent responses to the receipt of the answers φ and $\text{untell}(\varphi)$, respectively.

Secondly, the corresponding receipt of a question $\text{ask}(\varphi)$ along a channel c, will be handled by the addressed agent's communication facilitator Fac which satisfies the following recursive equation:

$$Fac :- c?\text{ask}(\varphi) \cdot ((e?\varphi \cdot d!\varphi) \ \& \ Fac),$$

where e denotes an internal channel connecting the facilitator with the agent. Note that consequently this facilitator in fact describes a bag of received requests (along channel c) for answering ψ.

Obviously, this basic form of asynchronous dialogue can be extended to more involved patterns of interaction.

As an additional example we consider the KQML speech acts ask_one, which is used to ask for one instantiation of the specified question. In the concurrency framework of ACP [3], value-passing can be modelled by synchronisation of actions and non-deterministic choice. Similarly, in our framework, we can model the generation and communication of solutions to constraints as described by the KQML speech acts like ask_one in the following way.

Example 14 Anticipated responses (to be received along channel c) to the KQML expression $\text{ask\_one}(\varphi)$ can be modelled as follows:

$$\sum_{i \in I} c?\varphi(\theta_i) \cdot S_i,$$

where $\sum$ represents non-deterministic choice and the set $\{\theta_i \mid i \in I\}$ denotes the set of all suitable substitutions, $\varphi(\theta_i)$ denotes the application of the substitution θ_i to φ and S_i represents the corresponding subsequent reaction.

For instance, consider the question $\text{ask\_one}(price(x, item464))$ to ask for the price of a particular item. Let us assume that prices can be any natural number between 0 and 1000. The reception of an answer to the question can then be described by:

$$\sum_{i \in [0..1000]} c?price(i, item464) \cdot S_i.$$

5   Conclusions and Further Reading

In this paper, we have considered the process algebra ACPL, which models the basics of agent communication. This algebra combines the information-processing aspects of CCP with a generalisation of the synchronous handshaking communication mechanism of CSP. The operational semantics of ACPL is given in terms of a transition system that consists of local and global transition rules. The local rules describe the operational behaviour of agents, like the local effects of communication actions. The global rules define the operational behaviour of multi-agent systems including the matching of communication actions. We have shown how ACPL provides a general basis to address the semantics of agent communication languages.

The basic algebra ACPL has been extended in several different directions. We conclude the paper by considering a number of these extensions.

Full Abstraction The operational semantics of ACPL describes the behaviour of a multi-agent system in terms of its computations. In general, however, we are not interested in all details of the behaviour that a particular system exhibits. That is, we want to reason about a multi-agent system at a higher level of abstraction, namely at a level that captures the aspects that are visible to an external observer. In [4], we consider the observable behaviour of a multi-agent system to be the final information stores as computed by the individual agents in a system. In order to describe this notion of observable behaviour in a compositional way, we have developed a form of denotational semantics, called *failure semantics*, which is shown to be a fully-abstract characterisation of the notion of observables. For instance, with respect to this observable behaviour, the following algebraic laws hold. If $\varphi \vdash \psi$ then:

$$c!\varphi = c!\varphi + c!\psi$$
$$c?\psi = c?\psi + c?\varphi$$

The crucial observation here is that any communication action that for instance matches $c \,!\, p$ also matches $c \,!\, p \wedge q$. In general, we could say that sending a message includes sending all messages that contain less information. Similarly, any communication action that matches $c \,?\, p \wedge q$ also matches $c \,?\, p$. In other words, anticipating the receipt of a messages includes anticipating the receipt of all messages that contain more information.

Specification and verification Once the semantics of a programming language has been established, it allows us to consider the *specification* and *verification* of agent communication. Verification amounts to the process of checking whether a program satisfies desired behaviour as expressed by a specification, like for instance the conversation policy [16] that if an agent A is asked by an agent B whether a particular proposition holds then A subsequently answers B whether it believes the proposition to hold or not. In [12], a compositional verification calculus for ACPL is defined. This calculus can be used to verify that a particular multi-agent system satisfies its specification. On the basis of this calculus it is possible to implement (semi-)automatic verification procedures. This is a subject of future research.

Translations In [11], we consider communicating agents that employ different vocabularies to represent information. In order to communicate some translations between these vocabularies need to generated. Instead of being defined in advance, we consider translations that are dynamically constructed during execution of the system. These translations are based both on the information that the agents exchange and the underlying ontologies that they employ. This yields a framework that can be used to study and analyse experiments as performed in the research on the origins of language, like for instance dialogue games in which the purpose of communication is to develop a mutual understanding of the agents' vocabularies [31]. This is also a subject of further research.

Agents and objects In [10], it is studied in which way concepts and techniques that have been developed in the object-oriented paradigm, can be adopted and adjusted for multi-agent systems. In particular, we study in which way the rendezvous communication mechanism of object-oriented programming can be generalised to structure the exchange of information between agents. A central concept of this chapter is the concept of a *question invocation* by analogy with the concept of a *method invocation* from object-oriented programming.

Groups Finally, we mention here some related work by De Vries *et al.* [33,34], where an abstract programming language for agent interaction is proposed, called GrAPL. This language contains constructs for coordinating group activity (group communication, formation, and collaboration). There are definite similarities between GrAPL and ACPL: both are given operational (process-algebraic) semantics, both employ the idea of a CSP-like synchronisation for communication between agents, and in both languages the communicated information is viewed as comprising constraints in a constraint system. The main difference is that in ACPL bilateral communication is used while in GrAPL this idea is extended to groups of agents that tell each other constraints about (parameters of) actions to be performed by them. In [33, Chapter 6] this idea is extended further to the communication of partial plans, i.e. orders on actions, as well as who is willing to do what, between agents in a group so that in effect the agents are able to perform distributive planning.

References

1. J.L. Austin. *How to do Things with Words*. Oxford University Press, Oxford, 1962. 114
2. J.C.M. Baeten and C.A. Middelburg. Process algebra with timing: real time and discrete time. In J.A. Bergstra, A. Ponse, and S.A. Smolka, editors, *Handbook of Process Algebra*. Elsevier, 1999. 115
3. J.A. Bergstra and J.W. Klop. Process algebra for synchronous communication. *Information and Control*, 60:109–137, 1984. 115, 118, 124
4. F.S. de Boer, R.M. van Eijk, W. van der Hoek, and J.-J.Ch. Meyer. Fully-abstract model for the exchange of information in multi-agent systems. *Theoretical Computer Science*, 290(3):1753–1773, 2003. To appear. 115, 125
5. F.S. de Boer and C. Palamidessi. A process algebra of concurrent constraint programming. In *Proceedings of the Joint International Conference and Symposium on Logic Programming (JICSLP'92*, pages 463–477, Cambridge, Massachusetts, 1992. MIT Press. 115

6. S.D. Brookes, C.A.R. Hoare, and W. Roscoe. A theory of communicating sequential processes. *Journal of ACM*, 31:499–560, 1984. 115

7. E.W. Dijkstra. Go to statement considered harmful. *Communications of the ACM*, 11(3):147–148, 1968. 114

8. E.W. Dijkstra. *A Discipline of Programming*. Prentice-Hall, Englewood Cliffs, N.J., 1976. 114

9. R.M. van Eijk, F.S. de Boer, W. van der Hoek, and J.-J.Ch. Meyer. Information-passing and belief revision in multi-agent systems. In J. P. M. Müller, M. P. Singh, and A. S. Rao, editors, *Intelligent Agents V, Proceedings of 5th International Workshop on Agent Theories, Architectures, and Languages (ATAL'98)*, volume 1555 of *Lecture Notes in Artificial Intelligence*, pages 29–45. Springer-Verlag, Heidelberg, 1999. 115

10. R.M. van Eijk, F.S. de Boer, W. van der Hoek, and J.-J.Ch. Meyer. Generalised object-oriented concepts for inter-agent communication. In C. Castelfranchi and Y. Lesperance, editors, *Intelligent Agents VII, Proceedings of 7th International Workshop on Agent Theories, Architectures, and Languages (ATAL 2000)*, volume 1986 of *Lecture Notes in Artificial Intelligence*, pages 260–274. Springer-Verlag, Heidelberg, 2001. 115, 126

11. R.M. van Eijk, F.S. de Boer, W. van der Hoek, and J.-J.Ch. Meyer. On dynamically generated ontology translators in agent communication. *International Journal of Intelligent Systems*, 16(5):587–607, 2001. 115, 126

12. R.M. van Eijk, F.S. de Boer, W. van der Hoek, and J.-J.Ch. Meyer. A verification framework for agent communication. *Journal of Autonomous Agents and Multi-Agent Systems*. To appear, 2003. 115, 125

13. T. Finin, D. McKay, R. Fritzson, and R. McEntire. KQML: An Information and Knowledge Exchange Protocol. In Kazuhiro Fuchi and Toshio Yokoi, editors, *Knowledge Building and Knowledge Sharing*. Ohmsha and IOS Press, 1994. 113

14. FIPA. Foundation for intelligent physical agents. Communicative act library specification. http://www.fipa.org, 2000. 113

15. P. Gärdenfors. *Knowledge in flux: Modelling the dynamics of epistemic states*. Bradford books, MIT, Cambridge, 1988. 116

16. M. Greaves, H. Holmback, and J. Bradshaw. What is a conversation policy? In F. Dignum and M. Greaves, editors, *Issues in Agent Communication*, volume 1916 of *Lecture Notes in Artificial Intelligence*, pages 118–131. Springer-Verlag, Heidelberg, 2000. 125

17. F. Guerin and J. Pitt. A semantic framework for specifying agent communication languages. In *Proceedings of fourth International Conference on Multi-Agent Systems (ICMAS-2000)*, pages 395–396, Los Alamitos, California, 2000. IEEE Computer Society. 114

18. L. Henkin, J.D. Monk, and A. Tarski. *Cylindric Algebras (Part I)*. North-Holland Publishing, Amsterdam, 1971. 116

19. C.A.R. Hoare. Communicating sequential processes. *Communications of the ACM*, 21(8):666–677, 1978. 115

20. H Jifeng, M.B. Josephs, and C.A.R. Hoare. A theory of synchrony and asynchrony. In *Proc. of the IFIP Working Conference on Programming Concepts and Methods*, pages 446–465, 1990. 124

21. Y. Labrou, T. Finin, and Y. Peng. Agent communication languages: The current landscape. *IEEE Intelligent Systems*, 14(2):45–52, 1999. 113

22. R. Milner. *A Calculus of Communicating Systems*, volume 92 of *Lecture Notes in Computer Science*. Springer-Verlag, 1980. 115

23. R. Milner. *Communicating and Mobile Systems: the π-Calculus*. Cambridge University Press, 1999. 115

24. J. Pitt and A. Mamdani. Some remarks on the semantics of FIPA's agent communication language. *Autonomous Agents and Multi-Agent Systems*, 2(4):333–356, 1999. 113

25. G. Plotkin. A structured approach to operational semantics. Technical Report DAIMI FN-19, Computer Science Department, Aarhus University, 1981. 115, 118

26. R. Reiter. On closed world data bases. In H. Gaillaire and J. Minker, editors, *Logic and Data Bases*, pages 55–76, New York, 1978. Plemum Press. 123

27. V.A. Saraswat. *Concurrent Constraint Programming*. The MIT Press, Cambridge, Massachusetts, 1993. 115

28. V.A. Saraswat, M. Rinard, and P. Panangaden. Semantic foundations of concurrent constraint programming. In *Proceedings of the 18th ACM Symposium on Principles of Programming Languages (POPL'91)*, pages 333–352, 1991. 116

29. J.R. Searle. *Speech acts: An essay in the philosophy of language*. Cambridge University Press, Cambridge, 1969. 114

30. M.P. Singh. Agent communication languages: Rethinking the principles. *IEEE Computer*, 31(12):40–47, 1998. 113

31. L. Steels. The origins of ontologies and communication conventions in multi-agent systems. *Journal of Autonomous Agents and Multi-Agent Systems*, 1(2):169–194, 1998. 126

32. B. Thomsen. A calculus of higher order communicating systems. In *Conference Record of the 16th Annual ACM Symposium on Principles of Programming Languages*, pages 143–153, 1989. 115

33. W. de Vries. *Agent Interaction: Approaches to Modelling, Abstraction, Programming and Verification of Multi-Agent Systems*. PhD thesis, Utrecht University, Mathematics and Computer Science, 2002. To Appear. 126, 126

34. W. de Vries, F.S. de Boer, K.V. Hindriks, W. der Hoek, and J.-J. Ch. Meyer. Programming language for coordinating group actions. In B. Dunin-Keplicz and E. Nawerecki, editors, *From Theory to Practice in Multi-Agent Systems*, volume 2296 of *Lecture Notes in Artificial Intelligence*, pages 313–321. Springer-Verlag, Heidelberg, 2002. 126

Hierarchical Information Combination in Large-Scale Multiagent Resource Management

Osher Yadgar[1], Sarit Kraus[2], and Charles L. Ortiz, Jr.[3]

[1] Dept. of CS, Bar Ilan University, Ramat Gan, 52900 Israel
yadgar@macs.biu.ac.il
[2] Dept. of CS, Bar Ilan University, Ramat Gan, 52900 Israel
sarit@macs.biu.ac.il
[3] Artificial Intelligence Center, SRI International, Menlo Park, CA 94025 USA
ortiz@ai.sri.com

Abstract. In this paper, we describe the Distributed Dispatcher Manager (DDM), a system for managing resource in very large-scale task and resource domains. In DDM, resources are modeled as cooperative mobile teams of agents and objects or tasks are assumed to be distributed over a virtual space. Each agent has direct access to only local and partial information about its immediate surroundings. DDM organizes teams hierarchically and addresses two important issues that are prerequisites for success in such domains: (i) how agents can extend local, partial information to arrive at a better local assessment of the situation and (ii) how the local assessments from teams of many agents can be integrated to form a global assessment of the situation. We conducted a large number of experiments in simulation and demonstrated the advantages of the DDM over other architectures in terms of accuracy and reduced inter-agent communication.[*]

1 Introduction

This paper presents a novel multiagent solution to the problem of resource management in very large-scale task and resource environments. We focus on domains of application in which resources are best modeled by mobile agents, each of which can decide, fairly autonomously, to take on new tasks in their immediate environment. Since agents are mobile, they can be redirected to other areas where resources are needed. However, since no single agent has global information regarding the distribution of tasks and resources, local information from agents must be pooled to obtain a more accurate understanding of the global situation. A typical domain that we have in mind is one involving sensor webs that must be jointly tasked for surveillance: sensors correspond to agents and objects that appear in the environment correspond to tasks. For these sorts of problem domains, we segment the problem solving proc-

---

[*] This work was supported by DARPA contract F30602-99-C-0169 and NSF grant 9820657. The second author is also affiliated with UMIACS.

M.-P. Huget (Ed.): Communications in Multiagent Systems, LNAI 2650, pp. 129–145, 2003.

ess into two stages: (1) a situation assessment stage in which information processed from individual agents is extended with causal knowledge about likely object behaviors and then combined to form a global situation assessment; and (2) a resource distribution stage in which agents are (re-)distributed for better task management. In this paper, we focus on the first stage; a companion paper addresses the second stage.

There are a number of ways one could approach the problem of achieving coordinated behavior in very large teams of agents. The various methods can range along several dimensions; as teams scale up, however, the degree of communication required for effective coordination is one important measure of system performance which one would like to minimize. The extent of communication can be measured, roughly, in terms of the number of rounds of communication needed between agents and the size of the messages exchanged. Complex protocols, such as contract nets, that involve *explicit coordination* in the form of cycles of announcements, bids and awards to determine an appropriate task allocation among team members can become costly, particularly after the number of tasks grows to the point that several rounds of each cycle is necessary to reach agreement on an appropriate division of labor. Methods that require a rich agent communication language (ACL) also place a burden on the communications medium, requiring larger messages and more complex processing by each agent; a consequence of the latter is the need for agents of a more complex design.

One of our goals has therefore been to develop methods that minimize such communication-related metrics by limiting the degree of explicit coordination required. A secondary goal was to also develop methods suitable for achieving coordinated behavior among very simple agents; hence, the ACL is extremely simple in design. To accomplish this we have designed a system which exploits agent autonomy in service of realtime reactivity. It assumes that agents are of a relatively simple design and organized hierarchically to reduce inter-agent communication. Agents are grouped into teams, each with a distinguished team leader; teams might be assigned to specific geographic sectors of interest. Teams are themselves grouped into larger teams. Communication is restricted to flow only between an agent (or team) and its team leader. State information from individual agents flows up to team leaders and sector assignments flow from the team leader to the agents. Each individual agent can position itself within an assigned sector depending on the tasks (objects) that it detects in its local environment. In this model, therefore, resources are not directly *allocated* to tasks but are rather distributed to sectors where it is believed that they are most needed: the sector leader need not know exactly which agent is going to take on a particular task. This design does not preclude the possibility of sector leader, for example, using a more complex ACL; however, it does simplify the style and extent of communication necessary between agents.

More abstractly, we can model such problems and their solution in the following way. We define a *resource management problem, MP*, as a tuple, $MP = \langle O, S, T, A, Sa, G, g, Comm, paths, ResBy \rangle$, such that O stands for a set of tasks or objects; S, a set of object/tasks states; T, a set of integer times; A, a set of agents; Sa, a set of agent states; G, a set of groups; $g: A \cup G \rightarrow G$, an assignment of agents and groups to groups; $Comm \subseteq A \times A$, a binary relation indicating a communication link between agents; $\sigma : T \times O \rightarrow S$ the actual states of tasks at given time. A causal relation, $ResBy \subseteq S \times T \times S \times T$, constrains the evolution of object states in terms of contiguous, legitimate paths, such that $ResBy(s1,t1,s2,t2)$ iff $s2$ at $t2$ could follow $s1$ at time $t1$.

For finding a solution to MP we consider the notion of an object state function f_o : $T \rightarrow S$ that associates with an object o its state change over time. If f_o is the actual path function then for any t, $f_o(t) = \sigma(t,o)$. We define an *information map*, I as a set of path functions. We define a *solution*, Σ, to a given *MP*, written $\Sigma(MP)$, such that $\Sigma(MP) \subseteq I$, iff each object in O is captured in an actual path function in $\Sigma(MP)$. We expand on this formalization in later sections. Schematically we have the following (the second stage of the problem is to distribute agents to sectors - see companion paper for details).

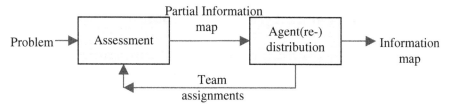

Figure 1: Solving the problem and redistributing the agents

The problem as described presents a number of difficult challenges: (1) there is a data association or object identification problem associated with connecting up task state measurements from one time point to the next; (2) local information obtained by an agent is incomplete and uncertain and must be combined with other agents' local information to improve the assessment; and (3) computing the information map and tracking objects must be accomplished in real time (this is one reason for giving individual agents the flexibility to act more or less autonomously within their sector: agents can react to nearby targets).

In this paper we describe the Distributed Dispatcher Model (DDM), a system that embodies these ideas. DDM is designed for efficient coordinated resource management in systems consisting of hundreds of agents; the model makes use of hierarchical group formation to restrict the degree of communication between agents and to guide processes for very quickly combine partial information to form a global assessment. Each level narrows the uncertainty based on the data obtained from lower levels. We show that the hierarchical processing of information reduces the time needed to form an accurate global assessment.

We have tested the performance of the DDM through extensive experimentation in a simulated environment involving many sensors. In the simulation models a suite of Doppler sensors are used to form a global information map of targets moving in a steady velocity. A Doppler sensor is a radar that is based on the Doppler effect. A Doppler sensor provides only partial information about a target, in terms of an arc on which a detected target might be located and the velocity towards it, that is, the *radial velocity* [3]. Given a single Doppler measurement, one cannot establish the exact location and velocity of a target; therefore, multiple measurements must be combined for each target. This problem was devised as a challenge problem by the DARPA Autonomous Negotiating Teams (ANTS) program to explore realtime distributed resource allocation algorithms in a two dimensional geographic environment. ANTS program uses Dopplers combined out of three different sectors, whereas only one sector may be activated at a time. The orientations of the sectors are 0, 120 and 240 degrees.

We have compared our hierarchical architecture to other architectures; in this paper we report on results that show that situation assessment is faster and more accurate in DDM. We have also shown that DDM can achieve these results while only using a low volume of possibly noisy communication.

2 Path Inference at the Agent Level in DDM

Each individual agent can extend its local information through the application of causal knowledge that constrains the set of possible paths that could be associated with a collection of data measurements.

2.1 Objects Movement and Agent Measurements

The ResBy function is meant to capture those constraints. The relation *ResBy* holds for two object-states s1 and s2 and two time points t1 and t2 where $t2 \geq t1$, if it is possible that if the state of an object was s1 at t1, then it could be s2 at t2. *ResBy* should also satisfy the following constraints:

Let $t_1, t_2, t_3 \in T$ and $s_1, s_2, s_3 \in S$, $t_1 < t_2 < t_3$ such that

(i)	if $ResBy(<t_1, s_1>, <t_2, s_2>)$	and
	$ResBy(<t_2, s_2>, <t_3, s_3>)$	then
	$ResBy(<t_1, s_1>, <t_3, s_3>)$	
(ii)	if $ResBy(<t_1, s_1>, <t_2, s_2>)$	and
	$ResBy(<t_1, s_1>, <t_3, s_3>)$	then
	$ResBy(<t_2, s_2>, <t_3, s_3>)$	
(iii)	if $ResBy(<t_1, s_1>, <t_3, s_3>)$	and
	$ResBy(<t_2, s_2>, <t_3, s_3>)$	then
	$ResBy(<t_1, s_1>, <t_2, s_2>)$	
(iv)	if $ResBy(<t, s_1>, <t, s_2>)$ then $s_1 = s_2$.	

The constraints (i)-(iii) on ResBy restrict the way the state of an object may change over time. They refer to three points of time t_1, t_2, t_3 in an increasing order and to the possibility that an object was at state s_1, s_2 and s_3 at these time points, respectively. If the object has been in these states at the corresponding times then s_2 at t_2 should be a result of s_1 at t_1, i.e. $ResBy(<t_1, s_1>, <t_2, s_2>)$. Similarly $ResBy(<t_2, s_2>, <t_3, s_3>)$ and $ResBy(<t_1, s_1>, <t_3, s_3>)$. The constraints indicate that it is enough to check that two out of the three relations hold, to verify that the object was really at s_1 at t_1, s_2 at t_2 and s_3 at t_3. That is, if two of the three relations hold, the third one does as well. The last constraint (iv) is based on the fact that an object cannot be in two different states at the same time.

2.1.1 Objects and *ResBy* Relation in the ANTS Domain

In the ANTS domain, objects correspond to targets. The target state structure is $s = <\bar{r}, \bar{v}>$. $\bar{r}$ is the location vector of the target and $\bar{v}$ is the velocity vector. If a target state s_2 at t_2 resulted from target state s_1 at t_1 and the velocity of the target remained constant during the period $t_i..t_j$, then $\bar{r}_2 = \bar{r}_1 + \bar{v}_1 \cdot (t_i - t_j)$. We assume that no target is likely to appear with the same exact properties as another target. That is, there cannot be two targets at the exact same location moving in the same velocity and direction. Thus, in ANTS where , $s_i = <\bar{r}_i, \bar{v}_i> ResBy(<t_1, s_1>, <t_2, s_2>)$ is true iff: (i) r_2 may be derived from r_1 using the motion equation of a target and given $\bar{v}_1$ during the period $t_2 - t_1$ and (ii) $\bar{v}_1 = \bar{v}_2$.

The physical motion of a moving body in a steady velocity follows the four constraints of the ResBy relation. In general, in any domain every object state that combines out of a singular state along with the first derivative of this state by time where this derivative is not depended on time satisfies the four constraints.

2.1.2 Agents' Measurements

Each agent is capable of taking measurements or sampling its nearby environment. In the ANTS domain a sampling agent state is represented by the location of the sensor and its orientation.

Object measurements provide only partial information on object-states and may be incorrect. When an agent takes measurements we refer to its agent state as the *viewpoint* from which a particular object state was measured. We assume that there is a function *PosS* that given k consecutive measurements taken by the same agent, up to time t returns a set of possible states, $S' \subseteq S$, for an object at time t where exactly one $s \in S'$ is the right object state and there is an $m \geq 1$ such that $|S'| \leq m$.

A *path*, p, is a sequence of triples $<<t_1, sa_1, s_1> ... <t_n, sa_n, s_n>>$ where $t_i \in T, s_i \in S, sa_i \in Sa$ and for all $1 \leq i < n$, either
(i) $t_i < t_{i+1}$ and $ResBy(<t_i, s_i>, <t_{i+1}, s_{i+1}>)$ is true or
(ii) $t_i = t_{i+1}$, $sa_i \neq sa_{i+1}$ and $s_i = s_{i+1}$.

Each path represents an object's discrete state change over time as measured by sampling-agents in states, $sa_1...sa_n$. Constraint (i) considers the case where two points in the path captures the change of the state of the object from s_i at time t_i to s_{i+1} at time t_{i+1}. In that case, where the path specifies the way the state was changed, $ResBy(<t_i, s_i>, <t_{i+1}, s_{i+1}>)$ must hold, i.e. the object could be at s_i at t_i and then at s_{i+1} at t_{i+1}. On the other hand, constraint (ii) considers the case of two points $<t_i, sa_i, s_i>$, $<t_{i+1}, sa_{i+1}, s_{i+1}>$ on the path that do not capture a change in the object's state but rather two different observations of the object. That is, the object was at a given state s_i at time t_i, but was observed by two agents. The two agents were, of course, in different states, and this is captured by the constraint that $sa_i \neq sa_{i+1}$.

A path often consists of only a very few states of an observed object. However, an agent would like to infer the state of the object at any given time from a path function. This is formalized as follows.

An object state function f_{π_s,π_e}, with respect to two path points $\pi_s = <t_s, sa_s, s_s>$, $\pi_e = <t_e, sa_e, s_e>$ where $t_s \leq t_e$, associates with each time point an object state (i.e. $f_{\pi_s,\pi_e} : T \to S$) such that

(i) $f_{\pi_s,\pi_e}(t_s) = s_s$ and $f_{\pi_e,\pi_e}(t_e) = s_e$

(ii) $\forall t_1, t_2$, $t_1 < t_2$ $ResBy(<t_1, f_{\pi_s,\pi_e}(t_1)>, <t_2, f_{\pi_s,\pi_e}(t_2)>)$.

An object state function represents object state change over time points in T with respect to two path points. To move from a path to an associated function, we assume that there is a function $pathToFunc: P \to F$ such that given a path $p \in P$,

$p = <<t_1, sa_1, s_1>, ..., <t_n, sa_n, s_n>>$, if $f_{\pi_s,\pi_e} = pathToFunc$ (p) then,

$\pi_s = <t_1, sa_1, s_1>$, $\pi_e = <t_n, sa_n, s_n>$ $\forall t_i, f_{\pi_s,\pi_e}(t_i) = s_i$.

In the rest of the paper we will use an object state function and its path interchangeably.

2.1.3 *PoSS* Implementation in ANTS

A measurement in the ANTS domain is a pair of amplitude and radial velocity values for each sensed target. Given a measurement of a Doppler radar the target is located by the Doppler equation:

$$r_i^2 = \frac{k \cdot e^{\frac{-(\vartheta_i - \beta)^2}{\sigma}}}{\eta_i}$$

where, for each sensed target, i, r_i is the distance between the sensor and i; θ_i is the angle between the sensor and i; η_i is the measured amplitude of i; β is the sensor beam angle; and k and σ are characteristics of the sensors and influence the shape of the sensor detecting area (1). Given k consecutive measurements one can use the Doppler equation to find the distance r_i. However, there are two possible θ_i angles for each such distance. Therefore, for PoSS function in ANTS domain returns two possible object states, i.e. *m*=2. For space reasons we do not present the proofs of the lemmas and theorems.

Theorem 1: *(PoSS in ANTS)* Assuming that the acceleration of a target in a short time period is zero. The next target location after a very short time is then given by

$$\theta_1 = \alpha_1 + \sqrt{-\sigma \cdot \ln\left(\frac{\eta_1}{k}(r_0 + v_{r0} \cdot t_{1,0})^2\right)} \qquad \frac{\bar{r}_2(\theta_0) - \bar{r}_1(\theta_0)}{t_{2,1}} = \frac{\bar{r}_1(\theta_0) - \bar{r}_0(\theta_0)}{t_{1,0}}$$

where $r_0, \theta_0, \eta_0, v_{r0}$ and α_0 are values of the target at time $t = 0$ and θ_1, η_1 and α_1 represent values of the target at time $t = 1$. $t_{i,j}$ is the time between t=i and t=j.

Only certain angles will solve the equations. To be more accurate, the sampling agent uses one more sample and applies the same mechanism to θ_1, θ_2 and θ_3. The angles are used to form a set of possible pairs of location and velocity of a target (i.e., the PosS function values). Only one of these target states is the correct one.

In addition, $pathToFunc$ (p) is calculated using in the following way

$$f_{\pi_s,\pi_e}(t) = < \overline{r}_s - \overline{v}_s \cdot (t - t_s), \overline{v}_s > \text{ which is equivalent to } < \overline{r}_e - \overline{v}_e \cdot (t - t_e), \overline{v}_e > .$$

2.2   Constructing an Information Map

DDM uses partial and local information to form an accurate global description of the changes in objects over time. The DDM model can be applied to many command, control and intelligence problems by mapping the DDM entities to the domain entities. As pointed out earlier, the goal of the DDM is to construct an information map.

Definition 1: An *information map, infoMap,* is a set of object state functions $< f^1_{\pi^1_s,\pi^1_e}, ..., f^h_{\pi^h_s,\pi^h_e} >$ such that for every $1 \leq i, j \leq h$ and $t \in T$ $f^i_{\pi^i_s,\pi^i_e}(t) \neq f^j_{\pi^j_s,\pi^j_e}(t)$

Intuitively, *infoMap* represents the way that the states of objects change over time. The condition on the information map specifies the assumption that two objects cannot be at the same state and time. Because each agent has only partial and uncertain information of its local surroundings an agent may need to construct the *infoMap* in stages. In some cases, an agent might not be able to construct the entire *infoMap*. The process of constructing the *infoMap* will use various intermediate structures.

As mentioned above, to capture the uncertainty associated with sensed information, each sampled object is associated with several possible *object states*. We introduce the notion of a capsule that represents a few possible states of an object at some time as derived from measurements taken by an agent in a given state.

Definition 2: A *capsule* is a triple of a time point, a sampler agent state and a sequence of up to m object-states, i.e., $c = < t, sa, \{s_1, ..., s_l\} >$ where $t \in T, sa \in Sa, s_i \in S, l \leq m$. We denote the set of all possible capsules by C.

Capsules are generated by the sampling agents using the domain dependent function *PosS* and k consecutive samples.

The assessment problem discussed earlier corresponds to the problem of how best to choose the right state from every capsule. It is impossible to determine which state is the correct state using only one viewpoint: measurements from one viewpoint can result in up to m object states, each of which could correspond to the correct state. Therefore, capsules from different viewpoints are needed. A different viewpoint may correspond to a different state of the same sampling agent or of different sampling agents. To choose the right object state from each capsule state, different capsules are connected using the *ResBy* relation to form a path. Each of these paths is evaluated and those with the best probability are chosen to represent the most likely sequence of object state transitions to form state functions.

Definition 3: *localInfo* is a pair of *infoMap* and a set of capsules, *<infoMap, unused-Capsules>* where *unusedCapsules*=$< c_1,...,c_m >$ s.t. for all $1 \le i \le m$ and for all $1 \le j \le l$ and $c_i = < t_i, sa_i, \{s_{i1},...,s_{i,l}\} >$ and for every $f_{\pi_s, \pi_e} \in$ infoMap $f_{\pi_s, \pi_e}(t_i) \ne s_{ij}$.

At any time, some capsules can be used to form object state functions that have a high probability of representing objects. These functions are recorded in *infoMap;* we refer to them as *accurate representations*. The remaining capsules are maintained in the *unusedCapsules* set and used to identify state functions. That is, the condition of definition 3 intuitively states that an object associated with a function f_{π_s, π_e} was not constructed using one of the measurements that were used to form the capsules in the *unusedCapsules* set.

2.3   The DDM Hierarchy Architecture

In a large-scale environment many capsules may have to be linked from each area. Applying the *ResBy* relation many times can be time consuming. However, there is a low probability that capsules created based on measurements taken far away from one another will be related. Therefore, it makes sense to distribute the solution. The DDM hierarchical structure guides the distributed construction of the global *infoMap*. The lower level of the hierarchy consists of sampling agents, which are grouped according to their associated area. Each group has a leader. Thus, the second level of the hierarchy consists of sampler group leaders. Sampler group leaders are also grouped according to their associated area. Each such group of sampler leaders is associated with a zone group leader. Thus, the third level of the hierarchy consists of zone group leaders, which in turn, are also grouped according to their associated area, with a zone group leader, and so on. Leader agents are responsible for retrieving and combining information from their group of agents. We refer to members of a group as group subordinates. Sampling agents are mobile; therefore, they may change their group when moving to a different area. The sampler leaders are responsible for the movements of sampling agents. For space reasons we do not discuss the agent distribution process here, but rather focus on the global *infoMap* formation. We also do not discuss the methods we have developed to replace group leaders that stop functioning. All communication takes place only between a group member and its leader.

A sampler agent takes measurements and forms capsules. These capsules are sent to the sampler leader at specified intervals. A sampler leader collects capsules from its sampler agents to represent its *localInfo*. In this computation, it uses the previous value of *localInfo*; it then sends its *localInfo* to its zone leader. A zone leader collects the *localInfo* of all the sub-leaders of its zone and forms a *localInfo* of its entire zone. It, in turn, sends it to its leader and so on. The top zone leader, whose zone consists of the entire area, forms a *localInfo* of all the objects in the entire area. In the next section we present the algorithms for these agent processes.

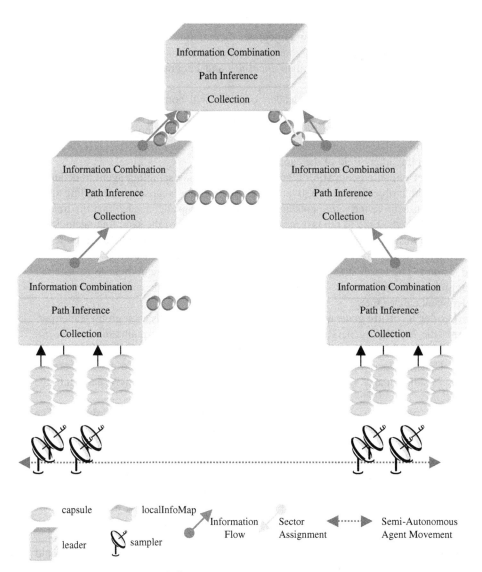

Figure 2: DDM hierarchy information flow diagram

3 Algorithm Description

The formation of a global information map integrates the following processes:
1. Each sampling agent gathers raw sensed data and generates capsules.

2. Every dT seconds each sampler group leader obtains capsules from all its sampling agents and integrates them into its *localInfo*.
3. Every dT seconds each zone group leader obtains from all its subordinate group leaders their *localInfo* and integrates them into its own *localInfo*.

As a result, the top-level group leader *localInfo* will contain a global information map.

We have developed several algorithms to implement each process. We will use a dot notation to describe a field in a structure, e.g., if $c =< t, sa, \{s_1, ..., s_l\} >$ then $c.sa$ is the sampling agent field of the capsule c.

Sampler capsule generation algorithm. We use one sampling agent to deduce a set of possible object states at a given time in the form of a capsule. A sampling agent takes k consecutive measurements and creates a new capsule, c, such that the time of the capsule is the time of the last measurement. The state of the sampling agent while taking the measurements is assigned to *c.sa*. The object states resulting from the application of the domain function *PosS* to the k consecutive measurements is assigned to *c.states*. The agent stores the capsules until it is time to send them to its sampler group leader asks for them. After delivering the capsules to the group leader the sampler agent deletes them.

Leader localInfo generation algorithm. Every dT seconds each group leader performs the *localInfo* generation algorithm. Each group leader maintains its own *localInfo*. The leader first purges any data older than τ seconds before processing new data. Updating *localInfo* involves three steps: (i) obtaining new information from the leader's subordinates; (ii) finding new paths; (iii) and merging the new paths into the *localInfo*.

In the first phase, every leader obtains information from its subordinates. The sampler group leader obtains information from all of its sampling agents for their *unusedCapsules* and adds them to its *unusedCapsules* set. The zone group leader obtains from its subordinates their *localInfo*. It adds the *unusedCapsules* to its *unusedCapsules* and merges the *infoMap* of that *localInfo* to its own *localInfo*.

Merging of functions is performed both in steps (i) and (iii). Merging is needed since, as we noted earlier, object state functions inserted by a leader into the information map are accepted by the system as correct and will not be removed. However, different agents may sense the same object and therefore it may be that different functions coming from different agents will refer to the same object. The agents should recognize such cases and keep only one of these functions in the *infoMap*. We use the following lemma to find identical functions and merge them.

Lemma 1:

Let $p^1 =< \pi_s^1, ..., \pi_e^1 >$, $p^2 =< \pi_s^2, ..., \pi_e^2 >$ be two paths, where $\pi_j^i =< t_j^i, sa_j^i, s_j^i >$ and $f_{\pi_s^1, \pi_e^1}^1 = pathToFunc(p^1)$, $f_{\pi_s^2, \pi_e^2}^2 = pathToFunc(p^2)$.

If $ResBy(< t_s^1, s_s^1 >, < t_s^2, s_s^2 >)$ then for any $f_{\pi_s^1, \pi_e^1}^1(t) = f_{\pi_s^2, \pi_e^2}^2(t)$

Leaders use lemma (1) and the *ResBy* relation to check whether the first state of an object state function resulted from the first state of a different object state function. If one of the states is related in such a way, the leader changes the minimum and the maximum triplets of the object state function. The minimum triplet is the starting triple that has the lowest time. The maximum triple is the ending triple that has the higher time. Intuitively, the two state functions are merged and the resulted function is associated with the combination of their ranges. If a leader cannot find an object state function to meet the subordinate's function, the leader will add it as a new function to its *infoMap*.

The second step is performed by every leader and corresponds to finding paths and extending current paths given a set of capsules. In order to form paths from capsules, the agent should choose only one object state out of each capsule. This constraint is based on the flowing lemma.

Lemma 2:

Let $C^1 = <t^1, sa^1, <s^1_1,...,s^1_{h^1}>>$, $C^2 = <t^2, sa^2, <s^2_1,...,s^2_{h^2}>>$ and
$ResBy(<t^1, s^1_i>, <t^2, s^2_j>)$ and $ResBy(<t^1, s^1_{i'}>, <t^2, s^2_{j'}>)$ then

(i) if $s^1_i \neq s^1_{i'}$ then $s^2_j \neq s^2_{j'}$ (ii) if $s^2_j \neq s^2_{j'}$ then $s^1_i \neq s^1_{i'}$ (iii) if $s^1_i = s^1_{i'}$ then $s^2_j = s^2_{j'}$
(iv) if $s^2_j = s^2_{j'}$ then $s^1_i = s^1_{i'}$

According to this lemma one state of one capsule cannot be in a ResBy relation with two different states in another capsule with respect to the capsule's time. Such a case of two different states violates the ResBy constraints.

Every leader stores the correct object state functions as part of its *infoMap* structure. In the top-level leader we would also like to have represented object state functions with an intermediate probability to represent objects. The top leader knows that some of the paths that he would like to use to form state functions are correct but it cannot decide which are correct. Paths with only one viewpoint are paths that may be correct. For instance, in the ANTS domain, paths with one viewpoint will have a 50% probability to be correct, due to the characteristics of the sensors. In other domains, the characteristics of the sensors may lead to different probabilities. The top-level leader will use these paths of intermediate probability to form a set of functions that have a partial probability of being correct.

3.1   Complexity

The main issue, which we would like to resolve, is whether a single level hierarchy or a multiple level one is best. If there is one level in the hierarchy then all the capsules are processed by the sampling leader agent. If there are, say, two levels, then there are several sampling agents that process the capsules simultaneously; this will save time. However, all of the capsules that the sampling leaders will not be able to use in building state functions will find their way into the *unusedCapsules* set and will then be transferred to the zone leader. The zone leader will collect all of the *unusedCapsules* and will process them one more time. Thus, the second level may waste the time saved by the distribution in the first level. Therefore, the time benefit of the hierarchy depends on the ratio of the capsules that the lower level is able to use.

In order to determine the ratio of capsules that have not been used at a given level for which it is still beneficial to have an additional level in the hierarchy we first state the complexity of the two main algorithms. First, we consider the algorithm for forming paths and then the algorithm that merges functions.

Lemma 3:

Let C be a set of capsules and m is the maximum number of states in a capsule. The time complexity of finding the paths by the algorithm of step 2 is in the worse case: $\dfrac{\left(|C| \cdot m\right)^2}{2}$.

Lemma 4:

The time complexity of merging two sets of object state functions F^1 and F^2 is in the worse case: $\dfrac{|F^1| \cdot |F^2|}{2}$.

The most time consuming process is the formation of new paths in step 2. It depends on the number of capsules generated by the agents. Thus in the next lemma we state this number.

Lemma 5:

Let O be the group of objects located in the area Λ in a given time period and A the set of agents located in the area. Let λ be the size of the sub-area sensed by a single sampling agent. Suppose that in a give τ time periods the sampling agent is activating its sensor for δ time periods. Let C be a set of capsules generated by agents in area Λ in the period τ . Then:

$$|C| \le \frac{\tau}{\delta} \cdot |O| \cdot |A|$$

Intuitively, lemma 5 says that the number of capsules is bound by the number of objects that the agents may observe in a given time period. Using the above lemmas we derive a bounds on the percentage of *unusedCapsule* that should be processed at a given level to make it beneficial to add additional level.

Theorem 1:

Let area Λ be divided into q subsections, Λ_i $1 \le i \le q$ such that $\Lambda = \bigcup_{1 \le i \le q} \Lambda_i$ and α be the capsule percentage that could not be used in the state function construction by the agents at a given level. Then, if $\alpha < \sqrt{\dfrac{q^2-1}{q^2}}$ it is beneficial, with respect to performance time, to increase the hierarchy by one level, given that there are at least two agents in each area.

As can be seen, even when α is very close to 1 it is still beneficial to consider adding an additional level.

4   Simulation, Experiments and Results

We wanted to explore several issues via simulations. First we wanted to ascertain the ability of the DDM model to identify state functions. Second, we wanted to check whether the hierarchy model improved the performance of the system. Third, we wanted to check how much the model was sensitive to noise. Finally, we wanted to examine whether increasing the number of agents and using better equipped sampling agents improved performance.

4.1 Simulation Environment

We developed a simulation of the ANTS domain to test the model. The simulation consists of an area of a fixed size in which Dopplers attempt to identify the object state functions of moving targets. Each target had an initial random location and an initial random velocity of up to 50 km. per hour. Targets leave the area when reaching the boundaries of the zone. Each target that leaves the area causes a new target to appear at the same location with the same velocity in a direction that leads it inwards. Therefore, each target may remain in the area for a random time period. Each Doppler has initial random location and a velocity that is less than 50 km. per hour. When a Doppler gets to the border of the controlled area it bounces back with the same velocity. This ensures an even distribution of Dopplers.

Evaluation Methods. We collected the state functions produced by agents during a simulation. We used two evaluation criteria in our simulations: (1) target tracking percentage and (2) average tracking time. We counted a target as tracked if the path identified by the agent satisfied the following: (a) the maximum distance between the calculated location and the real location of the target did not exceed 1 meter, and (b) the maximum difference between the calculated $v(t)$ vector and the real $v(t)$ vector was less than 0.1 meter per second and 0.1 radians in angle.

In addition, the identified object state functions could be divided into two categories: (1) Only a single function was associated with a particular target and was chosen to be part of *the infoMap*. Those functions were assigned a probability of 100% corresponding to the actual object state function. (2) Two possible object state functions based on one viewpoint were associated with a target. Each was assigned a 50% probability of corresponding to the actual function. We will say that one set of agents *did better* than another if they reached higher tracking percentage and lower tracking time with respect to the 100% functions and the total tracking percentage was at least the same.

The averages reported in the graphs below were computed for one hour of simulated time. The *target tracking percentage time* was calculated by dividing the number of targets that the agents succeeded in tracking, according to the above definitions, by the actual number of targets during the simulated hour. In total, 670 targets passed through the controlled area within an hour in the basic settings experiments described below. The *tracking time* was defined as the time that the agents needed to find the object state function of the target from the time the target entered the simulation. Tracking average time was calculated by dividing the sum of tracking time of the tracked targets by the number of tracked targets. Note that 29% of the targets in our experiments remained in the area less than 60 seconds in our basic settings.

Basic Settings. The *basic setting* for the environment corresponded to an area 1200 by 900 meters. In each experiment, we varied one of the parameters of the environment, keeping the other values of the environment parameters as in the basic settings. The Dopplers were mobile and moved randomly as described above. Each Doppler stopped every 10 seconds, varied its active sensor randomly, and took 10 measurements. The maximum detection range of a Doppler in the basic setting was 200 meters; the number of Dopplers was 20 and the number of targets at a given time point was 30. The DDM hierarchy consisted of only one level. That is, there was one sampler-leader that was responsible for the entire area.

We first compared several settings to test the hierarchy model and the sampling agents characterizations. Each setting was characterized by (i) whether we used a hierarchy model (H) or a flat model (F); (ii) whether the sampler-agents were mobile (M) or static (S); and (iii) whether Dopplers varied their active sectors from time to time (V) or used a constant one all the time (C). In the flat model the sampler agents used their local capsules to produce object state functions locally.

Mobile and dynamic vs. static Dopplers. In preliminary simulations (not presented here for space reasons) we experimented with all combinations of the parameters (i)-(iii) above. In each setting, keeping the other two variables fixed and varying only the mobility variable, the mobile agents did better than the static ones (with respect to the evaluation definition above).

Hierarchy vs. flat models. We examined the characteristics of 4 different settings: (A) FSC that involves static Dopplers with a constant active sector using a nonhierarchical model; (B) HSC as in (A) but using the hierarchical model; (C) FMV with mobile Dopplers that vary their active sectors from time to time, but with no hierarchy; (D) HMV as in (C) but using the hierarchical model. We tested FSC on two experimental arrangements: randomly located Dopplers and Dopplers arranged in a grid formation to achieve better coverage. There was no significant difference between these two FSC formations. Our hypothesis was that the agents in HMV would do better than the agents in all of the other settings.

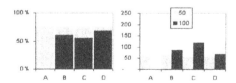

Figure 3: Target tracking percentage and average time by the settings

The first finding is presented in the left part of Figure 3. This indicates that the setting does not affect the overall tracking percentage (i.e., the tracking percentage of the 50% and 100% functions). The difference between the settings is with respect to the division of the detected target between accurate tracking and mediocre tracking. HMV performed significantly better than the other settings. It found significantly more 100% functions and did it faster than the others. This supports the hypothesis that a hierarchical organization leads to better performance. Further support for a hierarchical organization comes from HSC being significantly better than FMV even though, according to our preliminary results, HSC uses Dopplers that are more primitive than the Dopplers FMV.

Another aspect of the performance of the models is the average tracking time as shown in the right part of Figure 3. Once again, one can see that hierarchically based organizations lead to better results. We found that by considering only targets that stayed in the controlled zone at least 60 seconds, HMV reached 87% tracking percentage where 83% were accurately detected

We also considered a hierarchy with two levels: one zone leader leading four sampling leaders. The area was divided equally between the four sampling leaders, and each obtained information from the many mobile sampling agents located in its area. In this configuration Dopplers were able to move from one zone to another; Dopplers changed their sampling leader every time they moved from one zone to another. Comparing the results of the two-level hierarchy simulations (not presented here because of space reasons), with the one level hierarchy simulations we found that there was no significant difference in the performance (with respect to the evaluation definition) of the system when there were two levels of the hierarchy when there was only one level in the hierarchy. However, consistent with theorem 1, the computation time of the system was much lower.

Communication and noise. While the performance of the hierarchy-based models are significantly better than the non-hierarchy ones, the agents in the hierarchy model must communicate with one another, while no communication is needed for the flat models. Thus, if no communication is possible, then FMV should be used. When communication is possible, however, messages may be lost or corrupted. The data structure exchanged in messages is the capsule. In our simulations using a hierarchy model, each sampling agent transmitted 168 bytes per minute. We examined the influence of randomly corrupted capsules on the HMV's behavior. Figure 4 shows that as the percentage of the lost capsules increased the number of tracked targets decreased; however, up to a level of 10% noise, the detection percentages decreased only from 74% to 65% and the accurate tracking time increased from 69 seconds to only 80 seconds. Noise of 5% resulted in a smaller decrease to a tracking accuracy of 70% while the tracking time increased slightly to 71. DDM could even mange with noise of 30% and track 39% of targets with average tracking time of 115 seconds.

In the rest of the experiments we used the HMV settings without noise.

Varying the number of Dopplers and targets. We examined the effect of the number of Dopplers on performance. We found that, when the number of targets was fixed, then as the number of Dopplers increased the percentage of accurate tracking increased as well. The significance of this result is that it confirms that the system can make good use of additional resources. We also found out that as the number of Doppler sensors increased, the 50% probability paths decreased. This may be explained by the fact that 100% paths result from taking into consideration more than one sample viewpoint. We also found that increasing the number of targets, while keeping the

number of Dopplers fixed, does not influence the system's performance. We specu-
late that this is because an active sector could distinguish more than one target in that
sector.

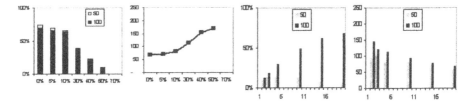

**Figure 4: Target detection percentage and
average time as function of the communication
noise**

**Figure 5: Tracking percentage and average
time as a function of the number of Dopplers**

Maximum detection range comparison. We also tested the influence of the detecting sector area on performance. The basic setting uses Dopplers with detection
range of 200 meters. We compared the basic setting to similar ones with detection
ranges of 50,100 and 150 meters. We found that as the maximum range increased the
tracking percentage increased up to the range covering the entire global area. As the
maximum radius of detection increased the tracking average time decreased. This is
a beneficial property, since it indicates that better equipment will lead to better performance.

5   Conclusions and Related Work

We have introduced a hierarchical approach for combining local and partial information of large-scale object and team environments where agents must identify the
changing states of objects. To apply the DDM model to a different environment, it is
only necessary to represent three domain-specific functions: *PosS,* that maps measurements to possible states; *ResBy,* that determines whether one given object state
associated with a time point can be the consequence of another given object state
associated with an earlier time point; and *pathToFunc,* that, given a path, returns a
function to represent it. Given these functions, all the DDM algorithms implemented
for the ANTS domain are applicable, as long as the complexity of these functions can
be kept low. Thus, we believe that the results obtained for the ANTS simulations will
carry over to any such domain.

The results reported in this paper support the following conclusions: (i) the hierarchy model outperforms a flat one; (ii) the flat mobile dynamic sector setting can be
used in situations where communication is not possible; (iii) increasing resources
increases performance; (iv) under the identified constraints, it is beneficial to add
more levels to the hierarchy; and (v) the DDM can handle situations of noisy communications.

In terms of related work, the benefits of hierarchical organizations have been argued by many. So and Durfee draw on contingency theory to examine the benefits of

a variety of hierarchical organizations; they discuss a hierarchically organized network monitoring system for object decomposition and also consider organizational self-design [6,7]. DDM differs in its use of organizational structure to dynamically balance computational load.

The idea of combining partial local solutions into a more complete global solution goes back to early work on the distributed vehicle monitoring testbed (DVMT) [5]. DVMT also operated in a domain of distributed sensors that tracked objects. However, the algorithms for support of mobile sensors and for the actual specifics of the Doppler sensors themselves is novel to the DDM system. Within the DVMT, Corkill and Lesser [2] investigated various team organizations in terms of *interest areas* which partitioned problem solving nodes according to roles and communication, but were not initially hierarchically organized [8]. Wagner and Lesser examined the role that knowledge of organizational structure can play in decisions [9].

All the alternative approaches to the ANTS problem (e.g., [4]) have been based on local assessment methods that require coordinated measurements from at least three Doppler sensors and intersecting the resulting arcs of each. Such coordination requires good synchronization of the clocks of the sensors and therefore communication among the Doppler agents to achieve that synchronization. In addition, communication is required for scheduling agent measurements. We have presented alternative methods, which can combine partial and uncertain local information.

References

1. ANTS Program Design Document, unpublished.
2. Corkill, Daniel, and Lesser, Victor. The use of meta-level control for coordination in a distributed problem solving network. In Proceedings of the Eighth International Joint Conference on Artificial Intelligence, pp. 748-756. August, Karlsruhe, Germany, 1983.
3. G. P. Thomas, The Doppler effect, London: Logos, 1965.
4. Leen-Kiat Soh, Costas Tsatsoulis, Reflective Negotiating Agents for Real-Time Multisensor Target Tracking. IJCAI 2001: 1121-1127.
5. Lesser V., Corkill D. and Durfee E., An update on the Distributed Vehicle Monitoring Testbed, CS Technical Report 87-111, University of Massachusetts, Amherst, 1987.
6. So Y., Durfee E., Designing Tree-Structured Organizations for Computational Agents, Computational and Mathematical Organization Theory, 2(3), pages 219-246, 1996.
7. So Y., Durfee E., A Distributed Problem-Solving Infrastructure for Computer Network Management. International Journal of Intelligent and Cooperative Information Systems, 1(2):363-392, 1992.
8. W. Richard Scott, Organizations: Rational, Natural and Open, Prentice-Hall, 1992.
9. Wagner Thomas and Lesser Victor. Relating Quantified Motivations for Organizationally Situated Agents. In Intelligent Agents VI --- Proceedings of the Sixth International Workshop on Agent Theories, Architectures, and Languages, Lecture Notes in Artificial Intelligence, pp. 334-348. April, 1999.

A Perspective on Multiagent Coordination Models

Laura Bocchi and Paolo Ciancarini

Dipartimento di Scienze dell'Informazione
Univ. of Bologna, Italy

Abstract. In this paper we present a guided tour of some research on the topic of agent coordination. We present an historical survey about some coordination models and languages for multiagent systems. We show how some cordination models have been adapted to different network infrastructures, distinguishing between pre-WWW and WWW-based coordination architectures. We show that the advent of the new programming paradigms of Web Services and the Semantic Web is prompting the definition of a new family of coordination models and languages, useful to describe multiagent systems suitable for these new infrastructures.

1 Introduction

Most attempts to determine which features a software entity should exhibit to be recognized to be an "agent" agree on the fact that an agent is an autonomous entity which performs an independent computational activity and interacts with its surrounding environment [4]. Then, a multi-agent system is a software system built by composing several independent computational activities, which have to interact with each other and with their environment.

An interesting consequence of such definitions is that, due to its intrinsically interactive nature, a comprehensive view of a multi-agent system should not rely upon the analysis of the internal behaviour of each agent only.

Actually multi-agent systems usually exhibit a complex global behaviour, emerging from the mutual interaction among their components, that is hard to be described and managed when communication is considered from a single agent viewpoint.

In this paper we take the view that the design, the implementation, and the subsequent management of a multi-agent system may take advantage from the choice and exploitation of a *coordination model*, that is, a high-level interaction abstraction aimed at globally ruling the behavior of the different system components. We have explored such a viewpoint in the last 15 years in a number of research projects: this paper is a sort of summary of such researches, including also references to similar works.

Basically, coordination models are abstractions for designing programming languages. In fact, all coordination models we know include primitives for concurrency and agent interaction control; they have been introduced to describe

M.-P. Huget (Ed.): Communications in Multiagent Systems, LNAI 2650, pp. 146–163, 2003.

non-sequential programming languages: in this sense they differ from conventional models for concurrency, that are usually oriented to study the formal semantics of concurrent programming languages [35].

The story of software agents begins with the idea of a 'soft robot' - semi-autonomous programmed entities capable of carrying out tasks toward a goal, while requesting and receiving advice and orders by humans in human terms. The first software agents were mostly natural language processors; the advent of the Internet added several dimensions to the concept [21].

A first dimension is *mobility*: agents can go around the net to find relevant data. A second, more important, dimension is *autonomy*: the agent has to be able to operate in unexpected conditions, far from the control of its "owner". A third dimension is *proactiveness*: the agent must be able to make efforts to reach its goals. A fourth, distinctive, dimension is *interaction* with other agents, and this is the typical field where coordination models are useful [37].

In recent years, a much narrower, e-commerce oriented, use of the term "agent" has emerged, with a fairly tenuous relationship to actual agent technologies and a steady growth despite some disappointing failures. This has lead to a partial transformation of the concept of agent into an anthropomorphized, self-customizing virtual servant designed for a single task: a pleasing interface to a world of information that does not please us.

Agents, like objects, are abstractions which encapsulate state and behavior. The main difference between an agent and an object is that an agent is autonomous, has full control on its behavior and can invoke services from the outside world, while objects are usually conceived as reactive abstractions. Agent-based systems can be studied at different abstraction levels. For instance, we can study which cooperation model is enacted by the agents (i.e., what kind of society - collaborative, authoritative, market-like, etc.); or we can study which interaction model is used by the agents (i.e., how, when, and with which roles is the dialogue among agents performed); or, from a software engineer viewpoint, we can study which software composition model is used to design a multiagent system (i.e., the technologies used for letting the agents execute, communicate, move, interoperate).

Many research efforts in the area of autonomous and intelligent agents have focused on intra-agent aspects, such as agent languages and architectures, which focus on the agent's internal structure [30]. However, multi-agent systems should not be simply considered as a sum of individuals. If a society of agents exists, a collective social behaviour is likely to emerge. Therefore, to fully understand multi-agent systems, theories for agent societies are needed. These theories should define what is the world that hosts the society, which laws rule the world, and which are the individuals that can populate it. In addition, if any intelligent global behaviour can emerge from a system, there should be a place where it should be found and monitored.

In a multi-agent world, this intelligence cannot reside inside agents only, but it should be somehow spread among agents and the interaction space among them. That is, the world where agents live is not composed of agents only, but also of the abstractions supporting the interactions, as well as of the history of these interactions. Therefore, a multi-agent system should define not only the world where agents live, but also the laws that permeate the interaction space or the communication media, and enable agent interactions.

Agents usually interact by exchanging complex symbolic information and possibly have to agree on complex interaction protocols. In addition, agents are autonomous, possibly designed separately in different times by different people, and including heterogeneous software components. These issues have led to the development of several proposals in the area of agent communication languages, such as the FIPA and the KQML proposals. From a different perspective, several middleware systems, notably CORBA, have been proposed as software layers enabling interoperability among software components. Although these works are important to achieve interoperability, they mainly focus on peer-to-peer communications and do not account for a more comprehensive view of the interaction as a primary component of agents' societies. Therefore, both agent communication languages and middleware systems have to somehow be extended in scope in order to include not only language and protocol specifications but also the definition of coordination laws, to allow for a global understanding and management of interactions.

When a multi-agent system is made up of a large number of independently designed components, may be very difficult to correctly design and managing the system as a whole. An approach that simply puts components together and lets them to interact is likely to degenerate into chaos. Instead, models and tools are needed to put components together in a structured way: as already recognised in the area of software engineering, the design and management of a large software project requires the definition and analysis of its software architecture. This includes defining the role of each component, the mechanisms upon which composition can be based, and their composition laws. A similar approach would be undoubtedly helpful also in the context of multi-agent systems. However, in this case, a more dynamic and flexible definition of the software architecture interaction-oriented rather than composition-oriented is needed.

2 Coordination in the Pre-Web Era

Coordination is a key concept for studying the activities of complex dynamic systems. Due to its fundamentality, this general notion encompasses several research fields such as robotics, biology, computational systems, and human societies.

In [32] we find a basic definition:

"Coordination is managing dependencies between activities".

Such a definition implies that all instances of coordination include *actors* performing *activities* that are interdependent. Activities can be dependant along a number of dimensions: temporal, spatial, causal.

Regarding computer science, we find coordination in operating systems in order to manage dependencies in exploiting hardware resources or in database management systems which coordinate accesses to shared data.

Conforming to the definition given above, the term *Coordination Theory* refers to

"the theories about how coordination can occur in diverse kind of systems" [32].

In our scope coordination is a theory about how to program the control of active and self contained software entities, which have to cooperate or to synchronize to perform some action on their own behalf. As the concept of agent becomes more defined with the web's advent, as we will see, it becomes natural to instantiate the concept of coordinable software entity with the concept of agent, involving coordination in multi-agent systems.

2.1   Coordination Models and Languages

Coordination of software entities can be expressed in terms of coordination models and languages. In the following we try to clarify these two different notions. For *coordination model* we prefer the following intuitive definition:

"A coordination model is the glue that binds separate activities into an ensemble" [15]

In other words, a coordination model provides a framework in which the interaction of individual agents can be expressed. This covers not only the aspect of communication of agents, but also those of creation and destruction of agents, spatial distribution of agents, as well as synchronization and distribution of actions over time. A more constructive approach to describe coordination models is to identify the components out of which they are built:

1. Coordination Entities. These are the building blocks which are coordinated. Ideally, these are the active agents.
2. Coordination Media. These are the media enabling the communication between the agents.
3. Coordination Laws. These laws describe how agents are coordinated making use of given coordination media.

A coordination model can be embodied in a (software)coordination architecture or in a coordination language. Examples of coordination architectures are the client-server architecture, the software pipeline, or the blackboard: software components are arranged in some special, well defined structures that enact specific cooperation protocols. Usually parallel programmers implicitly design a software architecture using low-level communication primitives. Due to this rather intuitive approach to software design, there is the need of high-level coordination languages to simplify the implementation of such systems. A *coordination language* is "the linguistic embodiment of a coordination model" [15]. Action performed by agents can be divided in two different classes:

1. *Inter-Agent actions* perform the communication among different agents. They are the subjects of coordination models.
2. *Intra-Agent actions* belong to a single agent, like e.g. internal computations. In the case of specialized interface agents, intra-agent actions may also comprise communication acts by an agent outside the coordination model, like primitive I/O operations or interactions with users.

Most coordination languages have their focus on a clear separation between coordination and computation, seen as orthogonal language design issues. Interestingly, these are also the two major dimensions under which a software agent world can be studied. A very famous metaphor in form of a simple equation establishes this orthogonality as follows:

Programming = Coordination + (sequential) Computation

Thus, according to such a metaphor a programming language should be composed of two orthogonal components: a coordination component and a computational component.

The *coordination component* concerns the actions of synchronization, communication and service usage and provision. The *Computation component* defines the actions of processes.

This separation facilitates the reuse of the coordination component with different computational models, as in Linda [8]. The separation is also effective from a software engineering viewpoint, because keeping the specification of coordination issues separate from computational issues, the programming task is simplified by bringing interaction to a higher level of abstraction.

2.2   The Tuple Space Coordination Model

Although a wide range of coordination models have been proposed in literature, a popular approach consists of defining some form of shared memory abstraction, which can be used as a message repository by a number of agents. Some of these models, like Gamma [5] and LO [3], are based on some form of concurrent "multiset rewriting". In fact, a Tuple Space is formally a multiset, because it can contain several identical tuples. Thus the evolution of a multiagent system based on a tuple space can be described by concurrent multiset rewriting rules. Another similar metaphor is the "chemical reaction" typical of the CHAM [7]. Gamma, LO and the CHAM are mainly theoretical frameworks to study the property of concurrent systems. A coordination model based on multiset rewriting and chemical reactions is the Interaction Abstract Machine [2]. The IAM was introduced as an object-based model for pattern based, associative coordination of either inter-agent or intra-agent entities. Possibly the most famous shared memory abstraction is the Tuple Space as in the Linda parallel programming language [15]. A Tuple Space is a global container of tuples. Tuples are similar to records in Pascal, however some fields can contain function invocations. Tuples are said to be *passive* if all their fields contain data only, whereas they are said to be *active* if at least a field contains a function invocation. When all active fields of an active tuple terminate, the tuple becomes passive. Agents cannot communicate directly but only in an asynchronous way by reading, consuming, writing or creating new tuples in the Tuple Space.

The coordination rules in Linda are defined by the four basic primitives:

out(t) inserts a new passive tuple *t* in the Tuple Space;

read(t) reads a passive tuple matching *t* from the Tuple Space, or blocks if no such tuple is found;

  in(t) reads and deletes a passive tuple matching *t* from the Tuple Space, or blocks if no such tuple is found;

eval(t) creates a new active tuple *t*.

Surprisingly, these four very simple primitives can support a wide range of coordination patterns [14]. This communication is defined *generative*, in the sense that when a message is emitted by an sender, it has an independent existence in the Tuple Space until it is explicitly withdrawn by a receiver. The access to tuples is *associative* in the sense that the receiver specifies via a template the kind of tuples (not the specific instance) in which it is interested, and one of the tuples matching the template, if available, is selected to be read or consumed from the Tuple Space. In other words, patterns allow to access data by saying *what* is needed rather than *how* it should be found.

The presumably most famous example of coordination model based on Tuple Space is Linda [29]. Linda consists of a few simple operations that have to be embedded in a host sequential language to obtain a parallel programming language; several linguistic embodiments exists, like C-Linda, FORTRAN-Linda or Java-Linda.

2.3   Models Based on the Tuple-Space

Many coordination languages have been proposed to extend the minimalistic Linda capabilities in different directions, either introducing more advanced *coordination primitives* which have the ability to manage groups of data, or giving the coordinable agents the ability of dynamically modify the *coordination rules*, thus obtaining a programmable coordination medium (TuCSoN [36], Law Governed Linda [34], and MARS [11]). Several other coordination models proposed a reshaping of the operational semantics of the coordination medium. Some of them are based on multiple flat tuple spaces identified by unique names (Klaim [28]), some other coordination models introduced the idea of multiple nested spaces, as PoliS.

PoliS was introduced in [16] as "a programming model for multiple tuple spaces"; its syntax and semantics have been formally defined in [20]. Introducing PoliS we generalized the idea of the single, monolithic Tuple Space in Linda with a whole hierarchy of nested multiple spaces that dynamically evolve in time.

In fact, a PoliS Tuple Space is a container which can contain three kinds of elements: other *spaces*, *program tuples* that contain behavior, and *ordinary tuples* that are ordered sequences of values representing the resources produced or consumed in some space by an agent executing a program tuple.

Program tuples manage activities inside the spaces; they are capable of modifying the space they belong to and their parent one by removing and adding tuples.

They can dynamically create new spaces through the primitive tsc (for *tuple space create*) that adds a new place as a child of the one where the rule was executed. Spaces can be eliminated through the execution of a special rule named *invariant*. Invariants are constraints which must ever hold inside a specific space, whenever they are violated the space "dies". By defining its own invariants a place is no more a passive entity; it has some control on activities that happen inside.

In [20] is showed how PoliS can be used to *specify* and *analyze* software architectures.

There is a mapping between the multiple tuple spaces structure of PoliS and the structure of software architectures. The former are based on the definition of components, which can be seen as the composition of several sub-components; they can be represented by PoliS places. The tuple based communication mechanism, moreover, let the focus be put on the structure as at the architectural level we would like to have an abstract view of the system, abstracting from communication details.

Last but not least, the multiple tuple spaces model in PoliS allows the specification of context-free components as independent spaces with their active rules. This means that every tuple space in PoliS can be seen either as a multithreaded agent, or as a multiagent system, composable with other agents or systems.

The PoliS mechanism of active rules scoping helps in the definition of the assumptions on the external environment.

In this way we can reason on which assumptions that components make on their context and analyze how different assumptions can match and how components can be interconnected. The help of automatic tools for testing of these properties made PoliS suitable for analyzing software architectures. In [20] a mapping between the PoliS operational semantics and TLA (Temporal Logic of Action) [31] has been studied. This allows to use a theorem prover for formal reasoning on PoliS specifications. In [18] a model checking technique is studied and exploited to perform analysis on PoliS specification documents. PoliS has been used to specify the architectures of complex systems.

2.4   Generative Communication for Web-Based Applications

Linda was the first language to focus solely on coordination, proving that coordination issues are orthogonal to computation issues. Separation of concerns simplifies the programming task by bringing interaction to a higher level of abstraction and allows both reuse of components and coordination specifications. But a Linda-like monolithic Tuple Space has still little to do with multi-agent systems. This notwithstanding, it has been successively extended and investigated as a model for multi agent and open systems design, because of the following features:

- Uncoupling of active entities: senders and receivers using the tuple space as channel/repository do not know about each other. The anonymous communication provides scalability because it is no more necessary to keep track of agents connected to a Tuple Space.
- Space uncoupling: associative addressing globally share the Tuple Space between all the agents, regardless of the particular machine of platform in which they are stored.
- Time uncoupling: tuples persistency is independent from the agents that generate or use them.
- Non determinism: anonymous associative addressing is intrinsically non-deterministic, that is appropriate to manage information dynamically changing.

Many coordination models based on Linda differ for the features they introduce to achieve the ability of programming open systems. In PoliS we have PoliS inherits all the benefits of generative communication that makes the always changing system structure transparent. Furthermore its multiple tuple spaces together with the possibility of creating and removing spaces allows to formally describe the dynamic topology of a network in which new localities are added and removed during the system's lifetime. The presence of a set of rules in a space defines the space features that can be dynamically modified during the system's life time and the possibility to transfer rules from one space to another allows to model systems in which nodes supply services not only by communicating data and performing remote computations but also transferring computation abilities to other nodes. Finally active entities can autonomously move from one space to another one.

A coordination model with all these added features, while maintaining a certain degree of transparency and simplicity, becomes suitable for the dynamic context of open systems and the WWW in particular. This has been shown by the KLAIM research group [28]. KLAIM is a coordination language which extends Linda with multiple tuple spaces; moreover agents can move from a tuple space to another, making KLAIM suitable to design and study multiagent systems including a concept of mobility.

3 The Web Advent

Although the original notion of software agent is not connected to the birth of the World Wide Web, it is the availability of such a worldwide information and communication technology which has increased the scientific and commercial interest in the agent concept.

Since potentially interesting data and documents are now spread all over the world, it becomes natural to study how computations over such data can also spread all over the world. Software agents seem a perfect solution for this problem, and we adopted this view quite rapidly [24].

3.1 The WWW, Java, and Coordination Technologies

Several multi-agent platforms were born in the early Web years by combining Java and a coordination language to build software agents for the WWW. The rapid developments in object-oriented programming and wide area networking has led to the integration of these technologies and the formation of distributed object-based computing platforms [17]. This has led to the development of several agent toolkits that are typically Java-based.

Although the typical Java operating environment is a distributed system, because Java is multithread and allows remote dynamic code loading, originally it was not a language for distributed programming. The only facility offered by the Java 1.0 version for supporting distributed processing was a sockets library. Programming distributed systems using sockets is notoriously boring, difficult and error-prone. An alternative strategy to manage coordination among remote Java components consists of adding to Java high-level coordination mechanisms. Is with this aim that we presented Jada [22], a combination of Java with the Linda coordination language. Jada, like Linda, is a minimalist coordination language. Differently from other Linda-like implementations, which usually include a preprocessor necessary because Linda slightly changes (i.e. it constrains) the host language syntax, Jada is based on a set of classes to be used to access a coordination medium that is an object space, thus allowing the users to continue using their standard Java development tools.

Interestingly, the idea of combining Java with a coordination medium more complex than Linda's Tuple Space has been pursued by some important software industries: shortly after Jada, Sun itself introduced JavaSpace [41], whereas IBM introduced TSpaces [42].

Both JavaSpaces and TSpaces introduce in Java the Tuple Space coordination model. Essentially they introduce tuple spaces among the primitive objects of Java, and then add a plethora of primitives to deal with them. In this way both systems abandon the minimalistic approach typical of Linda. In fact, JavaSpaces adds to Tuple Space several synchronization operations based on events, aiming at supporting long range transactions among agents. JavaSpaces are a component of the Jini reference architecture [40].

TSpaces also supports transactions, using a relational database management system as the implementation infrastructure for the Tuple Space.

3.2 Multi-agent Coordination Frameworks for the Web

In the last decade the Web as the dominating Internet service has evolved into the most popular and widespread platform for world wide global information systems. At its core, the Web is a static hypertext graph in which documents are offered by servers, retrieved by clients with the HTTP protocol, and displayed by graphical interfaces that are very easy to use. Because of its diffusion, it is desirable to use the Web as a platform for dynamic, distributed applications. The support offfered by the core Web platform for applications was initially very rudimentary, however several programming mechanisms are now available in order to make the Web a more effective platform for multiagent applications.

An interesting approach to multi-agent Web based applications consists of using middleware to connect the active parts in an application, which then can be located in Web clients and/or servers. Coordination technology takes the role of providing a uniform access and presentation mechanisms, providing an Application Programming Interface for posting messages and retrieve responses in forms of tuples or similar data strctures. The key concept is the use of Linda-like coordination to manage the interaction among agents.

3.2.1 A Multi-agent Groupware Platform Based on Linda-like Coordination

In order to manage the activity of groups of agents, a joint research of the University of Bologna and the Technical University of Berlin produced PageSpace [25]. PageSpace is a reference architecture for multiagent applications built on top of the WWW. PageSpace applications consists of a number of distributed agents that have to be coordinated to accomplish some cooperative tasks. The purpose is to allow the deployment of distributed applications using a coordination model, the communication among different modules, and the WWW as the underlying presentation platform. In the PageSpace reference architecture for multi-agent systems we distinguished several kinds of *agents*:

- *User interface agents* are the interfaces of applications. They are manifested as a display in the users browser and are delivered to the client by the other agents of the application according to the requests of the user. User interface agents are displayed within a general interface framework that provides support for the stable interface elements to manage the interaction with the homeagent.
- *Homeagents* are a persistent representation (avatar) of users in the PageSpace. Since at any moment users can be either present or absent in the shared workspace, it is necessary to collect, deliver, and possibly act on the messages and requests of the other agents. The homeagent receives all the messages bound to the user, and delivers them orderly to the user on request. Evolved homeagents can in some circumstances actively perform actions or provide answers on behalf of the user in her absence.
- *Application agents* are the agents that actually perform the working of the multiagent application. They are specific of one application, and can be started and interrupted according to the needs of the application. They live and communicate exploiting the coordination infrastructure, offer and use each other's services, interact with the shared data, and realize useful computations within the PageSpace.
- *Gateway agents* provide access to the external world for PageSpace applications. Applications needing to access other coordination environments, network services, legacy applications, middleware platforms, etc., may do so by requesting services to the appropriate gateway agent. Each gateway agent is specialized for dealing with one type of external environment, and will trans-

late and deliver externally the services requests of the application agents, and will deliver the corresponding response back to the appropriate agent.
- *Kernel agents* provide basic, reusable services to the application agents. They perform management and control task on the agents active within the PageSpace environment. They deal with the activation, interruption and movement of the agents within the physical configuration of connected nodes.

We called "agents" the entities present in the PageSpace architecture because they are autonomous and can be knowledge-based, work on behalf of the user, can be mobile, etc.

PageSpace was one of the first reference architectures for multiagent systems.

3.2.2   Some Applications of Coordinated Multi-agent Systems

In the last years have been developed several tools for mobile agents in Java that provide ad hoc communication and collaboration mechanisms for the agents. Here in Bologna we proposed the Macondo system, whose main feature is that the mobile agents support is completely decoupled from the coordination support [19]. Macondo can be considered as a framework for mobile agents written in Java. Macondo is a coordination language based on multiple nested Tuple Spaces. Using PageSpace as a reference architecture, and Macondo as coordination language, we developed MUDWeb, a groupware platform running on the WWW [23].

Macondo has proved to be a useful framework in the bioinformatics field to build an intelligent agents architecture for DNA-microarray data integration [33]. Integration and automatic analysis of a large amount of data distributed in many bioinformatics databases is a recent research topic that involves both biology and computer science. In molecular biology have been developed many techniques which can rapidly generate large amounts of data. One of them is DNA microarray, a highly parallel methodology to screen genome samples for the expression of particular DNA sequences. Since experimental data are disseminated in a myriad of different databases that are duplicated in several repositories, the experimental data integration and clustering imply the exploration of a network of sites from which the investigator can integrate (select and cluster) data of interest.

4   Towards a Co-ordinated Web

There is currently a huge, ever-increasing range of Internet-based applications and services that are *document-centric*, meaning that they are made of components that carry some contents, adhere to some document ontology, and exchange complex data structures that represent digital documents complying with such an ontology.

A relevant topic which involves all the kinds of digital documents, is the need of an unified, or at least understandable, format for the large amount of data. A very desirable feature would be making all data inside documents or databases "machine-readable" allowing agents to operate it instead of humans. A technique that is more and more used consists of annotating all information resources with semantic metadata. The expected result is commonly defined the *Semantic Web* [6].

People who are using Web technologies are mostly interested in communitating or accessing *contents*, that is information transmitted and stored in form of electronic documents. There is a wide, ever-increasing range of Internet-based applications and services that are document-centric, meaning that they are made of components which agree on some document ontology to exchange structured data in form of documents complying with such an ontology. Several Internet applications deal with document exchanges: for instance, CSCW systems typically deal with accesses to shared workplaces or document spaces. In order to be machine processable, documents have to include *metadata*, namely they gave to include semantic descriptions of their contents.

From a software design viewpoint, people are actively developing novel methods, tools and infrastructures for document-centric applications, because it is still unclear how they should be designed at a world-wide scale. Document-centric, network aware models are needed in order to study, compare and design these applications: documents enriched with computational activities are intrinsically mobile. We anticipate a conceptual shift from process- and object-oriented computing to document-centered multiagent system design. Such a conceptual shift makes it necessary to clarify the relationships between active documents and the underlying middleware.

Since several applications are multi-components and multi-documents, there is the need of suitable middleware to support the related coordination activities. Interestingly, the definition of a coordination middleware offers the possibility for the exploitation of XML in the framework at different levels. While the role of XML for defining documents can be either purely passive, namely structuring data, or behavioral, namely defining its rendering, it is also possible to exploit XML in middleware as an integral part of the underlying coordination framework and, say, use it to define the coordination space as well as the coordination laws.

4.1   Active Documents as Agents

In this context strongly centered upon the Web as universal platform we envision a trend toward computing and service models centered around the concept of *active and mobile documents*: documents can integrate active behavior and can be able to handle themselves and to coordinate with other application components, and possibly moving themselves over a network. When an active document integrates autonomous threads of control, it exhibits *proactive* behavior and can be assimilated to a software agent. Recently in the Displet project [9] we have explored some issues relating active documents and coordination in the design of both document and content management systems.

4.1.1   The Displets   The basic idea of the *Displet* approach is to provide an active document environment, where XML documents can be enriched with application-specific behavior in order to, say, let them be effectively rendered or transferred over a network. Specifically, Displets [27,10] are software modules that are attached to an XML document and activated when some pre-declared tags are parsed during the manipulation of the document: in short, a displet supports the specification of the treatment of either existing or new tags. A displet may print text strings, display images or make use of graphical primitives, or do any needed action in the context of a multi-document application.

The first release of Displets was proposed mainly for creating HTML extensions in a principled, general way. The idea was to be able to new tags on a per-document basis, without any explicit support from commercial browsers, and to provide the document with the procedural rendering support needed to create in a document and visualize any kind of graphical object with styles, font, images, and graphical primitives. With the advent of XML, the displet approach has been adopted as a tool for the rendering of XML documents. Now, Displets are going to become a general-purpose environment for the definition and the execution of XML document agents.

The central idea of Displets is to attach behaviors, in terms of Java classes, to XML documents. An XML transformation stylesheet can be defined to transform a "normal" XML document into an active one. The Displets parser transforms the document into a DOM tree, that the XML stylesheet can transform into a different tree, also by attaching to the tree specification of Java classes devoted to associated specific behaviors to specific portion of the tree. The new XML document obtained from this transformation can thus have become an active document. There, Java classes determine the behavior of the document when manipulated by external applications (e.g., browsers and printers), and runnable threads can determine the autonomous behavior of the document when launched for execution.

Displets document agents can have associated a private internal behavior, devoted to determine the behavior of the document itself, as a stand-alone entities. However, it is also possible to think attaching to a document a behavior related to the interaction of a document with other document, in the context of a multi-component application.

4.1.2 Middleware for Document-Agents Systems

4.1.2 Middleware for Document-Agents Systems Since several applications are multi-components and multi-documents, there is the need of a suitable middleware.

Middleware is conceived as a software layer that abstracts from the heterogenous characteristics of different architectures, operating systems, programming languages and networks in distributed systems. It integrates these into one system by providing services that provide functionality based on the given common abstraction and that are implemented on top of the named heterogeneous components. The goal of middleware is to support integrated distributed systems whose value is more than the sum of the parts.

Among the various services typically offered by middleware architectures, we are most interested in facilities for the coordination of document-centric activities. In this context, coordination is usually considered to be the management of dependencies among activities ([32]). As such, it integrates functionalities implemented as activities of heterogeneous components of software. Thus, it is a typical task of middleware.

Coordination middleware is difficult to design. The provided abstraction has to deal with the central issues of how data is communicated, how activities are started and synchronized. The heterogeneity found is very broad, ranging from RPCs, object invocations, component usage to agent interaction with different characteristics such as one-to-one or one-to-many communication and synchronization.

With XML, document-centric abstractions are revitalized. We are still exploring what role XML can play in coordination middleware for modern document-centric applications [26]. We look at document-centric middleware that uses XML. Our specific interest are the coordination services therein. The systems under review fall into three categories. They offer services for agents that process XML document, offer XML services for regular agents, or offer services in an XML integrated system.

In the coordination language Linda, tuples are primitive data without higher order values such as nested tuples, or mechanisms to express the intention of typing fields such as names etc. For Web-based systems, a richer form of data is needed. It has to be able to capture application specific higher data-structures easily without the need to encode them into primitive fields. The format has to be open so that new types of data can be specified. And it has to be standardized in some way, so that data-items can be exchanged between entities that have different design-origins. XML fulfills all those criteria.

XMLSpaces [38,39] is an extension to the Linda model which serves as middleware for XML. In XMLSpaces, XML documents serve as fields within the coordination space. Thus, ordinary tuples are supported, while XML documents can be represented as one-fielded tuples.

The MARS-X coordination architecture [12] defines a Linda-like middleware model to enable agent (specifically, mobile Java agents) to coordinate their activities via Linda-like access to shared spaces of XML documents. Unlike XMLSpaces, which operates at the granularity of XML documents, MARS-X adopts a more fine-grained approach, and considers any XML document in terms of an unstructured set of tuples. Accordingly to this perspective, a document and its data can be accessed and modified by exploiting the associative operation typical of the Linda model, and agents can coordinate with each other via exchange of document tuples, and via synchronization over tuple occurrences. Specifically, MARS-X provides agents a JavaSpace interface to access to a set of XML documents in terms of Java object tuples.

5   Conclusions

Traditional approaches to multiagent system design focus on the complexity related to the management of highly interactive multiagent applications. In fact, in most cases, the rules governing the interactions between the application agents are not explicitly modelled at the earlier design stages, and the design usually mixes computation and coordination issues into the code of the agents, in some sense without being able to define and separate "individual" and "social" application tasks. This usually undermines the openness and the reusability of both applications and their underlying software architectures, as well as their maintainability.

In this paper we have summarized some relevant consequences of adopting a coordination viewpoint on the engineering of a multiagent system. We have showed adopted an historical perspective centered upon our own research, which evolved from language design issues, to software architecture issues, to Web-based middleware issues, to more generally agent oriented software engineering issues.

Interestingly, these are all basically related to the *separation of concerns* between the computation and the coordination issues, or, in other terms, between individual and social tasks:

- *design focus* – agent interaction protocols can be designed by focussing on its individual task(s) (e.g., concentrating on the information needed and produced/inferred by the agent in the process of achieving its tasks), in many sense disregarding the social task(s) of the groups the agent belongs to;
- *coordination design* – social rules and collective behaviour can be represented in terms of coordination laws, charged upon the coordination media, and can be designed and implemented independently at the software architecture level, with no concern for the internal structure of the agents.
- *social intelligence* – social tasks can be achieved as the result of the mutual interaction of agents, each one pursuing its own aims. The interaction space can be exploited as a further source of intelligence for the multiagent system.
- *modularity and reusability* – autonomous agents focussing on their tasks, with no concern for coordination issues and designed around very straightforward interaction protocols, are a natural source of modularity for multiagent systems. They can be reused wherever their capabilities are needed, independently of the social rules. Dually, coordination rules can be exploited to achieve social tasks simply given the agent goals and protocols, independently of the internal structure of the agents.
- *incremental design and implementation* – once that social rules are designed and implemented, individual capabilities can be refined so as to improve the agent ability to achieve its task independently of the rest of the system. Analogously, once that agents tasks and interaction protocols are designed and implemented, coordination rules can be independently refined so as to improve the capability of the multiagent system to achieve its social goals.

The current trends in coordination research continue to develop and study novel coordination models suitable for designing network aware languages and applications [13]. Especially the Web and the new related technologies like Web

Services seem a promising application field. For instances, languages for orchestrating Web Services and the agents which use them are being developed, which are based on ideas based on coordination models [1].

Acknowledgments. We thank for support the Italian MIUR project SAHARA 40% on Software Architectures for MultiAgent Systems.

References

1. L. Andrade and J. Fiadeiro. Coordination Technology for Web Services. In *Proc. Int. OOPSLA Workshop on OO Web Services*, pages 566–583, Tampa, USA, 2001. 161
2. J. Andreoli, P. Ciancarini, and R. Pareschi. Interaction Abstract Machines. In G. Agha, P. Wegner, and A. Yonezawa, editors, *Trends in Object-Based Concurrent Computing*, pages 257–280. MIT Press, Cambridge, MA, 1993. 150
3. J. Andreoli and R. Pareschi. Linear Objects: Logical Processes with Built-in Inheritance. *New Generation Computing*, 9(3-4):445–473, 1991. 150
4. A.Omicini, F.Zambonelli, M.Klusch, and R.Tolksdorf, editors. *Coordination of Internet Agents: Models, Technologies, and Applications*. Springer-Verlag, Berlin, 2001. 146
5. J. Banatre and D. LeMetayer. The Gamma Model and its Discipline of Programming. *Science of Computer Programming*, 15:55–77, 1990. 150
6. T. BernersLee, J. Hendler, and O. Lassila. The Semantic Web. *Scientific American*, 284(5):34–43, 2001. 157
7. G. Berry and G. Boudol. The Chemical Abstract Machine. *Theoretical Computer Science*, 96:217–248, 1992. 150
8. R. Bjornson, N. Carriero, and D. Gelernter. From weaving threads to untangling the web: a view of coordination from Linda's perspective. In D. Garlan and D. LeMetayer, editors, *Proc. 2nd Int. Conf. on Coordination Models and Languages*, volume 1282 of *Lecture Notes in Computer Science*, pages 1–17, Berlin, Germany, September 1997. Springer-Verlag, Berlin. 150
9. L. Bompani, P. Ciancarini, and F. Vitali. Software Engineering on the Internet: A Roadmap. In A. Finkelstein, editor, *Proc. 22nd Int. Conf on Software Engineering - Track "The Future of Software Engineering"*, pages 303–318, Limerick, Ireland, 2000. 157
10. L. Bompani, P. Ciancarini, and F. Vitali. XML-based Hypertext Functionalities for Software Engineering. *Annals of Software Engineering*, 13:231–248, 2002. 158
11. G. Cabri, L. Leonardi, and F. Zambonelli. Reactive Tuple Spaces for Mobile Agent Coordination. In K. Rothermel and F. Hohl, editors, *Proc. 2nd Int. Workshop on Mobile Agents*, volume 1477 of *Lecture Notes in Computer Science*, pages 237–248, Stuttgart, Germany, 1998. Springer-Verlag, Berlin. 151
12. G. Cabri, L. Leonardi, and F. Zambonelli. MARS: A Programmable Coordination Architecture for Mobile Agents. *IEEE Internet Computing*, 4(4):26–35, July/August 2000. 159
13. L. Cardelli and A. Gordon. Mobile ambients. *Theoretical Computer Science*, 240(1):177–213, 2000. 160
14. N. Carriero and D. Gelernter. *How to Write Parallel Programs: A First Course.* MIT Press, Cambridge, MA, 1990. 151

15. N. Carriero and D. Gelernter. Coordination Languages and Their Significance. *Communications of the ACM*, 35(2):97–107, February 1992. 149, 149, 150
16. P. Ciancarini. PoliS: a Programming Model for Multiple Tuple Spaces. In C. Ghezzi and G. Roman, editors, *Proc. 6th ACM/IEEE Int. Workshop on Software Specification and Design (IWSSD)*, pages 44–51, Como, Italy, October 1991. IEEE Computer Society Press. 151
17. P. Ciancarini. Coordination Models and Languages as Software Integrators. *ACM Computing Surveys*, 28(2):300–302, 1996. 154
18. P. Ciancarini, F. Franzè, and C. Mascolo. Using a Coordination Language to Specify and Analyze Systems Containing Mobile Components. *ACM Transactions on Software Engineering and Methodology*, 9(2):167–198, 2000. 152
19. P. Ciancarini, A. Giovannini, and D. Rossi. Mobility and Coordination for Distributed Java Applications. In S. Krakowiak and S. Shrivastava, editors, *Recent Advances in Distributed Systems*, volume 1752 of *Lecture Notes in Computer Science*, pages 402–425. Springer-Verlag, Berlin, 2000. 156
20. P. Ciancarini, M. Mazza, and L. Pazzaglia. A Logic for a Coordination Model with Multiple Spaces. *Science of Computer Programming*, 31(2/3):231–262, July 1998. 151, 152, 152
21. P. Ciancarini, A. Omicini, and F. Zambonelli. Coordination Technologies for Internet Agents. *Nordic Journal of Computing*, 6(3):215–240, 1999. 147
22. P. Ciancarini and D. Rossi. Jada: a coordination toolkit for Java. Technical Report UBLCS-96-15, Dipartimento di Scienze dell'Informazione, Università di Bologna, Italy, 1996. 154
23. P. Ciancarini, D. Rossi, and F. Vitali. Designing a document-centric coordination application over the Internet. *Interacting with Computers*, 13:677–693, 2001. 156
24. P. Ciancarini, R. Tolksdorf, and F. Vitali. The World Wide Web as a Place for Agents. In M. Woolridge and M. Veloso, editors, *Artificial Intelligence Today. Recent Trends and Developments*, volume 1600 of *Lecture Notes in Artificial Intelligence*, pages 175–194. Springer-Verlag, Berlin, 1999. 153
25. P. Ciancarini, R. Tolksdorf, F. Vitali, D. Rossi, and A. Knoche. Coordinating Multiagent Applications on the WWW: a Reference Architecture. *IEEE Transactions on Software Engineering*, 24(5):362–375, 1998. 155
26. P. Ciancarini, R. Tolksdorf, and F. Zambonelli. Coordination Middleware for XML-centric Applications. In *Proc. ACM/SIGAPP Symp. on Applied Computing (SAC)*, pages 336–343. ACM Press, 2002. 159
27. P. Ciancarini, F. Vitali, and C. Mascolo. Managing complex documents over the WWW: a case study for XML. *IEEE Transactions on Knowledge and Data Engineering*, 11(4):629–638, July/August 1999. 158
28. R. DeNicola, G. Ferrari, and R. Pugliese. Klaim: a Kernel Language for Agents Interaction and Mobility. *IEEE Transactions on Software Engineering*, 24(5):315–330, 1998. 151, 153
29. D. Gelernter. Generative Communication in Linda. *ACM Transactions on Programming Languages and Systems*, 7(1):80–112, 1985. 151
30. N. Jennings and M. Wooldridge. Intelligents Agents: Theory and Practice. *Knowledge Engineering Review*, 10(2), 1999. 147
31. L. Lamport. The Temporal Logic of Actions. *ACM Transactions on Programming Languages and Systems*, 16(3):872–923, May 1994. 152
32. T. Malone and K. Crowstone. The Interdisciplinary Study of Coordination. *ACM Computing Surveys*, 26(1):87–119, 1994. 148, 149, 159

33. E. Merelli. An intelligent agents architecture for dna-microarray data integration. In *Proc. First Workshop on Network Tools and Applications in Biology (NETTAB)*, pages 145–155, Genoa, Italy, 2001. 156

34. N. Minsky and J. Leichter. Law-Governed Linda as a Coordination Model. In P. Ciancarini, O. Nierstrasz, and A. Yonezawa, editors, *Object-Based Models and Languages for Concurrent Systems*, volume 924 of *Lecture Notes in Computer Science*, pages 125–146. Springer-Verlag, Berlin, 1995. 151

35. P. C. N. Busi, R. Gorrieri, and G. Zavattaro. Models for Coordinating Agents: a Guided Tour. In A. Omicini, F. Zambonelli, , M. Klusch, and R. Tolksdorf, editors, *Coordination of Internet Agents: Models, Technologies, and Applications*, pages 6–24. Springer-Verlag, Berlin, 2001. 147

36. A. Omicini and F. Zambonelli. Coordination of mobile information agents in tucson. *Journal of Internet Research*, 8(5), 1998. 151

37. S. Ossowski. *Co-ordination in Artificial Agent Societies*, volume 1535 of *Lecture Notes in Computer Science*. Springer-Verlag, Berlin, 1999. 147

38. R. Tolksdorf and D. Glaubitz. Coordinating Web-based Systems with Documents in XMLSpaces. In *Proc. 6th IFCIS International Conference on Cooperative Information Systems (CoopIS)*, 2001. 159

39. R. Tolksdorf and D. Glaubitz. XMLSpaces for Coordination in Web-based Systems. In *Proc. 10th IEEE Int. Workshop on Enabling Technologies: Infrastructure for Collaborative Enterprises (WETICE)*. IEEE Computer Society Press, 2001. 159

40. J. Waldo. The Jini Architecture for Network-centric computing. *Communications of the ACM*, 42(7):76–82, July 1999. 154

41. J. Waldo et al. Javaspace specification - 1.0. Technical report, Sun Microsystems, March 1998. 154

42. P. Wyckoff, S. McLaughry, T. Lehman, and D. Ford. T spaces. *IBM Systems Journal*, 37(3):454–474, 1998. 154

Argumentation-Based Communication between Agents

Simon Parsons[1,2] and Peter McBurney[2]

[1] Department of Computer and Information Science
Brooklyn College, City University of New York
2900 Bedford Avenue, Brooklyn, NY 11210, USA
parsons@sci.brooklyn.cuny.edu

[2] Department of Computer Science
University of Liverpool
Liverpool, L69 7ZF, UK
{s.d.parsons,p.j.mcburney}@csc.liv.ac.uk

Abstract. One approach to agent communication is to insist that agents not only send messages, but support them with reasons why those messages are appropriate. This is argumentation-based communication. This chapter looks at some of our work on argumentation-based communication, focusing on issues which we think apply to all work in this area, and discussing what we feel are the important issues in developing systems for argumentation-based communication between agents.

1 Introduction

When we humans engage in any form of dialogue it is natural for us to do so in a somewhat skeptical manner. If someone informs us of a fact that we find surprising, we typically question it. Not in an aggressive way, but what might be described as an inquisitive way. When someone tells us "X is true"—where X can range across statements from "It is raining outside" to "The Dow Jones index will continue falling for the next six months"—we want to know "Where did you read that?", or "What makes you think that?". Typically we want to know the basis on which some conclusion was reached. In fact, this questioning is so ingrained that we often present information with some of the answer to the question we expect it to provoke already attached—"It is raining outside, I got soaked through", "The editorial in today's Guardian suggests that consumer confidence in the US is so low that the Dow Jones index will continue falling for the next six months." This is exactly argumentation-based communication. It is increasingly being applied to the design of agent communication languages and frameworks, for example: Dignum and colleagues [8,9]; Grosz and Kraus [14]; Parsons and Jennings [25,26]; Reed [28]; Schroeder *et al.* [30]; and Sycara [34]. Indeed, the idea that it is useful for agents to explain what they are doing is not just confined to research on argumentation-based communication [29].

Apart from its naturalness, there are two major advantages of this approach to agent communication. One is that it ensures that agents are *rational* in a certain sense. As we shall see, and as is argued at length in [21], argumentation-based communication allows us to define a form of rationality in which agents only accept statements that

M.-P. Huget (Ed.): Communications in Multiagent Systems, LNAI 2650, pp. 164–178, 2003.

they are unable to refute (the exact form of refutation depending on the particular formal properties of the argumentation system they use). In other words agents will only accept things if they don't have a good reason not to. The second advantage builds on this and, as discussed in more detail in [4], provides a way of giving agent communications a *social semantics* in the sense of Singh [32,33]. The essence of a social semantics is that agents state publicly their beliefs and intentions at the outset of a dialogue, so that future utterances and actions may be judged for consistency against these statements. The truth of an agent's expressions of its private beliefs or intentions can never be fully verified [37], but at least an agent's consistency can be assessed, and, with an argumentation-based dialogue system, the reasons supporting these expressions can be sought. Moreover, these reasons may be accepted or rejected, and possibly challenged and argued-against, by other agents.

This chapter sketches the state of the art in argumentation-based agent communication. We will do this not by describing all the relevant work in detail, but by identifying what we consider to be the main issues in building systems that communicate in this way, and briefly describing how our work has addressed them.

2   Philosophical Background

Our work on argumentation-based dialogue has been influenced by a model of human dialogues due to argumentation theorists Doug Walton and Erik Krabbe [35]. Walton and Krabbe set out to analyze the concept of commitment in dialogue, so as to "provide conceptual tools for the theory of argumentation" [35, page ix]. This led to a focus on persuasion dialogues, and their work presents formal models for such dialogues. In attempting this task, they recognized the need for a characterization of dialogues, and so they present a broad typology for inter-personal dialogue. They make no claims for its comprehensiveness. Their categorization identifies six primary types of dialogues and three mixed types. As defined by Walton and Krabbe, the six primary dialogue types are:

Information-Seeking Dialogues: One participant seeks the answer to some question(s) from another participant, who is believed by the first to know the answer(s).

Inquiry Dialogues: The participants collaborate to answer some question or questions whose answers are not known to any one participant.

Persuasion Dialogues: One party seeks to persuade another party to adopt a belief or point-of-view he or she does not currently hold.

Negotiation Dialogues: The participants bargain over the division of some scarce resource in a way acceptable to all, with each individual party aiming to maximize his or her share. [1]

Deliberation Dialogues: Participants collaborate to decide what course of action to take in some situation.

Eristic Dialogues: Participants quarrel verbally as a substitute for physical fighting, with each aiming to win the exchange.

---

[1] Note that this definition of Negotiation is that of Walton and Krabbe. Arguably negotiation dialogues may involve other issues besides the division of scarce resources.

This framework can be used in a number of ways. First, we have increasingly used this typology as a framework within which it is possible to compare and contrast different systems for argumentation. For example, in [3] we used the classification, and the description of the start conditions and aims of participants given in [35] to show that the argumentation system described in [3] could handle persuasion, information seeking and inquiry dialogues. Second, we have also used the classification as a means of classifying particular argumentation systems, for example identifying the system in [25] as including elements of deliberation (it is about joint action) and persuasion (one agent is attempting to persuade the other to do something different) rather than negotiation as it was originally billed. Third, we can use the typology as a means of distinguishing the focus (and thus the detailed requirements for) systems intended to be used for engaging in certain types of dialogue as in our work to define locutions to perform inquiry [22] and deliberation [16] dialogues.

The final aspect of this work that is relevant, in our view, is that it stresses the importance of being able to handle dialogues of one kind that include embedded dialogues of another kind. Thus a negotiation dialogue about the purchase of a car might include an embedded information seeking dialogue (to find the buyer's requirements), and an embedded persuasion dialogue (about the value of a particular model). This has led to formalisms in which dialogues can be combined [23,28].

3   Argumentation and Dialogue

The focus of attention by philosophers to argumentation has been on understanding and guiding human reasoning and argument. It is not surprising, therefore, that this work says little about how argumentation may be applied to the design of communication systems for artificial agents. In this section we consider some of the issues relevant to such application.

3.1   Languages and Argumentation

Considering two agents that are engaged in some dialogue, we can distinguish between three different languages that they use. Each agent has a *base language* that it uses as a means of knowledge representation, a language we might call L. This language can be unique to the agent, or may be the same for both agents. This is the language in which the designer of the agent provides the agent with its knowledge of the world, and it is the language in which the agent's beliefs, desires and intentions (or indeed any other mental notions with which the agent is equipped) are expressed. Given the broad scope of L, it may in practice be a set of languages—for example separate languages for handling beliefs, desires, and intentions—but since all such languages carry out the same function we will regard them as one for the purposes of this discussion.

Each agent is also equipped with a *meta-language ML* which expresses facts about the base language L. Agents need meta-languages because, amongst other things, they need to represent their preferences about elements of L. Again ML may in fact be a set of meta-languages and both agents can use different meta-languages. Furthermore, if the agent has no need to make statements about formulae of L, then it may have no meta-language (or, equivalently, it may have a meta-language which it does not make use of). If an agent does have a separate meta-language, then it, like *L*, is *internal* to the agent.

Finally, for dialogues, the agents need a shared communication language (or two languages such that it is possible to seamlessly translate between them). We will call this language *CL*. We can consider *CL* to be a "wrapper" around statements in *L* and *ML*, as is the case for KQML [11] or the FIPA ACL [12], or a dedicated language into which and from which statements in *L* or *CL* are translated. *CL* might even be *L* or *ML*, though, as with *ML*, we can consider it to be a conceptually different language. The difference, of course, is that *CL* is in some sense *external* to the agents—it is used to communicate between them. We can imagine an agent reasoning using *L* and *ML*, then constructing messages in *CL* and posting them off to the other agent. When a reply arrives in *CL*, it is turned into statements in *L* and *ML* and these are used in new reasoning.

Argumentation can be used with these languages in a number of ways. Agents can use argumentation as a means of performing their own internal reasoning either in *L*, *ML*, or both. Independently of whether argumentation is used internally, it can also be used externally, in the sense of being used in conjunction with *CL*—this is the sense in which Walton and Krabbe [35] consider the use of argumentation in human dialogue and is much more on the topic of this chapter.

3.2   Inter-agent Argumentation

External argumentation can happen in a number of ways. The main issue, the fact that makes it argumentation, is that the agents do not just exchange facts but also exchange additional information. In persuasion dialogues, which are by far the most studied type of argumentation-based dialogues, these reasons are typically the reasons why the facts are thought to be true. Thus, if agent *A* wants to persuade agent *B* that *p* is true, it does not just state the fact that *p*, but also gives, for example, a proof of *p* based on information (grounds) that *A* believes to be true. If the proof is sound then *B* can only disagree with *p* if either it disputes the truth of some of the grounds or if it has an alternative proof that *p* is false. The intuition behind the use of argumentation here is that a dialogue about the truth of a claim *p* moves to a dialogue about the supporting evidence or one about apparently-conflicting proofs. From the perspective of building argumentative agents, the focus is now on how we can bring about either of these kinds of discussion.

There are a number of aspects, in particular, that we need to focus on. These include:

- Clearly communication will be carried out in *CL*, but it is not clear how arguments will be passed in *CL*. Will arguments form separate locutions, or will they be included in the same kind of *CL* locution as every other piece of information passed between the agents?
- Clearly the exchange of arguments between agents will be subject to some protocol, but it is not clear how this is related, if at all, to the protocol used for the exchange of other messages. Do they use the same protocol? If the protocols are different, how do agents know when to move from one protocol to another?

– Clearly the arguments that agents make should be related to what they know, but it is not clear how best this might be done. Should an agent only be able to argue what it believes to be true? If not, what arguments is an agent allowed to make?

One approach to constructing argumentation-based agents is the way suggested in [31]. In this work *CL* contains two sets of illocutions. One set allows the communication of facts (in this case statements in *ML* that take the form of conjunctions of value/attribute pairs, intended as offers in a negotiation). The other set allows the expressions of arguments. These arguments are unrelated to the offers, but express reasons why the offers should be acceptable, appealing to a rich representation of the agent and its environment: the kinds of argument suggested in [31] are threats such as, "If you don't accept this I will tell your boss," promises like: "If you accept my offer I'll bring you repeat business," and appeals such as: "You should accept this because that is the deal we made before."

There is no doubt that this model of argumentation has a good deal of similarity with the kind of argumentation we engage in on a daily basis. However, it makes considerable demands on any implementation. For a start, agents which wish to argue in this manner need very rich representations of each other and their environments (especially compared with agents which simply wish to debate the truth of a proposition given what is in their knowledge-base). Such agents also require an answer to the second two points raised above, and the very richness of the model makes it hard (at least for the authors) to see how the third point can be addressed.

Now, the complicating factor in both of the bullet points raised above is the need to handle two types of information—those that are argument-based and those that aren't. One way to simplify the situation is to make all communication argument-based, and that is the approach that we have been following of late. In fact, we go a bit further than even this suggests, by considering agents that use argumentation both for internal reasoning and as a means of relating what they believe and what they communicate. We describe this approach in the next section.

3.3 Argumentation at All Levels

In more detail what we are proposing is the following. First of all, every agent carries out internal argumentation using *L*. This allows it to resolve any inconsistency in its knowledge base (which is important when dealing with information from many sources since such information is typically inconsistent) and to establish some notion of what it believes to be true (though this notion is defeasible since new information may come to light that provides a more compelling argument against some fact than there previously was for that fact). The upshot of this use of argumentation, however it is implemented, is that every agent can not only identify the facts it believes to be true but can supply a rationale for believing them.

This feature then provides us with a way of ensuring a kind of rationality of the agents—rationality in communication. It is natural that an agent which resolves inconsistencies in what it knows about the world uses the same technique to resolve inconsistencies between what it knows and what it is told. In other words the agent looks at the reasons for the things it is told and accepts these things provided they are supported by more compelling reasons than there are against the things. If agents are only going to accept things that are backed by arguments, then it makes sense for agents to only say things that are also backed by arguments. Both of us, separately in [21] and [4], have suggested that such an argumentation-based approach is a suitable form of rationality, and it was implicit in [3].[2]

The way that this form of rationality is formalized is, for example, to only permit agents to make assertions that are backed by some form of argument, and to only accept assertions that are so backed. In order words, the formation of arguments becomes a precondition of the locutions of the communication language *CL*, and the locutions are linked to the agents' knowledge bases.

Although it is not immediately obvious, this gives argumentation-based approaches a *social semantics* in the sense of Singh [32,33]. The naive reason for this is that since agents can only assert things that in their considered view are true (which is another way of putting the fact that the agents have more compelling reasons for thinking something is true than for thinking it is false), other agents have some guarantee that they are true. However agents may lie, and a suitably sophisticated agent will always be able to simulate truth-telling. A more sophisticated reason is that, assuming such locutions are built into *CL*, the agent on the receiving end of the assertion can always challenge statements, requiring that the reasons for them are stated. These reasons can be checked against what that agent knows, with the result that the agent will only accept things that it has no reason to doubt. This ability to question statements gives argumentation-based communication languages a degree of verifiability that other semantics, such as the original modal semantics for the FIPA ACL [12], lack.

3.4   Dialogue Games

Dialogues may be viewed as games between the participants, called *dialogue games* [18]. In this view, explained in greater detail in [24], each participant is a player with an objective they are trying to achieve and some finite set of moves that they might make. Just as in any game, there are rules about which player is allowed to make which move at any point in the game, and there are rules for starting and ending the game.

As a brief example, consider a persuasion dialogue. We can think of this as being captured by a game in which one player initially believes p to be true and tries to convince another player, who initially believes that p is false, of that fact. The game might start with the first player stating the reason why she believes that p is true, and the other player might be bound to either accept that this reason is true (if she can find no fault with it) or to respond with the reason she believes it to be false. The first player is then bound by the same rules as the second was—to find a reason why this second reason is false or to accept it—and the game continues until one of the players is forced to accept the most recent reason given and thus to concede the game.

---

[2] This meaning of rationality is also consistent with that commonly given in philosophy, see, e.g., [17].

4 A System for Argumentation-Based Communication

In this section we give a concrete instantiation of the rather terse description given in Section 3.3, providing an example of a system for carrying out argumentation-based communication of the kind first suggested in [25].

4.1 A System for Internal Argumentation

We start with a system for internal argumentation—this is an extended version of [10], where the extension allows for a notion of the strength of an argument [2], which is augmented to handle beliefs and intentions. To define this system we start with a propositional language which we call $\mathcal{L}$. From $\mathcal{L}$ we then construct formulae such as $B_i(p)$, $D_i(p)$ and $I_j(q)$ for any p and q which are formulae of $\mathcal{L}$. This extended propositional language, and the compound formulae that may be built from it using the usual logical connectives, is the base language L of the argumentation-based dialogue system we are describing. $B_i(\cdot)$ denotes a belief of agent i, $D_i(\cdot)$ denotes a desire of agent i, and $I_j(\cdot)$ denotes an intention of agent j, so the overall effect of this language is just to force every formula to be a belief, a desire, or an intention. We will denote formulae of L by ϕ, ψ, σ .... Since we are only interested in syntactic manipulation of beliefs, desires and intentions here, we will give no semantics for formulae such as $B_i(p)$ and $B_i(p) \rightarrow D_i(p)$— suitable ways of dealing with the semantics are given elsewhere (e.g. [26,36]). An agent has a knowledge base Σ which is allowed to be inconsistent, and has no deductive closure. The symbol $\vdash$ denotes classical inference and $\equiv$ denotes logical equivalence.

An argument is a formula of L and the set of formulae from which it can be inferred:

Definition 1. An *argument* is a pair $A = (H, h)$ where h is a formula of L and H a subset of Σ such that:

1. H is consistent;
2. $H \vdash h$; and
3. H is minimal, so no subset of H satisfying both 1. and 2. exists.

H is called the *support* of A, written $H = \text{Support}(A)$ and h is the *conclusion* of A written $h = \text{Conclusion}(A)$.

We talk of h being *supported* by the argument (H, h).

In general, since Σ is inconsistent, arguments in $\mathcal{A}(\Sigma)$, the set of all arguments which can be made from Σ, will conflict, and we make this idea precise with the notions of rebutting, undercutting and attacking.

Definition 2. Let A_1 and A_2 be two distinct arguments of $\mathcal{A}(\Sigma)$. A_1 *undercuts* A_2 iff $\exists h \in \text{Support}(A_2)$ such that $\text{Conclusion}(A_1)$ *attacks* h.

Definition 3. Let A_1 and A_2 be two distinct arguments of $\mathcal{A}(\Sigma)$. A_1 *rebuts* A_2 iff $\text{Conclusion}(A_1)$ *attacks* $\text{Conclusion}(A_2)$.

Definition 4. Given two distinct formulae h and g of $\mathcal{L}$ such that $h \equiv \neg g$, then, for any i and j:

- $B_i(h)$ *attacks* $B_j(g)$;
- $D_i(h)$ *attacks* $D_j(g)$; and
- $I_i(h)$ *attacks* $I_j(g)$.

With these definitions, an argument is rebutted if it has a conclusion $B_i(p)$ and there is another argument which has as its conclusion $B_j(\neg p)$ or $B_j(q)$ such that $q \equiv \neg p$. An argument with a desire as its conclusion can similarly be rebutted by another argument with a desire as its conclusion, and the same thing holds for intentions. Thus we recognize "Peter intends that this paper be written by the deadline" and "Simon intends this paper not to be written by the deadline" as rebutting each other, along with "Peter believes God exists" and "Simon does not believe God exists", but we do not recognize "Peter intends that this paper will be written by the deadline" and "Simon does not believe that this paper will be written by the deadline" as rebutting each other. Undercutting occurs in exactly the same situations, except that it holds between the conclusions of one argument and an element of the support of the other.[3]

To capture the fact that some facts are more strongly believed and intended than others, we assume that any set of facts has a preference order over it.[4] We suppose that this ordering derives from the fact that the knowledge base Σ is stratified into non-overlapping sets $\Sigma_1, \ldots, \Sigma_n$ such that facts in Σ_i are all equally preferred and are more preferred than those in Σ_j where $j > i$. The preference level of a nonempty subset H of Σ, $level(H)$, is the number of the highest numbered layer which has a member in H.

Definition 5. Let A_1 and A_2 be two arguments in $\mathcal{A}(\Sigma)$. A_1 is *preferred* to A_2 according to *Pref* iff $level(Support(A_1)) \leq level(Support(A_2))$.

By $\gg^{Pref}$ we denote the strict pre-order associated with *Pref*. If A_1 is strictly preferred to A_2, we say that A_1 is *stronger* than A_2. We can now define the argumentation system we will use:

Definition 6. An *argumentation system* (AS) is a triple

$$\langle \mathcal{A}(\Sigma), Undercut/Rebut, Pref \rangle$$

such that:

- $\mathcal{A}(\Sigma)$ is a set of the arguments built from Σ,
- *Undercut/Rebut* is a binary relation capturing the existence of an undercut or rebut holding between arguments, $Undercut/Rebut \subseteq \mathcal{A}(\Sigma) \times \mathcal{A}(\Sigma)$, and
- *Pref* is a (partial or complete) preordering on $\mathcal{A}(\Sigma) \times \mathcal{A}(\Sigma)$.

---

[3] Note that attacking and rebutting are symmetric but not reflexive or transitive, while undercutting is neither symmetric, reflexive nor transitive.

[4] We ignore for now the fact that we might require different preference orders over beliefs and intentions and indeed that different agents will almost certainly have different preference orders, noting that the problem of handling a number of different preference orders was considered in [5] and [7].

The preference order makes it possible to distinguish different types of relation between arguments:

Definition 7. Let A_1, A_2 be two arguments of $\mathcal{A}(\Sigma)$.

- If A_2 undercuts or rebuts A_1 then A_1 *defends itself* against A_2 iff $A_1 \gg^{Pref} A_2$. Otherwise, A_1 *does not defend itself.*
- A set of arguments S *defends* A iff: $\forall$ B such that B undercuts or rebuts A and A does not defend itself against B then $\exists\, C \in S$ such that C undercuts or rebuts B and B does not defend itself against C.

Henceforth, $C_{Undercut/Rebut,Pref}$ will gather all non-undercut and non-rebut arguments along with arguments defending themselves against all their undercutting and rebutting arguments. [1] showed that the set $\underline{S}$ of acceptable arguments of the argumentation system $\langle \mathcal{A}(\Sigma), Undercut/Rebut, Pref \rangle$ is the least fixpoint of a function $\mathcal{F}$:

$$\mathcal{F}(S) = \{(H, h) \in \mathcal{A}(\Sigma) | (H, h) \text{ is defended by } S\}$$

where $S \subseteq \mathcal{A}(\Sigma)$.

Definition 8. The set of *acceptable* arguments of an argumentation system $\langle \mathcal{A}(\Sigma), Undercut, Pref \rangle$ is:

$$\underline{S} = \bigcup \mathcal{F}_{i \geq 0}(\emptyset)$$
$$= C_{Undercut/Rebut,Pref} \cup \left[\bigcup \mathcal{F}_{i \geq 1}(C_{Undercut/Rebut,Pref}) \right]$$

An argument is acceptable if it is a member of the acceptable set.

If the argument (H, h) is acceptable, we talk of there being an acceptable argument for h. An acceptable argument is one which is, in some sense, proven since all the arguments which might undermine it are themselves undermined.

Note that while we have given a language L for this system, we have given no language ML. This particular system does not have a meta-language (and the notion of preferences it uses is not expressed in a meta-language). It is, of course, possible to add a meta-language to this system—for example, in [5] we added a meta-language which allowed us to express preferences over elements of L, thus making it possible to exchange (and indeed argue about, though this was not done in [5]) preferences between formulae.

4.2   Arguments between Agents

Now, this system is sufficient for internal argumentation within a single agent, and the agent can use it to, for example, perform nonmonotonic reasoning and to deal with inconsistent information. To allow for dialogues, we have to introduce some more machinery. Clearly part of this will be the communication language, but we need to introduce some additional elements first. These elements are datastructures which our system inherits from its dialogue game ancestors as well as previous presentations of this kind of system [3,6].

Dialogues are assumed to take place between two agents, P and C.[5] Each agent has a knowledge base, Σ_P and Σ_C respectively, containing their beliefs. In addition, following Hamblin [15], each agent has a further knowledge base, accessible to both agents, containing commitments made in the dialogue. These commitment stores are denoted $CS(P)$ and $CS(C)$ respectively, and in this dialogue system (unlike that of [6] for example) an agent's commitment store is just a subset of its knowledge base. Note that the union of the commitment stores can be viewed as the state of the dialogue at a given time. Each agent has access to their own private knowledge base and to both commitment stores. Thus P can make use of $\langle \mathcal{A}(\Sigma_P \cup CS(C)), Undercut/Rebut, Pref \rangle$, and C can make use of $\langle \mathcal{A}(\Sigma_C \cup CS(P), Undercut/Rebut, Pref \rangle$. All the knowledge bases contain propositional formulae and are not closed under deduction, and all are stratified by degree of belief as discussed above.

With this background, we can present the set of dialogue moves that we will use, the set which comprises the locutions of CL. For each move, we give what we call rationality rules, dialogue rules, and update rules. These locutions are those from [27] and are based on the rules suggested by [20] which, in turn, were based on those in the dialogue game DC introduced by MacKenzie [19]. The rationality rules specify the preconditions for making the move. The update rules specify how commitment stores are modified by the move.

In the following, player P addresses the move to player C. We start with the assertion of facts:

assert(ϕ) where ϕ is a formula of L.

> **rationality:** the usual assertion condition for the agent.
> **update:** $CS_i(P) = CS_{i-1}(P) \cup \{\phi\}$ and $CS_i(C) = CS_{i-1}(C)$

Here ϕ can be any formula of L, as well as the special character $\mathcal{U}$, discussed in the next sub-section.

assert(S) where S is a set of formulae of L representing the support of an argument.

> **rationality:** the usual assertion condition for the agent.
> **update:** $CS_i(P) = CS_{i-1} \cup S$ and $CS_i(C) = CS_{i-1}(C)$

The counterpart of these moves are the acceptance moves:

accept(ϕ) ϕ is a formula of L.

> **rationality:** The usual acceptance condition for the agent.
> **update:** $CS_i(P) = CS_{i-1}(P) \cup \{\phi\}$ and $CS_i(C) = CS_{i-1}(C)$

---

[5] The names stem from the study of persuasion dialogues—P argues "pro" some proposition, and C argues "con".

accept(S) S is a set of formulae of L.

> **rationality:** the usual acceptance condition for every $\sigma \in S$.
> **update:** $CS_i(P) = CS_{i-1}(P) \cup S$ and $CS_i(C) = CS_{i-1}(C)$

There are also moves which allow questions to be posed.

challenge(ϕ) where ϕ is a formula of L.

> **rationality:** $\emptyset$
> **update:** $CS_i(P) = CS_{i-1}(P)$ and $CS_i(C) = CS_{i-1}(C)$

A challenge is a means of making the other player explicitly state the argument support-ing a proposition. In contrast, a question can be used to query the other player about any proposition.

question(ϕ) where ϕ is a formula of L.

> **rationality:** $\emptyset$
> **update:** $CS_i(P) = CS_{i-1}(P)$ and $CS_i(C) = CS_{i-1}(C)$

We refer to this set of moves as the set $\mathcal{M}_{DC}^d$. These locutions are the bare minimum to carry out a dialogue, and, as we will see below, require a fairly rigid protocol with a lot of aspects implicit. Further locutions such as those discussed in [23], would be required to be able to debate the beginning and end of dialogues or to have an explicit representation of movement between embedded dialogues.

Clearly this set of moves/locutions defines the communication language CL, and hopefully it is reasonably clear from the description so far how argumentation between agents takes place; a prototypical dialogue might be as follows:

1. P has an acceptable argument $(S, B_p(p))$, built from Σ_P, and wants C to accept $B_p(p)$. Thus, P asserts $B_p(p)$.
2. C has an argument $(S', B_c(\neg p))$ and so cannot accept $B_p(p)$. Thus, C asserts $B_c(\neg p)$.
3. P cannot accept $B_c(\neg p)$ and challenges it.
4. C responds by asserting S'. and asserts $B_p(\neg q)$.
5. ...

At each stage in the dialogue agents can build arguments using information from their own private knowledge base, and the propositions made public (by assertion into com-mitment stores).

4.3   Rationality and Protocol

The final part of the abstract model we introduced above was the use of argumentation to relate what an agent "knows" (in this case what is in its knowledge-base and the com-mitment stores) and what it is allowed to "say" (in terms of which locutions from CL it is allowed to utter). We make this connection by specifying the rationality conditions in the definitions of the locutions and relating these to what arguments an agent can make. We do this as follows, essentially defining different types of rationality [27].

Definition 9. An agent may have one of three *assertion* attitudes.

- a *confident* agent can assert any formula ϕ for which there is an argument (S, ϕ).
- a *careful* agent can assert any formula ϕ for which there is an argument (S, ϕ) if no stronger rebutting argument exists.
- a *thoughtful* agent can assert any proposition ϕ for which there is an acceptable argument (S, ϕ).

Of course, defining when an agent can assert formulae is only one half of what is needed. The other part is to define the conditions on agents accepting formulae. Here we have the following [27].

Definition 10. An agent may have one of three *acceptance* attitudes.

- a *credulous* agent can accept any formula ϕ for which there is an argument (S, ϕ).
- a *cautious* agent can accept any proposition ϕ for which there is an argument (S, ϕ) if no stronger rebutting argument exists.
- a *skeptical* agent can accept any proposition ϕ for which there is an acceptable argument (S, ϕ).

In order to complete the definition of the system, we need only to give the protocol that specifies how a dialogue proceeds. This we do below, providing a protocol (which was not given in the original) for the kind of example dialogue given in [25,26]. As in those papers, the kind of dialogue we are interested in here is a dialogue about joint plans, and in order to describe the dialogue, we need an idea of what one of these plans looks like:

Definition 11. An *plan* is an argument $(S, I_i(p))$. $I_i(p)$ is known as the *subject* of the plan.

Thus a plan is just an argument for a proposition that is intended by some agent. The detail of "acceptable" and "attack" ensure that an agent will only be able to assert or accept a plan if there is no intention which is preferred to the subject of the plan so far as the that agent is aware, and there is no conflict between any elements of the support of the plan. We then have the following protocol, which we will call $\mathcal{D}$ for a dialogue between agents A and B.

1. If allowed by its assertion attitude, A asserts both the conclusion and support of a plan $(S, I_A(p))$. If A cannot assert any $I_A(p)$, the dialogue ends.
2. B accepts $I_A(p)$ and S if possible. If both are accepted, the dialogue terminates.
3. If the $I_A(p)$ and S are not accepted, then B asserts the conclusion and support of an argument (S', ψ) which undercuts or rebuts $(S, I_A(p))$.
4. A asserts either the conclusion and support of $(S''', I_A(p))$, which does not undercut or rebut (S', ψ), or the statement $\mathcal{U}$. In the first case, the dialogue returns to Step 2; in the second case, the dialogue terminates.

The utterance of a statement $\mathcal{U}$ indicates that an agent is unable to add anything to the dialogue, and so the dialogue terminates whenever either agent asserts this.

Note that in B's response it need not assert a plan (A is the only agent which has to mention plans). This allows B to disagree with A on matters such as the resources assumed by A ("No, I don't have the car that week"), or the tradeoff that A is proposing ("I don't want your Megatokyo T-shirt, I have one like that already"), even if they don't directly affect the plans that B has.

As it stands, the protocol is a rather minimalist but suffices to capture the kind of interaction in [25,26]. One agent makes a suggestion which suits it (and may involve the other agent). The second looks to see if the plan prevents it achieving any of its intentions, and if so has to put forward a plan which clashes in some way (we could easily extend the protocol so that B does not have to put forward this plan, but can instead engage A in a persuasion dialogue about A's plan in a way that was not considered in [25,26]). The first agent then has the chance to respond by either finding a non-clashing way of achieving what it wants to do or suggesting a way for the second agent to achieve its intention without clashing with the first agent's original plan. There is also much that is implicit in the protocol, for example: that the agents have previously agreed to carry out this kind of dialogue (since no preamble is required); that the agents are basically co-operative (since they accept suggestions if possible); and that they will end the dialogue as soon as a possible agreement is found or it is clear that no progress can be made (so neither agent will try to filibuster for its own advantage). Such assumptions are consistent with Grice's co-operative maxims for human conversation [13].

One advantage of such a minimal protocol is that it is easy to show that the resulting dialogues have some desirable properties. The first of these is that the dialogues terminate:

Proposition 1. *A dialogue under protocol $\mathcal{D}$ between two agents G and H with any acceptance and assertion attitudes will terminate.*

If both agents are thoughtful and skeptical, we can also obtain conditions on the result of the dialogue:

Proposition 2. *Consider a dialogue under protocol $\mathcal{D}$ between two thoughtful/skeptical agents G and H, where G starts by uttering a plan with the subject $I_G(p)$.*

- *If the dialogue terminates with the utterance of $\mathcal{U}$, then there is no plan with the subject $I_G(p)$ in $A(\Sigma_G \cup CS(H))$ that H can accept.*
- *If the dialogue terminates without the utterance of $\mathcal{U}$, then there is a plan with the subject $I_G(p)$ in $A(\Sigma_G \cup \Sigma_H)$ that is acceptable to both G and H.*

Note that since we can't determine exactly what H says, and therefore what are the contents of $CS(H)$, we are not able to make the two parts of the theorem symmetrical (or the second part an "if and only if", which would be the same thing).

Thus if the agents reach agreement, it is an agreement on a plan which neither of them has any reason to think problematic. In [25,26] we called this kind of dialogue a negotiation. From the perspective of Walton and Krabbe's typology it isn't a negotiation—it is closer to a deliberation with the agents discussing what they will do.

5   Summary

Argumentation-based approaches to inter-agent communication are becoming more widespread, and there are a variety of systems for argumentation-based communication that have been proposed. Many of these address different aspects of the communication problem, and it can be hard to see how they relate to one another. This chapter has attempted to put some of this work in context by describing in general terms how argumentation might be used in inter-agent communication, and then illustrating this general model by providing a concrete instantiation of it, finally describing all the aspects required by the example first introduced in [25].

Acknowledgements The authors would like to thank Leila Amgoud and Nicolas Maudet for their contribution to the development of many of the parts of the argumentation system described here.

References

1. L. Amgoud and C. Cayrol. On the acceptability of arguments in preference-based argumentation framework. In *Proc. 14th Conf. Uncertainty in AI*, pages 1–7, 1998. 172
2. L. Amgoud and C. Cayrol. A reasoning model based on the production of acceptable arguments. *Annals of Mathematics and AI*, 34:197–215, 2002. 170
3. L. Amgoud, N. Maudet, and S. Parsons. Modelling dialogues using argumentation. In E. Durfee, editor, *Proc. 4th Intern. Conf. on Multi-Agent Systems*, pages 31–38, Boston, MA, USA, 2000. IEEE Press. 166, 166, 169, 173
4. L. Amgoud, N. Maudet, and S. Parsons. An argumentation-based semantics for agent communication languages. In *Proc. 15th European Conf. on AI*, 2002. 165, 169
5. L. Amgoud and S. Parsons. Agent dialogues with conflicting preferences. In J.-J. Meyer and M. Tambe, editors, *Proc. 8th Intern. Workshop on Agent Theories, Architectures and Languages*, pages 1–15, 2001. 171, 172, 172
6. L. Amgoud, S. Parsons, and N. Maudet. Arguments, dialogue, and negotiation. In W. Horn, editor, *Proc. 14th European Conf. on AI*, pages 338–342, Berlin, Germany, 2000. IOS Press. 173, 173
7. L. Amgoud, S. Parsons, and L. Perrussel. An argumentation framework based on contextual preferences. In J. Cunningham, editor, *Proc. Intern. Conf. Pure and Applied Practical Reasoning*, London, UK, 2000. 171
8. F. Dignum, B. Dunin-Kęplicz, and R. Verbrugge. Agent theory for team formation by dialogue. In C. Castelfranchi and Y. Lespérance, editors, *Intelligent Agents VII*, pages 141–156, Berlin, Germany, 2001. Springer. 164
9. F. Dignum, B. Dunin-Kęplicz, and R. Verbrugge. Creating collective intention through dialogue. *Logic Journal of the IGPL*, 9(2):305–319, 2001. 164
10. P. M. Dung. On the acceptability of arguments and its fundamental role in nonmonotonic reasoning, logic programming and *n*-person games. *Artificial Intelligence*, 77:321–357, 1995. 170
11. T. Finin, Y. Labrou, and J. Mayfield. KQML as an agent communication language. In J. Bradshaw, editor, *Software Agents*. MIT Press, Cambridge, MA, 1995. 167
12. FIPA. Communicative Act Library Specification. Technical Report XC00037H, Foundation for Intelligent Physical Agents, 10 August 2001. 167, 169
13. H. P. Grice. Logic and conversation. In P. Cole and J. L. Morgan, editors, *Syntax and Semantics III: Speech Acts*, pages 41–58. Academic Press, New York City, NY, USA, 1975. 176
14. B. J. Grosz and S. Kraus. The evolution of SharedPlans. In M. J. Wooldridge and A. Rao, editors, *Foundations of Rational Agency*, volume 14 of *Applied Logic*. Kluwer, The Netherlands, 1999. 164
15. C. L. Hamblin. *Fallacies*. Methuen, London, UK, 1970. 173

16. D. Hitchcock, P. McBurney, and S. Parsons. A framework for deliberation dialogues. In H. V. Hansen, C. W. Tindale, J. A. Blair, and R. H. Johnson, editors, *Proc. 4th Biennial Conf. Ontario Soc. Study of Argumentation (OSSA 2001)*, Windsor, Ontario, Canada, 2001. 166

17. R. Johnson. *Manifest Rationality: A Pragmatic Theory of Argument.* Lawrence Erlbaum Associates, Mahwah, NJ, USA, 2000. 169

18. J. A. Levin and J. A. Moore. Dialogue-games: metacommunications structures for natural language interaction. *Cognitive Science*, 1(4):395–420, 1978. 169

19. J. D. MacKenzie. Question-begging in non-cumulative systems. *J. Philosophical Logic*, 8:117–133, 1979. 173

20. N. Maudet and F. Evrard. A generic framework for dialogue game implementation. In *Proc. 2nd Workshop on Formal Semantics and Pragmatics of Dialogue*, University of Twente, The Netherlands, May 1998. 173

21. P. McBurney. *Rational Interaction.* PhD thesis, Department of Computer Science, University of Liverpool, 2002. 164, 169

22. P. McBurney and S. Parsons. Risk agoras: Dialectical argumentation for scientific reasoning. In C. Boutilier and M. Goldszmidt, editors, *Proc. 16th Conf. on Uncertainty in AI*, Stanford, CA, USA, 2000. UAI. 166

23. P. McBurney and S. Parsons. Games that agents play: A formal framework for dialogues between autonomous agents. *J. Logic, Language, and Information*, 11(3):315–334, 2002. 166, 174

24. P. McBurney and S. Parsons. Dialogue game protocols. In Marc-Philippe Huget, editor, *Agent Communications Languages*, Berlin, Germany, 2003. Springer. (This volume.). 169

25. S. Parsons and N. R. Jennings. Negotiation through argumentation — a preliminary report. In *Proc. 2nd Intern. Conf. on Multi-Agent Systems*, pages 267–274, 1996. 164, 166, 170, 175, 176, 176, 176, 177

26. S. Parsons, C. Sierra, and N. R. Jennings. Agents that reason and negotiate by arguing. *Logic and Computation*, 8(3):261–292, 1998. 164, 170, 175, 176, 176, 176

27. S. Parsons, M. Wooldridge, and L. Amgoud. An analysis of formal interagent dialogues. In C. Castelfranchi and W. L. Johnson, editors, *Proc. First Intern. Joint Conf. on Autonomous Agents and Multi-Agent Systems (AAMAS 2002)*, pages 394–401, New York, USA, 2002. ACM Press. 173, 174, 175

28. C. Reed. Dialogue frames in agent communications. In Y. Demazeau, editor, *Proc. 3rd Intern. Conf. on Multi-Agent Systems*, pages 246–253. IEEE Press, 1998. 164, 166

29. P. Riley, P. Stone, and M. Veloso. Layered disclosure: Revealing agents' internals. In C. Castelfranchi and Y. Lespérance, editors, *Intelligent Agents VII*, pages 61–72, Berlin, Germany, 2001. Springer. 164

30. M. Schroeder, D. A. Plewe, and A. Raab. Ultima ratio: should Hamlet kill Claudius. In *Proc. 2nd Intern. Conf. on Autonomous Agents*, pages 467–468, 1998. 164

31. C. Sierra, N. R. Jennings, P. Noriega, and S. Parsons. A framework for argumentation-based negotiations. In M. P. Singh, A. Rao, and M. J. Wooldridge, editors, *Intelligent Agents IV*, pages 177–192, Berlin, Germany, 1998. Springer. 168, 168

32. M. P. Singh. Agent communication languages: Rethinking the principles. In *IEEE Computer 31*, pages 40–47, 1998. 165, 169

33. M. P. Singh. A social semantics for agent communication languages. In *Proc. IJCAI'99 Workshop on Agent Communication Languages*, pages 75–88, 1999. 165, 169

34. K. Sycara. Argumentation: Planning other agents' plans. In *Proc. 11th Joint Conf. on AI*, pages 517–523, 1989. 164

35. D. N. Walton and E. C. W. Krabbe. *Commitment in Dialogue: Basic Concepts of Interpersonal Reasoning.* SUNY Press, Albany, NY, 1995. 165, 165, 166, 167

36. M. J. Wooldridge. *Reasoning about Rational Agents.* MIT Press, Cambridge, MA, USA, 2000. 170

37. M. J. Wooldridge. Semantic issues in the verification of agent communication languages. *J. Autonomous Agents and Multi-Agent Systems*, 3(1):9–31, 2000. 165

Interaction Protocol Engineering

Marc-Philippe Huget[1] and Jean-Luc Koning[2]

[1] Agent ART Group
University of Liverpool
LIVERPOOL L69 7ZF
United Kingdom
M.P.Huget@csc.liv.ac.uk

[2] INPG-CoSy
50, rue Laffemas, BP 54
26902 VALENCE cedex 9, France
Jean-Luc.Koning@esisar.inpg.fr

Abstract. Several methodologies are supplied to multiagent system designers to help them defining their agents and their multiagent systems. These methodologies focus mainly on agents and on multiagent systems and barely consider how to design interaction protocols. A problem could emerge of this lack since interaction protocols are more and more complex. The aim of this article is to present our proposal of interaction protocol engineering which is based on the communication protocol engineering [10]. Interaction protocol engineering allows designers to define protocols from scratch. Our proposal is composed of five stages: analysis, formal description, validation, protocol synthesis and conformance testing.

1 Introduction

Interaction is a key component in multiagent systems which allows agents to exchange information, cooperate and coordinate in order to complete their tasks. One usual method for representing interaction is protocol. An agent interaction protocol is a set of rules that guide the interaction among several agents. For a given state of the protocol only a finite set of messages may be sent or received. If one agent is to use a given protocol, it must agree to conform to such a protocol and obey the various rules. Moreover, it must comply with its semantics. A thorough definition of interaction protocols can be found in [9].

Interaction protocols present similarities with communication protocols used in distributed systems [10]. Actually, early works on interaction in multiagent systems were adaptations of communication protocols. Communication protocols cannot be directly used within the multiagent framework since there are several differences between agents and processes. First of all, agents are autonomous and they are able to join groups to fulfill their tasks [1]. Moreover, messages in multiagent systems are richer than the ones in distributed systems. Agents use Speech Act theory [25] for their interaction. Other differences can be found in [15].

M.-P. Huget (Ed.): Communications in Multiagent Systems, LNAI 2650, pp. 179–193, 2003.

For the past, methodologies have been provided to help multiagent system designers to design agents as well as multiagent systems. Usually, methodologies do not take into consideration the design of interaction protocols. Only Gaia [30] and MAS-CommonKADS [14] can describe how to represent protocols. However, such methodologies are useful since protocols become more and more complex. This is particularly the case in the domain of negotiation or electronic commerce such as in the Fishmarket application [22].

The aim of this paper is to present a proposal for interaction protocol engineering. Such an engineering already exists for communication protocols [10]. Since interaction protocols present some differences with communication protocols, one cannot directly use communication protocol engineering. Our proposal consists in reusing communication protocol engineering when interaction protocols are similar to communication protocols and adapting communication protocol engineering when interaction protocols differ from communication protocols.

Our proposal is composed of five stages going all the way from requirement analysis to conformance testing via formal description, validation and protocol synthesis. We will particularly focus on formal description stage and to a lesser extent on the requirement analysis stage.

The remainder of this chapter is as follows. Section 2 presents the requirement analysis. This stage produces a natural language document which informally describes the purpose of the protocol. Section 3 deals with the formal description of a protocol. We propose a new formal description technique based on the CPDL language in order to add modularity and reusability in interaction protocol design. Section 4 describes the validation stage. Validation is important for checking whether protocols conform to the specifications. In our case, the validation is performed by making use od the SPIN model-checker [11]. Once a protocol has been formally described and checked, it is necessary to generate a program which behaves like the formal description. Section 5 presents this stage. As Holzmann notes it [10], some errors might appear during code generation, thus it is required to check the executable version of the protocol. Section 6 presents the conformance testing stage which checks if the executable version of the protocol conforms to the specifications. Section 7 describes the different tools associated to our proposal of interaction protocol engineering. Finally, Section 8 concludes the paper and presents future directions in our work.

2 The Requirement Analysis Stage

The first stage of our proposal deals with the requirement analysis. This stage defines an informal document which gathers all the features a protocol has to provide. This document also presents the different scenarios in the interaction. At this point, it is also useful to store what good properties have to be present and what bad properties must to be avoid.

Such a description is done through a natural language description. In our proposal, the analysis stage combines the specification of requirement stage and the design stage found in communication protocol engineering. We propose to merge these two stages since it appears to be important to describe together the unfolding and the messages used in this unfolding. We suggest that some analysis document gathers the following fields: the protocol's name, a set of keywords to characterize it, the agents' role involved in the interaction protocol, the agent that will initiate the interaction, some prerequisite, the protocol's function which is a summary of the purpose of the protocol, its behavior, constraints on the interaction, and conditions on termination.

These fields are used at different moments during a protocol's life cycle. Table 1 describes the use of these fields.

Table 1. Use of Analysis Document Fields in Interaction Protocol Engineering

	description	validation	protocol synthesis	conformance testing
name				
keywords				
agents	√			
initiator	√		√	
prerequisite		√	√	
function				
behavior	√	√	√	√
constraints		√	√	√
termination	√	√	√	√

Field like name, keywords and function are not used during this part of the life cycle but they are in the protocol reuse and maintenance stage.

In order to exemplify such analysis stage, let us introduce the agent-based NetBill [4] purchase protocol. The agent-based modeling of this protocol can be abstracted to involve only three agents, one customer, one merchant and a commonly trusted bank. Customers buy e-goods through a web-browser from the merchant. Payment between them is settled by the bank. NetBill protocol is tailored for the payment of electronic goods.

The corresponding analysis document could be the following:

Name: NetBill
Keywords: electronic commerce, secured transaction, purchase, low value e-goods
Agents' role: customer, merchant, bank (NetBill server)
Initiator: customer
Prerequisite: both the client and merchant must have an account at the bank
Function: Let us quote Cox et al.'s definition [4]. *We are building a system called and delivery of low-priced network goods. A customer, represented by a client computer, wishes to buy information from a merchant's server. An account server (the NetBill server), maintains accounts for both customers and merchants, linked to conventional financial institutions. A NetBill transaction transfers information goods from merchant to customer, debiting the*

customer's NetBill account and crediting the merchant's account for the value of the goods.

Behavior: While the previous field summarizes the whole protocol, this one provides a detailed description. The detailed description represents several pages so we can only give here a brief description of the different steps in the protocol.

The NetBill protocol may be decomposed into several steps:

1. The **Price Request Phase** takes place between the customer and the merchant agents. The former requires the price of a good and the latter sends it in return.

2. The **Goods Delivery Phase** takes place again between the customer and the merchant agents. The former requests the electronic good which the latter sends back in an encrypted form.

3. The **Payment Phase** takes place between the three agents role. The customer sends the merchant its signed electronic payment order. The merchant endorses it by including a key and sends it to the bank in order for the financial transfer to take place. Once completed, the bank gives back a payment slip to the merchant who in turn gives it (along with the encrypting key) to the customer.

Constraints: During the various interactions, all the agents must be authenticated

Termination: The customer possesses the electronic good as well as the encryption key, and the financial transactions have been completed or else no financial transaction has taken place

It seems that this stage is not really tackled in the literature neither with communication protocols nor interaction protocols. Generating a complete document for this stage requires practice.

3   The Formal Description Stage

A natural language specification of the requirements is described in the previous stage. As Holzmann notes it, using natural language can carry a misunderstanding of the protocol's properties or its unfolding [10]. Actually, if the specification of requirements is described by one designer and the design stage by another one, the document has to be without misunderstandings on the protocol's unfolding. Moreover, natural language does not make the reuse of such parts of the protocol easy. Finally, this approach does not allow to check whether some properties are present in the protocol. A convenient solution is to use an accurate and rigorous formal tool in order to represent a protocol. Therefore, the formal description stage consists in translating an informal description of a protocol into a formal one.

There does not exist any algorithm nor methodology that help designers write the formal description of a protocol given its specifications. Practice seems to be the only way to correctly handle this stage.

Communication protocol engineering provides several formal description techniques to design protocols: finite state machines [24], Petri nets [16] or languages such as LOTOS, ESTELLE or SDL [28]. Other formal description techniques are only used by interaction protocols such as temporal logic [8] or UML based modeling languages [23] [18] [6].

Reuse in multiagent systems is frequent. As a consequence, interaction protocol designers can claim for such reuse in protocol engineering. Unfortunately, this reuse is not handled by the current formal description techniques. Our proposal is to define a new formal description technique which takes into account reusability as well as modularity and lisibility [17]. A detailed comparison of the current formal description techniques according to a set of criteria such as reusability, modularity or concurrency can be found in [17]. The conclusion drawn shows that no formal description technique presents reusability, modularity and concurrency.

On proposal here is not to consider a protocol as a monolithic object but as an aggregation of objects. Each object performs a little part of the interaction. The objects are called *micro-protocols* in our approach. The language which links the micro-protocols is called CPDL (*Communication Protocol Description Language*).

3.1   Micro-protocols

Micro-protocols are the basic components for designing protocols. They represent actions or particular tasks. They are composed of performatives which are the atomic elements of Speech Act theory [25]. Several other elements can be used within micro-protocols such as loops, decisions, conditions and exceptions.

The following table exemplifies the Contract Net protocol [5] as a micro-protocol.

Name: ContractNet
Parameters' semantics:
A: sender
B: receiver
T: task
P: proposal
R: refuse
Definition:
cfp(A,B,T).token(*).time(10).(not-understood(B,A,T).exit |

refuse(B,A,R).exit | propose(B,A,P)).

(reject-proposal(A,B,R) |

accept-proposal(A,B,P).

exception{cancel=exit}.(failure(B,A,R) | inform(B,A,T)))

Semantics: ContractNet

The field *name* identifies a unique micro-protocol. The field *parameters' semantics* associates a semantics to the parameters used by the communicative acts. This information is useful for designers to know what kind of information has to be sent or received. A second use is to provide a link between our interaction module and agents for retrieving the value of variables (see Section 7). The field *semantics* gives the semantics of the micro-protocol. This information is used during maintenance for reusability. The field *definition* is the main one. It provides the meaning of the micro-protocol. It is composed of communicative acts, loops, time constraints, synchronization or decisions.

In this example, agents use FIPA's ACL [7]. Agent A proposes task T to agents B. The first communicative act *cfp* proposes task T to agents B. The next slot is composed of several pieces of information. One has the predicates *time* and *token* and a decision between several communicative acts: *not-understood*, *refuse* and *propose*. This means that agent A is waiting for several answers[1] from agents B and the communicative act used must be one of the three proposed. The predicate *time* is used to prevent agent A from indefinitely waiting for answers. If the deadline is passed, agent A follows the interaction. The special keyword *exit* is used for two communicative acts. It means that when agents reply with *not-understood* or *refuse*, the interaction is then ended. Agent A answers either by *accept-proposal* if a particular agent won the right to do the task or by *reject-proposal* if a particular agent lost the right to do the task. Agent B performs the task and informs agent A if it succeeds (with an *inform* message) or if it fails (with a *failure* message). We add an exception (the *cancel* message). This exception allows agents to stop the realization of the task at any time.

A detailed description of micro-protocols can be found in [17] and in [12].

3.2   The CPDL Language

Since designers have to handle several micro-protocols, it is necessary to provide a language for aggregating these micro-protocols. This language is called CPDL (*Communication Protocol Description Language*) [17] [12]. A protocol written with CPDL is described as a set of formulae.

CPDL is a description language for interaction protocols based on a finite state automata paradigm, which we have endowed with a set of features coming from other formalisms such as:

- **tokens** in order to synchronize several processes as this can be done with marked Petri nets.
- **timeouts** for the handling of time in the other agents' answers. This notion stems from temporal Petri nets.
- **beliefs** that must be taken into account prior to firing a transition. This notion is present in predicate/transition Petri nets as well as in temporal logic.
- **beliefs** within the protocol's components as it is the case in the AgenTalk application [19].

---

[1] As much as *cfp* message.

A CPDL well-formed formula looks like:

$$\alpha, \{b \in \mathcal{B}\}^\star, loop(\bigwedge p_i) \mapsto \text{micro-protocol}^\star, \beta$$

A CPDL formula corresponds to an edge going from an initial vertex to a final one in a state transition graph. Such an arc is labeled with the micro-protocols, the beliefs and the loop conditions.

α denotes the state the agent is in prior to firing the formula and β denotes the state it will arrive in once the formula has been fired. $\{b \in \mathcal{B}\}^\star$ represents the guard of a formula. Such a guard is a conjunction of first-order predicates that need to be evaluated to true in order for the formula to be used. $\mathcal{B}$ is the set of agent's beliefs. This guard is useful when the set of formulae contains more than one formula with a same initial state. Only one formula can have a guard evaluated to true at a given time, therefore it is fired. This requires that no formula be nondeterministic and that two formulae cannot be fired at the same time. In the current version of CPDL, predicates used for beliefs are defined within the language, and agents have to follow them.

As indicated earlier the loop predicate aims at handling loops within a formula. Its argument is a conjunction of predicates. It loops on the set of micro-protocols involved in the formula while it evaluates to true.

States *init* and *end* are reserved keywords. They correspond to the initial and final states of a protocol. Several final states may exist because several sequences of messages may take place from a single protocol. For example, with the Contract Net protocol [5] whether a bid is accepted or not leads to two different situations; one providing an actual result (accepted-proposal) and one stopping the negotiation process (rejected-proposal).

To exemplify the CPDL language, we present the example of Sian's protocol [26]. There are two kinds of agents involve in this protocol: agents which propose hypothesis and agents which confirm, modify or disconfirm this hypothesis. The principle of this protocol is that agents propose a hypothesis and wait for opinions of other agents. As soon as agents have gathered all the opinions. They decide with an heuristic if this hypothesis has to be considered as a knowledge or if this hypothesis has to be withdrawn.

The protocol in CPDL is as follows:

init $\mapsto$ queryif(A,B,C), A1
A1 $\mapsto$ collect(B,A,V), A2
A2, proposal=withdrawn $\mapsto$ end
A2, proposal=agreed $\mapsto$ inform(A,B,C), end

Agent A asks agents B whether the hypothesis C is true. Then, the interaction steps into state $A1$. Opinions are collected through the micro-protocol *collect*. Then, agent A passes into state $A2$. Agent A decides whether the hypothesis is true or not according to the opinions or a heuristic. If the proposal is true, then the variable *proposal* is set to *agreed* otherwise it is set to *withdrawn*.

If the hypothesis is false, agent A fires the first formula which ends the interaction since there is no micro-protocol and the next state is a final state. If the hypothesis is true, agent A uses the second formula which informs agents B that the hypothesis is now a piece of knowledge.

Conditions on formulas allow designers to get rid of nondeterminism. It is for instance the case for formulas beginning with state $A2$. The value of the variable *proposal* must not be both *withdrawn* and *agreed*.

3.3   The UAMLe Graphical Modeling Language

The CPDL language is a textual language. It is frequently more practical for designers to have a graphical representation of protocols. Such graphical representation for the CPDL language is done through the UAMLe graphical language [18] [17]. This language is an extension of the FIPA graphical modeling language UAML [6] that takes into account the notions of micro-protocols and some additions such as exceptions.

A protocol in UAMLe is rendered as a diagram as shown on Figure 1. Agents are represented by their roles in the interaction. Roles are rendered as lifelines which are denoted by boxes at the top of the diagram with the role name within and the vertical bar anchored to them. Such an approach allows designers to reduce the size of diagrams. It is then not required to represent as many lifelines as we have agents. If designers have n agents which share the same role: client, they only represent one lifeline for the role client. Messages in UAMLe go from a sender role to a receiver role. Constraints on messages in CPDL are present in UAMLe. It is possible to describe messages with cardinality, with constraints, sent in multicast. Readers may refer to [12] and [18] for a detailed description of UAMLe.

CPDL protocols and UAMLe protocols can be designed with the DIP tool (see Section 7).

4   The Validation Stage

Formal description of protocols does not avoid errors and some requested behaviors can be absent. Interaction protocol designers have two verification techniques to check if good properties are present, if wrong properties are missing and if the formal description conforms to the specifications. A first technique uses the notion of graph and defines the property to be checked as a property on a graph; this is called reachability analysis. For instance, checking the termination corresponds to checking whether the final states of the graph are reachable. The graph is obtained by a depth-first search of the protocol. A second technique defines a model of the protocol and a property defined by a temporal logic formula; this is called model checking [3]. Model checking tests if the model satisfies the temporal logic formula. The model of the protocol is simply the graph obtained during reachability analysis.

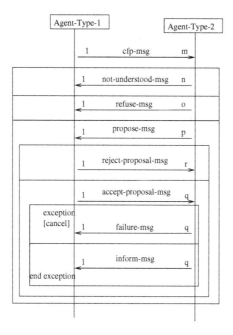

Fig. 1. Contract Net Protocol in UAMLe.

Reachability analysis is rather used to check structural properties such as deadlock freeness, liveliness, termination or acceptance cycle freeness. Model checking is a more powerful tool and allows designers to check properties related to the function of the protocol.

In our proposal of interaction protocol engineering, we use the model checker SPIN associated to the language PROMELA [10] [11]. We provide an algorithm for translating CPDL representations into Promela [12]. In a word, this algorithm unfolds micro-protocols into formulae and builds a graph based on this unfolding. Special cases appear when micro-protocols use constraints, loops or exceptions since several transitions have to be inserted whether constraints are valid or not. Such an example of validation can be found in [12].

The translation is performed by our TAP tool (see Section 7). This tool also allows designers to perform a reachability analysis of CPDL formulae. Moreover, it is possible to translate CPDL formulae into Petri nets [12].

5   The Protocol Synthesis Stage

By now, a designer will have a formal description of a protocol and a validation of it. It is time to realize an operational version of such formal protocols. Describing an operational version of a protocol is called protocol synthesis or more traditionally in software engineering, forward engineering.

A usual approach for protocol synthesis consists in generating a program which behaves like the formal description of the protocol [10] [21]. This program contains two levels of decisions. The external level represents states in the interaction. The internal level corresponds to messages to any interaction states. This program is built in a two step process. The first step uses an automatic algorithm [2]. This algorithm derives a program skeleton which only contains the protocol transitions. Actually, it is impossible for a program to derive the transitions' semantics. Generally, this semantics needs to conform to complex standards. The semantics is added by hand in a second step.

The downside of this approach is that errors can occur during these two steps. Deadlocks can arise. Moreover, some properties defined in the analysis document can disappear. For these reasons, we propose a second approach based on an interaction module. This approach stems from the fact that no errors can occur if agents directly execute the formal description. For executing a formal description, agents need a mechanism. This mechanism is called an interaction module (see Section 7). The interaction module manages the interaction within agents. It sends and receives the messages and keeps the interaction contexts updated.

The main advantage of this approach is to reduce the work for designers. They have less effort to do to implement interaction within agents. However, if agents use just a few protocols, this interaction module may overweight agents.

6   The Conformance Testing Stage

The previous stages in this proposal of interaction protocol engineering offer the possibility to formally design, to check some properties and to synthesize an operational version of the protocol. As noted by Löffler and Serhrouchni [20] and Holzmann [10], the translation from a formal description of a protocol into an operational one can insert errors and misconceptions and some features described in the specification of requirements can be absent. The conformance testing stage checks whether the operational version of the protocol still verifies the properties defined in the specification of requirements and, of course, checks the absence of wrong properties.

The conformance testing stage differs from the validation one in that it checks properties on an operational version whereas the validation stage checks properties on a formal version of the protocol.

The Conformance Testing test suite is derived from the formal description as shown on Figure 2. Designers take the formal description denoted by s on the figure. They generate a program denoted by i. This implementation will be checked by the conformance testing. The generation of the test suite denoted by Ts is done as follows. Designers track the state they want to check. The path to this state is then known. Designers note what are the outgoing messages for this state. The remaining of the test deals with the executable version of the protocol. The path to the state is applied to the executable version then designers test if the outgoing messages for the state of this executable version match the outgoing messages of the formal description. If it is the case then the test succeeds else the test fails.

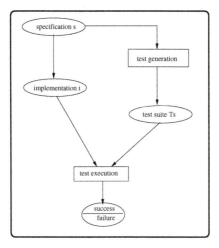

Fig. 2. Conformance Testing Algorithm

Obviously, if designers use the interaction module, they do not need to apply the conformance testing since no code has been generated.

Such an example of conformance testing can be found in [12].

7   Tools for Interaction Protocol Engineering

An interaction protocol engineering cannot be considered complete without tools to help designers. In the context of our proposal of interaction protocol engineering. We propose several tools working either for the design or the execution phase:

- the DIP tool for the requirement analysis stage, the formal description stage and the protocol synthesis stage.
- the TAP tool for the validation stage
- the CTP tool for the conformance testing stage
- the interaction module for the management of interaction within agents
- the message server for the management of messages between agents

Let us briefly describe the purpose of these tools.

The DIP (*Designing Interaction Protocols*) tool is a tool used during three stages: requirement analysis, formal description and protocol synthesis (see Figure 3). DIP allows designers to store their analysis document. As a consequence, it is easier for designers to design protocols and to have a look on the analysis document. The main activity of DIP is the formal description stage. DIP accepts several formal description techniques: CPDL, UAMLe, UAML and PDN. The two first are our proposal. UAML is FIPA's proposal. In these three cases, it is possible to handle and to modify protocols. PDN is FIPA's proposal and looks like a tree structure. PDN is only a visual representation that one cannot edit. It is easy to change of formal description technique during protocol design like starting with UAML and completing the protocol with UAMLe. The only limitation lies in the differences between the formal description techniques: UAMLe encompasses exceptions but not UAML. The last task of DIP is protocol synthesis. DIP generates a set of Java classes for the protocols.

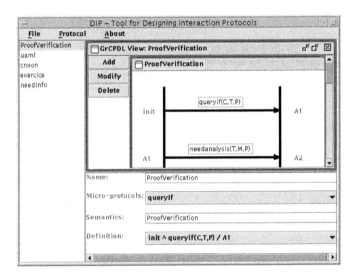

Fig. 3. DIP Tool

The TAP (*Testing Agents and Protocols*) tool intervenes during the validation stage. Several features are supplied in the tool. It is possible to do a reachability analysis of a CPDL representation of a protocol. Since reachability analysis is not enough for the validation, TAP translates CPDL representations as a PROMELA program and makes use of SPIN for model checking protocols. The last feature of TAP is the translation of CPDL protocols into Petri nets. This feature is only given in case designers want to get benefit of Petri net tools.

The CTP (*Conformance Testing Protocols*) tool realizes the conformance testing of protocols. It uses the algorithm defined in Section 6.

These three tools take place during the design phase and cover all the design cycle. The following two tools deal with the execution phase of protocols. The main one is the interaction module [13]. This interaction module manages the interaction within the agents. It handles protocols and interactions and matches incoming messages with expected messages. As long as the interaction module does not need any information from the agents, it operates in an autonomous way. For instance, if the values of various variables are known, the interaction module does not need to request the agents each time. The interaction module queries its agent when a decision between several outgoing messages has to be made or when the value of some variables used in the outgoing messages are unknown. The aim of this interaction module is to ease the way to implement the interaction within agents.

The second tool for the execution is less advanced. It is a message server. Our message server is a RMI object accessible to all agents. It manages incoming and outgoing messages and stores messages till the agents request them. The message server is able to handle mobile agents and the modification of addresses.

8   Conclusion and Future Work

Up to now, no thorough methodology has been put forward for the design of interaction protocols. Current multiagent methodologies prefer to focus on agents or on multiagent systems. The aim of this chapter is to present a proposal about interaction protocol engineering. Our proposal is composed of five stages: requirement analysis, formal description, validation, protocol synthesis and conformance testing. This proposal covers the design cycle of protocols. We have added several tools to help designers.

This proposal offers several contributions to the interaction protocol engineering:

1. An analysis document for specifying the requirements for the protocol. This document is organized as fields.
2. A modular and reusable formal description technique. CPDL also embodies the notion of exceptions.
3. An interaction module for the management of interaction within agents. It helps designers during the protocol synthesis stage. With this interaction module, designers no longer have to specifically implement interaction within the agents.
4. An interaction protocol engineering which covers the whole design cycle from the specification of requirements to the validation of the executable version of the protocol.

Our proposal of interaction protocol engineering has successfully been applied to the tele-teaching project Baghera[2] [29]. It helps designers design protocols. Moreover, our interaction module is used within agents to handle interaction between agents. This project is valuable for our work since it enables us to find errors within the interaction module which gives us a feedback on how to improve our proposal of interaction protocol engineering.

A second example of use of our interaction module is in the project of distributed agenda management [27].

---

[2] http://www-baghera.imag.fr

References

1. B. Bauer, J. P. Muller, and J. Odell. An extension of UML by protocols for multia-gent interaction. In *International Conference on MultiAgent Systems (ICMAS'00)*, pages 207–214, Boston, Massachussetts, july, 10-12 2000. 179

2. P.-Y. M. Chu. *Towards Automating Protocol Synthesis and Analysis*. PhD thesis, Ohio State University, 1989. 188

3. E. Clarke, O. Grumberg, and D. Peled. *Model Checking*. MIT Press, 2000. 186

4. B. Cox, J. Tygar, and M. Sirbu. Netbill security and transaction protocol. In *Proceedings of the First USENIX Workshop in Electronic Commerce*, july 1995. 181, 181

5. R. Davis and R. G. Smith. Negotiation as a metaphor for distributed problem-solving. *Artificial Intelligence*, 20:63–109, 1983. 183, 185

6. FIPA. *Specification: Agent Communication Language*. Foundation for Intelli-gent Physical Agents, http://www.fipa.org/spec/fipa99spec.htm, September 1999. Draft-2. 183, 186

7. FIPA. *Specification*. Foundation for Intelligent Physical Agents, http://www.fipa.org/repository/fipa2000.html, 2000. 184

8. M. Fisher and M. Wooldridge. Specifying and executing protocols for cooperative action. In *International Working Conference on Cooperating Knowledge-Based Systems (CKBS-94)*, Keele, 1994. 183

9. M. Greaves, H. Holmback, and J. Bradshaw. What is a conversation policy? In *Autonomous Agents'99 Special Workshop on Conversation Policies*, 1999. 179

10. G. J. Holzmann. *Design and Validation of Computer Protocols*. Prentice-Hall, 1991. 179, 179, 180, 180, 182, 187, 188, 188

11. G. J. Holzmann. The model checker spin. *IEEE Transactions on Software Engi-neering*, 23(5), May 1997. 180, 187

12. M.-P. Huget. *Une ingnierie des protocoles d'interaction pour les systmes multi-agents*. PhD thesis, Universit Paris 9 Dauphine, June 2001. 184, 184, 186, 187, 187, 187, 189

13. M.-P. Huget. Design agent interaction as a service to agents. In M.-P. Huget, F. Dignum, and J.-L. Koning, editors, *AAMAS Workshop on Agent Communica-tion Languages and Conversation Policies (ACL2002)*, Bologna, Italy, July 2002. 190

14. C. Iglesias, M. Garrijo, J. Gonzales, and J. Velasco. Design of multi-agent sys-tem using mas-commonkads. In Springer-Verlag, editor, *Proceedings of ATAL 98, Workshop on Agent Theories, Architectures, and Languages*, volume LNAI 1555, pages 163–176, Paris, France, July 1998. 180

15. N. R. Jennings and M. Wooldridge. Agent-oriented software engineering. In J. Bradshaw, editor, *Handbook in Agent Technology*. MIT Press, 2000. 179

16. K. Jensen. *High-Level Petri Nets, Theory and Application*. Springer-Verlag, 1991. 183

17. J.-L. Koning and M.-P. Huget. A semi-formal specification language dedicated to interaction protocols. In H. Kangassalo, H. Jaakkola, and E. Kawaguchi, editors, *Information Modelling and Knowledge Bases XII*, Frontiers in Artificial Intelligence and Applications. IOS Press, Amsterdam, 2001. 183, 183, 184, 184, 186

18. J.-L. Koning, M.-P. Huget, J. Wei, and X. Wang. Extended modeling languages for interaction protocol design. In *Proceedings of Agent-Oriented Software Engineering (AOSE 01)*, Montreal, Canada, May 2001. 183, 186, 186

19. K. Kuwabara, T. Ishida, and N. Osato. AgenTalk: Describing multiagent coordination protocols with inheritance. In *Seventh IEEE International Conference on Tools with Artificial Intelligence*, pages 460–465, Herndon, Virginia, November 1995. 184

20. S. Löffler and A. Serhrouchni. Protocol design: from specification to implementation. In *5th Open Workshop for High-Speed Networks*, Mar. 1996. 188

21. M. Narasimhan. An object oriented framework for composing communication protocols. Master's thesis, Department of Computing and Information Sciences, Kansas State University, Manhattan, Kansas, january 1997. 188

22. P. Noriega. *Agent mediated auctions: The Fishmarket Metaphor*. PhD thesis, Universitat Autnoma de Barcelona, 1998. 180

23. J. Odell, H. V. D. Parunak, and B. Bauer. Representing agent interaction protocols in UML. In P. Ciancarini and M. Wooldridge, editors, *Proceedings of First International Workshop on Agent-Oriented Software Engineering*, Limerick, Ireland, june, 10 2000. Springer-Verlag. 183

24. A. Salomaa. *Theory of Automata*. Pergamon Press, 1969. 183

25. J. Searle. *Speech Acts: An Essay in the Philosophy of Language*. Cambridge University Press, Cambridge, 1969. 179, 183

26. S. S. Sian. Adaptation based on cooperative learning in multi-agent systems. In Y. Demazeau and J.-P. Mller, editors, *Decentralized AI*, volume II, pages 257–272, Amsterdam, The Netherlands, 1991. Elsevier Science Publishers B.V. 185

27. J. L. Tavares da Silva and Y. Demazeau. Distributed agenda management through decentralised vowels co-ordination approach. In *8th Iberoamerican Conference on Artificial Intelligence (IBERAMIA'02)*, 2002. under submission. 191

28. K. J. Turner. *Using Formal Description Techniques - An Introduction to Estelle, LOTOS and SDL*. John Wiley and Sons, Ltd, 1993. 183

29. C. Webber and S. Pesty. A two-level multi-agent architecture for a distance learning environment. In E. B. Costa, editor, *ITS 2002/Workshop on Architectures and Methodologies for Building Agent-based Learning Environments*, pages 26–38, 2002. 191

30. M. Wooldridge, N. R. Jennings, and D. Kinny. The gaia methodology for agent-oriented analysis and design. *Journal of Autonomous Agents and Multi-Agent Systems*, 3(3):285–312, 2000. 180

An Organisational Approach to the Design of Interaction Protocols [*]

Juan Manuel Serrano and Sascha Ossowski

Artificial Intelligence Group
School of Engineering
University Rey Juan Carlos
{jserrano,s.ossowski}@escet.urjc.es
http://www.ia.escet.urjc.es

Abstract. Modern ACLs, such as FIPA ACL, provide standardised catalogues of performatives and protocols, designed as general purpose languages to ensure interoperability among agent systems. However, recent work reports a need for new ad-hoc sets of performatives and protocols in certain contexts, showing that FIPA ACL does not support adequately all relevant types of interactions. In this paper we first present a formal model that relates performatives and protocols, to the organisation of MAS. Then, the FIPA IPL is analysed from the perspective of this formal model and a principled method for the *design* of the IPL of a particular MAS is developed, which account for both, reusability and expressiveness. Finally, we illustrate our approach by an example in the domain of online stock brokering.

1 Introduction

Agent Communication Languages (ACLs) are considered to be one of the most relevant components of todays Multiagent Systems (MASs). Indeed, agents could be just conceived as software components which interact by means of an ACL. Traditionally, as established by the "de facto" standard KQML [5], ACLs make reference to two major concepts: performatives, which express the types of communicative actions (CAs), or "illocutionary actions" in the sense of speech act theory [11], performed by agents in the sending of some message, and interaction protocols (IPs), which codify prototypical patterns of message exchange. The ACL proposed by the Foundation of Intelligent Physical Agents (FIPA), named FIPA ACL, follows this scheme and comprises two major components: a catalogue of communicative actions (FIPA CAL) and a library of interaction protocols (FIPA IPL).

Similarly, organisational models (OMs) are proposed by current methodologies for MAS development as one of the central components in the analysis of this type of systems[15,3]. Up to some respect, these models already acknowledge the link between organisation and ACL: most of them make explicit reference

---

[*] Research sponsored by MCyT, project TIC2000-1370-C04-01, and by CAM, project 07T/0011/2000

M.-P. Huget (Ed.): Communications in Multiagent Systems, LNAI 2650, pp. 194–208, 2003.

to CAs and IPs as an essential part of the interaction within an organisation. However, their primary concern is usually the organisational model, whereas the communication language plays a subordinate, facilitating role. In [12], we proposed a method for the systematic analysis and design of communicative action catalogues for some MAS, explicitly driven by the organisational model of the application. This paper makes a similar attempt with respect to the library of interaction protocols.

More specifically, we tackle the practical problem of how to build expressive and reusable catalogues of protocols for the ACL of a *particular* multiagent applications, setting out from organisational concepts such as *social interaction* and *roles*. In order to do so, we will pay special attention to two major relationships between roles: roles can be *specialised*, and roles may *play* other roles [7]. On the other hand, the IPL design method proposed in this paper draws upon the ACL design method proposed in [12].

The paper is structured as follows: In Section 2 we summarise the RICA meta-model, a UML-based formal framework that defines an integrated view of OMs and ACLs, and show how the different elements of FIPA ACL can be structured according to this model. Section 3 proposes a re-design of FIPA IPL from the point of view of the RICA metamodel and the role model implicitly supported by FIPA ACL. Section 4 summarises our IPL design proposal, which will be illustrated by the example of a MAS that provides financial advice to investors in the domain of online brokering. Finally, we compare our approach to related work, and discuss future lines of research.

2   Organisational Structure of ACLs

In order to model the link between communicational and organisational components of MAS, the conceptual framework needs to be identified first. Respecting organisational terms, we draw from Ferber and Gutknecht's Agent/Group/Role metamodel [4], that highlights *Agent, Group* and *Role*, as organisational key concepts. As far as the concept of *Role* is concerned, it is customary to define it in terms of the functionality or behaviour associated to some type of agent, within an organisational context [4,15,3]. We employ the term "interaction" in the same way as "protocol" is used in [15]: it refers to the type of *Social Interaction* in which some group of roles participates, specified in terms of the *purpose* of that interaction, rather than to prototypical patterns of message exchange. We reserve the word "protocol" for this latter sense. The Role/Interaction/Communicative Action (RICA) metamodel [12] defines our view of the interrelation between these organisational concepts, in terms of UML class relations. Figure 1 shows the most relevant relations of this model with respect to the purpose of this paper. **Self** Associations. The usual generalisation and specialisation relationships within classes also apply to the classes of the RICA metamodel, particularly to agent roles [7]. In addition, the RICA metamodel includes the usual *plays*-relation between roles [3]. In the sequel, we will see that these self-associations are crucial for a consistent definition of the interrelation between communicative and organisational concepts.

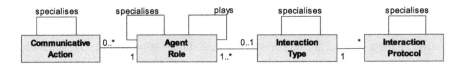

Fig. 1. UML diagram of the RICA metamodel

***Role/Communicative Action* Association.** In general, both the communicative and non-communicative behaviour , together with a set of rights or permissions, are necessary to fully specify a role [15]. As we are concerned with the interplay between organisational and communicative concepts, our standpoint in this paper is similar to [3], where agent interaction is purely dialogic and, consequently, roles are exclusively defined in terms of a set of illocutionary actions. An intelligent tutoring agent, for instance, may request students to perform some exercise, inform them about the examination day, etc. So, its role may be characterised by CAs such as FIPA *request, inform-ref*, etc.

Of course, there are roles in other application domains which will also issue *inform-ref* and *request* messages. This suggests the existence of more generic roles, call them *Requester* and *Information Provider* respectively, that the intelligent tutor and many others may play. Thus, although requests are performed by many different roles, we consider this CA (and others, such as FIPA *cancel, request-when* and *request-whenever*), to be exclusively *characteristic* to the requester role. The one-to-many Role/CA association of the RICA metamodel accounts for this relation between a CA and its *only* characteristic role. Table 1 shows a partition of the FIPA CAL in terms of the characteristic roles of their performatives.

Table 1. Classification Scheme for the FIPA ACL

FIPA ACL				
Message Exchange	Action Performing I	Information Exchange	Action Performing II	Brokering
FIPA CAL				
Communicator	Requester I	Information Seeker	Requester II	Brokering Requester
inform	*request*	*query-if*	*cfp*	*propagate*
confirm	*request-when*	*query-ref*	*accept-proposal*	*proxy*
disconfirm	*request-whenever*	*subscribe*	*reject-proposal*	
not-understood	*cancel*			
	Requestee I	Information Provider	Requestee II	Broker
	agree	*inform-if*	*propose*	
	refuse	*inform-ref*		
	failure			
FIPA IPL				
	Request-Prot.	*Query-Prot.*	*Propose-Prot.*	*Brokering-Prot.*
	Request-When-Prot.	*Subscribe-Prot.*	*ContractNet-Prot.*	*Recruiting-Prot.*
			IteratedContractNet-Prot.	
			English-Auction-Prot.	
			Dutch-Auction-Prot.	

If a role is a specialisation of another, the former obviously inherits the attributes of the latter, and in particular all the CAs that characterise the super-role. The sub-role can (but must not) add new illocutionary actions to the catalogue of the super-role, or may *specialise* some of these CAs. For instance, the FIPA *query-ref* message type is a specialisation of the FIPA *request* CA, obtained by overloading its propositional content. This goes in line with a specialisation relationship between the corresponding characteristic roles: the *Requester* and *Information Seeker*. The other specialisation relationships, which can be identified within the FIPA CAL, are shown in figure 2.

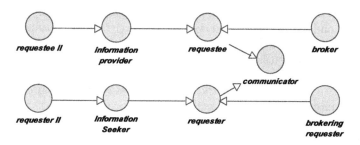

Fig. 2. Role model Implicit in the FIPA CAL

***Role/Social Interaction* Association.** Obviously, several roles may participate in a certain type of social interaction. For instance, the FIPA Requester and Requestee roles participate in an interaction about *Action Performing*, and *Exchange of Information* is a social interaction jointly performed by the FIPA Information Seeker and Information Provider roles. Table 1 shows the other types of social interaction supported by the FIPA ACL.

Still, it is also customary in the organisational literature to acknowledge that roles may participate in several types of interaction [4]. To account for this multiple cardinality, we make use of the *plays-* relation between roles. For instance, an intelligent tutor may both, exchange information and interact with the students regarding action performing. In this example, the intelligent tutor *indirectly* participates in both types of interaction while playing the Requester and Information Provider roles, respectively. The *Role/Social Interaction* relationship of the RICA metamodel accounts for the *only* characteristic social interaction in which some role(s) may *directly* participate.

Furthermore note that, as before, the specialisation relationship between roles also induces a specialisation relationship between the corresponding types of social interaction.

***Social Interaction/Protocol* Association.** This one-to-many relation account for that fact that usually *several* protocols are associated to the same topic, i.e. type of social interaction. For instance, the FIPA-Query-Protocol and FIPA-Subscribe-Protocol are prototypical patterns of information exchange among agents. Table 1 shows a partition of the FIPA IPL in terms of the types of social interaction supported by the FIPA ACL.

3   An Organisational Perspective on the FIPA IPL

As explained in section 3, the RICA meta-model prescribes the specialisation of protocols corresponding to generic types of social interactions. This section proposes a re-design of the protocols included in FIPA IPL, which takes advantage of this specialisation mechanism. The proposal will be illustrated taking into account the FIPA-Query-Protocol and FIPA-Request-Protocol, corresponding to the *Information Exchange* and *Action Performing I* interaction types, respectively.

The generalisation relationship described in figure 2, between the *Information Seeker* and the *Requester*, shows that the exchange of information can be considered as a particular case of interaction about action performing, where the action to be performed is to inform the requester about some fact. Therefore, information exchange protocols like the FIPA-Query-Protocol, could be defined based upon an specialisation of the FIPA-Request-Protocol. Moreover, action performing interactions, and any other interaction type, are particular cases of message exchange. Thus, the FIPA-Request-Protocol could be defined as a refinement of some protocol for message exchange (not defined by FIPA). The protocols for each type of social interaction will be defined in terms of their only characteristic types of CAs, which are described in table 1.

UML State diagrams is the chosen formalism to represent the interaction protocols, which differs from AUML– the one used by FIPA IPL. Moreover, the protocols are defined in accordance to [1], where state transitions are triggered by messages from both roles, and states are considered to be *interaction states*, and not *agent states*. The labels used for each role participating in the interaction, are defined in a simple UML *note* element. Figures 3, 4 and 5 show the corresponding protocols.

Message Exchange. As described in figure 3, any kind of interaction may be in two states: a normal one in which interaction flows smoothly, and one in which normal interaction has been interrupted, because of a message *not understood* by some party in the interaction. Then, the interaction will enter a clarification state. Exit from this state may take two alternative courses: either agents come back to the normal interaction state, or they finish the interaction.

Action Performing. Two different states can be identified in interactions about action performing (see figure 4). The first one is entered whenever the requester issues a request, and represents the situation in which this request is being evaluated by the requestee. Upon an agreement of the requestee, the interaction would enter into a state where the requester is waiting for the performance and the requestee is committed to it.

There are two major differences between this protocol and the FIPA-Request-Protocol. First, it might not be necessary to explicitly send an *agree* message in case that the requester grants the performance, if the action is to be performed immediately. Second, once the action has been performed, it may not be necessary to inform the requester that the action was successfully or unsuccess-

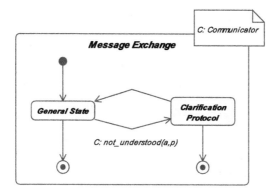

Fig. 3. Message-Exchange Interaction Protocol

fully performed, if the action performance was made publicly. In that case, the interaction would finish without any need of sending a message.

It should be noted that the state diagram shown in figure 4 does not represent the whole protocol of the action performing interaction. Rather, this state diagram should be considered as an specialisation of the *Message Exchange* state named *General State*. Thus, the whole protocol for action performing would include the *Clarification Protocol* state as well. In this way, the specialisation of protocols proceeds by adding new states and transitions to the generic protocol, similarly to [8].

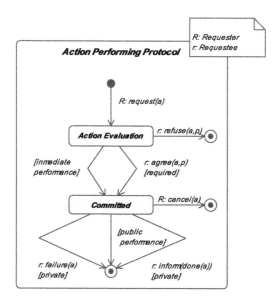

Fig. 4. Action Performing Interaction Protocol

Information Exchange. Figure 5 explains the FIPA-Query-Protocol as an specialisation of the Action-Performing-Protocol described previously. It has the same substates of the former, plus a number of new transitions. The first one, from the initial state to the *action evaluation* state, shows that the interaction may start with a *query-ref* message. As this type of CA is a kind of request, this transition overrides the *request* message which initiates action performing interactions. Last, the protocol may finish with the requestee *informing* the requester about some fact. This transition specialises the Action-Performing-Protocol transition corresponding to a public performance of the requested action. On the other hand, no new transitions from the *action evaluation* to the *committed* states are needed, besides those found in the generic protocol.

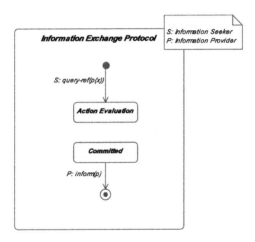

Fig. 5. Information Exchange Interaction Protocol

4   Organisational Design of the MAS IPL

Once the close relation between OMs and an ACLs is formalised, the question arises as to how an Interaction Protocol Library (IPL) for a *particular* Multiagent System (MAS) can be defined. In this section we provide a design method for MAS IPL based on the RICA metamodel. For this purpose, we set out from the general ACL design method proposed in [12].

This method is driven by an initial ("a priori") organisational model which specifies the domain-dependent roles and types of interaction played by the different classes of agents in the MAS. The other major input to the design method is the existing FIPA IPL. As a result, the MAS IPL is obtained, structured in terms of the types of interaction and roles included in a *refined* version of the initial OM. The design method is structured in four major steps:

Step 1: Collecting Sample Dialogues. The first step for obtaining the communication language is to collect natural language dialogues for the different domain-dependent types of interaction.

Step 2: Pragmatic Analysis. The second step is a pragmatic analysis, attempting to identify the types of CAs that best describe the communicative behaviour of the agents in the dialogues, by means of natural-language illocutionary expressions. Additionally, the particular patterns of message exchange for each dialogue will be also considered. UML sequence diagrams might be used to document these patterns.

Step 3: Reuse Analysis. In this step the preliminary set of natural-language speech act verbs is analysed in order to identify their artificial counterparts in the FIPA CAL. The same is performed with respect to the preliminary patterns of interaction and the FIPA IPL.

Step 4: Extension Design. The previous step may have uncovered limitations of the FIPA ACL to account for the different kinds of illocutionary expressions and/or dialogue patterns that are characteristic for the particular MAS. This step will provide a formalisation of the new interaction protocols and communicative actions, on the basis of a refinement of the initial organisational model.

5   The IPL of an Online Stock Broker: An Organisational Design

This section illustrates our IPL design method with an example in the domain of the online brokerage industry. More specifically, we focus on the design of the IPL for a kind of personal assistant, which extends an Online Stock Broker with advisory capabilities. The goal of the Online Stock Broker would be that investors choose the most suitable investments to their personal profile and stock portfolio.

In order to design the *Online Broker IPL*, we depart from a simplified organisational model of the application. Figure 6 shows this model, where the online stock broker and investor classes are identified. These agents play several roles as they participate in three different types of interaction: the exchange of financial information, the trading of stocks and the financial advisement of the investor.

Step 1: Collecting Sample Dialogues

Table 2 shows a natural language dialogue between some broker and investor, whose topic is the trading of a particular stock. The dialogue has been artificially created in order to cover the three types of interaction in which broker and investor participate (distinct levels of gray allow to identify their corresponding subdialogues, numbered I, II and III). Thus, the dialogue starts with a conversation about the trading of stocks (I), but it is immediately followed by an advisory interaction about the suitability of the trading order (II). The advisory dialogue is also interrupted by a short message exchange concerning the request of information about the stock being traded (III). Then, the conversation focuses again on advisory matters (II), and finishes by taking up again the theme of stock trading (I).

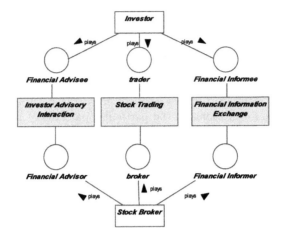

Fig. 6. Initial Organisational Model for the Online Broker Application

Table 2. Sample Dialogue between the Online Stock Broker and the Investor

(1) I-	I would like to buy 500 shares of TERRA
(2) B-	Be careful, this is a risky order
(3) I-	Can you explain why?
(4) B-	Because this stock has a high level of volatility
(5) I-	Which is exactly the volatility value of TERRA?
(6) B-	40%
(7) I-	Which stock would you recommend?
(8) B-	Some of these stocks might be suitable for you: S1, S2, ...
(9) I-	Could you recommend me a specific order for S1?
(10) B-	An order with 50 or 100 shares (current price per share: 10E)
(11) I-	Forget the initial order. I would like to buy 100 shares of S1
(12) B-	Ok....

(I) Stock Trading (II) Financial Advice (III) Exchange of Financial Information

Step 2: Pragmatic Analysis

In the next step, a preliminary version of the Online Broker CAL, including the English illocutionary expressions which describes the communicative behaviour of the investor and broker in the sample dialogue of table 2, will be obtained. For instance, the advisory interaction (subdialogue II) starts with the broker *warning* the investor *not to* request that order, and the investor *requesting* the broker *for an explanation* of that warning.

On the other hand, figure 7 shows a UML sequence diagram describing the flow of messages between the investor class and the broker roles. The messages are those preliminary extracted from the sample dialogues. This sequence diagram and many others, should be input to the design of the Online Broker IPL.

Step 3: Reuse Analysis

There is a number of illocutionary expressions included in the preliminary catalogue which does not show relevant differences in meaning with respect to some performatives of the FIPA CAL (cf. [14] and [6], respectively). For instance, the *query* and *inform* illocutionary verbs in subdialogue III corresponds to the *query-ref* and *inform-ref* performatives of FIPA. Thus, the information provider role implicit in the FIPA CAL can be considered a super-type of the financial informer. Indeed, these two roles are identical if we consider only their pragmatic competence. However, they are different roles as the financial informer has specific non-communicative competences and rights [15], such as the access to financial databases to provide the required stock information. Analogously, the FIPA requestee role is a super-type of the Broker role.

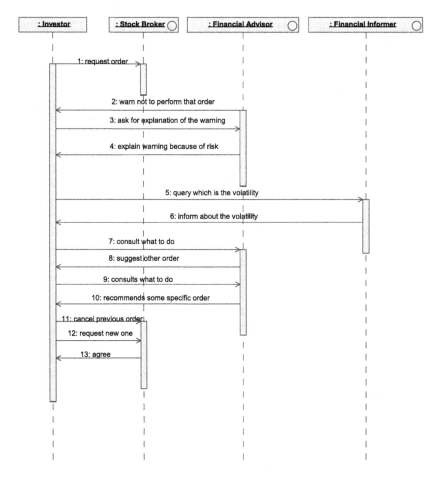

Fig. 7. Preliminary Sequence Diagrams for the Online Stock Broker IPL

Step 4: Extension Design

On the contrary, most of the English speech act expressions identified in sub-dialogue II are highly specific and there are no close correspondences between them and any of the FIPA performatives. Of course, *suggest* could be defined as *informing* about the possibility to do some action in order to reach some goal, and so the FIPA *inform* performative could be used instead of a new *suggest* performative. However, as we advocate the specification of expressive ACLs, we will consider the formalisation of these illocutionary expressions supporting financial advisory interactions. As this is a type of interaction not covered by FIPA ACL, we will proceed by refining the initial OM of the application.

Step 4.1: Organisational Model Refinement Suggestions and recommen-dations are *characteristic* types of CA for the abstract advisory role. Thus, the financial advisor can be considered as an specialisation of the advisory role. As part of the communicative competence of the financial advisor, we also found expressions such as *warn not to* and *explain*. The first one can also be considered to denote a characteristic type of CA of the advisory role. The other one gives rise to the *explainer*, a new role abstracted away from the financial advisor. Con-cerning the investor, the counterparts to the explainer and advisory roles will be the *explainee* and *advisee* roles.

On the other hand, as generic advisors also needs explanatory capabilities to reach their goals, the explainer can be considered a role that the advisor may *play*. This relationship between the explainer and the advisor is not of a gen-eralisation/specialisation nature, as the advisor will not be an explainer during its whole life-cycle, only sometimes. With regard to the interaction protocol, the advisory IP is not an specialisation of the explanatory one. Rather, there will be some points in the advisory protocol that will enact the explanatory protocol.

In summary, figure 8 shows the extended role model for the stock broker class, where abstract FIPA roles identified in Step 3 are represented in light gray, and the new explanatory and advisory abstract roles in a dark gray. A dashed line separates those roles and classes which are domain-dependent, from those potentially reusable such as the FIPA Roles, the explainer and the advisor.

Step 4.2: CAL Refinement The refinement of the preliminary Online Broker CAL is shown in table 3, which is structured according to the two FIPA-types of interaction identified in step 3, plus the explanatory and advisory interactions of step 4.1. The design of the explanatory and advisory subcatalogues is the subject of another paper [13]. In the following, we will concentrate on the refinement of the Online Broker IPL.

Step 4.3: IPL Refinement Protocols for the exchange of financial information and stock trading can be reused from the FIPA IPL. However, the interaction between the online broker and the investor concerning financial advice and ex-planatory dialogues require the design of new protocols. These protocols are shown in figures 9 and 10.

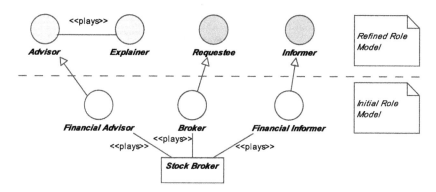

Fig. 8. Extended Role Model for the Stock Broker Class

Table 3. Communicative Act Library for the Online Broker Application

Online-Broker ACL			
Stock Trading	Financial Inf. Exchange	Financial Advice	
Action Performing I	Information Exchange	Advice Giving	Explanatory Dialogues
CAL			
Requestee	Information Provider	Advisor	Explainer
agree ...	inform ...	warn notify recommend ...	explain-inferred-fact explain-observed-fact ...
Requester	Information Seeker	Advisee	Explainee
request ...	query-ref ...	consult ...	request-for-explanation ...
IPL			
FIPA-Request Protocol ...	FIPA-Query Protocol ...	Advisory Protocol ...	Explanatory Protocol ...

FIPACALReuse   PotentiallyReusable

Explanatory Protocol. Explanatory interactions are parameterised with respect to some proposition to be explained, and start with a *request-for-explanation* message. The explainer may have come to know that proposition either by: (1) directly observing that fact from some observation source (*explain-observed-fact* message), or (2) by inferring this fact from a set of premises $p_1, p_2, ...$ and a knowledge base consisting of the set of propositions $k_1, k_2, ...$ (*explain-inferred-fact* message). In this latter case, the explainee may request further explanation of some premise p_i.

Advisory Protocol. Advisory interactions might be initiated both by the advisor and the advisee. In the first case, the advisor may warn the user not to perform some action s/he intends to perform, which may have as a consequence some fact which is against some goal of the user. On the contrary, the interaction may also start with the advisor notifying the user that some event makes possible the achievement of some goal. In the second case, the advisee may start an advisory interaction by consulting the advisor about the best way to achieve some goal p.

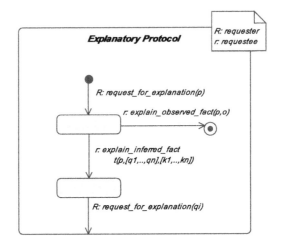

Fig. 9. Explanatory Interaction Protocol

In this latter case, the interaction enters a state parameterised by the goal to be achieved by the user. The interaction may enter this state from a warning or a notification as well. In case of a warning, the user may consult the advisor the best way to achieve the goal q', which was the reason to plan the performance of action a. In case of a notification, the user may just consult the advisor the best way to achieve the notified fact. The consultation might be answered with a suggestion or a recommendation of the advisor, to perform some action. This may cause further consultations about how to perform that action.

In this way, this protocols might be interleaved as the online broker switch roles between the advisor and the explainer. Thus, in the sample dialogue, the advisor switch to the explainer role (and therefore, to the explanatory interaction), whenever it receives a *request-for-explanation* message. When this interaction is finished, it may continue the conversation about financial advisement.

6   Discussion

This paper has described a method for designing the IPL of a particular MAS, which is explicitly driven by the domain-dependent types of interaction and roles included in the OM of the MAS. We argue that our proposal not only helps to bridge the gap between the organisational and communicative components of the MAS architecture, ensuring their consistency, but also best account for the satisfaction of two major requirements of the design process: expressiveness and reusability.

On the one hand, following [10], our method departs from FIPA ACL (our *core* language) and advocates the inclusion in the MAS ACL of types of CA and protocols not included in the standard (which may correspond to new types of

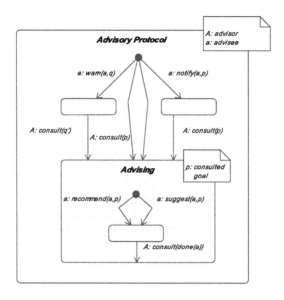

Fig. 10. Advisory Interaction Protocol

interaction). In this way, we intend the resulting MAS ACL to be a more anthropomorphic or expressive language than FIPA ACL [1]. Expressive catalogues of CAs makes the protocol descriptions more understandable and synthetic, as the performatives convey the extra meaning that should be supplied as part of the propositional content of more abstract message types (such as *inform*).

Nevertheless, our proposal still attempts to foster reusability of both, FIPA ACL and the extended components of the MAS ACL. On the one hand, an organisational analysis of FIPA ACL, showing its supported types of interaction and abstract roles, makes possible to identify which components of FIPA ACL could be reused. This is in contrast with [10], where the extension of a core-ACL is also driven by the need to support more specific social interactions, but no organisational analysis is provided of that core language. On the other hand, we also attempt to support further reusability of the new CAs and protocols by identifying their characteristic generic roles and types of interaction. This have been shown through the identification of roles such as the *advisor* and the *explainer*, which could be re-used in other application domains.

Moreover, we address extension and composition of IPs [2] as a process guided by the generalisation and "role playing" relationships of roles. The role playing relationship allows to partition the complex behaviour of some class or role into more simpler ones. Consequently, IPs descriptions become simpler. Concerning generalisation hierarchies of roles, they allow to infer a corresponding generalisation hierarchy between IPs, which also have as a consequence the simplification of their specification. In this way, our approach follows [10], [9] and [8], in important respects. However, our approach goes beyond their work in that the decomposition of protocols is guided by organisational concepts. Thus, a principled and systematic decomposition method is provided, i.e. not only for exceptional cases (e.g. error handling, etc.). Last, despite the use of UML state diagrams, the proposed method does not constraint the use of other formalism like AUML.

References

1. J. M. Bradshaw, S. Dutfield, P. Benoit, and J. D. Woolley. KAoS: Toward an industrial-strength open agent architecture. In J. M. Bradshaw, editor, *Software Agents*, chapter 17, pages 375–418. AAAI Press / The MIT Press, 1997. 198, 207
2. B. Chaib-Draa and F. Dignum. Trends in agent communication language. *Computational Intelligence*, 18(2):1–14, 2002. 207
3. M. Esteva, J. A. Rodriguez, C. Sierra, P. Garcia, and J. L. Arcos. On the formal specifications of electronic institutions. In F. Dignum and C. Sierra, editors, *Agent-mediated Electronic Commerce (The European AgentLink Perspective)*, volume 1191 of *LNAI*, pages 126–147, Berlin, 2001. Springer. 194, 195, 195, 196
4. J. Ferber and O. Gutknetch. A meta-model for the analysis of organizations in multi-agent systems. In Y. Demazeau, editor, *ICMAS'98*, pages 128–135. IEEE Press, 1998. 195, 195, 197
5. T. Finin, Y. Labrou, and J. Mayfield. Kqml as an agent communication language. In J. M. Bradshaw, editor, *Software Agents*. AAAI Press / The MIT Press, 1997. 194
6. F. for Intelligent Physical Agents. *FIPA Communicative Act Library Specification*. http://www.fipa.org/specs/fipa00037, 2000. 203
7. G. Gottlob, M. Schrefl, and B. Röck. Extending object-oriented systems with roles. *ACM Transactions on Information Systems*, 14:268–296, 1996. 195, 195
8. K. Kuwabara, T. Ishida, and N. Osato. Agentalk: Coordination protocol description for multiagent systems. In V. Lesser, editor, *Proceedings of the First International Conference on Multi–Agent Systems*, page 455, San Francisco, CA, 1995. MIT Press. 199, 207
9. M. H. Nodine and A. Unruh. Constructing robust conversation policies in dynamic agent communities. In F. Dignum and M. Greaves, editors, *Issues in Agent Communication*, pages 205–219. Springer-Verlag: Heidelberg, Germany, 2000. 207
10. J. Pitt and A. Mamdani. Designing agent communication languages for multi-agent systems. *Lecture Notes in Computer Science*, 1647:102–114, 1999. 206, 207, 207
11. J. Searle. *Speech Acts*. Cambridge University Press, 1969. 194
12. J. M. Serrano and S. Ossowski. An organizational metamodel for the design of catalogues of communicative actions. *Lecture Notes in Computer Science*, 2413:92–108, 2002. 195, 195, 195, 200
13. J. M. Serrano and S. Ossowski. Towards structured libraries of communicative acts. In P. Petta and J. P. Müller, editors, *Proceedings of the Third International Symposium: From Agent Theory to Agent Implementation*, Vienna, 2002. Austrian Society for Cybernetic Studies. 204
14. A. Wierzbicka. *English speech act verbs. A semantic dictionary*. Academic Press, Australia, 1987. 203
15. M. Wooldridge, N. R. Jennings, and D. Kinny. The gaia methodology for agent-oriented analysis and design. *Autonomous Agents and Multi-Agent Systems*, 3(3):285–312, Sept. 2000. 194, 195, 195, 196, 203

Design Agent Interaction as a Service to Agents

Marc-Philippe Huget

Agent ART Group
University of Liverpool
LIVERPOOL L69 7ZF
United Kingdom
M.P.Huget@csc.liv.ac.uk

Abstract. A common feature of agents is their interaction ability. They need this interaction in order to fulfill their tasks or to cooperate for fulfilling them. This paper presents our approach where the interaction is defined within an interaction module. This interaction module handles protocols and manages interactions between agents. The interaction module is inserted into agents. The paper describes the requirements for such an interaction module and the advantages and drawbacks of the approach. Since a link is required between the reasoning part of the agents and the interaction module, we propose a language for the interconnection based on XML. A second domain of use of the interaction module is given: mobile agents. If the interaction module is defined as a service, agents can use it. In this case, agents do not have to bring an interaction module when moving from site to site.

1 Introduction

Multiagent systems are frequently decomposed in four parts: agents, environment, interactions and organizations [2] [3]. Interaction is one of the key components in multiagent systems since it allows agents to cooperate, to coordinate and to exchange information in order to complete their tasks. The notion of reuse is well established in the domain of multiagent systems and, usually, it is possible to reuse agents between projects. Unfortunately, it is more difficult to do this for interaction and to reuse it between projects. It is quite difficult to define where the interaction is since interaction is often defined in agent behavior. Protocols and semantics of agent communication languages are diluted in agents.

In order to ease the reuse, we present our approach where we extract protocols and semantics from agents and put them into a framework called an *interaction module*. The aim of this interaction module is to handle protocols and to manage interaction between agents. A first version of the interaction module inserts it into agents but we will see in the second part of the paper that this interaction module can be defined as a service to agents and implemented outside agents.

The aim of this paper is to present our interaction module and discuss how to insert it into agents. We indicate above that the main interest in this approach is to ease the reuse of interaction between projects. A second advantage is for

M.-P. Huget (Ed.): Communications in Multiagent Systems, LNAI 2650, pp. 209–222, 2003.

mobile agents, if we define the interaction module as a service to agents. The Internet and particularly, the World-Wide Web grow every day and traffic is some time slow since numerous users try to access them. Users have to wait more and more in order to have their information. A solution which is already in use is to send mobile agents on the Internet [11]. Mobile agents can go from site to site without needing a continuous link to their users' computers. However, mobile agents are sometimes user assistant agents and as a consequence, encompass a lot of data such as user profiles, requests, etc. Thus, they need more time to go from sites to sites since they are "heavier".

It is thus possible to reduce the weight of mobile agents if designers define the interaction module as a service and supply it to agents. Indeed, agents do not need communication facilities when they go from site to site, they only need it on sites, before leaving sites and when entering sites. If they can delete their interaction module before leaving a site and get one when entering a site, they are lighter when moving.

The paper is structured as follows. Section 2 presents the interaction module. Section 3 describes the requirements for using this interaction module. Section 4 shows the advantages and the drawbacks of such an approach. Section 5 describes the language for the link between the reasoning part of agents and the interaction module. Section 6 presents one example in the domain of mobile agents where the interaction module might have an interest. If designers define the interaction module as a service, it is then possible for mobile agents not to incorporate an interaction module, and as a consequence, to be lighter when moving from site to site. Section 7 concludes the paper and presents future work.

2   Extracting Interaction from Agents

Usually, interaction protocols and semantics associated with agent communication languages are diluted in agents. It is difficult to extract these elements easily. Describing protocols and semantics in agents' behaviors is due to the origin of interaction protocols. Interaction protocols are based on communication protocols [7]. Generating code for communication protocols implies the realization of a program where the code corresponds to the protocol [1]. A common approach is to realize the protocol as a program with two levels of *if*. The first level corresponds to the states of the interaction and the nested level corresponds to the different allowed messages for interaction states.

We follow the same approach as Müller [12] and Ferguson [4] for the definition of the interaction. It means that agents have a reasoning component, a perception component as well as an interaction module [8]. The interaction module encompasses both protocols and semantics for agent communication languages. The interaction module sends and receives messages and acts on behalf of agents. It is linked to the reasoning component of agents in order to receive further information. This information is used for completing the sending of messages. The interaction module receives the messages directly from other agents. Since interaction is now defined in an interaction module, agents are not aware of protocols and do not know the structure of the protocols such as next messages for the current state of the interaction. This information is provided by the interaction module if needed.

As soon as, agents want to begin a new interaction, they ask the interaction module to begin an interaction and provide it with information such as receivers, message contents, etc. The interaction module creates a new context for this interaction, completes the first message for the interaction then sends it to receivers. If the interaction module cannot solve the non determinism between several messages, it asks agents to choose between these messages.

The interaction module actions are the following:

1. beginning an interaction where the agent is initiator
2. beginning an interaction where the agent is participant
3. receiving messages
4. sending messages
5. updating interaction contexts
6. asking agents for the name of the receivers and the message contents
7. choosing the next message according to conditions
8. asking agents when non determinism between several messages does not allow it to choose the next message

Interaction contexts are used in order to save the information of a current interaction, i.e. agents usually have several interactions in parallel with several other agents. It is then necessary to store the information about the interactions such as the name of the protocol, the participants, the current state in the interaction and the data used in the protocol.

The interaction module is divided in three parts as shown on Figure 1:

1. an interaction mechanism
2. protocols
3. contexts

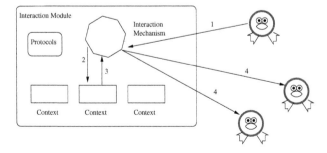

Fig. 1. Interaction Module Architecture

The interaction module takes a different approach for storing protocols. Usually, protocols are described through code but here, we define protocols by their formal descriptions. This method allows us to reduce the errors when designing protocols. Holzmann signaled that generating code for protocols implies incorporating flaws and errors which are only detected by conformance testing [7] [14]. The main advantage of this approach is to reduce the effort for designing interaction protocols. Designers are sure to have an execution which matches the formal description, since it is the formal description which is used. Several formal description techniques are available in the literature such as automata, Petri nets [7] or Agent UML [13]. In our approach, we follow our specific formal description technique called CPDL (*Communication Protocol Description Language*) [9] [10] [8]. The main advantage of the CPDL language is to consider a protocol as an aggregation of components called micro-protocols. As a consequence, it is easier to reuse protocols or parts of protocols. The CPDL language is a textual language. A detailed description of the CPDL language can be found at [8] [9]. We just give here some examples. For instance, here is the CPDL protocol for the request to connect to a server:

```
NAME: cnxon
MUP:
queryif,
inform.
SEM: cnxon
DEF:
init ^ queryif(C,T,P).inform(T,C,R)/ end
```

The field NAME corresponds to the name of the protocol. The field MUP gives the needed micro-protocols for executing the protocol. The field SEM describes the semantics of the protocol. This field is free format so, designers can define it as a textual string or as a logic formula. The main field is the field DEF. This field describes the protocol as a set of formulae. These formulae adopt a finite state machine approach since formulae contain an initial state, a final state and a set of micro-protocols which label the transition from the initial state to the final state. Conditions and loops can be inserted in order to modify the execution. In our example given above, we have just one formula from the initial state *init* to the final state *end*. This formula has two micro-protocols: *query-if* and *inform*.

The micro-protocol *queryif* is described as follows:

```
NAME: queryif
SEMPARAM:
A: sender,
B: receiver,
C: content.
DEF: query-if(A,B,C)
SEM: query-if
```

This above example is simple but micro-protocols can contain loops, beliefs, timeout and options within micro-protocols.

The field NAME gives the name of the micro-protocol. The field SEMPARAM represents the semantics of parameters for communicative acts. For instance, if the parameter A is used in the definition of the micro-protocol, it is easy to know the semantics of this parameter in reading the field SEMPARAM. The parameter A means that A is a sender. The field DEF is the most important one since it contains the set of communicative acts.

Here is a more complex example where the field DEF contains a loop. The loop follows while the conditions $a \wedge b \wedge c$ hold.

```
NAME: loop
SEMPARAM:
A:sender,
B:receiver,
C:content.
DEF: [a@b@c@d]{query-if(A,B,C).inform(B,A,C)}
SEM: loop
```

The interaction mechanism is the active part of the interaction module. It is responsible for the management of protocols and for the management of inter-actions. It uses protocols and contexts in order to handle interactions. Figure 1 presents an example of the use of the interaction module. First the agent invokes the interaction module (*step 1*) about an existing interaction since the context already exists. The interaction mechanism looks for this context (*step 2*) and obtains the next communicative act (*step 3*). Then, the interaction mechanism sends the message to receivers (*step 4*).

Moreover, the interaction mechanism stores previous data during this inter-action, so if we have twice the variable A, the interaction mechanism asks once. The second time, it assumes that this variable has still the same value. This approach is particularly interesting for the parameters corresponding to senders and receivers. The interaction mechanism does not have to ask each time.

For the moment, the interaction module is placed within agents but it is possible to insert it into the environment and to define it as a service to agents.

3   Requirements for This Approach

Before considering the pros and the cons of this approach (see Section 4), one has to define the requirements for using the interaction module. Indeed, if the service is defined as one available for agents, a common agreement is required among multiagent designers.

1. A common semantics for agent communication languages has to be used by agents. Such works already exist either the well-known FIPA's initiatives and the ACL language [5]; DARPA with KQML, van Eijk's approach [15], Wooldridge's approach [17] or Guerin's approach [6]. As a consequence of this requirement, the agent communication language has to be the same or it might require agents to share an ontology. In our approach, we refer to

the FIPA approach. The FIPA ACL has a formal semantics, in terms of a Semantic Language (SL). SL is a quantified multimodal logic, which contains modal operators for referring to the *beliefs*, *desires* and *uncertain beliefs* of agents, as well as a simple dynamic logic-style apparatus for representing actions. The semantics of the FIPA ACL maps each ACL message to a formula of SL, which defines a constraint that the sender of the message must satisfy if it is to be considered as conforming to the FIPA ACL standard. FIPA refers to this constraint as the *feasibility* condition. The semantics also map each message to an SL-formula that defines the *rational effect* of the action: the purpose of the message [18].

2. Agents must be able to interact with this interaction module. Communication must be established between the interaction module and the reasoning part of agents in order to exchange data. In order to describe the interaction between the interaction module and agents, we use XML [19]. For instance:

```
<to> agent1 </to>
<from> interaction service </from>
<protocol> auction-information </protocol>
<performative> inform </performative>
<unknown> receiver </unknown>
```

This communication concerns the protocol *auction-information* between the interaction service and the agent *agent1*. The interaction service wants to know who is the receiver of the performative *inform*. The field *unknown* represents the unknown value.

3. If the interaction module is defined as a service to agents, some precautions have to be taken since it is unclear that the owner of the interaction module can be trusted. It might be a malicious host. A trusted tier is required to provide a certain level of security.

4 Advantages and Drawbacks of an Interaction Module

This approach is quite attractive as it reduces network overloads but this is not the only advantage. Let us now define the advantages and the drawbacks of this method.

Advantages of Interaction as a Service

1. If agent designers remove the interaction part from agents, then agents will be lighter and therefore, they reduce the required bandwidth on the network. Presently, interaction and interaction mechanisms represent a big part in agents.

2. Agent designers do not have to worry about interaction modules since this one is provided by the destination host. They can focus on the description of users' profiles. Indeed, one can consider this service is also available on user's computer so, agent designers do not have to design it.

3. Protocols and electronic commerce protocols tend to be more and more complex. Actually, in such a domain like electronic commerce, protocols need to be secured and safe. Moreover, protocols are often modified so if users want to continue to use some Internet web sites, for instance, they have to download the latest version of agents. This operation might be boring and if repeated really frequently, they might be dissatisfaction grounds. If interaction is defined as a service provided on web site, web site designers can easily modify protocols, they just have to put them in the interaction service.

Drawbacks of Interaction as a Service

1. The main difficulty of this approach is to deal with interoperability and agents coming from different agent designers. One has to find a common agreement and a common background to agents can use the interaction module. This problem is solved for most part since it is possible to use FIPA agent communication language and this already provides a suitable semantics.
2. The second problem is about knowledge management and knowledge sharing between the reasoning part of the agent and the interaction module. This problem is twofold: (1) how to link reasoning parts to the interaction module and (2) how to represent data in order to be used by interaction module. The former problem is solved by our language (see Section 5) which can be considered as an API for accessing the interaction module. The latter problem is solved when representing data with XML [19]. Tags are to be defined and known by agent designers. Moreover, XML allows designers to define hierarchical data or data composed of several fields. For instance,

```
<to> agent1 </to>
<from> interaction service </from>
<protocol> auction-information </protocol>
<performative> inform </performative>
<description>
    <item> computer </item>
    <brand> dream of computer </brand>
    <model> 404 </model>
    <price> 1000 dollars </price>
</description>
```

3. One problem arises when using mobile agents on the Internet. It is not sure that hosts can be trusted. It is possible to have malicious hosts. These malicious hosts can modify interaction protocols so as to increase their benefits or to avoid negotiation between the host and the mobile agents. We see that the problem is located on the protocols and the semantics associated to these protocols. Since protocols are provided by the hosts, all misbehaviors are possible. As far as we are concerned, the problem with malicious hosts does not deal with the interaction as a service but with the agents' behavior and their ability to prevent some misbehaviors.

4. The last problem is a technical problem. What are the requirements for agent designers if they want to be sure that their agents can link to the interaction module? The given solution is to consider agents are represented by Java classes and the interaction service is represented as a RMI service. Obviously, if agent designers do not use Java, this drawback still remains. In a future version of this approach, it will be possible to describe the interaction module as a CORBA service so this problem does no longer hold.

5   The Language for the Interconnection

We provide a language for the interconnection since in two cases, the interaction module needs information: lack of information and non determinism. Each time the interaction module has to send messages, it has to give the receivers and the message contents. From time to time, this information is not known. In this case, the interaction module asks the reasoning part of agents in order to know the values. The second use for the language is when it is not possible for the interaction module to know what is the next message since there are several messages and it is unable to determine between them.

Messages between agents and interaction service are described in XML. Several fields are common for all messages.

The tag

```
<to>...</to>
```

represents the receiver of the message, either one agent or the interaction service.

The tag

```
<from>...</from>
```

represents the sender of the message, either one agent or the interaction service.

The tag

```
<protocol>...</protocol>
```

is always present and gives the protocol used. This information helps both agents and the interaction service to know which contexts this message deals with.

After these tags, we have several options for the remainder of the message. A current option is to create a new interaction for a given protocol. Agents indicate this as follows:

```
<to> interaction service </to>
<from> agent1 </from>
<protocol> ContractNet </protocol>
<action> creation </action>
```

This message is coming from the agent *agent1* to the interaction service. The protocol is the protocol *Contract Net*. The action about this protocol is described in the tag

```
<action>...</action>
```

Here is the term *creation* which explains the interaction service has to create a new interaction using the protocol *ContractNet*.

Of course, the interaction service needs extra information about the receiver and the content of the message, and optionally, what message must be used.

The information is always requested according to the same schema:

```
<to> agent1 </to>
<from> interaction service </from>
<protocol> ContractNet </protocol>
<performative> cfp </performative>
<unknown> receiver </unknown>
```

All unknown information is stored between the tag

```
<unknown> </unknown>
```

It might be *receiver* if the receiver is unknown or *content* if the content of the message is unknown.

The answer is given as follows:

```
<to> interaction service </to>
<from> agent1 </from>
<protocol> ContractNet </protocol>
<performative> cfp </performative>
<receiver> agent2, agent3, agent5 </receiver>
```

In Section 4, we give one example where the interaction service gives some information about the on-going interaction, there the price of a computer.

A second case where interaction service needs information is when it does not know what performative must be used. The following example describes an example where the choice between several performatives is requested:

```
<to> agent1 </to>
<from> interaction service </from>
<protocol> ContractNet </protocol>
<performatives>
      agree, disagree, not-understood
</performatives>
```

The interaction service asks what performative has to be used in the next message, either *agree, disagree* or *not-understood*.

5.1   Requesting the Interaction Service

As we saw above, agents lose their interaction service when moving, so they have to request another one. We define for that a small set of communicative acts, agents can understand even if they do not have interaction facilities. These communicative acts are:

➤ the communicative act *request* when the agent requests the access of the interaction service or the unlink of this interaction service.

➤ the communicative act *agree* if the interaction service can be accessed by this agent.

➤ the communicative act *disagree* if the interaction service cannot be accessed by this agent.

➤ the communicative act *not-understood* if the interaction service cannot understand what the agent requests[1].

Obviously, agents have to understand XML in order to parse the answer of the interaction service.

6   Example

Mobile agents are a convenient solution when users do not want to wait for the information since the network is stalled. They can send their agents on the Internet in order to retrieve the information then they shutdown their computers. They can switch on their computers from time to time to check if their agents have some information. A second interest in mobile agents is for distributed computing, it is sometimes better to send agents to the site where the computation is and to send back agents when the computation is completed.

When considering mobile agents, one can argue that communication facilities are not used during the translation from site to site (shown on Figure 2). Figure illustrates the transportation and the method proposed in this article: agents leave the interaction module and interaction service when leaving a site and get a new one when entering a site.

The advantage is to reduce the weight of agents and as a consequence, they are lighter when moving from site to site. The main drawback is to define a trusted tier for checking if the interaction service conforms to a set of policies since it is possible that site hosts are malicious and provide an interaction module which is designed to retrieve information from mobile agents or force purchases.

Let us take a small example of using interaction as a service. Let us suppose users want to send agents on the Internet in order to find information on several sites. Then, they shutdown their PC.

We omit the step when users inform agents what the search is and when agents contact destination host and have an agreement to be downloaded there.

Figure 3 presents the steps of our example.

The first step represents the loss of the Interaction service by agents just before they are downloaded to the destination host. The second step is the transportation from one site to another one.

The next step corresponds to the agent's waking. Until now, agents do not need to interact but now they have to ask about their search of information. In step four, they try to connect to the interaction service. Here is the request by agent *agent1*:

---

[1] This communicative act is used for compatibility with FIPA which requires that this communicative act must be recognized by agents.

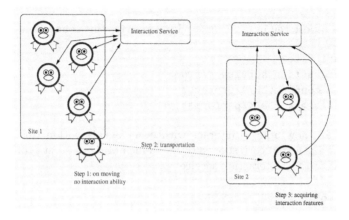

Fig. 2. Interaction seen as a Service

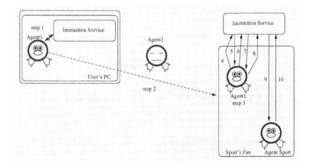

Fig. 3. Example of using Interaction as a Service

```
<to> interaction service</to>
<from> agent1 </from>
<protocol> connection </protocol>
<performative> request </performative>
```

Let us suppose the interaction service agrees for this connection. It answers:

```
<to> agent1 </to>
<from> interaction service </from>
<protocol> connection </protocol>
<performative> agree </performative>
```

Agents are now able to interact with other agents within this multiagent system. The sixth step corresponds to the launch of the request protocol by the agent *agent1* to the interaction service.

```
<to> interaction service </to>
<from> agent1 </from>
<protocol> RequestInformation </protocol>
<action> creation </creation>
```

Obviously, the interaction service needs some information in order to send the first message: the receiver and the content (step seven):

```
<to> agent1 </to>
<from> interaction service </from>
<protocol> RequestInformation </protocol>
<unknown> receiver, content </unknown>
```

The eighth step corresponds to the answer of the interaction service's request:

```
<to> interaction service </to>
<from> agent1 </from>
<protocol> RequestInformation </protocol>
<receiver> agent\_sport </receiver>
<content> who is the player at the second base?
</content>
```

Then, in ninth step, the interaction service sends the message to the agent *agent1*:

```
<to> agent2 </to>
<from> agent1 </from>
<protocol> RequestInformation </protocol>
<performative> request </performative>
<content> who is the player at the second base?
</content>
```

The tenth step is the answer of the agent_sport:

```
<to> agent1 </to>
<from> agent2 </from>
<protocol> RequestInformation </protocol>
<performative> inform </performative>
<content> nobody, it's a joke! </content>
```

The protocol ends after this message. Agent *agent1* has just to collect information from the interaction service and will come back as soon as its user is connected to Internet.

7   Conclusion and Future Work

In this paper, we present a new approach in order to consider interaction. The interaction is clearly defined and located in an interaction module. A first advantage for such an approach is to reduce work for designers. They do not have to code from scratch the management of interaction protocols since a framewrok already exists. Designers can focus on the agents. A second advantage is when the interaction module is defined as a service supplied to agents –mobile agents do not have to bring the interaction module with them when moving from site to site.

This interaction service is provided with a set of requirements in order to link agents with this service. Moreover, a link language is used between agents and the service using XML features.

The interaction module is currently used in the tele-teaching project Baghera[2] where the agents use the interaction module for their communication [16].

Future work might follow several directions:

1. Some additions have to be made to the interaction mechanism: the ability to use timeout, broadcast and acknowledgment avoiding the loss of messages.
2. For the moment, the interaction module is a Java application, and if agents want to use this module, they have to be written in Java as well. A future work will be to define this interaction module as a CORBA service, so agents either written in Java or another language is, can access this module.
3. The link language and the set of fields used in XML must be improved and use existing work, particularly in the ontology domain.
4. In this version of the interaction service, it is only possible to interact inside the system and not with outside agents, We have to define a link between interaction services.
5. This approach does not take into account for the moment how to interact when the interaction service has to interact with agents which want to keep its communicative features, how the communication might be done.

---

[2] http://www-baghera.imag.fr

References

1. P.-Y. M. Chu. *Towards Automating Protocol Synthesis and Analysis*. PhD thesis, Ohio State University, 1989. 210
2. Y. Demazeau. Steps towards multi-agent oriented programming. slides Workshop, 1st International Workshop on Multi-Agent Systems, IWMAS '97, October 1997. 209
3. Y. Demazeau. *VOYELLES*. Habilitation diriger les recherches, Institut National Polytechnique de Grenoble, Grenoble, avril 2001. 209
4. I. Ferguson. Towards an architecture for adaptive, rational, mobile agents. In E. Werner and Y. Demazeau, editors, *Decentralized AI 3 — Proceedings of the Third European Workshop on Modelling Autonomous Agents in a Multi-Agent World (MAAMAW 91)*, pages 249–262. Elsevier Science Publishers, 1991. 210
5. FIPA. *Specification: Agent Communication Language*. Foundation for Intelligent Physical Agents, http://www.fipa.org/spec/fipa99spec.htm, September 1999. Draft-2. 213
6. F. Guerin and J. Pitt. Denotational semantics for agent communication languages. In *Proceedings of the Fifth International Conference on Autonomous Agents (AA 2001)*, pages 497–504, Montreal, May 2001. 213
7. G. J. Holzmann. *Design and Validation of Computer Protocols*. Prentice-Hall, 1991. 210, 212, 212
8. M.-P. Huget. *Une ingnierie des protocoles d'interaction pour les systmes multi-agents*. PhD thesis, Universit Paris 9 Dauphine, June 2001. 210, 212, 212
9. J.-L. Koning and M.-P. Huget. A semi-formal specification language dedicated to interaction protocols. In H. Kangassalo, H. Jaakkola, and E. Kawaguchi, editors, *Information Modelling and Knowledge Bases XII*, Frontiers in Artificial Intelligence and Applications. IOS Press, Amsterdam, 2001. 212, 212
10. J.-L. Koning, M.-P. Huget, J. Wei, and X. Wang. Engineering electronic commerce interaction protocols. In *Proceedings of Intelligent Agents, Web Technologies and Internet Commerce (IAWTIC 01)*, Las Vegas, NV, USA, July 2001. 212
11. D. Kotz and R. S. Gray. Mobile agents and the future of internet. *ACM Operating Systems Review*, 33(3):7–13, August 1999. 210
12. J. Müller. *The Design of Intelligent Agents - a layered approach*. Number LNAI 1177 in Lecture Notes in Artificial Intelligence. Springer-Verlag, Berlin, 1996. 210
13. J. Odell, H. V. D. Parunak, and B. Bauer. Representing agent interaction protocols in UML. In P. Ciancarini and M. Wooldridge, editors, *Proceedings of First International Workshop on Agent-Oriented Software Engineering*, Limerick, Ireland, june, 10 2000. Springer-Verlag. 212
14. J. Tretmans. *A Formal Approach to Conformance Testing*. PhD thesis, University of Twente, Enschede, The Netherlands, 1992. 212
15. R. van Eijk, F. S. de Boer, and W. van der Hoek. Operational semantics for agent communication languages. Technical Report UU-1999-08, University of Utrecht, 1999. 213
16. C. Webber, L. Bergia, S. Pesty, and N. Balacheff. The baghera project: a multi-agent architecture for human learning. In *Proceedings of the Workshop Multi-Agent Architectures for Distributed Learning Environments, AIED2001*, pages 12–17, San Antonio, TX, 2001. 221
17. M. Wooldridge. Verifiable semantics for agent communication languages. In Y. Demazeau, editor, *Third International Conference on Multiagent Systems (ICMAS-98)*, pages 349–356, Paris, France, July 1998. IEEE. 213
18. M. Wooldridge. *Reasoning about Rational Agents*. MIT Press, 2000. 214
19. XML. The xtensible markup language. See http://www.xml.org/. 214, 215

A FIPA Compliant Goal Delegation Protocol

Federico Bergenti[1], Giovanni Rimassa[1], Matteo Somacher[1],
and Luis Miguel Botelho[2]

[1] AOT Lab, Dipartimento di Ingengeria dell'Informazione, Parco Area delle Scienze 181/A,
43100 Parma, Italy
{bergenti, somacher, rimassa}@ce.unipr.it
[2] Department of Computer Science of ISCTE, Av. Das Forças Armadas, Edifício ISCTE,
1600 Lisbon, Portugal
Luis.Botelho@iscte.pt

Abstract. This paper presents an interaction protocol, built on top of FIPA ACL, allowing an agent to delegate a goal to another agent, in the form of a proposition that the delegating agent intends its delegate to bring about. The proposed protocol addresses the concrete needs of a service that is to be deployed within the AgentCities network, but also helps to highlight some issues that are related to the FIPA ACL itself and its usage to build more complex agent interaction blocks.

1 Introduction

The AgentCities project aims at building an open, worldwide network [1] of agent based services, relying on FIPA compliant agent platforms. The participants to the various incarnations of AgentCities project believe that such a widespread and heterogeneous test bed is key to support the transition of Multi Agent Systems technologies from research labs to actual, deployed applications. The AgentCities effort is also quite interesting for the FIPA organization, because it will validate the whole set of the FIPA specifications (not just the FIPA ACL) on the widest scale so far.

Within the arena of distributed software infrastructures, FIPA promotes a landscape where applications are composed by *agents* receiving life support from *platforms*; FIPA tries to support both *agent-level* and *platform-level* interoperability through a comprehensive set of specification. At the agent level, FIPA mainly deals with ACL, interaction protocols, message content and message ontology issues. Though the FIPA ACL is provided with a semantics formally rooted in multi-modal BDI logics, it is generally accepted that FIPA does not mandate a BDI architecture for agents, but only that observable agent behaviour can be interpreted within a BDI framework. Recognizing this suggests that a major feature of the FIPA infrastructure is the support for heterogeneous agent societies, where different members have different levels of internal complexity. All of them will enjoy autonomy and sociality, but only a subset of them will be gifted with an internal architecture providing reasoning capabilities.

M.-P. Huget (Ed.): Communications in Multiagent Systems, LNAI 2650, pp. 223–238, 2003.

Such a vision strives for *semantic scalability*, where software components of different internal complexity still exhibit behaviour compliant with the FIPA ACL semantics; this becomes even more important when MAS technology tackles the new deployment scenarios arising from the convergence and integration between the Internet and the wireless environments [3].

This paper proposes an interaction protocol to perform goal delegation between two agents, in the form of a proposition that the delegating agent wants the delegate agent to bring about. Section 2 explains the traits and usefulness of the goal delegation operation in the context of MAS, and clarifies the reasons for implementing goal delegation as an interaction protocol in the FIPA infrastructure environment.

Section 3 describes the interaction protocol as a Finite State Machine decorated with semantic annotations, and shows its FIPA compliance and soundness. Lastly, section 4 puts the protocol in the practical context that caused its design in the first place: an Event Organizer service that is to be set up in the framework of the Agent-Cities project.

2   Motivation and Requirements

Goal delegation arises quite naturally in a cooperative, rational agents environment: every agent pursues its own goals, goal partitioning is a standard divide-and-conquer strategy, and in a collaborative environment there generally are enough hierarchy and trust relationships, so that an agent is likely to find some other one to delegate a sub goal to. When considered from an agent coordination perspective, goal delegation has two main facets:

1. *Delegation of commitment.* This means that the delegate agent should embrace the intentions of the delegating agent, trying to achieve the goal as if it were one of its own. From the delegating agent point of view, this requires a kind of trust in the delegate good will: the delegating agent has to believe that the delegate is trustworthy and will honestly try to achieve the goal.
2. *Delegation of strategy.* Delegating a declarative goal instead of an operational plan means that the delegating agent is interested only in the resulting outcome and not in the specific way the delegate achieves it. Thus, the delegating agent not only trusts the delegate good will, but also its skills. The delegating agent has to believe the delegate agent knows how to achieve the delegated goal.

In [5] the authors analyse several aspects of trust in the perspective of the Information Society, taking into account both human and software agents, relating the theory of trust to computer security issues and stressing how computer mediated communication creates several new trust related issues. Our paper only deals with software agents, following a rather rigid and precise behaviour that relies on FIPA ACL semantics and the proposed interaction protocol; however, a major aim of the Agent-Cities project is to insert such agents within the global Information Society, made by software, hardware and human participants. So, though the general considerations about trust at large don't directly affect the subject of this paper, they still remain in its conceptual landscape.

The two aforementioned facets of the goal delegation operation correspond to the *core trust* in *competence* and *disposition*, discussed in [7] as the basis for a trust relationship between two agents. In [5], the authors also observe that some additional mental attitudes are required in the delegating agent, in order for it to develop a delegation disposition toward its (about to become) delegate. These mental attitudes are the *dependence belief* and the *fulfilment belief*. *Dependence belief* amounts to believing that the goal achievement critically depends on the delegate agent, or at least that the goal can be achieved more efficiently by relying on the delegate agent. *Fulfilment belief* consists of believing that the goal will be achieved due to the delegate contribution. The dependence belief is not directly addressed by our protocol, but stays implicit in the acquaintance structure of a specific application. For instance, performing a yellow pages search or running a service discovery protocol could result in the delegating agent getting a list of agents it can rely on for the task to delegate. The fulfilment belief, instead, is taken into account in our protocol, in that the goal delegation proper is decoupled from result notification. More clearly, when the goal is delegated, the delegating agent believes the goal will be achieved, but the delegate agent, after finding a plan and trying to execute it, tells the delegating agent whether the goal has been achieved or not, thus providing a chance for fulfilment belief revision.

FIPA agents are autonomous social software components whose external behaviour can be described with a BDI model. While designing multi agent systems, the semantic scalability promoted by FIPA suggests to take different approaches for different agent roles, depending on the needed sophistication and internal complexity levels. Recognizing this suggests that a major feature of the FIPA infrastructure is the support for heterogeneous agent societies, where different members have different levels of internal complexity. While the plan execution delegation can obviously be implemented using FIPA ACL *request* communicative act and the *FIPA-Request* interaction protocol, there is no similar ready-made support for goal delegation.

In principle, a goal delegation design component can use any layer of the FIPA communication model: since we want our goal delegation component to be reusable across application domains, we avoid introducing ontological entities. Our goal delegation protocol is based on a FIPA ACL communicative act, named *achieve* after the KQML performative [11], but which is really a macro-act defined in term of the existing ones, so that the FIPA ACL semantics is left untouched. Moreover, from previous considerations stems that goal delegation is a complex, high-level conversation that involves much more than a single speech act; therefore we define a complete interaction protocol to carry out goal delegation.

The protocol definition, given in section 3, uses FIPA SL to define the *achieve* communicative act; this does not clash with our requirement of application domain independence, however, because the subset of FIPA SL we use is only the one required by [9] to specify the FIPA ACL semantics. So, any content language that can express the content of the primitive FIPA ACL communicative acts can replace FIPA SL in the definition of our protocol semantics.

During the past few years, several researchers [14], [6], [13] pointed out that the FIPA ACL semantics, being based on internal mental states of the communicating agents, was not really suited to drive interactions among independently developed agents, acting in open environments. Within the scope of this paper, the authors are more concerned with protocol design than with protocol verification. Therefore, they stay neutral with respect to the mentalistic vs. observable dilemma; the following section defines the goal delegation protocol using the mentalistic FIPA ACL semantics just because it is the official one. The authors are aware that FIPA set up a Semantics TC [10] to design a semantic framework taking into account social notions, and they believe that the ideas and techniques described in this paper could also be easily restated in a social semantics.

3 Protocol Description

This section has four objectives: define the *achieve* performative, which can be used for goal delegation, design a goal delegation protocol, propose a framework for protocol analysis, and analyse the goal delegation protocol using the presented framework.

3.1 Goal Delegation

If agent i has a goal G it wants to delegate to another agent r, then i may ask r to exe-cute some plan of action whose execution r believes to result in a state of the world in which G is true. Without loss of generality, this section uses FIPA SL in order to keep the presentation more concrete.

In SL, the *Feasible* operator can be used to express the idea that it is possible to execute a given action resulting in the achievement of some state of the world. If an agent believes there is a plan of action ?p such that (Feasible ?p G), the agent believes ?p will bring about G. In SL, the *Done* operator can be used to express the idea that a certain action has been done. If an agent believes Done(A), it believes to be in a state of the world in which the action A has just been executed.

Given the semantics of the ACL inform performative, agent r can only send mes-sage <r, inform(i, P)> if r believes P to be true. If r informs i that a certain plan of action has just been executed, r must believe that the plan has actually been executed. The above elements are about all it takes to express goal-delegation messages. The delegating agent must request the delegate to inform it that some plan whose execu-tion is believed to achieve the desired goal has been executed.

In dynamic and uncertain environments, the execution of a plan believed to bring about G does not ensure that G is actually achieved. Therefore, after the execution of the selected plan, the delegate agent must also check that the goal has actually been achieved. The complete message is

<i, request(r, <r, inform(i, ∃p(Done(p,Feasible(p, G)) ∧ G))>)>

That is, i requests r to inform it that some plan believed to achieve G has been per-formed and G has been achieved. According to the semantics of the *inform* performa-tive, r will only send the inform message if it believes those conditions to hold. We propose to extend FIPA ACL with the new performative *achieve* defined as above

$\langle i, achieve(r, G)\rangle \equiv \langle i, request(r, \langle r, inform(i, \exists p(Done(p,Feasible(p, G)) \wedge G))\rangle)\rangle$

In the remaining of this section, we analyse the feasibility preconditions and the rational effect of the *achieve* performative; and propose a protocol to be used for goal delegation. The analysis will rely on the proposed definition. Since the *achieve* performative is defined in terms of the *request* performative, its semantics will result of replacing the content of the request with

$\langle r, inform(i, \exists p(Done(p,Feasible(p, G)) \wedge G))\rangle$.

In the FIPA Specifications [9], the semantics of the *request* message is defined by the following feasibility preconditions and rational effect:

FP of $\langle i, request(r, A)\rangle$
- FP(A)[i\r]. The subset of the feasibility preconditions of action A that are mental attitudes of i;
- $B_i(Agent(r, A))$. The sender believes the receiver to be the agent of the requested action;
- $\neg B_i(I_r Done(A))$. The sender does not believe that the receiver already intends to perform the requested action otherwise there would be no point in requesting.

RE of $\langle i, request(r, A)\rangle$
- Done(A). The sender i can reasonably expect that the requested action will be done.

Replacing A by $\langle r, inform(i, \varphi)\rangle$ in which

$\varphi \equiv \exists p(Done(p, Feasible(p, G)) \wedge G)$

we obtain:

FP of $\langle i, achieve(r, G)\rangle \equiv$ FP of
$\langle i, request(r, \langle r, inform(i, \exists p(Done(p,Feasible(p, G)) \wedge G))\rangle)\rangle$
- FP($\langle r, inform(i, \exists p(Done(p,Feasible(p, G)) \wedge G))\rangle$)[i\r]. The subset of the feasibility preconditions of $\langle r, inform(i, \exists p(Done(p,Feasible(p, G)) \wedge G))\rangle$ that are mental attitudes of i. The feasibility preconditions of the inform message are mental attitudes of the sender alone, which is the responder agent r. Therefore, this is the empty set;
- $B_i(Agent(r, \langle r, inform(i, \exists p(Done(p,Feasible(p, G)) \wedge G))\rangle))$. The sender believes the receiver to be the agent of the specified inform message;
- $\neg B_i(I_r Done(\langle r, inform(i, \exists p(Done(p,Feasible(p, G)) \wedge G))\rangle))$. The sender does not believe that the receiver already intends to send the specified inform message.

RE of $\langle i, achieve(r, G)\rangle \equiv$ RE of
$\langle i, request(r, \langle r, inform(i, \exists p(Done(p,Feasible(p, G)) \wedge G))\rangle)\rangle$
- Done($\langle r, inform(i, \exists p(Done(p,Feasible(p, G)) \wedge G))\rangle$). The sender i can reasonably expect that the *inform* communicative act will be done.

The above semantics of the *achieve* performative nearly fulfil all the requirements of protocol delegation as defined in section 2:

1. The initiator believes that the responder is skilled enough to achieve the goal;
2. The initiator believes the responder does not already intend to achieve the goal;
3. The initiator does not care about the plan to be used to achieve the goal.

The first requirement can be shown to be implied by the *achieve* feasibility preconditions, because the initiator can only send the *achieve* message if it believes the responder to be the sender of the message informing that the plan has been executed and the goal has been achieved. Following the semantics of the *inform* performative, the responder can only send such a message if it believes to have actually achieved the desired goal. If we assume the responder is aware of the feasibility preconditions of the *inform* performative, the initiator can only believe the responder will be the sender of the message if it also believes the responder to be capable of achieving the goal.

The second requirement is not a consequence of the feasibility preconditions of the *achieve* performative. Actually, the initiator can't believe that the responder already has the intention of informing it that the goal has been achieved. But it is allowed to believe that the responder already intended to achieve the desired goal. This aspect will be the subject of section 3.4.

The third requirement is captured by the proposition the initiator is requesting the responder to send

$$\exists p(Done(p, Feasible(p, G)) \wedge G)$$

The existential quantifier in this proposition means that the plan to be executed will be any plan believed by the responder to achieve the desired goal. Therefore, the initiator does not care about the specific plan that is used. Examples of possible types of plans are:

1. *Ask around, just in case.* Being lazy, r could ask its acquaintances if the goal is already achieved. Notice that this does indeed delegate the strategy but not the commitment. If anyone among the acquaintances of agent r answers positively, then the goal has been achieved, even if r doesn't know how.
2. *Do it yourself.* r could find out a feasible plan for the goal, which hasn't been executed yet, and then execute it. This will of course achieve the goal.
3. *Who's going to keep my promises?* r can further delegate the goal (both strategy and commitment), using the goal delegation protocol recursively. By induction on the nesting level, if there is a finite number of nested delegations that complete successfully, the goal will be achieved.

Since *achieve* has been defined in terms of the *request* message, we will analyse the FIPA-Request protocol as the basis for the goal delegation protocol. The FIPA-Request protocol is started by the initiator sending the *request* message to the responder. When the responder receives the *request* message, it has three alternatives. It may send a *not-understood* message; it may send a *refuse* message; or it may send an *agree* message. If the responder sends the *agree* message, it becomes committed to try to execute the requested action. When executing the requested action, the responder may send a *failure* message in case it fails to successfully execute the action; it may send an *inform-ref* message; and it may send an *inform-done* message. Given the above, in case of successful termination of the FIPA-Request protocol, the responder sends an *agree* message and then it sends an *inform-ref* or an *inform-done*.

Adapting the FIPA-Request for the goal delegation case, it would result in the protocol described in figure 1.

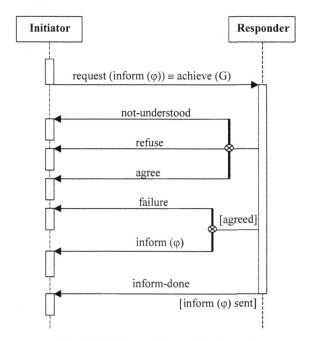

Fig. 1. FIPA Request Protocol for the goal

Clearly, this protocol is not totally adequate for goal delegation. The first obvious inconvenience is that the *inform-done* in the last step of the successful protocol execution is not necessary because the responder would have already informed the initiator that the plan has been performed and the goal has been achieved. There is no point in informing the initiator that the requested *inform* message has already been sent. Less obvious is the content of the *failure* message in case something fails. There are three possible types of failure: (i) the responder may fail sending the inform message; (ii) the responder may fail to execute the plan; and (iii) the responder executed the plan but, due to unforeseen events or due to insufficient knowledge about the results of available actions, the plan failed to attain the desired result.

Considering the above three aspects we propose the following goal delegation protocol. Let G be the goal to be achieved, and let's define the proposition

φ≡∃?plan (Done(?plan,Feasible(?plan, G)) ∧ G

Notice that, although this looks like a higher order formula, it is not because, in each concrete case, G will be instantiated with a specific goal to be achieved. Therefore the formula is a proposition schema, not a higher order formula.

The protocol works as follows (see also figure 2):

1. <i, request(r, <r, inform(i, φ)>)>
2. Action Alternatives
   (a) <r, not_understood(i, (<i, request(r, <r, inform(i, φ)>>, reason for not under-
        standing))>
   (b) <r, refuse(i, (<r, inform(i, φ)>, Reason for refusing))>
   (c) <r, agree(i, (<r, inform(i, φ)>, Condition of action execution))>
3. [agreed] Action Alternatives
   (a) <r, failure(i, (<r, inform(i, φ)>, Reason for the failure of the inform))>
   (b) <r, failure(i, (<r, inform(i, φ)>, *Plan* was not completely executed))>
   (c) <r, failure(i, (<r, inform(i, φ)>, *Goal* has not been achieved))>
   (d) <r, inform(i, φ)>

Some details of the above specification are worth noting. The protocol specification is richer than AUML diagrams [2] currently used in the FIPA specifications, because it specifies parts of the contents of some of the involved messages. Symbols *Plan* and *Goal* appearing in messages 3(b) and 3(c) will be instantiated with concrete plan and goal expression, at the time the messages are actually sent. This specification should be part of the protocol description. The conversation identifiers in all of the possible messages must be the same. It is the responsibility of the protocol initiator to create that identifier. This specification should also be part of the formal protocol description. Finally, each set of alternative courses of action is available only at certain junctures, that is, in certain protocol states. For example, alternative actions 3(a) to 3(d) are available to the agent only if the agent has agreed to perform the requested action. It is necessary to explicitly and formally specify protocol state changes [8].

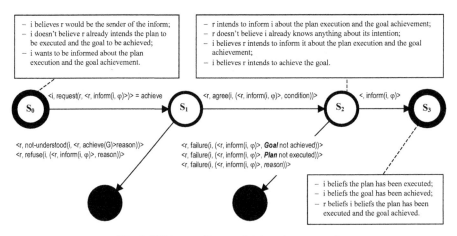

Fig. 2. FIPA compliant goal delegation protocol

In the following subsections we present a framework for protocol analysis and we analyse the proposed goal delegation protocol.

3.2   Protocol Analysis

This section provides a framework that may be used to analyse interaction protocols with respect to the set of propositions that should be true in each protocol state. This proposal lays down the basis for a protocol verification system, which could be built in a Court Agent that could be developed in agent societies.

The main ideas behind our protocol analysis methodology are *compliance* and *intentional action*. We assume that when an agent sends a message (i) it does so intentionally, and (ii) it is desirable that it complies with the message semantics. It results from the above assumptions that, when a message is observed, the message feasibility preconditions should hold (because the sender should comply with the message semantics) and the sender intended the message rational effects (because it sent the message intentionally). For instance, when agent i receives message $<r, inform(i, P)>$, it may assume that

$B_r P \wedge \neg B_r(Bif_i P \vee Uif_i P)$ (*inform* feasibility preconditions)
and
$I_r B_i P$ (the agent intends the rational effects of the message).

Given the above reasons, and acknowledging the fact that protocol state changes reflect message sending/receiving, we may attach to each protocol state, a set of propositions that should be true from a normative point of view. The state that results of a state transition from state S due to message $<i, M>$ is the union of state S with the feasibility preconditions of M and I(i, RE(M)), in which RE(M) is the set of rational effects of M, and $I(i, \Delta)=\{I_i(p): p \in \Delta\}$ represents the fact that the sender intends all the propositions in Δ.

$S_l = S_k \cup FP(i, j, M_{l,k}) \cup I(i, RE(i, j, M_{l,k}))$, in which S_l and S_k are protocol states, $M_{l,k}$ is the message that resulted in the protocol state transition from state S_l to state S_k, $RE(i, j, M_{l,k})$ is the set of Rational Effects of message $M_{l,k}$, indexed to the sender i and the receiver j, and $FP(i, j, M_{l,k})$ is the set of Feasibility Preconditions of message $M_{l,k}$ indexed to sender i and receiver j. All protocols have an initial empty state, the state before the initiating message is sent.

In the following sections, we analyse the case of successful execution of the goal delegation protocol, as defined in section 3.1, using the concept of protocol-state just presented.

3.3   Goal-Delegation Analysis

Step 1: Protocol initiation. Before the protocol is initiated, the protocol is in the initial state (S_0), which is the empty set. The protocol initiator (agent i) sends message $<i, request(r, <r, inform(i, \varphi)>)>$, resulting in a protocol state transition to state S_1.

According to the definitions presented in subsections 3.1 and 3.2, S_1 is composed by the *achieve* feasibility preconditions and the intention of its rational effects.

$S_1 = \{B_i(Agent(r, <r, inform(i, \varphi)>), \neg B_i(I_r\ Done(<r, inform(i, \varphi)>)), I_iDone(<r, inform(i, \varphi)>)\}$

That is, the observer is entitled to conclude that (i) the initiator believes that the responder will be the agent of the inform message; (ii) the initiator does not believe that the responder already has the intention of having informed the initiator that the plan has been executed and the goal has been achieved; and (iii) the initiator wants the responder to inform it that the plan has been executed and the goal achieved.

Step 2: The responder agrees. In the second step, the responder agrees to inform the initiator that the plan has been executed and the goal has been achieved. This message results in a new state transition to state S_2. S_2 is the union of S_1 with the feasibility preconditions of the *agree* message and the intention of its rational effects. The feasibility preconditions and the rational effects of the *agree* message are those specified in [9].

$S_2 = S_1 \cup \{B_rI_r\ Done(<r, inform(i, \varphi)>, \phi), \neg B_r(Bif_i\ I_r\ Done(<r, inform(i, \varphi)>, \phi) \vee Uif_i\ I_r\ Done(<r, inform(i, \varphi)>, \phi)), I_rB_i\ I_r\ Done(<r, inform(i, \varphi)>, \phi)\}$

in which ϕ is the condition under which the inform message will be sent.

The observer of the *agree* message is now entitled to have additional beliefs. The responder believes it has the intention to inform the initiator that the plan has been executed and the goal has been achieved. The responder does not believe the initiator already knows anything about its intention. The responder intends the initiator to believe it has the intention of informing it of the success of the goal delegation process.

In order to check the soundness of the designed protocol, it could be determined if each protocol state is consistent. S_2 is obviously consistent since the beliefs and intentions ascribed to each participant are not contradictory.

Step 3: Success. In the third step, the responder agent informs the initiator that it has successfully executed the plan believed to achieve the delegated goal and the goal has been achieved. This message produces another protocol-state transition resulting in state S_3. Given the semantics of the inform message, as defined in [9], the new state will be defined as follows

$S_3 = S_2 \cup \{B_r\varphi, \neg B_r(Bif_i\varphi \vee Uif_i\varphi), I_rB_i\varphi\}$

in which

$\varphi \equiv \exists plan(Done(plan, Feasible(plan, G)) \wedge G)$
$S_3 = \{B_i(Agent(r, <r, inform(i, \varphi)>), \neg B_i(I_r\ Done(<r, inform(i, \varphi)>)), I_iDone$
$(<r, inform(i, \varphi)>), B_rI_r\ Done(<r, inform(i, \varphi)>, \phi), \neg B_r\ (Bif_i\ I_r\ Done(<r, inform(i, \varphi)>, \phi) \vee Uif_i\ I_r\ Done(<r, inform(i, \varphi)>, \phi)), I_rB_i\ I_r\ Done(<r, inform(i, \varphi)>, \phi), B_r\varphi, \neg B_r(Bif_i\varphi \vee Urf_i\varphi), I_rB_i\varphi\}$

Among other things, the observer of this state will know that the responder believes there is a plan that results in the delegated goal becoming achieved; it also believes that plan has been executed; and it also believes the goal to have been achieved. By virtue of being the receiver of the message that caused this last state transition, the protocol initiator is an observer of the last protocol state (S_3). Therefore, the initiator concludes the responder believes to have achieved the desired goal. That is, in case of successful termination, the goal delegation protocol fulfils the purpose of its design.

Using a similar analysis, it could easily be shown that the protocol also works appropriately in the other termination conditions. From the point of view of protocol soundness, it can also be seen that S_3 does not contain contradictions. This is a good criterion to assume the protocol to be well formed.

As can be seen, the last state of the protocol clearly shows that it is legitimate to assume that the initiator knows the plan has already been executed and the goal has been achieved. Therefore, as previously argued (see section 3.1), the inform-done message that would be generally necessary in the request protocol is not needed in the goal delegation protocol.

3.4 Alternative Design

As argued in section 3.1, the proposed definition of the *achieve* performative does not fulfil all requirements for goal delegation. Specifically, it does not follow from the semantics of the performative that the protocol initiator does not believe the responder to already have the intention to achieve the desired goal. The proposed definition can only ensure that the responder agent (the delegate) does not already intend to inform the initiator that the goal has been achieved. Although this is not a very important drawback, it would be desirable if it could e fixed.

The referred problem arises because SL, the language used to express the semantics of the performative, is not rich enough to overcome that difficulty. This subsection proposes to extend SL with a new action operator that enables overcoming the mentioned problem. The new operator, execute, has also been proposed in [4].

Execute is a general-purpose action operator used to express the action of executing a given action description passed as an argument. Using execute, the protocol initiator can ask the responder to execute any plan that achieves the desired goal, instead of asking the responder to inform it that the plan has been executed. Using this design, all goal delegation requirements will be met, and the goal delegation protocol will more closely mirror the request protocol.

We start analysing the way of expressing the action of executing a plan that achieves the goal. Feasible(p, G) means that p can be executed and achieves G. Any(p, Feasible(p, G)) refers a plan (anyone) that can achieve G. Execute(Any(p, Feasible(p, G))) is the action of executing the plan referred by Any(p, Feasible(p, G)), that is a plan that achieves the desired goal.

Given the above elements, the achieve performative could have the alternative definition

<i, achieve(r, G> ≡ <i, request(r, <r, execute(any(p, Feasible(p, G)))>>

that is characterized by:

FP of <i, achieve(r, G)>

– FP execute(any(p, Feasible(p, G))) [i\r]. The subset of the feasibility preconditions of <r, execute(any(p, Feasible(p, G)))> that are mental attitudes of i;

– B_i(Agent(r, <r, execute(any(p, Feasible(p, G)))>)). The sender believes the receiver to be the agent of the action of executing the plan;

– ¬B_i(I_r Done(<r, execute(any(p, Feasible(p, G)))>)). The sender does not believe
that the receiver already intends execute a plan that achieves the goal.

RE of <i, achieve(r, G)>

– Done(<r, execute(any(p, Feasible(p, G)))>). The sender i can reasonably expect
that a plan that achieves the goal will be done.

This alternative definition fulfils all the goal delegation requirements presented in
section 2:

1. The initiator believes that the responder is skilled enough to achieve the goal;
2. The initiator believes the responder does not already intend to achieve the goal;
3. The initiator does not care about the plan to be used to achieve the goal.

The first requirement can be shown to be implied by the *achieve* feasibility preconditions, because the initiator can only send the *achieve* message if it believes the responder to be the agent of the action of executing the plan believed to achieve the
goal. Therefore it must believe the responder can do it.

The second requirement is exactly the second feasibility precondition of the
achieve performative.

The third requirement is captured by the action the initiator is requesting the responder to perform: any plan that is believed to achieve the goal.

This alternative definition has a consequence that must be handled. The initiator
does not ask the responder to inform it that the plan has been executed and the goal
has been achieved. This will be handled at the protocol level, not at the performative
level. The new protocol definition is defined below, in which
$\psi \equiv$ any(p, Feasible(p, G)):

1. <i, request(r, <r, execute(ψ)>)>
2. Action Alternatives
   (a) <r, not-understood(i, (<i, request(r, <r, execute(ψ)>>, Reason for not under-
       standing))>
   (b) <r, refuse(i, (<r, execute(ψ)>, Reason for refusing))>
   (c) <r, agree(i, (<r, execute(ψ)>, Condition of action execution))>
3. [agreed] Action Alternatives
   (a) <r, failure(i, (<r, execute(ψ)>, **Plan** was not completely executed))>
   (b) <r, failure(i, (<r, execute(ψ)>, **Goal** has not been achieved))>
   (c) <r, inform(i, Done(ψ))>

The new protocol design is simpler because it has less alternatives in step 30. Besides, it is more closely related to the request protocol. This protocol specifies two
cases of failure messages.

Although this alternative definition of the goal delegation protocol is better than the one proposed in section 3.1, it relies upon an extension of the SL language. Therefore, in the case study described in the next section we assume the initial definition.

4 Case Study: Agentcities Event Organizer Service

The Agentcities event organizer fulfils service compositions using the services, provided by the Agentcities network, needed to set up a social event. It shows that agents offer dynamic and flexible solutions for supply chains, especially to deal with unexpected events and chain reorganization. In the reference scenario, a conference chair attempts to develop a schedule for her conference and to book the venues and services that she requires, e.g., hotel, restaurant and amusement events. She delegates to the event organizer the work, monitoring the progress of arrangements. The event organizer service is available in the Parma Agentcities node [1]. The main actors involved in the event organizer are:

1. the user, i.e., the conference chair;
2. the event organizer agent, i.e., the agent that tries to achieve the global goal that the user submitted;
3. the solvers, i.e., the skilled agents that search the needed services and negotiate the contracts for buying them with the service provider agents;
4. the service provider agents.

The process starts when the chair decides to organize the conference and requests the event organizer agent to set up a set of needed services, fixing some constraints and a priority for each service. It finishes when all mandatory services are bought or reserved. These interactions are governed thanks to the FIPA-Request protocol for the goal delegation case proposed in section 3.1, where the event organizer plays the role of the initiator and the solver plays the one of the responder. Due to some limitations in the FIPA-ACL semantics, some interaction rules are implicitly defined in the agent code, e.g., the deadlines that the solver has to respect for the plan execution. The following step can be iterated until the conference is fully organized.

Conversation 1: Goal Delegation. This conversation is carried out between the event organizer and the solver.

Protocol initiation. The chair fixes through a Web page the finite set of services that she wants to buy for the conference and a finite set of associated constraints. These parameters are translated in a global goal assigned to the event organizer, e.g., "make it so that all the 20 attendees have a dinner together and rooms booked for five nights in nearby hotels".

For the sake of simplicity we assume that the idea of "constraints" or "service priority" will not be exchanged among the agents. Only the event organizer agent knows about the full set of required constraints and the priorities of the services. This eases the problem solving process because the event organizer agent centralizes the validation of constraints without delegating it to solvers.

Then, the event organizer decomposes its given global goal into sub-goals, each of which is proposed, with the following performative, to one particular problem solving agent (so-called solver), based on its functional capabilities to achieve the goal assigned.

The solvers are either newly created by the event organizer as instances of functional agent classes or have been spawned in the past and therefore already exist. In our scenario a sub-goal corresponds to the search of suitable contracts for the services asked by the chair, without considering the cross-services constraints, e.g., the solver searching for restaurants does not consider that the restaurant cannot be too far away from the hotel, only the event organizer agent deals with such a constraint.

The solver agrees. The solver agrees to achieve the assigned sub-goals and builds a plan.

The solver executes the plan. Each solver uses the search infrastructure services offered by the Agentcities network architecture to find suitable service providers. The solver chooses the providers that fit its tasks best. This can be done through a direct interaction or through a market place. Once a suitable service provider is found, the solver negotiates with it to reach a preliminary agreement for a contract that regulates the requested service.

The solver informs the event organizer about the contract. The solver informs the event organizer the sub-goal is achieved and it knows about some contracts.

Converstion 2: Contract Retrieval. This conversation is carried out between the event organizer and the solver. The event organizer believes that the solver has negotiated at least one contract to purchase the assigned service. It starts a FIPA-Query protocol, where it plays the role of initiator and the solver plays the role of responder, to get such a contract. The solver gives its best proposal back to the event organizer for a subsequent use.

Conversation 3: Services Acceptance. This conversation is carried out between the event organizer and the chair. Once each instance of the protocol with the solvers ended, the event organizer agent has enough information to build the global plan satisfying the chair's requirements. To do so, it first composes the proposals received from the solvers and validates the cross-service constraints. If a consistent solution is found, it is proposed to the chair for a final acceptance.

Now, the event organizer agent informs the chair about the contracts she has to sign for achieving the global goal. If no consistent solution is found, the event organizer agent iterates the previous steps until an acceptable solution is found or until the chair decides to change some constraint.

The iteration consists of assigning new sub-goals to the solvers exploiting the knowledge about which cross-service constraints has not been satisfied. For example, if the process failed because the restaurant and the hotel were too far from each other, the new sub-goal will be "operate so that the attendees have dinner in a restaurant within 1 Kilometre from the hotel and give me back a new suitable contract for that".

Conversation 4: Services Purchase. This conversation is carried out between the event organizer and the service provider agents. Once the chair accepted the proposed solution, the event organizer agent starts a FIPA-Request protocol with the service provider agents in order to buy the service directly from them.

Conclusion

In this paper we proposed a FIPA compliant protocol to perform goal delegation between two agents. The motivation of this work starts from a real need, i.e. to build an application for the Agentcities.RTD project where agents delegated to other skilled agents their goals We approached the problem with the idea to only use what FIPA provides.

We proposed a framework for protocol analysis and we used it to validate our goal delegation protocol that uses the FIPA ACL semantics as it is. We argued that the protocol still have a minor drawback and we proposed a new SL operator *execute* that allows to fulfil all the requirements for goal delegation pointed out in the first part of the paper.

Finally we described the concrete application that was realized thanks to the effort of this work.

Acknowledgements

The research described in this paper is partly supported by the EC project Agent-cities.RTD, reference IST-2000-28385. The opinions expressed in this paper are those of the authors and are not necessarily those of the Agentcities.RTD partners.

References

1. Agentcities.RTD, reference IST-2000-28385, http://www.agentcities.net
2. Bauer B., Müller J.P., Odell J.R.E, Agent UML: A Formalism for Specifying Multiagent Interaction, In Paolo Ciancarini and Michael Wooldridge (eds) Agent-Oriented Software Engineering (Berlin 2001), Springer, 91-103.
3. Bergenti F., Burg B., Caire G., Poggi A. Deploying FIPA-compliant systems on handheld devices. IEEE Internet Computing, Volume 5 Issue 4 (July-Aug. 2001), 20-25.
4. L.M. Botelho L. M., Antunes N., Ebrahim M., Ramos P. Greeks and Trojans Together, Submitted paper, 2002.
5. C. Castelfranchi C., Falcone R. Socio-Cognitive Theory of Trust.
   http://alfebiite.ee.ic.ac.uk/docs/papers/D1/ab-d1-cas+fal-soccog.pdf.
6. Colombetti M. A Commitment-Based Approach to Agent Speech Acts and Conversations. In Proc. Workshop on Agent Languages and Communication Policies, 4th International Conference on Autonomous Agents (Barcelona 2000), 21-29.
7. C. Castelfranchi C., Pedone R. A Review on Trust in Information Technology.
   http://alfebiite.ee.ic.ac.uk/docs/papers/D1/ab-d1-cas+ped-trust.pdf.
8. J. Freire J., Botelho L. M. Executing explicitly represented protocols. Submitted paper, 2002.
9. FIPA spec. XC00037H. FIPA Communicative Act Library Specification.
   http://www.fipa.org/specs/fipa00037/.
10.FIPA TC Semantics Call for Information,
   http://www.fipa.org/docs/output/f-out-00099/f-out-00099.pdf.

11. T. Finin T., Labrou Y. KQML as an agent communication language. In J.M. Bradshaw (ed.), Software Agents, MIT Press, (Cambridge, MA, 1997), 291-316.

12. F. Giunchiglia F., Mylopoulos J., Perini A.. The Tropos Development Methodology: Processes, Models and Diagrams. Submitted at AAMAS 2002.

13. J. Pitt J., Kamara L., Artikis A.. Interaction Patterns and Observable Commitments in a Multi-Agent Trading Scenario.
http://alfebiite.ee.ic.ac.uk/docs/papers/D1/ab-d1-pitkamart-ipoc.pdf.

14. Singh M. P. Agent Communication languages: Rethinking the principles. IEEE Computer, 31 (12) (1998), 40-47.

Communication for Goal Directed Agents

Mehdi Dastani, Jeroen van der Ham, and Frank Dignum

Institute of Information and Computing Sciences
Utrecht University,
P.O.Box 80.089
3508 TB Utrecht
The Netherlands
{mehdi,jham,dignum}@cs.uu.nl

Abstract. This paper discusses some modeling issues concerning the communication between goal-directed agents. In particular, the role of performatives in agent communication is discussed. It is argued that the specification of the effect of performatives, as prescribed by FIPA, is sometimes too weak or unrealistic. The alternative, proposed in this paper, suggests a two phase modeling of the effect of the communication. A minimum effect can be hardwired in the semantics of sending and receiving messages. And the performative related part is achieved by executing a number of rules which are under the control of the agent and made accessible to the agent programmer. These issues are discussed in the context of 3APL which is a goal directed agent programming language.

1 Introduction

In any multi-agent system the communication between the agents will be an important aspect. Some work has been done on the formalization of the communication (see e.g. [1]). Most of the early work has concentrated on formalizing the messages, such that a precise and unambiguous meaning of them could be established. (see e.g. [2,3]). However, one of the main problems was (and still is) to determine the exact effects of a message. If we look at the specification of the "inform" message in the FIPA agent communication language (ACL) it states only a precondition that the sender should believe the contents of the inform message and do not believe that the receiver has knowledge about the content already and a rational effect (which should be interpreted as an intended effect of the inform) that the receiver will believe the content of the inform message. FIPA does not, however, give a formal specification of what a "rational effect" exactly means. It is not a direct consequence of performing the communicative act, but seems to be more like a goal of the sender of the message.

On the other hand the FIPA specification states informally that the receiver is "entitled" to believe that the sender believes the contents of the inform message and wishes the receiver to believe the contents of the inform message as well. However, this effect is not specified in the formal specifications of the message. It is therefore unclear whether these points could/should be seen as effects

M.-P. Huget (Ed.): Communications in Multiagent Systems, LNAI 2650, pp. 239–252, 2003.
© Springer-Verlag Berlin Heidelberg 2003

of sending the message. The above example quite clearly shows some of the major problems in formalizing agent communication. Although the FIPA ACL specification already formalizes some aspects of the ACL it also contains some gaps at crucial points. Most of these gaps are related to the exact preconditions and postconditions of the communicative act. It has been argued in [7] that preconditions of a communicative act in which the sender is supposed to have knowledge about the state of mind of the receiver are not very realistic. These preconditions can never be checked, because the sender cannot verify whether they actually hold (she cannot "look inside the head of the receiver"). Therefore the preconditions are relatively weak.

The postconditions are also difficult to specify. As in the example above, the sender certainly has an intended purpose with sending the message, but one cannot guarantee that this purpose is actually achieved. This depends for a large part on the receiver, which is autonomous. So, the effect of receiving a message is for the largest part determined by the receiving agent. If we want to give strict postconditions for a communicative act this would also pose heavy constraints on the way agents would have to handle messages and the mental updates they have to make. This seems overly restrictive to be practical.

The crux of the matter seems to lie in the balance between the autonomy of the agents on the one hand and the wish to predict the effects of a communicative act on the other hand. The first is of prime importance for two reasons. First, because autonomy is one of the most important characteristics of agents. Secondly, in open agent systems one cannot predict how other agents work internally and therefore are seemingly completely autonomous. However, one also would like to give precise semantics for the messages and their effects in order to standardize agent communication and for agents to be able to reflect about communicative acts.

In this paper we explore the balance between the autonomy of the agents and agent communication in the practical setting of the agent programming language 3APL. We give a short overview of 3APL and its semantics in the next section. In section 3 we indicate the issues that have to be dealt with in order to extend 3APL with a communication component (without solving issues in the implementation in a way that is not covered by the formal semantics of 3APL). In section 4 we show how the practical reasoning rules of 3APL can be used to add (more restrictive) effects to the communicative acts in a stepwise way. This allows the programmer to implement an agent, which minimally fulfills the FIPA specification, to draw more elaborate conclusions. In section 5 we will some preliminary conclusions and indicate areas for further research.

2   3APL Specification

3APL is an implementation language for cognitive agents that have beliefs and goals as mental attitudes and can revise or modify their goals. Moreover, 3APL agents are assumed to be capable of performing a set of basic actions such as mental updates. Each basic action is defined in terms of pre- and post-conditions and can be executed if the pre-condition is true. After the execution of a basic action the post-condition is set to be true. For example, a 3APL agent may have a goal to buy a computer and thereafter buy a book. The agent has the capability of buying computers and books (basic actions). The agent may believe he has not enough money to buy the computer but enough to buy the book. The agent can also delay the purchase of the computer if he believes he has not enough money by doing other things first.

A 3APL agent starts its deliberation with a number of goals to achieve. If the goals are basic actions for which the pre-conditions are true, then the goals are achieved by executing the basic actions; otherwise the goals are revised. In the above example, a 3APL agent aims at buying the computer first, but it realizes that he has not enough money. Therefore, he delays the purchase of the computer and buy the book first. In the rest of this section, we will briefly explain the formal syntax and semantics of 3APL. The complete formal specification of 3APL is described in [5]. We introduce only the minimum definitions needed to explain the working of the agents and the links with the communication between the agents. Those who are familiar with the 3APL specification can skip this section.

2.1   3APL Syntax

3APL [5] consists of languages for beliefs, basic actions, goals, and practical reasoning rules. A 3APL agent can be specified (programmed) by expressions of these languages. A set of expressions of a language implements one 3APL module. Below is an overview of these languages.

Definition 1. *Given a set of domain variables and functions, the set of domain terms T_D is defined as usual. Let $t_1, \ldots, t_n \in T_D$, $Pred_b$ be the set of predicates that constitute the belief expressions, $p \in Pred_b$, and ϕ and ψ be belief expressions. The belief language $\mathcal{L}_B$ is defined as follows:*

- $p(t_1, \ldots, t_n)$, $\neg \phi$, $\phi \wedge \psi \in \mathcal{L}_B$

All variables in $\phi \in \mathcal{L}_B$ are universally quantified with maximum scope. The belief-base module of a 3APL program is a set of belief formulae.

The set of basic actions is a set of (parameterized) actions that can be executed if certain preconditions hold. After execution of an action certain post-conditions must hold. These actions can be, for example, physical actions or belief update operations.

Definition 2. *Let Act be an action name, $t_1, \ldots, t_n \in T_D$, and $\phi, \psi \in \mathcal{L}_B$. Then, the action language $\mathcal{L}_A$ is defined as follows:*

- $\langle \phi, Act(t_1, \ldots, t_n), \psi \rangle \in \mathcal{L}_A$

The basic action module of a 3APL program is a set of basic actions.

The set of goals consists of different types of goals: Basic action goals (Baction-Goal), predicate goal (PredGoal), Test goal (TestGoal), skip goal (SkipGoal), sequence goal (SeqGoal), if-then-else goal (IfGoal), and while-do goal (While-Goal).

Definition 3. *Let* $t_1, \ldots, t_n \in T_D, Pred_g$ *be the set of predicates such that* $Pred_b \cap Pred_g = \emptyset$, $q \in Pred_g$, $\alpha \in \mathcal{L}_A$, *and* $\phi \in \mathcal{L}_B$. *Then, the set of goals* $\mathcal{L}_G$ *is defined as follows:*

   - skip , α , $q(t_1, \ldots, t_n)$, ϕ? $\in \mathcal{L}_G$,
   - $\pi_1; \ldots; \pi_n$, IF ϕ THEN π_1 ELSE π_2 , WHILE ϕ DO π $\in \mathcal{L}_G$.

The goal base module of a 3APL program is a set of goals.

Before we define practical reasoning rules, a set of goal variables, $GVAR$, is introduced. These variables are different from the domain variables used in the belief language. The goal variables may occur in the head and the body of practical reasoning rules and will be instantiated with a goal. Note that the domain variables are instantiated with the belief terms. We extend the language $\mathcal{L}_G$ with goal variables. The resulting language $\mathcal{L}_{G_v}$ extends $\mathcal{L}_G$ with the following clause: if $X \in GVAR$, then $X \in \mathcal{L}_{G_v}$.

Definition 4. *Let* $\pi_h, \pi_b \in \mathcal{L}_{G_v}$ *and* $\phi \in \mathcal{L}_B$, *then a practical reasoning rule is defined as:* $\pi_h \leftarrow \phi \mid \pi_b$.
This practical reasoning rule can be read as follows: if the agent's goal is π_h *and the agent believes* ϕ, *then* π_h *can be replaced by* π_b. *The practical reasoning module of a 3APL program is a set of practical reasoning rule.*

A practical reasoning rule can be applied to a goal by unifying the head of the rule with the goal. Since goal variables may occur in the head and the body of practical reasoning rules, the unification results in a substitution for goal variables. The resulting substitution will be applied to the body of the practical reasoning rule and the resulting goal will replace the goal to which the rule was applied. Consider the practical reasoning rule $A(); X; C() \leftarrow \top \mid X; X$ and the goal $\pi = A(); B(); C()$. The application of the rule to π results the substitution $[X/B()]$ which, when applied to the body of the rule, results the goal $B(); B()$. This goal will replace π.

Given the definition of beliefs, basic actions, goals and practical reasoning rules, a 3APL agent can be specified as follows:

Definition 5. *A 3APL agent is a tuple* $< \mathcal{A}, \Pi, \sigma, \Gamma >$, *where* $\mathcal{A}$ *is the set of basic actions that the agent can perform,* Π *is a set of goals,* σ *is a set of belief formula, and* Γ *is a set of practical reasoning rules.*

The following is an example of a 3APL agent.

Example 1. Let $A()$ be a basic action with pre-condition $\neg p(a)$ and postcondition $p(a)$ (i.e. $\{\neg p(a)\} A() \{p(a)\}$), and $B()$ be an action with precondition $p(a)$ and postcondition $\neg p(a)$ (i.e. $\{p(a)\} B() \{\neg p(a)\}$). The following agent has one goal which is "first do $A()$ and then $B()$". The agent also believes $p(a)$, and has a goal revision rule which states that whenever it has to do $A()$ and after that something else, (X) and also believes $p(a)$ (i.e. the precondition of $A()$ is not satisfied), then it delays the execution of $A()$ and does X first.

$$< \ \mathcal{A} = \{A(), B()\} \ ,$$
$$\Pi = \{ \ A(); B() \ \} \ ,$$
$$\sigma = \{ \ p(a) \ \} \ ,$$
$$\Gamma = \{ \ A(); X \leftarrow p(a) \mid X; A() \ \} \ >$$

2.2   3APL Semantics

In [5] an operational semantics for the 3APL language is proposed which is defined by means of a transition system. This semantics specifies transitions between the agent's states by means of transition rules. The state of an agent is defined as follows:

Definition 6. *The state of a 3APL agent is defined as a tuple $< \Pi, \sigma, \theta >$, where Π is the set of the agent's goals, σ is the agent's beliefs, and θ is a substitution consisting of binding of variables that occur in the agent's beliefs and goals.*

The substitution θ is passed through from one state to the next state by means of transition rules. Some transition rules generate new variable bindings, update the substitution with it and pass the updated substitution to the next state; other transition rules pass the substitution to the next state without updating it. For example, the substitution is updated by the transition rules for the execution of test goals and the application of practical reasoning rules while it is not updated by the transition rules for sequence and choice operators. In this section, we illustrate only some of the transition rules that help the understanding of this paper. The reader will find the complete set of transition rules in [5].

The first transition rule is for the execution of the set Π of agents' goals. This transition rule states that the execution of a set of goals can be accomplished by the execution of each goal separately. Let $\Pi = \{\pi_0, \ldots, \pi_i, \ldots \pi_n\}$, and θ and θ' be ground substitutions. Then,

$$\frac{< \{\pi_i\}, \sigma, \theta > \rightarrow < \{\pi_i'\}, \sigma', \theta' >}{< \{\pi_0, \ldots, \pi_i, \ldots \pi_n\}, \sigma, \theta > \rightarrow < \{\pi_0, \ldots, \pi_i', \ldots \pi_n\}, \sigma', \theta' >}$$

The transition rule for basic actions updates the belief base but does not update the substitution. Let $A(\overrightarrow{t})$ be a basic action with a sequence of domain terms $\overrightarrow{t}$ and τ be an update function that specifies the effect of the basic action on agent's beliefs. The semantics of basic actions is captured by the following transition rule. This update function is defined when the pre-condition of the action holds; otherwise undefined such that the transition cannot take place.

$$\frac{\tau(A(\overrightarrow{t})\theta, \sigma) = \sigma'}{< \{A(\overrightarrow{t})\}, \sigma, \theta > \rightarrow < \emptyset, \sigma', \theta >}$$

Finally, we present the transition rule for the execution of the while goal. Note that the substitution is not passed through and it is only applied to the first execution of the while body.

$$\frac{\sigma \models \phi\gamma}{< \{WHILE\ \phi\ DO\ \alpha\}, \sigma, \theta > \rightarrow < \alpha\gamma; WHILE\ \phi\ DO\ \alpha, \sigma, \theta >}$$

The complete set of transition rules can be found in [5]. Given the 3APL transitions rules the following is a possible execution trace, i.e. the transitions between agent states, of the agent that is specified in Example 1.

$$< \{A(); B()\}, \{p(a)\}, \emptyset > \Rightarrow < \{B(); A()\}, \{p(a)\}, \emptyset > \Rightarrow < \{A()\}, \{\neg p(a)\}, \emptyset >$$
$$\Rightarrow < \emptyset, \{p(a)\}, \emptyset >$$

3   Extending 3APL with Communication

The specification of 3APL agents is basically designed for single agents. As a consequence there is no account for agent communication. There are two ways to extend 3APL specification to account for communication. The first way is to extend the set of basic actions with synchronous communication actions such as $\mathtt{tell}(\psi)$ and $\mathtt{ask}(\varphi)$ or $\mathtt{offer}(\psi)$ and $\mathtt{require}(\varphi)$. The arguments φ and ψ of the synchronized actions are unified and the resulting variable bindings are the result of the communication and form the contents of the messages. In these approaches, the synchronized actions are matched on the basis of the performatives they enact. I.e. the $\mathtt{tell}$ action is a speech act with performative 'tell'. It should be matched with a speech act with the complementary performative 'ask'. This account of agent communication is proposed in [4,6].

A disadvantage of the above synchronous communication approach is that we would have to categorize all performatives in pairs that should be synchronized. Although a pair like $\mathtt{tell}$ and $\mathtt{ask}$ looks very natural it is difficult to model, e.g. all FIPA-ACL performatives in such a way. Moreover, in many multi-agent applications it is not realistic to determine the unique pairs of performatives beforehand as the agents need to deliberate on how to respond to a certain message. For example, when an agent receives a request it needs to deliberate on the content of the message to decide whether it reacts with an agree, refuse or not-understood message. If we consider all the different pairs possible then it becomes impossible to use the synchronous model described above. In that case we have to indicate with a particular instance of the $\mathtt{request}$ action which of the three possible answers should synchronize with this request. I.e. we determine the answer on forehand when sending the request. As a final disadvantage we want to mention that not all communication takes place in pairs as indicated above. Sometimes an agent just wants to inform another agent of some fact without the other agent having explicitly asked for the fact. These 'spur' messages are not be possible in the above synchronous model.

In this paper we propose an alternative approach to incorporate communication in the 3APL framework. The main feature is that it is based on asynchronous communication and supports modeling of FIPA-ACL performatives separately from the sending and receiving of the messages. In this approach, 3APL agents send and receive messages containing contents compliant to the FIPA specification. I.e. the message contains a message identifier, an explicit performative, the content, and the sender and receiver identifiers. In order to model asynchronous communication in the 3APL framework, the 3APL specification is extended with a buffer, called a message-base. The message-base of a 3APL agent contains messages that either are sent to other agents or are received from other agents. The message-base makes it possible for an agent to continue with its own goals after sending a message. It does not have to wait for the receiving agent to synchronize before it continues. In the same way, the receiving agent can receive messages at any time and does not have to form a goal to receive a message.

3.1   Communication Actions

Agents communicate by means of sending and receiving messages consisting of a message identifier, sender and receiver identifiers, a performative, and content information. The content information can be beliefs, basic actions, or goals. Sending and receiving messages is considered as communication actions (not basic actions) in the 3APL framework. The goal language, as defined in Definition 3, is extended to include these types of actions.

Definition 7. *The set of possible 3APL goals is extended with two communication actions* $\mathtt{Send}(\iota, \alpha, \beta, \rho, \psi)$ *and* $\mathtt{Receive}(\iota, \alpha, \beta, \rho, \psi)$, *where ι is a term that denotes the message identifier, α and β are terms denoting the identifiers for sender and receiver of the message, ρ denotes a FIPA performative, and ψ is the content information.*

We also extend the definition of an agent state in 3APL by including a message-base in the state.

Definition 8. *The message-base Ω of an agent is a set consisting of sent and received messages having the form* $\mathtt{sent}(\iota, \alpha, \beta, \rho, \psi)$ *and* $\mathtt{received}(\iota, \alpha, \beta, \rho, \psi)$. *The arguments are the same as described in definition 7. The state of a 3APL agent can now be defined as a tuple* $< id, \Pi, \sigma, \theta, \Omega >$, *where id is the agent's identifier, Π is the set of agent's goals, σ is agent's beliefs, θ is a substitution consisting of binding of first order variables that denote domain elements, and Ω is the message-base.*

We use a synchronization mechanism for sending and receiving messages. But this synchronization mechanism only takes care of simultaneously taking the messages from the sending agent and putting it in the receiving agent's message-base. At what time the receiving agent checks its message-base and how the messages are interpreted is treated in a completely asynchronous fashion.

This differs from other approaches, such as [4], since we do not synchronize performatives but only the sending and receiving actions of messages. As we see later, the exchange of information is based on unification of arguments of synchronized Send and Receive actions. The unification of the first four arguments of the communication actions is trivial since these arguments are terms. However, the fifth argument of these communication actions, the content, can be belief formula, basic actions, or even complex goals. For these complex objects unification is not trivial. For this reason, we introduce a set of so-called constraint variables that stand for belief formula, basic actions and complex goals, and assume that the fifth argument of one of the two synchronizing communication actions is such a variable. Therefore, the unification of arguments of synchronizing communication actions consists always of a pair $[X/c]$ where X is a constraint variable and c is the content information.

The semantics of Send and Receive is specified in terms of transition rules. The idea is that the sending agent removes the communication action Send from its goal-base after the execution of the send action, and stores the information concerning the sending action in its message-base. Although storing this information is not a part of the semantics of the send action, we believe that the agent may need this information for its future deliberation or its ongoing communications.

The receiving agent also stores its incoming messages in its message-base. In general, we assume that agents can receive messages at any moment. In fact, we assume that the goal of an agent a is of the form $\Pi \parallel \mathtt{Receive}(\iota, a, \beta, \rho, \psi)$, which indicates that the agent is concurrently waiting to receive messages.

Definition 9. *The following three transition rules specify the semantics for sending and receiving messages between agents and their synchronization, respectively.*

$$\frac{\varphi = <\iota, a, \beta, \rho, \psi>}{< a, Send(\varphi), \sigma, \theta, \Omega > \xrightarrow{\varphi!} < a, E, \sigma, \theta, \Omega \cup \{sent(\varphi)\} >}$$

$$\frac{\varphi = <\iota, \alpha, b, \rho, \psi>}{< b, Receive(\varphi), \sigma, \theta, \Omega > \xrightarrow{\varphi\tau?} < b, Receive(\varphi), \sigma, \theta, \Omega \cup \{received(\varphi\tau)\} >}$$

$$\frac{A \xrightarrow{\psi\tau?} A' \ , \ B \xrightarrow{\varphi!} B' \ , \ \psi\tau = \varphi}{M \cup \{A, B\} \to M \cup \{A', B'\}}$$

Note that in the second transition rule the concurrent receive action is not removed from the goal-base such that agents can continuously receive messages. Also note that the unification process takes care that an agent only receives messages (store them in his message-base) when they are sent to him. So, an agent does not have to check explicitly whether a certain message is meant for him.

4   Interpreting Messages by Practical Reasoning-Rules

Once a message is stored in the message-base of an agent, it can be interpreted by applying practical reasoning rules. The effect of the specific performative in the message is thus realised by the application of practical reasoning rules of the receiving agent. We can force the interpretation of the message (and thus the effects) to take place immediately by using so-called reactive rules. These rules do not have a head and are thus executed whenever the guard of the rule is true. In the case of practical reasoning rules pertaining to communication the guard of these rules is evaluated with respect to the message-base instead of the belief-base. For this reason, we index these rules with the label 'MB' to indicate that the guard should be evaluated with respect to the message-base rather than the belief-base. The rules have the following form:

$$\overset{MB}{\longleftarrow} \varphi \mid \pi$$

where φ refers to a received (or sent) message in the message-base and π will determine the effects of receiving (or sending) the message φ. E.g.

$$\overset{MB}{\longleftarrow} received(\iota, a, b, inform, p) \mid Update(B_a(p))$$

states that when agent b receives message ι from agent a informing that p holds, agent b updates its beliefs with the fact that agent a believes p (it assumes a to be sincere).

In many cases we do not want the agent to react immediately to the reception of a message. E.g. we only want an agent to react to an agree message if it is waiting for such a message. One could test a few of these things in the guard, but it seems more natural that some messages are handled as part of a protocol. The specification of the protocol in terms of subsequent goals of the agent leads to points where the agent will check its message-base for incoming messages. In order to model this situation we use (more general) rules of the following form:

$$handle\_performative(\overrightarrow{X}) \overset{MB}{\longleftarrow} \varphi \mid \pi$$

where $handle\_performative(\overrightarrow{X})$ can be used by the programmer to invoke the processing of a certain performative, π is the goal indicating how a message should be interpreted and φ is a logical formula that should be evaluated with respect to the message-base. The variable vector $\overrightarrow{X}$ is used to determine the parameters needed to execute a certain performative. We illustrate the use of these variables in the example given in the next subsection. Note that the programmer has to decide when messages with a certain performative should be processed since the head of the practical reasoning rule is not empty. Of course, these rules can also be reactive rules, in the sense that they can have empty head, such that the programmer has no influence on when a certain message is processed. Although both approaches are possible, we believe the programmer should be able to decide about the message processing.

Let us see how the process of interpreting a message in which the performative is a *request* can be specified by means of practical reasoning rules. According to the FIPA semantics for the request performative, a sending agent can request a receiving agent to perform an action. The receiving agent has to deliberate on the request to decide if it is granted or not. If so, the receiving agent sends an agree message to the sending agent, then performs the requested action, and finally informs the requesting agent that the action has been performed. This is achieved by applying the following rule.

$$
\begin{aligned}
handle\_request(f) &\xleftarrow{MB} \\
&received(\iota, \alpha, \beta, request, Action)\ | \\
&(\neg f(Action)?; \\
&\quad Send(reply(\iota), \beta, \alpha, refuse, Action)) \\
&+ \\
&(\ f(Action)?; \\
&\quad Send(reply(\iota), \beta, \alpha, agree, Action); \\
&\quad Action; \\
&\quad Send(reply(\iota), \beta, \alpha, inform, done(Action)))
\end{aligned}
$$

This rule for request handling implements the protocol as shown in figure 1. The head of the rule is an achievement goal and has one argument, f. This function, $f : G \rightarrow BF$, maps a goal to a formula, which is considered as the constraint for granting requests. This function is used in test-goals, so that when used in combination with the choice $(+)$, we can define what happens when an agent does not grant a request and when he does. In the first case he replies with a *refuse* message and goes his own way. In the latter case, he first replies with an *agree* message, executes the action and then informs the requester that the action has been done. Note that the *not-understood* message is not defined here, as it is only sent when the parsing of the message has failed.

4.1   An Example

In this section we show an example of a request conversation using the semantics as explained before. This example is not the trace of an execution of implemented agents, but it is constructed by hand to illustrate the expected trace. The semantics do not only follow the standard FIPA semantics, but also the standard FIPA request protocol as shown in Figure 1.

The conversation itself is in Table 1. This table has four columns, the first indicates the step-number, the second indicates the name of the mental states of the agents (GB:goal-base, MB:message-base) and the third and fourth column indicate the mental states of the communicating agents. For simplicity we assume that each agent executes one action at each step. This restriction is only for the ease of representation, the communication protocol does not require it.

During the conversation, the agents have the following belief-bases, unless noted otherwise: $BB_a=\{salesPerson(b), action(b, SellPC)\}$, meaning that agent a believes agent b is a salesperson and he also believes that b is able to sell

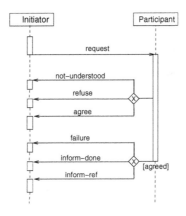

Fig. 1. FIPA Request Protocol

computers ('SellPC'), and $BB_b = \{$customer(a), pc(c1), pc(c2), pc(c3), available(c1,400), available(c2,500), available(c3,600)$\}$, meaning that agent b believes agent a is customer and b also believes that he has three different PCs, which are available for €400, €500 and €600 respectively. Finally, agent b has one basic action, SellPC:

$$PreCondition : \{customer(A), pc(C), available(C, P)\}$$
$$SellPC(A, C, P)$$
$$PostCondition : \{\neg available(C, P), sold(A, C, P)\}$$

In the first step we see that agent a starts with buyPC(500) in his goal-base and agent b with the startSelling() goal. Agent a has one practical reasoning rule that matches with this goal:

$$buyPC(X) \leftarrow salesPerson(B) \mid Send(1, a, B, request, SellPC(a, C, X))$$

This means that given a salesPerson, buyPC(500) is revised to the goal given in step 2. Then, agent a uses the transition rule for the Send action to go to step 3, sending out a request for a computer for €500 to agent b. The fact that a sent a request to b is then kept in the message-base using the sent predicate.

Meanwhile, agent b starts off with a startSelling() achievement goal in step 1. This is revised at step 2 through the following rule:

$$startSelling() \leftarrow \top \mid handle\_request(condition)$$

with

$$condition(SellPC(A, C, P)) \iff customer(A) \wedge pc(C) \wedge available(C, P)$$

The handle_request() is an achievement goal to handle the procedure of deciding to agree or refuse incoming requests as defined earlier. Here, the function

	Agent a	Agent b
1. GB:	buyPC(500)	startSelling()
2. GB:	Send(1,a,b,request,SellPC(a,C,500))	handleRequest(f)
3. GB: MB:	sent(1,a,b,request,SellPC(a,C,500))	handleRequest(f) received(1,a,b,request,SellPC(a,C,500))
4. GB: MB:	 sent(1,a,b,request,SellPC(a,C,500))	(¬(f(SellPC(a,C,500)))?; Send(2,b,a,refuse,SellPC(a,C,500))) + (f(SellPC(a,C,500))?; Send(2,b,a,agree,SellPC(a,C,500)); SellPC(a,C,500); Send(2,b,a,inform,done(SellPC(a,C,500)))) received(1,a,b,request,SellPC(a,C,500))
5. GB: MB:	 sent(1,a,b,request,SellPC(a,C,500))	Send(2,b,a,agree,SellPC(a,c2,500)); SellPC(a,c2,500); Send(2,b,a,inform,done(SellPC(a,c2,500))) received(1,a,b,request,SellPC(a,C,500))
6. GB: MB:	 sent(1,a,b,request,SellPC(a,c2,500)), received(2,b,a,agree,SellPC(a,c2,500))	SellPC(a,c2,500); Send(2,b,a,inform,done(SellPC(a,c2,500))) received(1,a,b,request,SellPC(a,c2,500)), sent(2,b,a,agree,SellPC(a,c2,500))
7. GB: MB:	 sent(1,a,b,request,SellPC(a,c2,500)), received(2,b,a,agree,SellPC(a,c2,500))	Send(3,b,a,inform,done(SellPC(a,c2,500))) received(1,a,b,request,SellPC(a,c2,500)), sent(2,b,a,agree,SellPC(a,c2,500))
8. GB: MB:	 sent(1,a,b,request,SellPC(a,c2,500)), received(2,b,a,agree,SellPC(a,c2,500)) received(3,b,a,inform,done(SellPC(a,c2,500)))	 received(1,a,b,request,SellPC(a,c2,500)), sent(2,b,a,agree,SellPC(a,c2,500)) sent(3,b,a,inform,done(SellPC(a,c2,500)))

Table 1. Example of a request conversation

condition is defined as the preconditions of the basic action SellPC, but in general this need not be the case. When for example an achievement goal is requested, which can trigger a whole set of basic actions, the relation between the actions and the preconditions may not be as straightforward as in this case.

In step 3 a request comes into the message-base of agent b and this triggers the revision of the handleRequest goal to the choice we see in step 4. And since agent b believes agent a is costumer and that he has a PC available for €500 (c2), he agrees to the request. Also due to this test-goal, he has now found a substitution for the variable C so that with the agree-message he can let agent a know what kind of PC to expect.

Going from step 4 to step 5, agent b has rewritten his goal-base because he has chosen to agree to the request. The first thing he has to do now is to inform agent a of his choice, the choice of agreeing to the request, as well as the choice for the PC he is going to sell to agent a. This message is received by agent a in step 6. He applies the substitution for C and waits for agent b to inform him about the result of the requested action.

Agent b on the other hand goes on processing his goal-base and is just about to execute this action. This results in step 7, where the belief-base of agent b is also updated: he removes the fact 'available(c2,500)' and adds 'sold$(a,$c2,500)'.

The last part of the request protocol is that agent b informs agent a that the action has been done. This is what happens when going from step 7 to step 8, where we see the final result. This, however, does not mean that the agents are finished now. They will still have to agree on a payment and delivery method, but that is outside the scope of this example.

The relations between the message-base and the belief-base have been left out from this example to keep it simple. Possible updates related to the incoming messages are for example after step 3. Agent b has received a request and could add $G_a buyPC(500)$ to his belief-base, meaning that agent a has the goal $buyPC(500)$. Similarly when agent a has received the request in step 6, he could add $G_b SellPC(a, c2, 500)$ to his belief-base. These possible belief-updates are all not defined in the FIPA semantics. The only belief-update that is defined in the FIPA ACL semantics is an update after an agent has received an **inform**, e.g. after step 8, agent a can add $B_b done(SellPC(a, c2, 500))$ to his belief-base. A possible update for the sender of this inform, like $B_a B_b done(SellPC(a, c2, 500))$ is, however, not defined in FIPA.

5   Conclusion

In this paper we have discussed some practical issues concerning the communication between goal directed agents. The first fundamental issue that we discussed is the fact that although the sending agent chooses the time to send a message, the receiving agent does not have the goal to receive that message. Therefore we created a message-base for each agent such that the transport of the message is performed synchronously while the handling of the message is asynchronous. We have shown how the specification of the effects of that depend on the performative of the message and how this is incorporated in practical reasoning rules that are invoked by the agents. The parts of the semantics of the communication that are undisputed and should take immediate effect are modelled using reactive rules that are invoked at the moment the message arrives in the message-base of the agent.

The parts of the intended effects of the communication over which the receiving agent needs to have control are modelled by reasoning rules that are invoked whenever the agent decides to pursue the trigger goal of that rule. E.g., the receiving agent decides itself when it wants to handle an inform message and whether it believes the contents of this message or even whether it believes that the sending agent believes the content.

By splitting up the 'standard' semantics of the messages given by FIPA in this way, it becomes possible to make agents that strictly conform to the FIPA specifications, but also deviate from this specification in circumstances where that might be necessary (e.g. the sincerity condition cannot be guaranteed in many open systems). The second advantage of incorporating the message handling in the practical reasoning rules is that the agent can incorporate them in a natural way among its other goals and can handle the messages at the point where it is most suitable for the agent.

Although the framework has been set up, a number of details still have to be taken care of. For instance, the unification of the content between the sent and received message is not trivial. Of course in this paper we only specified a few messages and their effects in 3APL. We intend to implement the complete set of FIPA messages in 3APL and implement the communication process. Finally there is a practical issue of how large the message-bases should be and what happens if received messages are never handled by the agent.

6   Acknowledgments

Special thanks go to Frank de Boer, Wiebe van der Hoek, Meindert Kroese, and John-Jules Meyer for many discussions and suggestions.

References

1. F. Dignum and M. Greaves. Issues in agent communication. In *LNCS-1916*. Springer-Verlag, 2000. 239
2. T. Finin, Y. Labrou, and J. Mayfield. KQML as an agent communication language. In J. Bradshaw, editor, *Software Agents*. MIT Press, Cambridge, 1995. 239
3. FIPA. http://www.fipa.org/. 239
4. K. Hindriks, F. de Boer, W. van der Hoek, and J.-J. Meyer. Semantics of communicating agents based on deduction and abduction. In *IJCAI'99, Workshop on Agent Communication Languages*, 1999. 244, 245
5. K. V. Hindriks, F. S. D. Boer, W. V. der Hoek, and J.-J. C. Meyer. Agent programming in 3APL. *Autonomous Agents and Multi-Agent Systems*, 2(4):357–401, 1999. 241, 241, 243, 243, 244
6. R. van Eijk, F. de Boer, W. van der Hoek, , and J.-J. Meyer. Generalised object-oriented concepts for inter-agent communication. In *Intelligent Agents VII, Proceedings of 7th International Workshop on Agent Theories, Architectures, and Languages (ATAL 2000)*, volume 1986 of LNAI, pages 260–274. Springer-Verlag, 2001. 244
7. M. Wooldridge. Semantic issues in the verification of agent communication languages. In *Autonomous Agents and Multi-Agent Systems*, volume 3, pages 9–32, 2000. 240

When Are Two Protocols the Same?

Mark W. Johnson[1], Peter McBurney[2], and Simon Parsons[2,3]

[1] Department of Mathematics
Pennsylvania State University Altoona
Altoona PA 16601-3760 USA
mwj3@psu.edu
[2] Department of Computer Science
University of Liverpool
Liverpool L69 7ZF UK
{p.j.mcburney,s.d.parsons}@csc.liv.ac.uk
[3] Department of Computer and Information Science
Brooklyn College
City University of New York
Brooklyn NY 11210 USA
parsons@sci.brooklyn.cuny.edu

Abstract. A number of protocols based on the formal dialogue games of philosophy have recently been proposed for interactions between autonomous agents. Several of these proposals purport to assist agents engaged in the same types of interactions, such as persuasions and negotiations, and are superficially different. How are we to determine whether or not these proposals are substantially different? This chapter considers this question and explores several alternative definitions of equivalence of protocols.

1   Introduction

Recently, several authors have proposed agent communications protocols based on the formal dialogue games of philosophy. These are interactions between two or more players, where each player "moves" by making utterances, selected from a finite set of possible locutions, according to a defined set of rules. These games have been studied by philosophers since at least the time of Aristotle [5], and have recently been the focus of renewed attention in philosophy [15].

Because dialogues conducted according to these games are rule-governed, they have been of particular interest to computer scientists, for modeling human-computer interaction [7], for modeling complex reasoning, such as that in legal domains [24], and for the task of software specification [10]. Recently, dialogue game formalisms have been proposed as protocols for interaction between autonomous software agents. In this domain, such protocols have been proposed for agent dialogues involving: persuasion [1,8,9]; joint inquiry [18]; negotiations over the division of scarce resources [4,22,30]; deliberations over a course of action [16]; and discovery of rare events [17].

As can be seen from this list of citations, more than one dialogue game protocol has sometimes been proposed for the same type of agent interaction. This presents a user or potential user of such protocols with a number of questions, including:

M.-P. Huget (Ed.): Communications in Multiagent Systems, LNAI 2650, pp. 253–268, 2003.

- How might one choose between two protocols?
- When is one protocol preferable to another?
- When do two protocols differ?

The first of these questions is of interest to agent designers who are considering how to allow their agents to interact—how do they pick one protocol from the many that have been proposed? Answering it involves, at the very least, having some way of describing the various features of protocols. In other work, two of us have taken a step towards answering this question by proposing a set of desirable properties for dialogue game protocols for agent interactions [21], and assessing various protocols against these properties.[1]

Such assessments could also provide a partial answer to the second question above. This question is again of interest to agent designers for much the same reason as the first, but goes a little further in that it also requires an understanding of what makes protocols good, and what makes them good for particular tasks (since it seems clear from the wide variety of extant protocols that some are good for some tasks and others are good for other tasks).

However, perhaps a more fundamental question is the third question given above—when do two protocols differ. Not only is an answer to this a prerequisite to being able to choose between two protocols, but it is also essential if we are to be able to tell if a protocol is new (in the sense of providing a different functionality from an existing protocol rather than just having equivalent locutions with different names) and if a protocol conforms to some specification, such as that laid down as the standard for interacting within some electronic institution [29]. Mention of functionality of a protocol leads naturally to considerations of semantics: what effects does a protocol, or rather, the dialogues conducted under it, have?[2]

In this paper, we present a preliminary exploration of this third question, including several alternative definitions for protocol equivalence. In order to do this, we first need to define what we mean by a dialogue game protocol (defined in Section 2) and to classify types of dialogues and types of locutions. We then present a classification of dialogue types, essentially a standard one from the philosophy of argumentation, due to Walton and Krabbe. Our classification of agent dialogue locutions (presented in Section 3), although based on a typology of speech acts due to Habermas, is novel. Section 4 presents our various definitions of dialogue game protocol equivalence, and explores their relationships to one another. Section 5 discusses possible extensions of the work of this paper.

2   Dialogue Game Protocols

Elsewhere [19], we identified the key elements of a dialogue game protocol, in a generic model of a formal dialogue game. We assume the dialogue occurs between autonomous

---

[1] For comparison, we also assessed the FIPA ACL [11] against these criteria.

[2] Thus our focus differs from that of traditional communications theory, which ignores the semantics of messages, e.g., *"Frequently the messages have meaning; that is they refer to or are correlated according to some system with certain physical or conceptual entities. These semantic aspects of communication are irrelevant to the engineering problem."* [32, p. 31].

software agents, and that the topics of their discussion can be represented in some logical language; we represent these topics with well-formed formulae denoted by lowercase Greek letters, θ, ϕ, etc. The specification of a dialogue game protocol then requires specification of:

Commencement Rules: Rules that define the circumstances under which the dialogue commences.

Locutions: Rules that indicate what utterances are permitted. Typically, legal locutions permit participants to assert propositions, permit others to question or contest prior assertions, and permit those asserting propositions which are subsequently questioned or contested to justify their assertions. Justifications may involve the presentation of a proof of the proposition or an argument for it. The dialogue game rules may also permit participants to utter propositions to which they assign differing degrees of belief or commitment, for example: one may merely *propose* a proposition, a speech act which entails less commitment than would an *assertion* of the same proposition.

Combination Rules: Rules that define the dialogical contexts under which particular locutions are permitted or not, or obligatory or not. For instance, it may not be permitted for a participant to assert a proposition θ and subsequently the proposition $\neg\theta$ in the same dialogue, without in the interim having retracted the former assertion.

Commitments: Rules that define the circumstances under which participants express commitment to a proposition in the dialogue. Typically, the assertion of a claim θ in the debate is defined as indicating to the other participants some level of commitment to, or support for, the claim. Since [15], formal dialogue systems typically establish and maintain public sets of commitments, called *commitment stores*, for each participant. When a participant utters a locution which incurs a commitment, the corresponding proposition is inserted into that participant's commitment store, where it is visible to the other participants. These stores are usually non-monotonic, in the sense that participants can also retract committed claims, although possibly only under defined circumstances. Fully specifying a protocol includes specification of the ways in which potentially-conflicting commitments may interact with one another.

Termination Rules: Rules that define the circumstances under which the dialogue ends.

Some comments on this model are in order. Firstly, the circumstances which may lead to the commencement of a specific dialogue under a given protocol are, strictly speaking, not part of that dialogue or protocol. Accordingly, it is reasonable to consider a meta-dialogue, where discussions about which dialogues to enter are undertaken [19] or a hierarchy of nested sequential dialogues [27]. Alternatively, participating agents may select a dialogue from some agreed library of dialogue types, as in [6]. Secondly, dialogue games are different from conversation policies [12], which are short sequences of legal utterances with a common purpose. Thus a conversation policy sits between a single utterance and a complete dialogue in length; it governs a portion of a complete dialogue, rather than the whole, as is the case with a dialogue game.

Thirdly, it is worth noting that more than one notion of *commitment* is present in the literature on dialogue games. For example, Hamblin treats commitments in a purely dialogical sense: *"A speaker who is obliged to maintain consistency needs to keep a store of statements representing his previous commitments, and require of each new statement he makes that it may be added without inconsistency to this store. The store represents a kind of persona of beliefs; it need not correspond with his real beliefs . . ."* [15, p. 257]. In contrast, Walton and Krabbe [36, Chapter 1] treat commitments as obligations to (execute, incur or maintain) a course of action, which they term action commitments. These actions may be utterances in a dialogue, as when a speaker is forced to defend a proposition he has asserted against attack from others; so Walton and Krabbe also consider propositional commitment as a special case of action commitment [36, p. 23]. As with Hamblin's treatment, such dialogical commitments to propositions may not necessarily represent a participant's true beliefs. In contrast, Singh's social semantics [35], requires agent participants to an interaction to express publicly their beliefs and intentions, and these expressions are called *social commitments*. These include both expressions of belief in some propositions and expressions of intent to execute or incur some future actions.[3]

Our primary motivation is the use of dialogue games as the basis for interaction protocols between autonomous agents. Because such agents will typically enter into these interactions in order to achieve some wider objectives, and not just for the enjoyment of the interaction itself, we believe it is reasonable to define commitments in terms of future actions or propositions external to the dialogue. In a commercial negotiation dialogue, for instance, the utterance of an offer may express a willingness by the speaker to undertake a subsequent transaction on the terms contained in the offer. For this reason, we can view commitments as mappings between locutions and subsets of some set of action-statements.

Classifying Dialogues

What different sorts of agent dialogues are there? If we assume that agents enter dialogues with each other in order to achieve specific objectives, it would seem reasonable to classify the dialogues in terms of the private and shared objectives of the participants. Indeed, these criteria — the private objectives and the shared objectives — were used by argumentation theorists Doug Walton and Erik Krabbe in their influential typology of human dialogues [36].[4] In addition, their typology is based on what information each participant has at the commencement of the dialogue (of relevance to the topic under discussion). The result was six primary types of dialogue, as follows: **Information-Seeking Dialogues** are those where one participant seeks the answer to some question(s) from another participant, who is believed by the first to know the answer(s). In

---

[3] It is worth noting that all these notions of *commitment* differ from that commonly used in discussion of agent's internal states, namely the idea of the persistence of a belief or an intention [38, p. 205]. As Singh [33] argues, there is a qualitative difference between social commitments of the kind discussed here, and personal commitments of the kind encoded in beliefs, desires, and intentions. He further argues that one kind of commitment cannot be derived from another.

[4] This typology is described in more detail in another chapter of this volume [20].

Inquiry Dialogues the participants collaborate to answer some question or questions whose answers are not known to any one participant. **Persuasion Dialogues** involve one participant seeking to persuade another to accept a proposition he or she does not currently endorse. In **Negotiation Dialogues**, the participants bargain over the division of some scarce resource. Here, the goal of the dialogue — a division of the resource acceptable to all — may be in conflict with the individual goals of the participants – to maximize their individual shares. Participants of **Deliberation Dialogues** collaborate to decide what action or course of action should be adopted in some situation. Here, participants share a responsibility to decide the course of action, or, at least, they share a willingness to discuss whether they have such a shared responsibility. Note that the best course of action for a group may conflict with the preferences or intentions of each individual member of the group; moreover, no one participant may have all the information required to decide what is best for the group. In **Eristic Dialogues**, participants quarrel verbally as a substitute for physical fighting, aiming to vent perceived grievances.

For our purposes, we note that the termination rules for these different dialogue types can be expressed succinctly in terms of utterances of support within each dialogue for certain propositions. An Information-seeking dialogue, for example, can terminate normally once the participant who sought the answer to some question indicates publicly that a given proposition provides a satisfactory answer. For normal termination of an Inquiry dialogue, all (or some designated subset) of participants must express such public indication. For a Persuasion dialogue, normal termination will occur when the participant being persuaded publicly endorses (via an appropriate locution) support for the proposition at issue. Similarly, normal termination rules for Negotiation and Deliberation dialogues may be articulated in terms of participant support for particular propositions — in these two cases, for propositions which express commitments to future actions external to the dialogues.

3   Classifying Locutions

The agent dialogue types above involve agents seeking to reach a common understanding of some situation or a collective agreement to undertake certain actions. The theory of Communicative Action of the philosopher Jürgen Habermas [14] attempts to understand how human participants achieve these goals through dialogue, and, as part of this theory, Habermas proposes a typology of statements made in such dialogues [14, pp. 325–326].[5] We have used this typology as the basis for our own classification of locutions in agent dialogues (with Habermas' labels given in parentheses):

Factual Statements (Constative Speech Acts): These are statements which seek to represent the state of the objective, external world. Statements of belief about factual matters are examples of these utterances. Contesting such a statement means denying that it is a true description of the reality external to the dialogue.

Value Statements (Expressive Acts): These are statements which seek to represent the state of the speaker's internal world, i.e., they reveal publicly a subjective preference or value assignments. Such statements may only be contested by doubting the sincerity of the speaker.

---

[5] Habermas' classification is derived from the typology of speech acts of Searle [31].

Connection Statements (Regulative Acts): These are statements which assert some social or other relationship between different participants.

Requests: These are statements about a desired state of the external world, in which an agent seeks another agent to act so as to bring about this state. Requests may be criticized on the grounds of effectiveness, i.e., that the requested action will not, in fact, bring about the desired world state. In addition, they may be refused, with or without a reason being expressed.

Promises: These are statements about a desired state of the external world, in which an agent itself agrees to act so as to bring about this state. As with requests, promises may be criticized on the grounds of effectiveness, and may be accepted or rejected, with or without reasons.

Inferences (Operative Acts): These are statements which refer to the content of earlier statements in a dialogue, drawing inferences from them or assessing their implications. Contestation of such statements can take the form of questioning the appropriateness or the validity of the inferences made.[6]

Procedural Statements (Communicative Acts): These are statements about the activity of dialogue itself, such as the rules for participation and debate. In many human discourses, these often themselves become the focus of debate, dominating the issues of substance. In some dialogues, the participants may agree to submit such issues to a chairperson or other authority for determination.

By distinguishing between Requests and Promises in the way we have, our classification differs from that of Habermas. He does not include promises in his structure, and requests are treated as commands (Imperative Acts) rather than as requests. We believe our approach is more appropriate in a context of agent autonomy. Complete autonomy, as may occur for example in open multi-agent systems, means that imperative statements may have no force: other agents can only be requested to perform some action, and never commanded to do it. In closed multi-agent systems, agents may have an hierarchical relationship with one another, and so not have complete autonomy, as for example, when they represent different departments of the same company. However, even in such applications, agents may still exercise some autonomy over a limited domain, and so a classification which includes both Requests and Promises is appropriate.

Of the seven types of locutions in this typology, only Factual statements, Promises and Requests relate to propositions with referants in the world external to the dialogue: Factual statements express beliefs about the world, while Promises and Requests concern propositions linked to actions in the world. Of these, only promises seek to *change* the external world in any way. Promises may be made by more than one participant (i.e., they may be joint promises) and may be viewed as commitments to create or to maintain a state of the world in which specified propositions are true [34,35]. In the next section, we will map Factual Statements and Promises to sets of propositions which represent external reality.

---

[6] Our definition departs slightly from that of Habermas, in that we permit Inferential Statements to have *"genuine communicative intent."*

4 Protocol Similarity

4.1 Concepts of Equivalence

In this section, we explore the question as to when two dialogue game protocols may be considered the same. To fix ideas, we first assume a finite set $\mathcal{A} = \{P_i | i = 1, \ldots, p\}$, of dialogue participants, or agents. Dialogues conducted by this set of agents are assumed to concern a finite set $\Phi = \{\phi_i | i = 1, \ldots, q\}$ of well-formed formulae in some propositional language, which we call the set of discussion topics. For this paper, both the set of agents and the set of topics are assumed fixed throughout. We denote dialogue game protocols by upper case script Roman letters, $\mathcal{D}, \mathcal{E}$, etc. Each protocol $\mathcal{D}$ comprises a finite set of legal locution-types, denoted $\mathcal{L}_\mathcal{D} = \{L_j | j = 1, \ldots, l\}$, and a number of combination, commitment and termination rules, denoted $\mathcal{R}_\mathcal{D} = \{R_j | j = 1, \ldots, r\}$. We assume that time can be represented by the non-negative real numbers, $[0, \infty)$, with locutions in a dialogue uttered simultaneously with the positive integers, i.e., the first utterance in the dialogue occurs at time $t = 1$, the second at time $t = 2$, etc. We define dialogues and partial dialogues as follows:

Definition 1. *A dialogue $\tilde{d}$ under dialogue-game protocol $\mathcal{D}$ is an ordered and possibly-infinite sequence of valid locutions, each possibly instantiated by one or more discussion topics, thus:*

$$\tilde{d} = (\ L_{d,t}(\theta_t)\ |\ t = 1, 2, \ldots)$$

with each $L_{d,t} \in \mathcal{L}_\mathcal{D}$ and each $\theta_t \in \Phi$. For any integer time-point $k > 0$, we say a partial dialogue to time k, $\tilde{d}_k$, is an ordered and finite sequence of valid possibly-instantiated locutions $(\ L_{d,t}(\theta_t)\ |\ t = 1, \ldots, k)$, with each utterance valid under the combination rules of protocol $\mathcal{D}$, and such that $L_{d,k}(\theta_k)$ does not terminate the dialogue $\tilde{d}$ under the termination rules of $\mathcal{D}$.

Drawing on the general structure of a dialogue game protocol presented in Section 2 we can make an initial attempt at defining protocol similarity as follows:

Definition 2. *(**Syntactic Equivalence**) Two protocols $\mathcal{D}$ and $\mathcal{E}$ are syntactically equivalent if their locutions, combination rules, commitment rules and termination rules are (respectively) the same, i.e., if $\mathcal{L}_\mathcal{D} = \mathcal{L}_\mathcal{E}$ and $\mathcal{R}_\mathcal{D} = \mathcal{R}_\mathcal{E}$.*

Thus, under this definition, two protocols are the same if their syntax is identical. This definition seems too strict, as it precludes us identifying two protocols which may differ in small but superficial ways, for example if one protocol has redundant locutions or rules.

Indeed, given a strictly syntactic notion of equality, it will classify two protocols which have sets of locutions which differ only in the names given to the locutions, as different. As an example of such a pair of dialogues, consider the two in [2] and [3]. The latter paper is a French language version of the former, and the protocol discussed in the two papers has locutions with exactly the same properties, but with different names (the names in the latter paper are the translation of the names in the former paper). The two protocols are not syntactically equivalent, despite the fact that they have exactly the same properties. Thus we need a less strict notion of equivalence. However, to achieve this we will need some notion of semantics, or meaning, for the dialogues under a protocol. We now present such a notion.

As mentioned in the previous section, Factual statements and Promises relate to propositions with referants in the world external to the dialogue. In each case, we may view the instantiated locution as invoking a subset of the elements of Φ, the set of discussion topics, and so each utterance comprising a Factual statement or a Promise defines a subset of Φ. For a given instantiated locution $L_j(\theta)$ in a protocol $\mathcal{D}$, we denote this subset by $\Phi_{\mathcal{D}}(L_j(\theta))$, and call it *the commitment set of $L_j(\theta)$ in $\mathcal{D}$*. Because a dialogue $\tilde{d}$ is an ordered sequence of instantiated locutions, we may consider the sequence of commitment subsets of Φ which arise from this particular sequence as a set of state transitions:

$$\emptyset \cup \{\Phi_{\mathcal{D}}(L_{d,t}(\theta_t)) \mid t = 1, 2, \dots \}$$

where each $L_{d,t}(\theta_t)$ is the (instantiated) t-th utterance in dialogue $\tilde{d}$. We append the empty set at the start of this sequence to represent the state of the commitments prior to utterance of the first locution in any dialogue. This means that all dialogues are assumed to commence with the same initial state.

We now have the means by which to identify two dialogues and two dialogue protocols in a semantic sense. In doing so, we are motivated by semantic notions from the theory of programming languages [13]. For example, we may consider two protocols as equivalent if any state transition achievable in one is also achievable in the other, a property known as bisimulation [23]:[7]

Definition 3. (***Bisimulation Equivalence***) *For any positive integers j and k, suppose that two partial dialogues $\tilde{d}_j$ and $\tilde{e}_k$ conducted under protocols $\mathcal{D}$ and $\mathcal{E}$ respectively have respective state transitions $\Phi_{\mathcal{D}}(L_{d,j}(\delta_j))$ and $\Phi_{\mathcal{E}}(L_{e,k}(\theta_k))$ such that*

$$\Phi_{\mathcal{D}}(L_{d,j}(\delta_j)) = \Phi_{\mathcal{E}}(L_{e,k}(\theta_k)).$$

Then $\mathcal{D}$ and $\mathcal{E}$ are bisimulation equivalent *if, for any instantiated locution $L_{d,j+1}(\delta_{j+1})$ valid under $\mathcal{D}$, there is an instantiated locution $L_{e,k+1}(\theta_{k+1})$ valid under $\mathcal{D}$ such that*

$$\Phi_{\mathcal{D}}(L_{d,j+1}(\delta_{j+1})) = \Phi_{\mathcal{E}}(L_{e,k+1}(\theta_{k+1}))$$

and conversely.

In other words, bisimulation equivalence says that any transition in commitment states achievable under one protocol by uttering a single instantiated locution can also be achieved under the other using only one instantiated locution. Note that the locutions and the topics with which they are instantiated may differ in the two protocols.

Many protocols permit participants to retract prior utterances. If so, then not all the beliefs expressed or action-commitments incurred during the course of a terminating dialogue may still be current at the end of that dialogue. We therefore distinguish the particular subset of Φ consisting of those beliefs or action-commitments made in the

---

[7] Strictly, the equivalence defined here is strong bisimulation [23, Chapter 4].

course of a dialogue which are still standing at the normal termination of the dialogue. For a terminating dialogue $\tilde{d}$ conducted under a protocol $\mathcal{D}$, we denote this set by $\Phi_{\mathcal{D},\tilde{d}}$, and we call it the *final commitment-set of $\tilde{d}$ under $\mathcal{D}$*. Note that this set may be empty. We therefore have available another notion of protocol equivalence:

Definition 4. *(Final-State Equivalence) Two protocols $\mathcal{D}$ and $\mathcal{E}$ are* final-state equivalent *if, for any terminating dialogue $\tilde{d}$ conducted under protocol $\mathcal{D}$, there is a terminating dialogue $\tilde{e}$ conducted under protocol $\mathcal{E}$ such that $\Phi_{\mathcal{D},\tilde{d}} = \Phi_{\mathcal{E},\tilde{e}}$, and conversely.*

This definition ignores the length of dialogues under each protocol. It would be possible for a dialogue under one protocol to terminate after five utterances (say) and to achieve an outcome for which a dialogue under the second protocol would require 500 locutions. So, we might wish to modify the previous definition as follows:

Definition 5. *(Equal-length Final-state Equivalence) Two protocols $\mathcal{D}$ and $\mathcal{E}$ are* equal-length final-state equivalent *if, for any terminating dialogue $\tilde{d}$ conducted under protocol $\mathcal{D}$, there is a terminating dialogue $\tilde{e}$ conducted under protocol $\mathcal{E}$ and comprising the same number of utterances as $\tilde{d}$, such that $\Phi_{\mathcal{D},\tilde{d}} = \Phi_{\mathcal{E},\tilde{e}}$, and conversely.*

For most applications, however, this definition may be too strict. Ideally, we desire a notion of final-state equivalence which would permit terminating dialogues under one protocol to be considered equivalent to terminating dialogues under the other protocol when these had the same outcomes and of similar length. For this notion, we would require a precise definition of the word *"similar."* Moreover, it would be desirable to define this notion so that transitivity is maintained, i.e., so that if protocols $\mathcal{D}$ and $\mathcal{E}$ are similar-length operationally equivalent and if $\mathcal{E}$ and $\mathcal{F}$ are similar-length operational equivalent, then so too are $\mathcal{D}$ and $\mathcal{F}$. We achieve this by partitioning time into a sequence of non-overlapping intervals, as follows:

Definition 6. *Let $(x_i \mid i = 1, 2, \ldots)$ be a finite or countably-infinite sequence of strictly increasing non-negative real numbers, with the first element being $x_1 = 0$. In the case where the sequence is finite with n elements, assume that ∞ is appended to the sequence as the $n+1$-th element, x_{n+1}. A* **time partition** *$\mathcal{T}$ is a collection of closed-open subsets $\{T_i \mid i = 1, 2, \ldots\}$ of the non-negative real numbers $[0, \infty)$, such that each $T_i = [x_i, x_{i+1})$. If $\mathcal{T} = [0, \infty)$, we say it is a degenerate* time-partition.

We now use this idea of a partition of time to define a notion of similarity of length for two dialogues. Essentially, two terminating dialogues are said to be of similar length when they both end in the same element of the partition.

Definition 7. *(T-Similar Final-state Equivalence) Let $\mathcal{T}$ be any time partition. Two protocols $\mathcal{D}$ and $\mathcal{E}$ are $\mathcal{T}$-similar final-state equivalent with respect to $\mathcal{T}$ if, for any terminating dialogue $\tilde{d}$ conducted under protocol $\mathcal{D}$, there is a terminating dialogue $\tilde{e}$ conducted under protocol $\mathcal{E}$, such that $\Phi_{\mathcal{D},\tilde{d}} = \Phi_{\mathcal{E},\tilde{e}}$, and such that the final utterance of $\tilde{e}$ occurs in the same element of time partition $\mathcal{T}$ as the final utterance of $\tilde{d}$, and conversely.*

It is clear that this notion of equivalence is transitive. Moreover, it can be readily seen that Final-state Equivalence and Equal-length Final-state Equivalence are special cases of $\mathcal{T}$-Similar Final-state Equivalence. In the first case, the partition is the degenerate case of the whole non-negative real line: $\mathcal{T} = [0, \infty)$. In the second case, because dialogue utterances occur only at integer time-points, the relevant partitions are those where each element of the partition includes precisely one integer, for example:

$$\mathcal{T} = [0, 0.5) \cup \bigcup_{k=1}^{\infty} [k - 0.5, k + 0.5).$$

As a final comment regarding these definitions, we note that recent work in abstract concurrency theory has argued that sequential behavior is distinguished from concurrent behavior because the former synchronizes information flows and time, while the latter allows these to evolve independently of one another [25]. If we allow the number of locutions in a dialogue to be a surrogate for time, then we can see that our definition of Final-state Equivalence treats time and information flows as completely independent, since the numbers of locutions in the dialogues under each pair of protocols is not mentioned in Definition 4. In contrast, non-degenerate $\mathcal{T}$-Similar Final-state Equivalence — i.e., all cases where $\mathcal{T} \neq [0, \infty)$ — attempts to re-couple time and information-flows in the pairing of dialogues under the two protocols being considered. Protocols deemed $\mathcal{T}$-similar final-state equivalent do not allow their respective information-flows (in the form of their final commitment sets) and the time taken to achieve these information flows to evolve independently: whatever the link between time and information-flow in any terminating dialogue under one protocol is preserved in the paired dialogue under the other protocol.

4.2   Comparison of Equivalences

We now consider the relationships between these various types of equivalence. We write $\Delta(\Pi)$ to denote the class of all protocols, and $\Delta(P)$ to denote the class of all pairs of protocols $\langle \mathcal{D}, \mathcal{E} \rangle$ where $\mathcal{D}, \mathcal{E} \in \Delta(\Pi)$. Then we write $\Delta(P_{\mathrm{syn}})$ to denote the class of all pairs of protocols $\mathcal{D}, \mathcal{E} \in \Delta(\Pi)$ such that $\mathcal{D}$ and $\mathcal{E}$ are syntactically equivalent, and $\Delta(P_{\mathrm{bi}})$, $\Delta(P_{\mathrm{fin}})$, and $\Delta(P_{\mathrm{eq}})$ to denote the classes of pairs of protocols which are bisimulation equivalent, final-state equivalent, and equal-length final-state equivalent respectively. Moreover, we write $\Delta(P_{\mathrm{sim}})$ to denote the class of all pairs of protocols $\mathcal{D}, \mathcal{E} \in \Delta(\Pi)$ such that there exists a non-degenerate time partition $\mathcal{T}$ for which $\mathcal{D}$ and $\mathcal{E}$ are $\mathcal{T}$-similar final-state equivalent. Call these five classes the *equivalence partitions* of $\Delta(\Pi)$. Then we have the following results:

Proposition 1. *The following set inclusions hold, and each inclusion is strict:*

$$\Delta(P_{\mathrm{syn}}) \subset \Delta(P_{\mathrm{bi}})$$

and

$$\Delta(P_{\mathrm{eq}}) \subset \Delta(P_{\mathrm{sim}}) \subset \Delta(P_{\mathrm{fin}}).$$

Proof. Straightforward from the definitions.   □

This proposition says that the class of syntactically-equivalent protocol pairs is a proper subset of the class of bisimulation equivalent protocol pairs. Likewise, the class of equal-length final-state equivalent protocol pairs is a proper subset of the class of non-degenerate $\mathcal{T}$-similar final-state equivalent pairs, which is in turn a proper subset of the class of final-state equivalent protocol pairs.

However, the relationship between bisimulation equivalence and the various forms of final-state equivalence is not straightforward, as the following two results reveal.

Proposition 2. *There exist protocols $\mathcal{D}$ and $\mathcal{E}$ which are bisimulation equivalent but not final-state equivalent.*

Proof. We proceed by demonstrating two such protocols. Consider a protocol $\mathcal{D}$, which contains just one locution, $do(P_i, \theta)$, a locution which expresses a promise by agent P_i to undertake the action represented by θ, for $\Phi = \{\theta\}$, and for $i = 1, 2$. Further suppose that protocol $\mathcal{D}$ has one rule, a termination rule, which causes the dialogue to terminate normally after any three successive utterances of locution $do(.)$. Thus, there are $2^3 = 8$ terminating dialogues under $\mathcal{D}$, and each has the form:

Utterance 1: $do(P_i, \theta)$
Utterance 2: $do(P_j, \theta)$
Utterance 3: $do(P_k, \theta)$

for possibly-identical agents P_i, P_j and P_k. The final commitment set for each dialogue is either $\{ (P_1, \theta), (P_2, \theta) \}$, in the case where both agents have uttered something in the dialogue, or simply $\{ (P_i, \theta) \}$, in the case where all three utterances were made by agent P_i, for $i = 1$ or 2.

Now consider a second protocol $\mathcal{E}$ which has the same locution set as protocol $\mathcal{D}$, but has no termination rules. All dialogues under $\mathcal{E}$ are infinite, and so partial dialogues may have any finite length. However, because Φ consists of a single element, and because there are only two agents, the commitment set for a partial dialogue at any time after commencement has either one or two elements, namely either or both of (P_1, θ) or (P_2, θ). Because there are no retraction locutions, elements in the commitment set cannot be removed once inserted. For protocol $\mathcal{D}$, all partial dialogues have length either one or two locutions. Because the two protocols have the same locutions, it can be readily seen that any transition in commitment states in a partial dialogue achievable under one protocol by uttering a single instantiated locution can also be achieved under the other using the same instantiated locution, and so the two protocols are bisimulation equivalent.

However, the two protocols are not final-state equivalent, since $\mathcal{E}$ has no terminating dialogues. Thus, there do not exist terminating dialogues under $\mathcal{E}$ which can be matched to each of the eight terminating dialogues under $\mathcal{D}$.   □

We can also construct a counter-example in the reverse direction, as follows.

Proposition 3. *There exist protocols $\mathcal{D}$ and $\mathcal{E}$ which are equal-length final-state equivalent but not bisimulation equivalent.*

Proof. Again, we demonstrate two such protocols. Consider a protocol $\mathcal{D}$, which contains just one locution, $do(P_i, \theta)$, a locution which expresses a promise by agent P_i to undertake the action represented by θ, for $\theta \in \Phi$. Here, the set Φ may have more than one element. Further suppose that protocol $\mathcal{D}$ has one rule, a termination rule, which causes the dialogue to terminate normally after any two successive utterances of locution $do(.)$. Thus, all terminating dialogues under $\mathcal{D}$ have the form, for agents P_i, P_j (possibly identical) and $\theta, \delta \in \Phi$:

Utterance 1: $do(P_i, \theta)$

Utterance 2: $do(P_j, \delta)$

The final commitment set for this dialogue is $\{\theta, \delta\}$.

Now consider a second protocol $\mathcal{E}$ which also contains the locution $do(.)$, with the same syntax. But suppose $\mathcal{E}$ also has a second locution $undo(P_i, \theta)$, which retracts any prior promise by agent P_i to undertake the action represented by θ. Thus, the dialogue sequence:

Utterance 1: $do(P_i, \theta)$

Utterance 2: $undo(P_i, \theta)$

.

.

generates the following sequence of commitment states:

$$\emptyset, \{\theta\}, \emptyset, \ldots$$

Next, assume that protocol $\mathcal{E}$ has three combination rules, the first of which states that a valid dialogue must commence with an instantiated utterance of the locution $do(.)$. The second combination rule says that this utterance may be followed either by another instantiated utterance of $do(.)$ or by an instantiated utterance of $undo(.)$. The third rule says that subsequent utterances may be instantiations of either locution, subject only to the termination rule. Finally, we assume that $\mathcal{E}$ has one termination rule, which causes a dialogue to terminate normally only in the case of dialogues containing no $undo(.)$ locutions, with this termination occurring after two successive utterances of locution $do(.)$.

It can be seen that all terminating dialogues under both protocols $\mathcal{D}$ and $\mathcal{E}$ have the same form, namely:

Utterance 1: $do(P_i, \theta)$

Utterance 2: $do(P_j, \delta)$

Under both protocols, these dialogues are the same length and lead to the same final commitment set: $\{\theta, \delta\}$. Thus, the two protocols are equal-length final-state equivalent. However, protocol $\mathcal{E}$ contains a commitment state transition which cannot be simulated by any locution in $\mathcal{D}$, namely that effected by the execution of the $undo(.)$ locution in the following dialogue sequence:

Utterance k: $do(P_i, \theta)$

Utterance $k + 1$: $undo(P_i, \theta)$

Thus, the two protocols are not bisimulation equivalent.   □

It is worth noting that it may be possible to represent similar-length dialogues using order of magnitude reasoning methods, such as those developed in the qualitative physics area of Artificial Intelligence [37]. For example, the system FOG of Olivier Raiman [26], defines three operators to represent the relative values of two physical variables: one variable is negligible relative to the other; their difference is negligible;

and both variables are the same size and order of magnitude. Raiman has defined axioms for these three operators, and given the FOG system a semantics based on the calculus of infinitesimals [28].

5 Conclusions

Dialogue game protocols have recently been proposed as the basis for interaction between autonomous agents in a number of situations. As these proposals proliferate, potential protocol users will require guidance in selecting protocols for specified tasks and in choosing between different protocols suitable for the same task. In this paper, we have taken some preliminary steps towards a formal theory of protocols capable of providing such guidance. Building on earlier work classifying dialogues and locutions, we have identified several dimensions by which protocols may be compared, including: the rules which comprise a protocol; the length of dialogues conducted according to a protocol; and the commitments incurred by participants in the course of a dialogue. Our classification of locutions, presented here for the first time, allows for statements of belief about factual matters, and for requests for and promises of actions. Because these locutions connect to external reality (descriptions of the world, and actions in that world) we were able to consider dialogues from the perspective of their semantic effects.

With these dimensions we were able to define several reasonable notions of equivalence of protocols, and to study their relationships to one another. These notions included: syntactic equivalence, where two protocols have identical locutions and rules; bisimulation equivalence, where any semantic transition able to be effected under one protocol can also be effected under the other; and several versions of final-state equivalence, where any final state achievable by a terminating dialogue under one protocol can also be achieved by a terminating dialogue under the other. The various notions of final-state equivalence differ according to whether the matched dialogues are required to have the same, or similar, numbers of locutions, or not. We believe these five notions of equivalence are appropriate for protocols with only terminating dialogues. More work, however, is required on understanding equivalence where one or both protocols permits non-terminating dialogues; this may lead us, in future work, to refine these definitions.

Although the work in this paper is preliminary, we hope it will lead to a complete theory of dialogue-game protocol equivalence for agent communications protocols, and thus provide guidance to protocol designers and users. To our knowledge, these issues have not previously been considered in the agent communications languages community. However, there is much to be done before these initial ideas will comprise a complete theory. Firstly, although we have drawn on notions of equivalence from the theory of programming languages and concurrency theory, there are other notions we could also borrow, such as weak equivalence or congruency [23]. To this end, it may be valuable to further explore the relationships, if any, between interaction protocols and process algebras. Secondly, our definitions of equivalence abstracted away from the details of dialogue game protocols, of dialogues and of locutions presented in Sections 2, 3 and 4. It would be interesting, therefore, to explore notions of equivalence which pertain to specific types of dialogue-games. Thirdly, in developing multiple notions of equivalence it may be useful to articulate desirable properties of such notions, in the same way that two of us have recently identified desirable properties of protocols themselves [21]. In discussing similar-length equivalence in Section 5.1, we mentioned one of these, namely that we believe that protocol-equivalence should be transitive.

These various lines of inquiry may be facilitated by the development of a mathematical language in which to represent protocols, along with a denotational semantics for them [13]. We are currently exploring a category-theoretic semantics for interaction protocols, under which protocols are represented by objects in an appropriate category of protocols. Studying this category and its properties will, we hope, allow us to better understand the space of protocols, and the landscape of this space. For example, we would hope eventually to achieve a denotational characterization of our different notions of equivalence of protocols. Once achieved, we would then seek to identify the best protocol or protocols *within* each equivalence class, according to some reasonable criteria. In addition, for those protocols which are not equivalent, a quantitative measure of their difference would provide guidance to protocol users and designers.

Acknowledgments   An earlier version of this work was presented at the Workshop on *Agent Communications Languages and Conversational Policies*, held in Bologna, Italy, in July 2002, as part of the First International Conference on Autonomous Agents and Multi-Agent Systems (AAMAS-2002). We thank the anonymous referees and the participants in the workshop for their comments. We also thank Rogier van Eijk and Michael Wooldridge for discussions on these topics.

References

1. L. Amgoud, N. Maudet, and S. Parsons. Modelling dialogues using argumentation. In E. Durfee, editor, *Proceedings of the Fourth International Conference on Multi-Agent Systems (ICMAS 2000)*, pages 31–38, Boston, MA, USA, 2000. IEEE Press. 253
2. L. Amgoud and S. Parsons. Agent dialogues with conflicting preferences. In J.-J. Meyer and M. Tambe, editors, *Proceedings of the Eighth International Workshop on Agent Theories, Architectures and Languages (ATAL 2001)*, pages 1–15, 2001. 259
3. L. Amgoud and S. Parsons. Les dialogues entre agents avec des préférences conflictuelles. In B. Chaib-draa and P. Enjalbert, editors, *Proceedings of the 1 eres Journées Francophones des Modèles Formels de l'Interaction*, pages 3–14, 2001. 259
4. L. Amgoud, S. Parsons, and N. Maudet. Arguments, dialogue, and negotiation. In W. Horn, editor, *Proceedings of the Fourteenth European Conference on Artificial Intelligence (ECAI 2000)*, pages 338–342, Berlin, Germany, 2000. IOS Press. 253
5. Aristotle. *Topics*. Clarendon Press, Oxford, UK, 1928. (W. D. Ross, Editor). 253
6. M. Barbuceanu and M. S. Fox. COOL: A language for describing co-ordination in multi agent systems. In V. Lesser, editor, *Proceedings of the First International Conference on Multi-Agent Systems (ICMAS-95)*, pages 17–24, Cambridge, MA, USA, 1995. MIT Press. 255
7. T. J. M. Bench-Capon, P. E. Dunne, and P. H. Leng. Interacting with knowledge-based systems through dialogue games. In *Proceedings of the Eleventh International Conference on Expert Systems and Applications*, pages 123–140, Avignon, France, 1991. 253

8. F. Dignum, B. Dunin-Kęplicz, and R. Verbrugge. Agent theory for team formation by dialogue. In C. Castelfranchi and Y. Lespérance, editors, *Intelligent Agents VII: Proceedings of the Seventh International Workshop on Agent Theories, Architectures, and Languages (ATAL 2000)*, Lecture Notes in Artificial Intelligence 1986, pages 150–166, Berlin, Germany, 2000. Springer. 253

9. F. Dignum, B. Dunin-Kęplicz, and R. Verbrugge. Creating collective intention through dialogue. *Logic Journal of the IGPL*, 9(2):305–319, 2001. 253

10. A. Finkelstein and H. Fuks. Multi-party specification. In *Proceedings of the Fifth International Workshop on Software Specification and Design*, Pittsburgh, PA, USA, 1989. ACM Sigsoft Engineering Notes. 253

11. FIPA. Communicative Act Library Specification. Technical Report XC00037H, Foundation for Intelligent Physical Agents, 10 August 2001. 254

12. M. Greaves, H. Holmback, and J. Bradshaw. What is a conversation policy? In F. Dignum and M. Greaves, editors, *Issues in Agent Communication*, Lecture Notes in Artificial Intelligence 1916, pages 118–131. Springer, Berlin, Germany, 2000. 255

13. C. A. Gunter. *Semantics of Programming Languages: Structures and Techniques*. MIT Press, Cambridge, MA, USA, 1992. 260, 266

14. J. Habermas. *The Theory of Communicative Action: Volume 1: Reason and the Rationalization of Society*. Heinemann, London, UK, 1984. Translation by T. McCarthy of: *Theorie des Kommunikativen Handelns, Band I, Handlungsrationalitat und gesellschaftliche Rationalisierung*. Suhrkamp, Frankfurt, Germany. 1981. 257, 257

15. C. L. Hamblin. *Fallacies*. Methuen, London, UK, 1970. 253, 255, 256

16. D. Hitchcock, P. McBurney, and S. Parsons. A framework for deliberation dialogues. In H. V. Hansen, C. W. Tindale, J. A. Blair, and R. H. Johnson, editors, *Proceedings of the Fourth Biennial Conference of the Ontario Society for Study of Argumentation (OSSA 2001)*, Windsor, Ontario, Canada, 2001. OSSA. 253

17. P. McBurney and S. Parsons. Chance discovery using dialectical argumentation. In T. Terano, T. Nishida, A. Namatame, S. Tsumoto, Y. Ohsawa, and T. Washio, editors, *New Frontiers in Artificial Intelligence: Joint JSAI 2001 Workshop Post Proceedings*, Lecture Notes in Artificial Intelligence 2253, pages 414–424. Springer, Berlin, Germany, 2001. 253

18. P. McBurney and S. Parsons. Representing epistemic uncertainty by means of dialectical argumentation. *Annals of Mathematics and AI*, 32(1–4):125–169, 2001. 253

19. P. McBurney and S. Parsons. Games that agents play: A formal framework for dialogues between autonomous agents. *Journal of Logic, Language and Information*, 11(3):315–334, 2002. 254, 255

20. P. McBurney and S. Parsons. Dialogue game protocols. In M.-P. Huget, editor, *Agent Communications Languages*, Lecture Notes in Artificial Intelligence, Berlin, Germany, 2003. Springer. *This volume*. 256

21. P. McBurney, S. Parsons, and M. Wooldridge. Desiderata for agent argumentation protocols. In C. Castelfranchi and W. L. Johnson, editors, *Proceedings of the First International Joint Conference on Autonomous Agents and Multi-Agent Systems (AAMAS 2002), Bologna, Italy*, pages 402–409, New York City, NY, USA, 2002. ACM Press. 254, 266

22. P. McBurney, R. van Eijk, S. Parsons, and L. Amgoud. A dialogue-game protocol for agent purchase negotiations. *Journal of Autonomous Agents and Multi-Agent Systems*, 2003. *In press*. 253

23. R. Milner. *Communication and Concurrency*. International Series in Computer Science. Prentice Hall, Hemel Hempstead, UK, 1989. 260, 260, 265

24. H. Prakken. On dialogue systems with speech acts, arguments, and counterarguments. In M. Ojeda-Aciego, M. I. P. de Guzman, G. Brewka, and L. M. Pereira, editors, *Proceedings of the Seventh European Workshop on Logic in Artificial Intelligence (JELIA-2000)*, Lecture Notes in Artificial Intelligence 1919, pages 224–238, Berlin, Germany, 2000. Springer. 253

25. V. R. Pratt. Transition and cancellation in concurrency and branching time. *Mathematical Structures in Computer Science*, 2002. *Forthcoming.* 262

26. O. Raiman. Order of magnitude reasoning. In *Proceedings of the Fifth National Conference on Artificial Intelligence (AAAI-86)*, pages 100–104, San Mateo, CA, USA, 1986. Morgan Kaufmann. Reprinted in [37]. 264

27. C. Reed. Dialogue frames in agent communications. In Y. Demazeau, editor, *Proceedings of the Third International Conference on Multi-Agent Systems (ICMAS-98)*, pages 246–253. IEEE Press, 1998. 255

28. A. Robinson. *Non-Standard Analysis*. North-Holland, Amsterdam, The Netherlands, 1966. 265

29. J. A. Rodríguez, F. J. Martin, P. Noriega, P. Garcia, and C. Sierra. Towards a test-bed for trading agents in electronic auction markets. *AI Communications*, 11(1):5–19, 1998. 254

30. F. Sadri, F. Toni, and P. Torroni. Logic agents, dialogues and negotiation: an abductive approach. In M. Schroeder and K. Stathis, editors, *Proceedings of the Symposium on Information Agents for E-Commerce, Artificial Intelligence and the Simulation of Behaviour Conference (AISB-2001)*, York, UK, 2001. AISB. 253

31. J. Searle. *Speech Acts: An Essay in the Philosophy of Language*. Cambridge University Press, Cambridge, UK, 1969. 257

32. C. E. Shannon. The mathematical theory of communication. In C. E. Shannon and W. Weaver, editors, *The Mathematical Theory of Communication*, pages 29–125. University of Illinois Press, Chicago, IL, USA, 1963. Originally published in the *Bell System Technical Journal*, October and November 1948. 254

33. M. P. Singh. A conceptual analysis of commitments in multiagent systems. Technical Report 96-09, Department of Computer Science, North Carolina State University, 1996. 256

34. M. P. Singh. An ontology for commitments in multiagent systems: toward a unification of normative concepts. *Artificial Intelligence and Law*, 7:97–113, 1999. 258

35. M. P. Singh. A social semantics for agent communications languages. In F. Dignum, B. Chaib-draa, and H. Weigand, editors, *Proceedings of the Workshop on Agent Communication Languages, International Joint Conference on Artificial Intelligence (IJCAI-99)*, Berlin, Germany, 2000. Springer. 256, 258

36. D. N. Walton and E. C. W. Krabbe. *Commitment in Dialogue: Basic Concepts of Interpersonal Reasoning*. State University of New York Press, Albany, NY, USA, 1995. 256, 256, 256

37. D. S. Weld and J. de Kleer, editors. *Readings in Qualitative Reasoning about Physical Systems*. Morgan Kaufmann, San Mateo, CA, USA, 1990. 264, 268

38. M. J. Wooldridge. *Introduction to Multiagent Systems*. John Wiley and Sons, New York, NY, USA, 2002. 256

Dialogue Game Protocols

Peter McBurney[1] and Simon Parsons[2]

[1] Department of Computer Science
University of Liverpool
Liverpool L69 7ZF U. K.
p.j.mcburney@csc.liv.ac.uk
[2] Center for Co-ordination Science
Sloan School of Management
Massachusetts Institute of Technology
Cambridge, MA 02142, USA
sparsons@mit.edu

Abstract. Formal dialogue games have been studied in philosophy since at least the time of Aristotle. Recently they have been used as the basis for agent interaction protocols. We review these applications and examine some of the protocols which have been proposed for agent interactions. We discuss the many open questions and challenges, including issues of automatability of agent dialogues, and the semantics of protocols.

1 Introduction

Dialogue game protocols for agent interactions lie between auction mechanisms and generic agent communications languages. Dialogue game protocols are more expressive than auction and game-theoretic mechanisms, typically allowing participants to question and contest assertions, to advance supporting arguments and counter-arguments, and to retract prior assertions, none of which are normally possible under auction mechanisms. Because such questions and arguments are likely to increase understanding by the participants of each other's positions, we would expect dialogue game protocols both to increase the chance of a successful resolution of an interaction, and to hasten it along, relative to auction mechanisms. It is for just these reasons that argumentation approaches were proposed for agent communications protocols in [43]. Moreover, in many decision contexts, determination of an agent's preferences between alternative decision-options may well depend upon the preferences of other participants [31], as for example when participants to a public policy decision consider the totality of consequences of each option, not merely those consequences which are of direct personal concern. In such circumstances, agents do not necessarily enter the interaction with their utilities and preferences fully formed; rather, their utilities and preferences are generated in the very act of interaction itself [47]. Auction mechanisms, because of their impoverished expressiveness, are particularly unsuitable for such "on-the-fly" preference-generation. Marketing theorists, modeling real-world consumer decision-making, have known this for a long time [28];

M.-P. Huget (Ed.): Communications in Multiagent Systems, LNAI 2650, pp. 269–283, 2003.

political theorists, now viewing democratic decision-making as a process of deliberation rather than one of economic choice, have also realized it [9].

At the other extreme, dialogue game protocols usually do not permit absolutely any contributions whatsoever, and participants may be required to respond to particular utterances in particular ways. Dialogues conducted according to such protocols are therefore more constrained than interactions using generic agent communications languages, such as FIPA's ACL [18]. In addition to allowing belligerent, malicious or badly-coded participants to disrupt conversations, the freedom of generic languages such as FIPA ACL also complicates the task of analysis of utterances and conversations. After all, any given sequence of utterances in the FIPA ACL may be followed by any one of the 22 locutions, and each of them in turn followed by one of 22 locutions, and so on. This creates a state-explosion problem for participants analysing a sequence of utterances, for example, to decide what locution to utter next, or seeking to infer the future utterances of other participants. One attempt to deal with this problem has sought to identify short sequences of utterances, called *conversation policies*, which have some common intention, and with rules connecting the ordering of locutions within them [20,54]. Thus, a request for information may be followed only by the provision of that information (via an *inform* locution in FIPA ACL) or a statement that the information is not known (also via an *inform* locution), and not any other statement. Conversation policies therefore sit between individual utterances and entire conversations; in particular, each participant may maintain several different conversation policies concurrently, implementing them as and when required, and these policies may differ from the policies of other participants in the same dialogue. Such an approach creates problems of global coherence across the entire conversation [16]. It also distinguishes conversational policies from formal dialogue games, whose rules apply to all participants in the interaction, and to all dialogues conducted under the protocol.

Formal dialogue games are interactions between two or more players, where each player "moves" by making utterances, according to a defined set of rules. Although their study dates at least from Aristotle [5], they have found recent application in philosophy, computational linguistics and Artificial Intelligence (AI). In philosophy, dialogue games have been used to study fallacious reasoning [21,30] and to develop a game-theoretic semantics for intuitionistic and classical logic [29] and quantum logic [41]. In linguistics, they have been used to explain sequences of human utterances [27], with subsequent application to machine-based natural language processing and generation [24], and to human-computer interaction [7]. Within computer science and AI, they have been applied to modeling complex human reasoning, for example in legal domains [8,45], and to requirements specification for complex software projects [17]. Dialogue games differ from the games of economic game theory [42] in that payoffs for winning or losing a game are not considered, and because there is no use of uncertainty measures, such as probabilities, to model the possible moves of opponents. They also differ from the abstract games recently used as a semantics for interactive computation [1], since these latter games do not share the rich rule structure of dialogue games, nor are they intended to have themselves a semantic interpretation involving the co-ordination of actions among a group of agents.

This chapter reviews the application of formal dialogue games to the design of agent interaction protocols. We begin, in Section 2, with a brief overview of an influential typology of human dialogues, which will be useful in classifying agent interactions. Section 3 then presents a model of a formal dialogue game protocol, following which we consider, in Section 4, several recent proposals for agent interaction protocols based on dialogue games. In Section 5, we discuss some of the many open issues and the research and development challenges current in this domain.

2   Types of Dialogues

An influential model of human dialogues is the typology of primary dialogue types of argumentation theorists Doug Walton and Erik Krabbe [55]. This categorization is based upon the information the participants have at the commencement of a dialogue (of relevance to the topic of discussion), their individual goals for the dialogue, and the goals they share. **Information-Seeking Dialogues** are those where one participant seeks the answer to some question(s) from another participant, who is believed by the first to know the answer(s). In **Inquiry Dialogues** the participants collaborate to answer some question or questions whose answers are not known to any one participant. **Persuasion Dialogues** involve one participant seeking to persuade another to accept a proposition he or she does not currently endorse. In **Negotiation Dialogues**, the participants bargain over the division of some scarce resource. Here, the goal of the dialogue — a division of the resource acceptable to all — may be in conflict with the individual goals of the participants. Participants of **Deliberation Dialogues** collaborate to decide what action or course of action should be adopted in some situation. Here, participants share a responsibility to decide the course of action, or, at least, they share a willingness to discuss whether they have such a shared responsibility. Note that the best course of action for a group may conflict with the preferences or intentions of each individual member of the group; moreover, no one participant may have all the information required to decide what is best for the group. In **Eristic Dialogues**, participants quarrel verbally as a substitute for physical fighting, aiming to vent perceived grievances.

Most actual dialogue occurrences — both human and agent — involve mixtures of these dialogue types. A purchase transaction, for example, may commence with a request from a potential buyer for information from a seller, proceed to a persuasion dialogue, where the seller seeks to persuade the potential buyer of the importance of some feature of the product, and then transition to a negotiation, where each party offers to give up something he or she desires in return for something else. The two parties may or may not be aware of the different nature of their discussions at each phase, or of the transitions between phases. Instances of individual dialogue types contained entirely within other dialogue types are said to be *embedded* [55].

3   Formal Dialogue Games

We now present a model of a generic formal dialogue game in terms of the components of its specification, taken from [36]. We first assume that the topics of discussion between the agents can be represented in some logical language, whose well-formed formulae are denoted by the lower-case Roman letters, p, q, r, etc. A dialogue game specification then consists of the following elements:

Commencement Rules: Rules which define the circumstances under which the dialogue commences.

Locutions: Rules which indicate what utterances are permitted. Typically, legal locutions permit participants to assert propositions, permit others to question or contest prior assertions, and permit those asserting propositions which are subsequently questioned or contested to justify their assertions. Justifications may involve the presentation of a proof of the proposition or an argument for it. The dialogue game rules may also permit participants to utter propositions to which they assign differing degrees of commitment, for example: one may merely *propose* a proposition, a speech act which entails less commitment than would an *assertion* of the same proposition.

Combination Rules: Rules which define the dialogical contexts under which particular locutions are permitted or not, or obligatory or not. For instance, it may not be permitted for a participant to assert a proposition p and subsequently the proposition $\neg p$ in the same dialogue, without in the interim having retracted the former assertion.

Commitments: Rules which define the circumstances under which participants express commitment to a proposition. Typically, the assertion of a claim p in the debate is defined as indicating to the other participants some level of commitment to, or support for, the claim. Since the work of philosopher Charles Hamblin [21], formal dialogue systems typically establish and maintain public sets of commitments, called *commitment stores*, for each participant; these stores are usually non-monotonic, in the sense that participants can also retract committed claims, although possibly only under defined circumstances.

Termination Rules: Rules that define the circumstances under which the dialogue ends.

It is worth noting here that more than one notion of *commitment* is present in the literature on dialogue games. For example, Hamblin treats commitments in a purely dialogical sense: *"A speaker who is obliged to maintain consistency needs to keep a store of statements representing his previous commitments, and require of each new statement he makes that it may be added without inconsistency to this store. The store represents a kind of persona of beliefs; it need not correspond with his real beliefs . . ."* [21, p. 257]. In contrast, Walton and Krabbe [55, Chapter 1] treat commitments as obligations to (execute, incur or maintain) a course of action, which they term action commitments. These actions may be utterances in a dialogue, as when a speaker is forced to defend a proposition he has asserted against attack from others; so Walton and Krabbe also consider propositional commitment as a special case of action commitment [55, p. 23]. As with Hamblin's treatment, such dialogical commitments to propositions may not necessarily represent a participant's true beliefs. In contrast, Munindar Singh's social semantics [52], requires participants in an interaction to express publicly their beliefs and intentions, and these expressions are called *social commitments*. These include both expressions of belief in some propositions and expressions of intent to execute or incur some future actions.[1] Our primary motivation is the use of dialogue games as the basis for interaction protocols between autonomous agents. Because such agents will typically enter into these interactions in order to achieve some wider objectives, and not just for the enjoyment of the interaction itself, we believe it is reasonable to define commitments in terms of future actions or propositions external to the dialogue. In a commercial negotiation dialogue, for instance, the utterance of an offer may express a willingness by the speaker to undertake a subsequent transaction on the terms contained in the offer. For this reason, we can view commitments as semantic mappings between locutions and subsets of some set of statements expressing actions or beliefs external to the dialogue.

Dialogue game protocols have been articulated for each of the rule-governed primary types of dialogues in the typology of Walton and Krabbe: information-seeking dialogues [24,55]; inquiries [35]; persuasion dialogues [2,11]; negotiation dialogues [4,24,33,49]; and deliberations [23]. Some of these proposals are discussed in the next section. There has even been some work on non-co-operation in dialogues [19], work which may yield dialogue game protocols for eristic dialogues. However, as mentioned earlier, most real-world dialogues (whether human or agent) involve aspects of more than one of these primary types. Two formalisms have been suggested for computational representation of combinations of dialogue: the *Dialogue Frames* of Chris Reed [46], which enable iterated, sequential and embedded dialogues to be represented; and our own *Agent Dialogue Frameworks* [36], which permit iterated, sequential, parallel and embedded dialogues to be represented. Both these formalisms are neutral with regard to the modeling of the primary dialogue types themselves, allowing the primary types to be represented in any convenient form, and allowing for types other than the six of the Walton and Krabbe typology to be included.

4 Examples of Dialogue Game Protocols

We now briefly review several of the proposals for dialogue game protocols published in the agent literature. The first of these is the protocol of Leila Amgoud,

---

[1] It is worth noting that all these notions of *commitment* differ from that commonly used in discussion of agent's internal states, namely the idea of the persistence of a belief or an intention [58, p. 205]. As Singh [51] argues, there is a qualitative difference between social commitments of the kind discussed here, and personal commitments of the kind encoded in beliefs, desires, and intentions. He further argues that one kind of commitment cannot be derived from another.

Nicolas Maudet and Simon Parsons [2]. This protocol is based on James MacKenzie's philosophical dialogue game DC [30], a game for two players, both subject to the same rules. DC enables the participants to argue about the truth of a proposition and was designed to study the fallacy of begging the question (*petitio principii*, or circular reasoning). The agent interaction protocol of [2] based on DC allows four distinct locutions: *assert, accept, question* and *challenge*; these can be instantiated with a single proposition, and also, for the locutions *assert* and *accept*, with a set of propositions which together constitute an argument for a proposition. Thus the participants may communicate both propositional statements and arguments about these statements, where arguments may be considered as tentative proofs (i.e., logical inferences from assumptions which may not all be confirmed). The locutions of this protocol are similar to those of DC except that they do not include a locution for retraction of assertions (called *withdrawal* in DC). As with MacKenzie's game, the protocol of [2] establishes commitment stores which record, in full public view, the statements each participant has asserted. The syntax for this protocol has only been provided for dialogues between two participants, but could be readily extended to more agents, as the same authors did subsequently in [3].

Amgoud *et al.* demonstrate that their system enables persuasion, inquiry and information-seeking dialogues [2]. However, as the authors note, to permit negotiation dialogues, the protocol requires additional locutions.[2] These are proposed in a subsequent paper by the same authors [4], in which three additional locutions are proposed, *request, promise* and *refuse*, making seven in all. In addition to instantiation with propositions and with arguments for propositions, several of these locution can also be instantiated with a two-valued function expressing a relationship between two resources. For example, the locution $promise(p \Rightarrow q)$ indicates a promise by the speaker to provide resource q in return for receiving resource p.

Building on the protocol of Amgoud *et al.* [4], Fariba Sadri, Francesca Toni and Paolo Torroni [49] propose a similar protocol but with fewer locutions. The legal locutions proposed here are: *request, promise, accept, refuse, challenge,* and *justify*. The contents of the locutions *request* and *promise* are resources, while the contents for the other four locutions are any of the six locutions. In addition, the locution *justify* allows the utterance of some support for a previous locution.

The dialogue-game protocols presented in the work of Frank Dignum, Barbara Dunin-Kȩplicz and Rineke Verbrugge [11,12] are intended to enable agents to form teams and to agree joint intentions, respectively. For both protocols, the authors assume that one agent, an *initiator* or *proponent*, seeks to persuade others (*opponents*) to join a team, and that another initiator (possibly the same agent) seeks to persuade team members to adopt a group belief or intention. The team-formation dialogue is modeled as an information-seeking dialogue followed by a persuasion, while the joint-intentions-formation dialogue is modeled as a persuasion dialogue, which may include embedded negotiation

---

[2] It may also require additional locutions for deliberation dialogues, although the authors suggest otherwise.

dialogues. For the persuasion dialogues, the authors adapt the rigorous persuasion dialogue game of Walton and Krabbe [55]. This game is a formalization of a critical discussion — i.e., a rigorous persuasion — in philosophy. Such dialogues involve two parties, one seeking to prove a proposition, and one seeking to disprove it.[3] Unfortunately, the authors do not specify their dialogue game models completely, for example, nowhere stating the set of locutions available to the participating agents. The protocol for joint intention formation dialogues [12] includes seven locutions: *statement, question, challenge, challenge-with-statement, question-with-statement* and *final remarks*; these last include: *"quit"* and *"won."* The statements associated with challenges and questions may be concessions made by the speaker. The protocol for team formation dialogues [11] may also use the same set of locutions, although this is not absolutely clear.

Finally, we briefly mention some of our own proposals for dialogue game agent interaction protocols. Firstly, in joint work with Rogier van Eijk and Leila Amgoud [33], we articulated a dialogue game protocol for negotiation dialogues between potential buyers and sellers of consumer durables; this work drew on a standard model of consumer decision-making. Secondly, together with David Hitchcock [23], we presented a dialogue game protocol for deliberation dialogues, drawing on a theory of deliberative argument from the philosophy of argumentation. Thirdly, in [35], we articulated a dialogue game protocol for agents engaged in an inquiry dialogue; this protocol enables the participants to express uncertain beliefs about claims and to resolve these on the basis of the arguments for and against the claims presented in the dialogue. Inquiries involve a disinterested search for the truthful answer to some question. In many instances, however, we may desire *particular* answers to a question, such as when we seek to identify the possible risks of a new technology. In these cases our search is overlaid with values we impose on the answer-space; in [34], we proposed a dialogue game protocol for agents engaged in such a search.

5   Issues and Challenges

The use of formal dialogue games as the basis for agent interaction protocols has only just begun, and there are many challenging issues still open. In this section we consider some of these.

5.1   Protocol Semantics

One of the reasons for the popularity of the FIPA ACL is the fact that it has been given a well-defined semantics [26]. This semantics, based on speech act theory from the philosophy of language [6,50,10], is defined in terms of the certain beliefs, uncertain beliefs and intentions of the participating agents. Having defined such a semantics means that participants know precisely what other speakers

---

[3] Note that the persuasion dialogues of Walton and Krabbe [55] deal only with beliefs, not intentions.

mean and intend by their utterances, *assuming those others are conforming to the semantics*. However, verifying conformance to the semantics is a conceptually challenging task [57], since it is always possible for a sufficiently-clever agent to simulate insincerely any required semantic state.

The development of appropriate semantics for dialogue game protocols is still very immature, although several different types of semantics have been defined for these protocols. The first of these involves defining locutions in terms of the pre-conditions necessary for, and the post-conditions arising from, their utterance, i.e., what is termed an *axiomatic* semantics in computer programming language theory [53]. We can distinguish, as in [32], between two types of axiomatic semantics. In a *public* axiomatic semantics, the pre-conditions and post-conditions of each locution are given only in terms of observable linguistic behaviour, and so conformity with the protocol can be verified by anyone observing the dialogue. The protocols in [23,33,34,35] have been given a public axiomatic semantics. A *private* axiomatic semantics, on the other hand, is one in which some or all locutions have pre- or post-conditions defined in terms of the internal states of the participants. The protocols of Amgoud *et al.* [2,4], of Sadri *et al.* [49] and of Dignum *et al.* [12] have been given such a semantics. For the protocols of Amgoud *et al.* [2,4], each participating agent is assumed to be vested with a private argumentation-based reasoning mechanism, which generates defeasible arguments from premises according to defined procedures, as in [13]. The mechanism also permits a preference ordering over the arguments. An agent can only utter a locution $assert(p)$, for p a proposition, if that agent has an acceptable argument for p in its own knowledge base, or in its knowledge base combined with the public commitment stores of the other participants. Here, *acceptable arguments* are those which survive a specified process of attack and defence within an argumentation framework [13].

In the case of the protocol of Sadri *et al.* [49], which is designed for dialogues over scarce resources (i.e, negotiation dialogues), utterances are linked to a first-order logic describing resources. In this semantics, the knowledge of an agent is described [49, Section 3.1] as an abductive logic program consisting of if-then rules and of statements regarding the resources owned by the agent. Integrity constraints are placed on this knowledge in the form of rules[4] which provide an agent with possible responses to utterances it receives. An example of such a rule is: *Accept a request*. The abducibles of this logic program are then the possible locutions which the agent may utter in response to a message it receives. For the protocol of Dignum *et al.* [12], the authors assume that the participating agents have a Belief-Desire-Intention (BDI) mental architecture [56] and vest the locutions with a private axiomatic semantics: as with the speech-act semantics of the FIPA ACL [18], locutions are defined in terms of their impacts on, and pre-conditions of, these private mental states.

One may also view a dialogue under a given protocol as a sequence of commands in a programming language which operates on the states of a virtual machine comprising the internal states of the agents participating in the dialogue.

---

[4] Confusingly called *dialogue protocols* by these authors.

This view leads to the definition of an *operational* semantics for the protocol [53] in which locutions are defined in terms of their state transitions. Operational semantics have recently been defined for various agent communications languages, e.g., [15,22]. To our knowledge, the only dialogue game protocol provided with an operational semantics is the consumer negotiation protocol of [33].

Programming language theory also entertains the concept of a *denotational* semantics [53], in which a translation is given between the commands in a programming language and the objects in some mathematical domain. In [37], we defined a denotational semantics for protocols in terms of sub-spaces of n-dimensional euclidean space; in this semantics, dialogues conducted according to a given protocol are mapped to directed paths in the associated sub-space. Another denotational approach arises from viewing agents engaged in dialogue as jointly constructing meaning as the dialogue proceeds, in the same way that humans using natural language may be thought to do. Thus, there may be value in defining a denotational semantics which is constructed incrementally in the course of a dialogue, in a manner analogous to the Discourse Representation Structures of natural language semantics in theoretical linguistics [25]. This is a line of research we are pursuing.

5.2   Formal Properties

Why define a semantics for a protocol? One reason, mentioned above, is so that the participants share common meanings for utterances. Another reason is to enable a better understanding of the formal properties of protocols and of the dialogues conducted under them. The study of the formal properties of dialogues and protocols is, like the development of formal semantics, still very immature, and considerable scope exists for further research in this area.

One property of great interest is *termination*: under what circumstances will dialogues conducted under a given protocol terminate? For instance, Sadri and her colleagues [49] demonstrate that a dialogue under their protocol requesting the use of some resource will always terminate in a finite number of steps, if conducted between agents vested with the abductive logic program mechanisms described in the paper.[5] Similarly, Parsons *et al.* [44] consider the termination properties of the protocols of [2,4] for agents vested with argumentation-based decision architectures.

A related property is *computational complexity*: how many dialogue utterances are required for normal termination of a dialogue under a given protocol? To our knowledge, the only work considering computational complexity of dialogue game protocols is that of Paul Dunne and Trevor Bench-Capon [14], who consider a particular two-party, persuasion dialogue protocol. The computational complexity of general negotiation mechanisms (not only those involving dialogue game protocols) were presented by one of us in [59].

---

[5] To some extent this result is not surprising since these mechanisms require the agents to be co-operative.

A third property of importance in practical applications concerns the degree to which a dialogue protocol may support automated dialogues between suitably-equipped software agents, what may be called *automatability*. In [33] we showed, using an operational semantics, that agents vested with appropriate, domain-specific, internal decision mechanisms could undertake fully automated consumer negotiation dialogues using the dialogue game protocol we defined. The internal decision mechanisms were derived from standard models of buyer and seller decision-making taken from marketing theory [28]. No other dialogue game protocol so far proposed has been proven to be automatable.

5.3   Protocol Design and Assessment

One reason a more thorough study of protocol properties is needed is to provide assistance to designers and users of agent interaction protocols. At present, designers of dialogue game protocols currently have no guidance for issues such as:

- How many locutions should there be?
- What types of locutions should be included? For example: assertions, questions, etc.
- What are the appropriate rules for the combination of locutions?
- When should behavior be forbidden, e.g., repeated utterance of one locution?
- Under what conditions should dialogues be made to terminate?
- When are dialogues conducted according to a particular protocol guaranteed to terminate?

Similarly, the absence of formal studies of dialogue game protocols means that agents (or their human principals) intending to use such protocols have no guidance for issues such as:

- When are two protocols the same? With the proliferation of protocols, it will become important for agents to decide which protocol should be used for particular interactions.
- How may different protocols be compared and how may differences be measured?
- Which protocols are to be preferred under which circumstances? In other words, what are their advantages and disadvantages?
- What is the formal relationship between dialogue game protocols and general agent communications languages, e.g., FIPA ACL.
- When are dialogue game protocols preferable to other forms of agent interaction, such as auction mechanisms or general agent communications languages?

As part of a longer-term project to develop a formal theory of interaction protocols, we have taken initial steps towards answering some of these questions. In work with Michael Wooldridge [39], we proposed thirteen desirable properties of interaction protocols using dialogue games. These properties included: *Separation of syntax and semantics*, so that conformance with the protocol could be assessed on the basis only of observable behaviour; *Clarity of argumentation theory*, so that participants would know in advance their dialectical obligations when making assertions, contesting others' assertions, etc; and *Enablement of self-transformation*, so that participants would be able to change their beliefs, preferences or intentions, and readily express such changes, in the course of an interaction. We applied these 13 properties to assess several existing dialogue game protocols and to the FIPA ACL; all were found wanting, to a greater or lesser extent.

In another step towards a formal theory of interaction protocols we have considered when two protocols may be considered the same. Not only is an answer to this question necessary for choosing between two protocols, but it is also essential in order to assess if a protocol is new (in the sense of providing a different functionality to an existing protocol rather than just having equivalent locutions with different names) or to assess if a protocol conforms to some specification (such as that laid down as the standard for interacting within some electronic institution [48]). In work with Mark Johnson [38], we have recently defined several reasonable notions of protocol equivalence and shown that these lead to distinct classes of protocols. Some of these notions were derived from ideas of process equivalence [40], and the links between protocols and processes are worth further exploration.

6   Conclusion

In this chapter, we have provided a brief overview of agent interaction protocols based on formal dialogue games. These games have almost 2500 years of study in philosophy behind them, and have recently found application in the design of autonomous software agent protocols. Only a handful of such protocols have so far been proposed, and only a few of their properties yet studied formally. This area of Artificial Intelligence therefore still has open many questions, research challenges and implementation issues. We believe that dialogue game protocols have great potential for multi-agent systems applications because they represent an effective compromise between the strict rule-governed nature of economic auction mechanisms and the greater expressiveness of generic agent communications languages. Proving this claim conclusively will need to await a formal theory of interaction protocols connecting dialogue game protocols, auction mechanisms and agent communications languages in a single coherent framework.

References

1. S. Abramsky. Semantics of interaction: an introduction to game semantics. In A. M. Pitts and P. Dybjer, editors, *Semantics and Logics of Computation*, pages 1–31. Cambridge University Press, Cambridge, UK, 1997. 270

2. L. Amgoud, N. Maudet, and S. Parsons. Modelling dialogues using argumentation. In E. Durfee, editor, *Proceedings of the Fourth International Conference on Multi-Agent Systems (ICMAS 2000)*, pages 31–38, Boston, MA, USA, 2000. IEEE Press. 273, 274, 274, 274, 274, 276, 276, 277

3. L. Amgoud and S. Parsons. Agent dialogues with conflicting preferences. In J-J. Meyer and M. Tambe, editors, *Pre-Proceedings of the Eighth International Workshop on Agent Theories, Architectures, and Languages (ATAL 2001)*, pages 1–14, Seattle, WA, USA, 2001. 274

4. L. Amgoud, S. Parsons, and N. Maudet. Arguments, dialogue, and negotiation. In W. Horn, editor, *Proceedings of the Fourteenth European Conference on Artificial Intelligence (ECAI 2000)*, pages 338–342, Berlin, Germany, 2000. IOS Press. 273, 274, 274, 276, 276, 277

5. Aristotle. *Topics*. Clarendon Press, Oxford, UK, 1928. W. D. Ross, Editor. 270

6. J. L. Austin. *How To Do Things with Words*. Oxford University Press, Oxford, UK, 1962. 275

7. T. J. M. Bench-Capon, P. E. Dunne, and P. H. Leng. Interacting with knowledge-based systems through dialogue games. In *Proceedings of the Eleventh International Conference on Expert Systems and Applications*, pages 123–140, Avignon, France, 1991. 270

8. T. J. M. Bench-Capon, T. Geldard, and P. H. Leng. A method for the computational modelling of dialectical argument with dialogue games. *Artificial Intelligence and Law*, 8:233–254, 2000. 270

9. J. Bohman and W. Rehg, editors. *Deliberative Democracy: Essays on Reason and Politics*. MIT Press, Cambridge, MA, USA, 1997. 270

10. P. R. Cohen and C. R. Perrault. Elements of a plan-based theory of speech acts. *Cognitive Science*, 3:177–212, 1979. 275

11. F. Dignum, B. Dunin-Kęplicz, and R. Verbrugge. Agent theory for team formation by dialogue. In C. Castelfranchi and Y. Lespérance, editors, *Intelligent Agents VII: Proceedings of the Seventh International Workshop on Agent Theories, Architectures, and Languages (ATAL 2000)*, LNAI 1986, pages 150–166, Berlin, Germany, 2000. Springer. 273, 274, 275

12. F. Dignum, B. Dunin-Kęplicz, and R. Verbrugge. Creating collective intention through dialogue. *Logic Journal of the IGPL*, 9(2):305–319, 2001. 274, 275, 276, 276

13. P. M. Dung. On the acceptability of arguments and its fundamental role in non-monotonic reasoning, logic programming and n-persons games. *Artificial Intelligence*, 77:321–357, 1995. 276, 276

14. P. E. Dunne and T. J. M. Bench-Capon. Two party immediate response disputes: properties and efficiency. Technical Report ULCS-01-005, Department of Computer Science, University of Liverpool, Liverpool, UK, 2001. 277

15. R. van Eijk, F. S. de Boer, W. van der Hoek, and J-J. Ch. Meyer. A fully abstract model for the exchange of information in multi-agent systems. *Theoretical Computer Science*, April 2002. *In press*. 277

16. R. Elio, A. Haddadi, and A. Singh. Task models, intentions, and agent conversation policies. In R. Mizoguchi and J. K. Slaney, editors, *Topics in Artificial Intelligence: Proceedings of the Sixth Pacific Rim Conference in Artificial Intelligence (PRICAI-2000)*, LNAI 1886, pages 394–403, Berlin, Germany, 2000. Springer. 270

17. A. Finkelstein and H. Fuks. Multi-party specification. In *Proceedings of the Fifth International Workshop on Software Specification and Design*, Pittsburgh, PA, USA, 1989. ACM Sigsoft Engineering Notes. 270

18. FIPA. Communicative Act Library Specification. Technical Report XC00037H, Foundation for Intelligent Physical Agents, 10 August 2001. 270, 276
19. D. M. Gabbay and J. Woods. Non-cooperation in dialogue logic. *Synthese*, 127(1-2):161–186, 2001. 273
20. M. Greaves, H. Holmback, and J. Bradshaw. What is a conversation policy? In F. Dignum and M. Greaves, editors, *Issues in Agent Communication*, LNAI 1916, pages 118–131. Springer, Berlin, Germany, 2000. 270
21. C. L. Hamblin. *Fallacies*. Methuen, London, UK, 1970. 270, 272, 272
22. K. V. Hindriks, F. S. de Boer, W. van der Hoek, and J-J. Ch. Meyer. Formal semantics for an abstract agent progamming language. In M. P. Singh, A. S. Rao, and M. J. Wooldridge, editors, *Intelligent Agents IV: Proceedings of the Fourth International Workshop on Agent Theories, Architectures and Languages (ATAL-97)*, LNAI 1365, pages 215–229. Springer, Berlin, Germany, 1998. 277
23. D. Hitchcock, P. McBurney, and S. Parsons. A framework for deliberation dialogues. In H. V. Hansen, C. W. Tindale, J. A. Blair, and R. H. Johnson, editors, *Proceedings of the Fourth Biennial Conference of the Ontario Society for the Study of Argumentation (OSSA 2001)*, Windsor, Ontario, Canada, 2001. 273, 275, 276
24. J. Hulstijn. *Dialogue Models for Inquiry and Transaction*. PhD thesis, Universiteit Twente, Enschede, The Netherlands, 2000. 270, 273, 273
25. H. Kamp and U. Reyle. *From Discourse to Logic: Introduction to Modeltheoretic Semantics of Natural Language, Formal Logic and Discourse Representation Theory*. Kluwer, Dordrecht, The Netherlands, 1993. Two Volumes. 277
26. Y. Labrou, T. Finin, and Y. Peng. Agent communication languages: The current landscape. *IEEE Intelligent Systems*, 14(2):45–52, March/April 1999. 275
27. J. A. Levin and J. A. Moore. Dialogue-games: metacommunications structures for natural language interaction. *Cognitive Science*, 1(4):395–420, 1978. 270
28. G. L. Lilien, P. Kotler, and K. S. Moorthy. *Marketing Models*. Prentice-Hall, Englewood Cliffs, NJ, USA, 1992. 269, 278
29. P. Lorenzen and K. Lorenz. *Dialogische Logik*. Wissenschaftliche Buchgesellschaft, Darmstadt, Germany, 1978. 270
30. J. D. MacKenzie. Question-begging in non-cumulative systems. *Journal of Philosophical Logic*, 8:117–133, 1979. 270, 274
31. M. Mandler. A difficult choice in preference theory: rationality implies completeness or transitivity but not both. In Elijah Millgram, editor, *Varieties of Practical Reasoning*, pages 373–402. MIT Press, Cambridge, MA, USA, 2001. 269
32. P. McBurney. *Rational Interaction*. PhD thesis, Department of Computer Science, University of Liverpool, Liverpool, UK, 2002. 276
33. P. McBurney, R. M. van Eijk, S. Parsons, and L. Amgoud. A dialogue-game protocol for agent purchase negotiations. *Journal of Autonomous Agents and Multi-Agent Systems*, 2002. *In press*. 273, 275, 276, 277, 278
34. P. McBurney and S. Parsons. Chance discovery using dialectical argumentation. In T. Terano, T. Nishida, A. Namatame, S. Tsumoto, Y. Ohsawa, and T. Washio, editors, *New Frontiers in Artificial Intelligence: Joint JSAI 2001 Workshop Post Proceedings*, LNAI 2253, pages 414–424. Springer, Berlin, Germany, 2001. 275, 276
35. P. McBurney and S. Parsons. Representing epistemic uncertainty by means of dialectical argumentation. *Annals of Mathematics and Artificial Intelligence*, 32(1-4):125–169, 2001. 273, 275, 276
36. P. McBurney and S. Parsons. Games that agents play: a formal framework for dialogues between autonomous agents. *Journal of Logic, Language and Information*, 11(3):315–334, 2002. 272, 273

37. P. McBurney and S. Parsons. A geometric semantics for dialogue-game protocols for autonomous agent interactions. *Electronic Notes in Theoretical Computer Science*, 52(2), 2002. 277

38. P. McBurney, S. Parsons, and M. W. Johnson. When are two protocols the same? In M. P. Huget, F. Dignum, and J. L. Koning, editors, *Agent Communications Languages and Conversation Policies. Proceedings of a Workshop at the First International Joint Conference on Autonomous Agents and Multi-Agent Systems (AAMAS 2002)*, Bologna, Italy, 2002. 279

39. P. McBurney, S. Parsons, and M. Wooldridge. Desiderata for agent argumentation protocols. In C. Castelfranchi and W. L. Johnson, editors, *Proceedings of the First International Joint Conference on Autonomous Agents and Multi-Agent Systems (AAMAS 2002)*, Bologna, Italy, 2002. 278

40. R. Milner. *Communication and Concurrency*. Prentice Hall, Hemel Hempstead, UK, 1989. 279

41. P. Mittelstaedt. *Quantum Logic*. D. Reidel, Dordrecht, The Netherlands, 1979. 270

42. M. J. Osborne and A. Rubinstein. *A Course in Game Theory*. MIT Press, Cambridge, MA, USA, 1994. 270

43. S. Parsons, C. Sierra, and N. R. Jennings. Agents that reason and negotiate by arguing. *Journal of Logic and Computation*, 8(3):261–292, 1998. 269

44. S. Parsons, M. Wooldridge, and L. Amgoud. An analysis of formal interagent dialogues. In C. Castelfranchi and W. L. Johnson, editors, *Proceedings of the First International Joint Conference on Autonomous Agents and Multi-Agent Systems (AAMAS 2002)*, Bologna, Italy, 2002. (*In press*). 277

45. H. Prakken and G. Sartor. Modelling reasoning with precedents in a formal dialogue game. *Artificial Intelligence and Law*, 6:231–287, 1998. 270

46. C. Reed. Dialogue frames in agent communications. In Y. Demazeau, editor, *Proceedings of the Third International Conference on Multi-Agent Systems (ICMAS-98)*, pages 246–253. IEEE Press, 1998. 273

47. W. Rehg. The argumentation theorist in deliberative democracy. *Controversia*, 2002. (*In press*). 269

48. J. A. Rodríguez, F. J. Martin, P. Noriega, P. Garcia, and C. Sierra. Towards a test-bed for trading agents in electronic auction markets. *AI Communications*, 11(1):5–19, 1998. 279

49. F. Sadri, F. Toni, and P. Torroni. Logic agents, dialogues and negotiation: an abductive approach. In M. Schroeder and K. Stathis, editors, *Proceedings of the Symposium on Information Agents for E-Commerce, Artificial Intelligence and the Simulation of Behaviour Conference (AISB-2001)*, York, UK, 2001. AISB. 273, 274, 276, 276, 276, 277

50. J. Searle. *Speech Acts: An Essay in the Philosophy of Language*. Cambridge University Press, Cambridge, UK, 1969. 275

51. M. P. Singh. A conceptual analysis of commitments in multiagent systems. Technical Report 96-09, Department of Computer Science, North Carolina State University, Raleigh, NC, USA, 1996. 273

52. M. P. Singh. A social semantics for agent communications languages. In F. Dignum, B. Chaib-draa, and H. Weigand, editors, *Proceedings of the Workshop on Agent Communication Languages, International Joint Conference on Artificial Intelligence (IJCAI-99)*, Berlin, Germany, 2000. Springer. 273

53. R. D. Tennent. *Semantics of Programming Languages*. Prentice-Hall, Hemel Hempstead, UK, 1991. 276, 277, 277

54. A. Unruh and M. Nodine. Industrial-strength conversations. In F. Dignum and M. Greaves, editors, *Issues in Agent Communication*, LNAI 1916. Springer, Berlin, Germany, 2000. 270

55. D. N. Walton and E. C. W. Krabbe. *Commitment in Dialogue: Basic Concepts of Interpersonal Reasoning*. SUNY Press, Albany, NY, USA, 1995. 271, 271, 272, 273, 273, 275, 275

56. M. Wooldridge. *Reasoning about Rational Agents*. MIT Press, Cambridge, MA, USA, 2000. 276

57. M. Wooldridge. Semantic issues in the verification of agent communication languages. *Journal of Autonomous Agents and Multi-Agent Systems*, 3(1):9–31, 2000. 276

58. M. Wooldridge. *Introduction to Multiagent Systems*. John Wiley and Sons, New York, NY, USA, 2002. 273

59. M. Wooldridge and S. Parsons. Languages for negotiation. In W. Horn, editor, *Proceedings of the Fourteenth European Conference on Artificial Intelligence (ECAI 2000)*, pages 393–397, Berlin, Germany, 2000. IOS Press. 277

Request for Action Reconsidered as a Dialogue Game Based on Commitments

Brahim Chaib-draa[1], Marc-André Labrie[1], and Nicholas Maudet[2]

[1] Dépt. Informatique et Génie Logiciel,
Université Laval, Ste-Foy, PQ, Canada
{chaib,labrie}@iad.ift.ulaval.ca
[2] IRIT, Université Paul Sabatier
Toulouse, France
maudet@irit.fr

Abstract. This paper follows recent work in the field of dialectical models of inter-agent communication. The request action as proposed by Winograd & Flores is reconsidered in an original dialogue game framework, as a composition of different basic games (small conversation policies). These basic games are based on commitments of participants and are handled through a "contextualization game" which aims at defining how games are opened or closed through the dialogue, and what combinations are legal. We show how such a model offers more practical flexibility, and covers more situations than the classical protocol. Finally, we give an overview on the game simulator that we are currently developing.

1 Introduction

Many authors have convincingly argued that classical approaches to agent communication languages (ACL) [7,9] suffer from a lack of verifiability (due to their mentalistic semantics) [18,3,24] and still require to be used with protocols (because there is simply to much continuations to be explored in practice) [11]. An interesting approach is then to use protocols as a basis to define (some part of) the semantics of ACL. The problem is that protocols usually lack of practical flexibility, genericness, and compositionality, as well as rigorous specifications (due to their underlying models, often finite state machines in the case of sequential interactions). Recently, researchers have begun to address these issues and have explored means to define more appropriate conversation policies (CPs), *i.e.* general constraints on the sequences of semantically coherent messages leading to a goal [11] —as opposed to protocols which refer too often to some specific underlying formalism. A significant amount of approaches on CPs have been inspired, more or less directly, by the work of formal dialectic of Hamblin [12] and Walton and Krabbe [22]. This trend of research really now forms a field of dialectical models of interaction (*computational dialectics*) [10,17]. We have argued elsewhere that this influence has in fact produced two sorts of approaches: *commitment-based* and *dialogue-game-based* CPs [14]. Commitment-based CPs aims at defining semantics of the communicative acts in terms of public notions,

M.-P. Huget (Ed.): Communications in Multiagent Systems, LNAI 2650, pp. 284–299, 2003.

e.g. social commitments. Dialogue-game-based CPs, in addition, consider that protocols are captured within appropriate structures (games), and that these structures can be composed in different ways to form the global structure of dialogue. In this paper, we aim at exploring in practice (on the classical request for action interaction) why and how such a dialogue-game-based approach can be useful.

The rest of the paper is as follows: Section 2 presents the case for conversation policies, using the "request for action" described in [23] as a motivating example. Section 3 introduces the basic material of the dialogue-game-based framework that forms the backbone of our approach. Section 4 reconsiders "request for action" within our framework. A discussion concludes the paper.

2 A Case for Conversation Policies

As suggested by speech-act-based tradition to interagent communication, we assume that messages exchanged between agents have the form of some *dialogue moves*, composed of a dialogue move *type* —or *performative* to use FIPA terminology— (*e.g.* assertion, question, etc.) accompanied with some *content* expressed in a content language. Until recently ACL research issues have primarily related to the generation and interpretation of individual of these ACL messages. Nowadays researchers on ACLs try to address the gap between these individual messages and the extended message sequences, or dialogues, that arise between agents. As part of its program code, every agent must implement tractable decision procedures that allow that agent to select and produce ACL messages that are appropriate to its private state. But these decision procedures must also take into consideration the context of prior ACL messages and other agent events, so that the agent produce messages that are appropriate to this interactional context. While the private state of its agent is not accessible, the interactional context is typically public and accessible to all dialogue participants, which makes easier to verify that the agent indeed conforms to the semantics of its communicative acts. The other advantage is that taking this context into account can actually *simplify* the computational complexity of ACL message selection for an agent. By engaging in preplanned or stereotypical conversations, much of the search space of possible agent responses can indeed be eliminated. The specification of these conversations is usually accomplished by means of protocols. In this paper, we will be interested in interactions between agents where no concurrency is involved (that is, mainly, interactions between two agents involved in a single dialogue). In this context, finite state machines (FSMs) are arguably an adequate and popular formalism to define these protocols. The states of the automaton maps the possible state of the conversation given a message by the participants and the previous state of the conversation. Carefully designed and highly complex protocols have been proposed using these techniques in the literature, and implemented in real applications, see for instance COOL [2]. The Winograd and Flores's [23] (see Fig. 1) "request for action" is a classical example of such protocols.

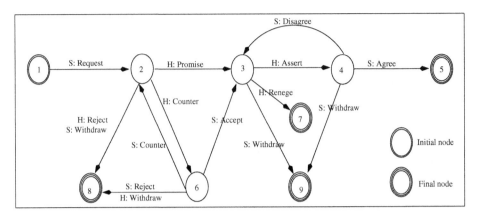

Fig. 1. The request for action protocol

Since this example is central in our paper, we will focus on this latter protocol and describe the dialogue behavior specified by this protocol. Conversation
begins in the initial state (1), by a request from speaker S. In state (2), the
dialogue can successfully be followed by the promise from H to realize the requested action, or come into a "negotiation cycle" with a counter-proposal from
H, or fail with a reject leading to state (8). At state (3), the addressee will signal
that the task has been achieved, or eventually decide to renege (leading to the
final state (7)) and S will in turn positively (state(5)) or negatively evaluate
the achievement of the action (state(3)). Now, in light of the above description
and also of the critics and discussion of [11,16,18,19,21,25], we list below some
problems encountered by protocols when described as FSMs:

- The state of the conversation is *practically* difficult to describe on the basis
  of several previous moves. As a result, protocols often describes very tightly
  constrained interactions (*e.g.* avoiding backtracking moves) and designers
  possibly omit transitions that may be, intuitively, allowed.
  Example: To determine the state of the dialogue, the "request for action"
  protocol refers in most cases to *the* previous move only. An exception is the
  "withdraw" move by S, which can lead to different states of the dialogue
  (however, all these states are final unsuccessful nodes, so the distinction
  seems rather misleading). Also one can argue, following [19], that S could
  make an offer to H without any explicit request from S, in which case the
  protocol would effectively starts at state (2), and this case is not covered by
  the protocol.
- The state of the conversation is only the result of the sequence of dialogue
  move types while in some cases it can be necessary to describe more expres-
  sively the state of the conversation.
  Example: Typically, it can useful to constrain the interaction on the basis
  of some information related to the content of the move. In our example,
  it could the case that the initial request of the agent also determines a

deadline, and consequently that the declaration that the action is done will be considered legal only if it occurs before this deadline. Alternatively the counter-proposals made by the agents during the negotiation cycle can be required to meet some constraints (for instance, S could only *postpone* the deadline for the action, etc.).

- The protocol is composed of different phases which could be used in the definition of others protocols.

  Example: When considered carefully, our example protocol seems to be composed of different "phases" (or small protocols), not identified as such and not specific to the particular case of the request for action (firstly, the agents will try to negotiate a task for H to do. Next S and H will discuss the correct achievement of this task.)

- Protocols don't allow the agents to consider possibilities to misbehave wrt. the specified interaction (even if this should be discouraged in general).

  Example: The agent which has been requested to undertake the action may decide (on the basis of some private reasons) that it is crucial to postpone its answer. The consequences of this unexpected behaviour should be made explicit, so that the agent can take this parameter into consideration when making its decision.

These remarks emphasis the need to define declarative *conversation policies* (CPs), which are *"general constraints on the sequences of semantically coherent messages leading to a goal"* [11]. The now popular commitment-based approach argues that protocols can be viewed as a set of commitments associated with each state of the dialogue. In this paper, we take more specifically the road of an approach mixing dialogue games and commitments. In the final section of the paper, we discuss whether this approach is appropriate to tackle the problems discussed earlier. But let us start by describing the details of our framework.

3 A Dialogue Game Framework Based on Commitments

We take the picture of two software agents involved in some interaction. To communicate, our agents exchange some communicative acts as can be found in the KQML or FIPA-ACL frameworks. As explained earlier, we assume that their communicative behavior is handled through a notion of dialogue game. The main features of this approach is that the notion of commitments (Sect. 3.1) is used to express the different notions defining the game structure (Sect. 3.2), and that these games can be are grounded (Sect. 3.3) and composed in different ways (Sect. 3.4).

3.1 Commitments

To start with, we give some details about the notion of commitment that we use in our approach. The notion of commitment is a social one, and should not be confused with some psychological notion of commitment. Crucially, commitments are contracted towards a partner or a group. More precisely, commitments are expressed as predicates with an arity of 6:

$$C(x, y, \alpha, t, s_x, s_y)$$

meaning that x is committed towards y to α at time t, under the sanctions s_x and s_y. The first sanction specifies conditions under which x can withdraw from this commitment, and the second specifies conditions under which y reneges the considered commitment. For instance, the following commitment

$$c_1 = C(Al, Bob, sing(Al, midnight), now, 10, 20)$$

states that agent Al is committed towards agent Bob to $sing$ at $midnight$. If Al eventually decides to withdraw the commitment he will pay the penalty 10. If Al decides to renege the commitment to sing, he will pay 20. We concede that this account of penalties is extremely simple in this version. A more complete account could be similar to the one of Toledo and al. [6]

The notation is inspired from [19], and allows us to compose the actions involved in the commitments: $\alpha_1 | \alpha_2$ classically stands for the choice, and $\alpha_1 \Rightarrow \alpha_2$ for the conditional statement that the action α_2 will occur in case of the occurrence of the event α_1. Finally, the operations on the commitments are just creation and cancellation.

$$c_2 = C(Al, Bob, sing(Al, midnight) | dance(Al, midnight), now, 10, 20)$$

and

$$c_3 = C(Al, Bob, music(Bob, midnight) \Rightarrow create(c_2), now, 10, 20)$$

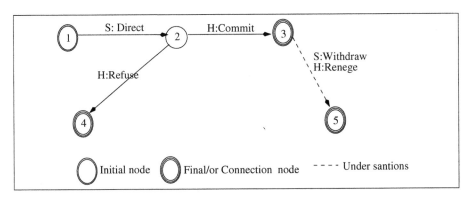

Fig. 2. The different status of the commitments

The commitment c_2 captures that the agent Al is committed towards Bob to $sing$ or $dance$ at midnight. The commitment c_3 captures that the agent Al is committed to contract the preceding commitment (c_2) if agent Bob plays $music$. All commitments hold a time concerning when they were contracted (now). From now, for the sake of readability, we will ignore the $create$ operation. We also permit propositional commitments, that we regard as collections of commitments centering on some proposition p, in the line of [22]. Such commitments are typically the result of assertive moves.

Now we need to describe the mechanism by which the commitments are discussed and created during the dialogue. This mechanism is precisely captured within our game structure. To account for the fact that some commitments are established within the contexts of some games *and only make sense within this context*, we make explicit the fact that this commitments are specialized to game g. This will typically be the case of the dialogue rules involved in the games, as we will see below.

3.2   Game Structure

We share with others [8,4,15] the view of dialogue games as structures regulating the mechanism under which some commitments are discussed through the dialogue. Unlike [4,15] however, we adopt a strict commitment-based approach within game structure and express the dialogue rules in terms of commitments. Unlike [8] on the other hand, we consider different ways to combine the structures of the games, and we precise how to derive all other games from some *basic* dialogue games —considering only the degree of strength [21].

In our approach, games are considered as bilateral structures defined by *entry conditions* (which must be fulfilled at the beginning of the game, possibly by some accommodation mechanism), *success conditions* (defining the goals of the participants when engaged in the game), *failure conditions* (under which the participants consider that the game reached a state of failure), and *dialogue rules*. As previously explained, all these notions, even dialogue rules, are defined in terms of (possibly conditional) commitments. Technically, games are conceived as structures capturing the different commitments created during the dialogue.

To sum up, we have Entry conditions (E), Success conditions of initiator (SI) and partner (SP), Failure conditions of initiator (FI) and partner (FP), and dialogues Rules (R) for each game. We also assume that there is a constant sanction s_g to penalize the agents that will not follow the expected dialogic behavior (as described in the Dialogue Rules). Within games, conversational actions are time-stamped as "turns" (t_0 being the first turn of dialogue within this game, t_f the last). To make things more concrete, let us illustrate these ideas with a directive game presented in Fig. 3.

Imagine that agent *Al* and agent *Bob* have entered the directive game. *Al* is committed to play a directive move towards agent *Bob*, and *Bob* is committed to create a commitment to play a commit (i.e., an accept) or a refuse if *Al* honors his commitment. The game follows the automata as described in Fig. 2, but note that the agents have the possibility to play some moves not expected (in this case, they have the penalty s_g). When the game expires (successfully or not), the commitments that were specialized to this game, those which are dependent on the context "g", are automatically cancelled. The others are known as "persistent" commitments. Thereafter, we will omit the sanctions in our games specifications for better readability.

$$
\begin{array}{l|l}
E_{bd} & \neg C(y, x, \alpha, t_0, s_y, s_x) \\
Si_{bd} & C(y, x, \alpha, t_f, s_y, s_x) \\
SP_{bd} & \text{Nil} \\
FI_{bd} & C(y, x, \neg\alpha, t_f, s_y, s_x) \\
FP_{bd} & \text{Nil} \\
R_{bd} & C_g(x, y, direct(x, y, \alpha), t_0, s_g, s_g) \\
& C_g(y, x, direct(x, y, \alpha)) \Rightarrow \\
& C_g(y, x, commit(y, x, \alpha) | refuse(y, x, \alpha), t_1, s_g, s_g), t_0, s_g, s_g) \\
& C_g(y, x, commit(y, x, \alpha)) \Rightarrow \\
& C(y, x, \alpha, t_2, s_y, s_x), t_0, s_g, s_g) \\
& C_g(y, x, refuse(y, x, \alpha)) \Rightarrow \\
& C(y, x, \neg\alpha, t_2, s_y, s_x), t_0, s_g, s_g)
\end{array}
$$

Fig. 3. Definition of a basic directive game.

Now, from this basic directive game, all other combinations as *S: direct*, *S: request*, *S: demand*, *S: order*, *S: command*, etc., and *H: commit*, *H: accept*, *H: promise*, *H: certify*, etc. can be negotiated between the two participants. To do that, S and H should negotiate the degree of strength of the two main speech acts composing the game. Now, let us explain what do we mean by the degree of strength. Speech acts are expressed with different *degrees of strength* depending on the illocutionary force. For example, the degree of strength of a supplications is greater than that of a request, because an initiator who supplicates expresses a stronger desire than a speaker who requests. According to this, the relations of comparative strength that exist between English illocutionary forces in virtue of semantic definitions of English performative verbs can be exhibited in semantic tables by constructing logical trees in accordance with the following rules [20]:

1. All nodes of a semantic table are speech act verbs with the same force;
2. A verb is the immediate successor of another verb if and only if the force that it names can be obtained from the force named by the other verb by adding new composants or increasing the degree of strength.

Such tree exhibits in fact relations of comparative strength between illocutionary forces. These trees can be reflected by some integers which measure the degree of strength of illocutionary forces. By convention, we select 0 (zero) to represent the *neutral* degree of strength that is characteristic of the primitive illocutionary force, $+1$ the next stronger degree, $+2$ the next stronger, etc. Similarly, -1 represents the greatest degree of strength smaller than zero, etc. Now, if we consider "assert", "commit", "direct", "declare", as the *primitives* of assertives, commissives, directives and declaratives, we can represent the four trees as follows:

- *for assertives:* suggest(degree $= -1$), assert(degree $= 0$), tell(degree $= +1$), inform(degree $= +2$), reveal(degree $= +3$), divulge(degree $= +4$), etc.
- *for commissives:* commit(degree $= 0$), accept(degree $= +1$), promise(degree $= +2$), certify(degree $= +3$), etc.

- *for directives:* suggest(degree = −1), direct(degree = 0), request(degree = +1), demand(degree = +2), order(degree = +3), etc.
- *for declaratives:* declare(degree = 0), renonce(degree = +1), terminate(degree = +2), cancel(degree = +3), etc.

Our assumption here is that this degree of strength will define in turn the sanctions (s_x, s_y) under which agents can withdraw, renonce, renege, etc. their commitments, as well as the sanctions s_g applied to the rules of the game. Both participants in conversation can then negotiate this degree of strength before entering the game. Formally, a game g is then represented by the following statement

$$\langle basic\_game(ds_I, ds_P), (E, S, F, R) \rangle$$

where *basic_game*, reflects some basic game as the directive game; (ds_I, ds_P) reflects degrees of strength from the basic type game for the initiator (I) and the partner (P), and the tuple (E, S, F, R) reflects the structure of the proposed game. Note that in any game, we only take into account the speech act of initiator as *request, ask, etc.* and the "acceptance" of partner as *commit, promise, assert, etc.* In other words, we do not take into account the "refusal" of partner and that is why we only consider two degrees of strength.

3.3   Grounding the Games

The specific question of how games are grounded through the dialogue is certainly one of the most delicate [13]. Following [17], we assume that the agents can use some meta-acts acts of dialogue to handle game structure and thus propose to enter in a game, propose to quit the game, and so on. Thus agents can exchange messages as

$$propose.enter(Al, Bob, g_1)$$

where g_1 describes a well-formed game structure (as detailed above). This message is a proposal of the agent Al to agent Bob to enter the game g_1. This means that games can have different status: they can be *open, closed,* or simply *proposed.* How this status is discussed in practice is described in a *contextualization* game which regulates this meta-level communication. As a simple first account of this game, we could adopt the intuitive view of games simply opened through the successful exchange of a propose/accept sequence. However, things are getting more complicate if we want to take account different kinds of combinations. All these kinds of structurations are considered within a contextualization game that we do not detail here.

3.4   Composing the Games

As explained before, the possibility to combine the games is a very attractive feature of the approach. The seminal work of [22] and the follow-up formalisation of [17] have focused on the classical notions of *embedding* and *sequencing*, but recent works extends the kinds of combinations studied [15]. We now detail the games' compositions that we use in our framework. Describing these kinds of combinations, we precise the conditions under which they can be obtained, and their consequences. Ultimately, such conditions and consequences should be included in the contextualization game we are working on [13].

Sequencing noted $g_1; g_2$, which means that g_2 starts immediately after termination of g_1.
Conditions: game g_1 is *closed*.
Effects: termination of game g_1 involves entering g_2.

Choice noted $g_1|g_2$, which means that participants play either g_1 or g_2 non-deterministically. Not surprisingly, this combination has no specific conditions nor consequences.

Pre-sequencing noted $g_2 \rightsquigarrow g_1$, which means that g_2 is opened while g_1 is proposed.
Conditions: game g_1 is *proposed*.
Effects: successful termination of game g_1 involves entering game g_2.
Such pre-sequencing games can be played to ensure that entry conditions of a forthcoming game are actually established —for instance to make public a conflictuel position before entering a persuasion game. In case that the first game is not successful, the second game is simply ignored.

Embedding noted $g_1 < g_2$, which means that g_1 is now opened while g_2 was already opened.
Conditions: game g_1 is *open*.
Effects: (conversational) commitments of the embedded games are considered having priority over those of the embedding game. Much work needs to be done to precisely define this notion within this framework, but this may be captured by constraining the sanctions related to the embedded game to be greater than those of the embedding game ($s_{g2} > s_{g1}$).

4   Request for Action

Our aim in this paper is to reconsider the famous "request for action" (see Fig. 1) protocol within our dialogue-game-based framework. Considering the protocol as initially stated by Winograd and Flores (see figure), we have found that such protocol requires four basics building dialogue games : (1) a "request" game (rg); (2) an "offer" game (og), (3) an "inform" game (ig) and (4) an "ask" game (ag).

4.1   Request Game (rg)

The request game as specified by Winograd and Flores captures the idea that the initiator (I) "request" the partner (P) and this latter can "promise" or "reject".

In our framework, this starts with the contextualization game in which I and P negotiate the establishment of the following game

$$\langle basic\_directive(+1, +2), (E_{rg}, S_{rg}, F_{rg}, R_{rg})\rangle$$

Both agents should also adapt their new conditions and rules from those of the primitive directive. The new conditions and rules are described in Fig. 4.

$$
\begin{array}{l|l}
E_{rg} & \neg C(y, x, \alpha, t_0) \\
SI_{rg} & C(y, x, \alpha, t_f) \\
SP_{rg} & \text{Nil} \\
FI_{rg} & C(y, x, \neg\alpha, t_f) \\
FP_{rg} & \text{Nil} \\
R_{rg} & C_g(x, y, request(x, y, \alpha), t_0) \\
& C_g(y, x, request(x, y, \alpha)) \Rightarrow \\
& C_g(y, x, promise(y, x, \alpha)|refuse(y, x, \alpha), t_1), t_0) \\
& C_g(y, x, promise(y, x, \alpha) \Rightarrow C(y, x, \alpha, t_2), t_0) \\
& C_g(y, x, refuse(y, x, \alpha) \Rightarrow C(y, x, \neg\alpha, t_2), t_0)
\end{array}
$$

Fig. 4. Conditions and rules for the request game.

Notice that I and P "request" and "promise" and consequently they should be more committed in this case than in the case where the first one "suggest" and the second "commit". Such increase in the degree of commitment should be reflected by sanctions which should be greater in the first case than in the second case.

4.2   Offer Game (*og*)

An offer is a promise that is conditional upon the partner's acceptance. To make an offer is to put something forward for another's choice (of acceptance or refusal). To offer then, is to perform a conditional commissive. The game can be described as

$$\langle basic\_offer(0, +1), (E_{og}, S_{og}, F_{og}, R_{og})\rangle$$

Precisely, to offer α on condition that the partner accept α. Conditions and rules are in this case are described in Fig. 5.

4.3   Information Game (*ig*)

This game starts with the couple $I : assert$ and $P : agree$ or $P : disagree$ which denotes in fact the couple with $(0,+1)$ according to the tree of strength.

$$\langle basic\_assertive(0, 0), (E_{ig}, S_{ig}, F_{ig}, R_{ig})\rangle$$

$$
\begin{array}{l|l}
E_{og} & \neg C(x, y, \alpha, t_0) \\
SI_{og} & C(x, y, \alpha, t_f) \\
SP_{og} & \text{Nil} \\
FI_{og} & C(x, y, \neg\alpha, t_f) \\
FP_{og} & \text{Nil} \\
R_{og} & C_g(x, y, \mathit{offer}(x, y, \alpha), t_0) \\
& C_g(y, x, \mathit{offer}(x, y, \alpha)) \Rightarrow \\
& C_g(y, x, \mathit{accept}(y, x, \alpha) | \mathit{refuse}(y, x, \alpha), t_1), t_0) \\
& C_g(x, y, \mathit{accept}(y, x, \alpha) \Rightarrow C(x, y, \alpha, t_2), t_0) \\
& C_g(x, y, \mathit{refuse}(y, x, \alpha) \Rightarrow C(x, y, \neg\alpha, t_2), t_0)
\end{array}
$$

Fig. 5. Conditions and rules for the offer game

Notice that a partner can be in the disposition of being in accord or agreement with someone without uttering any words. He can also agree by doing a speech act. In this case, he agrees when he can assert a proposition p while presupposing that the initiator has previously put forward p and while expressing his accord or agreement with this initiator as regards p. To disagree is to assert $\neg p$ when the other has previously put forward p. In this game, we assume that the successful termination is when an agreement is reached about the proposition p. The conditions and rules for this couple are detailed in Fig. 6.

$$
\begin{array}{l|l}
E_{ig} & C(y, x, p, t_0) \text{ or } C(y, x, \neg p, t_0) \\
SI_{ig} & C(y, x, p, t_f) \text{ and } C(x, y, p, t_f) \\
SP_{ig} & \text{Nil} \\
FI_{ig} & \text{Nil} \\
FP_{ig} & \text{Nil} \\
R_{ig} & C_g(x, y, \mathit{assert}(x, y, p), t_0) \\
& C_g(y, x, \mathit{assert}(x, y, p)) \Rightarrow \\
& C_g(y, x, \mathit{assert}(y, x, p) | \mathit{assert}(y, x, \neg p), t_1), t_0) \\
& C_g(x, y, \mathit{assert}(x, y, p) \Rightarrow C(x, y, p, t_1), t_0) \\
& C_g(y, x, \mathit{assert}(y, x, p) \Rightarrow C(y, x, p, t_2), t_0)
\end{array}
$$

Fig. 6. Conditions and rules for the inform game

4.4 Ask Game (*ag*)

We use "ask" in the sense of asking a question, which consists to request the partner to perform a future speech act that would give the initiator a correct answer to his question (in the context of this protocol, the questions will have the form "is the work W finished" and will expect an assertion or a denial that W is finished as a possible answers). According to these remarks, we propose for the *ask* game, described as

$\langle basic\_question(0,0), (E_{ag}, S_{ag}, F_{ag}, R_{ag})\rangle$

The structure pertaining to this game is described in Fig. 7.

$$
\begin{array}{l|l}
E_{ag} & \text{Nil} \\
SI_{ag} & C(y, x, p, t_f) \text{ or } C(y, x, \neg p, t_f) \\
SP_{ag} & \text{Nil} \\
FI_{ag} & \text{Nil} \\
FP_{ag} & \text{Nil} \\
R_{ag} & C_g(x, y, question(x, y, p), t_0) \\
& C_g(y, x, question(x, y, p)) \Rightarrow \\
& C_g(y, assert(y, x, p)|assert(y, x, \neg p), t_1), t_0) \\
& C_g(y, x, assert(y, x, p)) \Rightarrow C(y, x, p, t_2), t_0)
\end{array}
$$

Fig. 7. Conditions and rules for the ask game

4.5 Request Action Reconsidered

Taking for granted that our agents both have access to the basic building games as described above —and handle these games through the use of a contextualization game that we have sketched— we will now first study the detail of how a conversational behavior following the Winograd and Flores (WF) request for action protocol can be captured. We also illustrates the flexibility of the formalism by adding situations not considered in the initial protocol. An example concludes the section.

To start with, it is clear that WF basically consists of a request game followed with an evaluation phase. How will the result of the action be evaluated? In the WF protocol, it is assumed that the partner informs the initiator when the action is done. The combination is typically a pre-sequencing, since it only makes sense to play the *inform* game in case of acceptance of the request.

$rg \rightsquigarrow ig$

Now, as illustrated by the WF, it is possible that the agents enter some negotiation cycle about the requested action. This means that, after the initial request, we could find a sequence of different offers and requests made by the agents. We use the shortcut $(*)$ to stipulate that the sequence can be repeated a number of times, with different *request* and *offer* games, of course (conditions on these requests and offers are not detailed here).

$(rg; og)^* \rightsquigarrow ig$

As described so far, the resulting structure simply captures the classical WF protocol. Now, we consider in addition that the initiator may want to ask himself whether the action is completed. Thus we have the following amended structure, capturing that participants may choose an *inform* or an *ask* game to trigger the evaluation.

$(rg; og)^* \rightsquigarrow (ig|ag)$

Also, an important possibility not considered is that the agents may have some conflictuel position about the achievement of the action. In this case, they may want to enter some *persuasion* game to convince the other. Such a *persuasion* game (*pg*) is not detailed here, but can be regarded as another subtype of a directive game, where the initiator challenges the partner and demands some justification to support some proposition *p*. Thus we may have the following combination of games, where it is possible to embed in the *inform* (or *ask*) game a *persuasion* game to reach agreement:

$(rg; og)^* \rightsquigarrow (ig|ag) < (pg)^*$

All this assumes that the basic WF is initially described as a pre-sequence of a *request* and an *evaluation* game. Note that others combinations might be considered. For instance, we could assume that the initiator's request will be honored without any explicit feedback from the partner. In this case, the combination of games could be

$rg < (ig|ag)$

4.6 Example

To make things more concrete, we include an example involving *Al* and *Bob*. The dialogue starts when *Al* requests *Bob* to support him in the course of a reviewing process.

$propose.enter(Al, Bob, rg \rightsquigarrow ig)$

Bob would like to help his friend, but he is very busy at the moment so he wouldn't like to be penalize at this level. *Bob* refuses. *Al* proposes as an alternative the game *suggest* (*sg*) where the penalties are more acceptable (the *suggest* game is just another subtype of the basic directive game).

$propose.enter(Al, Bob, sg \rightsquigarrow ig)$

$accept.enter(Bob, Al, sg \rightsquigarrow ig)$

The preceding moves are examples of the game-level negotiation that we have discussed in the paper. The immediate consequence is that all the commitments described in the game are created. In particular, *Bob* has contracted the following commitment :

$C(Bob, Al, review(Bob, monday), now, 10)$

Now it is Monday in the world of our agents, and *Bob* informs *Al* that he has completed the review.

$inform(Bob, Al, done(review))$

Unfortunately, agent *Al* does not seem quite satisfied with the received review form. He does not agree that the action was done as requested.

$$assert(Al, Bob, not(done(review)))$$

Note that the current state of the dialogue (where a conflict of opinion is explicit) makes possible to enter a persuasion game, where for instance, agent *Bob* would challenge *Al* and ask why he is not happy with the review form. *Al* could in turn explains that *Bob* has choosen a borderline recommendation, a case forbidden by the review guidelines. The detail of how such persuasion dialogue can be managed within dialogue game framework might be found in [1]. In case of successful termination of the persuasion game, an agreement is found and the protocol ends.

4.7   Towards a Game Simulator

The currently in progress agent Dialogue Game Simulator adopts some facets presented in this paper. In particular, it offers a graphical environment which is able to simulate conversations between agents with dialogue games. Precisely, each user must initially choose a "scenario file" which is assigned to his agent. This file, created beforehand, contains the actions than he will carry out during simulation at a predetermined time. A file which describes a game is composed of entry conditions, success conditions, failures conditions, as well as rules of the game. Moreover, for each speech act forming part of a game, we can define a constraint which indicates the hierarchical relation which must exist between the sender and the receiver to be able to play the action in question.

For each initiated dialogue, a workspace is created containing the following: implicated agents, a stack of dialogue games as well as a chart of sent messages (similar to the sequence diagram of UML). The management of most of the compositions of dialogues is ensured by the stack which is in charge to keep the trace of dialectical shifts allowing thus to (a) manage the coherence of the conversation, (b) avoid conflict situations and, (c) possibly detect fallacies.

Notice also that each agent has an agenda, a structure containing its commitments in action as well as the propositional commitments that this agent had contract during the simulation. An agent's agenda also contain commitments of others agents which were contracted in a dialogue with him. As mentioned previously, the commitments established in a particular context are withdrawn from the agendas when the game which generated them, is closed.

The simulator is coded in JAVA, agents are developed with JACK —an agent development tool in JAVA, and files concerning the games are written in XML.

5   Discussion

Let us now return to the problems discussed in section 2, and investigate whether dialogue-game-based approaches as the one suggested here can help to meet these requirements:

- Identifying the state of the dialogue as a set of commitments (precisely those commitments that are relevant to constrain the interaction at this stage) is a key point to make CPs more easy to design. It allows the designer to use some declarative rules referring to these meaningful commitments, thus facilitating the design of most games while improving clarity and expressiveness. As a consequence, the resulting CPs are practically more flexible.
- Keeping track of the commitments of the participants also makes possible future references to these commitments instead of just referring to the previous moves of dialogue. For instance, it is possible to design dialogue rules where a request can obligates the other agent to promise to undertake an action before a given deadline.
- The use of small CPs offers more flexibility and genericness in the sense that those basic games can be composed for any other complex game. The contextualization game sketched in the paper offers the possibility to shift from game to game during conversation, but needs to be studied more carefully. One can specify, for instance the case where the initiator's request can be honored without an explicit acceptation of the partner; or the case where the initiator can ask if the commitment is satisfied.
- Public commitments as suggested in our approach motivates agents to conform to some expected behavior and thus facilitate coordination in the dialogue. However, agents remain autonomous and may decide to violate the commitments and pay the sanctions if they find good reasons to do so, offering a promising balance between normativeness and autonomy.

It is clear that much work needs to be done regarding some foundational aspects of the approach: the mechanisms of the commitments and the sanctions need to be explored to be exploitable by some computational agents, the contextualization and combinations of games will certainly need corrections when faced with to others case studies. However, by trying to investigate in the light of a classical example how this promising dialogue-game-based approach can be used, we feel that this paper contributes to the development of future flexible conversational policies.

References

1. L. Amgoud, N. Maudet, and S. Parsons. Modelling dialogues using argumentation. In *Proceedings of the 4th International Conference on Multi-Agent Systems (ICMAS00)*, pages 31–38, Berlin, 2000. IEEE Press. 297
2. M. Barbuceanu and M. Fox. Cool: A language for describing coordination in multiagent systems. In *Proceedings of the first International Conference on Multi-Agent Systems (ICMAS)*, pages 17–25, 1995. 285
3. M. Colombetti. Commitment-based semantics for agent communication languages. In *Proceedings of the First Workshop on the History and Philosophy of Logic, Mathematics and Computation (HPLMC00)*, San-sebastian, 2000. 284
4. M. Dastani, J. Hulstijn, and L. V. der Torre. Negotiation protocols and dialogue games. In *Proceedings of the 5th International Conference on Autonomous Agents (Agents2001)*, pages 180–181, Montreal, Canada, 2001. ACM Press. 289, 289

5. F. Dignum and M. Greaves, editors. *Issues in agent communication*, volume 1916 of *Lecture Notes in Computer Science*. Springer-Verlag, 2000. 299, 299, 299

6. C. Excelente-Toledo, R. A. Bourne, and N. R. Jennings. Reasoning about commitments and penalties for coordination between autonomous agents. In *Proceedings of fifth International Conference on Autonomous Agents (Agents2001)*, pages 131–138, Montreal, Canada, 2001. ACM Press. 288

7. T. Finin, Y. Labrou, and J. Mayfield. KQML as an agent communication language. In J. Bradshaw, editor, *Software agents*, pages 291–316. AAAI/MIT Press, 1997. 284

8. R. F. Flores and R. C. Kremer. To commit or not to commit: Modelling agent conversations for action. *Computational intelligence —Special Issue on Agent Communication Languages*, 18(2), 2002. 289, 289

9. Foundation for Intelligent and Physical Agents (FIPA). Communicative act library specification (xc00037h). http://www.fipa.org/spec, 2001. 284

10. T. F. Gordon. Computational dialectics. In P. Hoschka, editor, *Computers as assistants - A new generation of support systems*, pages 186–203. Lawrence Erlbaum Associates, 1996. 284

11. M. Greaves, H. Holmback, and J. Bradshaw. What is a conversation policy? In *[5]*, pages 118–131. 2000. 284, 284, 286, 287

12. C. L. Hamblin. *Fallacies*. Methuen, 1970. 284

13. N. Maudet. Negotiating games. *Journal of autonoumous agents and multi-agent systems* (research note, to appear). 291, 292

14. N. Maudet and B. Chaib-draa. Commitment-based and dialogue-game based protocols: new trends in agent communication languages. *The Knowledge Engineering Review*, 17(2), 2002. 284

15. P. McBurney and S. Parsons. Games that agents play: a formal framework for dialogue between autonomous agents. *Journal of Logic, Language, and Information —Special issue on logic and games*, 11(3), 2002. 289, 289, 292

16. P. McBurney, S. Parsons, and M. Wooldridge. Desiderata for agent argumentation protocols. In C. Castelfranchi and W. L. Johnson, editors, *Proceedings of the First International Joint Conference on Autonomous Agents and Multi-Agent Systems (AAMAS 2002)*, pages 402–409, Bologna, Italy, 2002. AAMAS. 286

17. C. Reed. Dialogue frames in agent communication. In *Proceedings of the Third International Conference on MultiAgent Systems (ICMAS98)*, pages 246–253, Paris, France, 1998. IEEE Press. 284, 291, 292

18. M. P. Singh. Agent communication languages: rethinking the principles. *IEEE Computer*, pages 40–47, 1998. 284, 286

19. M. P. Singh. A social semantics for agent communication language. In *[5]*, pages 31–45. 2000. 286, 286, 288

20. D. Vanderveken. *Meaning and speech acts*. Cambridge University Press, 1991. 290

21. L. Vongkasem and B. Chaib-draa. Acl as a joint project between participants. In *[5]*, pages 235–248. 2000. 286, 289

22. D. Walton and E. Krabbe. *Commitment in dialogue: basic concepts of interpersonal reasoning*. State University of New York Press, Albany, NY, 1995. 284, 289, 291

23. T. Winograd and F. Flores. *Understanding computers and cognition: a new foundation for design*. Addison-Wesley, MA, 1986. 285, 285

24. M. Wooldridge. Semantic issues in the verification of agent communication languages. *Journal of Autonomous Agents and Multi-Agent Systems*, 3(1):9–31, 2000. 284

25. P. Yolum and M. P. Singh. Flexible protocol specification and execution: applying event calculus planning using commitments. In *Proceedings of the first International Conference on Autonomous Agents and Multi-agent Systems (AAMAS2002)*, pages 527–534, 2002. 286

Computational Model of Believable Conversational Agents

Catherine Pelachaud[1] and Massimo Bilvi[2]

[1] LINC - Paragraphe
IUT of Montreuil - University of Paris 8
c.pelachaud@iut.univ-paris8.fr
[2] Department of Computer and System Science
University of Rome "La Sapienza"
bilvi@dis.uniroma1.it

Abstract. In this chapter we present the issues and problems involved in the creation of Embodied Conversational Agents (ECAs). These agents may have a humanoid aspect and may be embedded in a user interface with the capacity to interact with the user; that is they are able to perceive and understand what the user is saying, but also to answer verbally and nonverbally to the user. ECAs are expected to interact with users as in human-human conversation. They should smile, raise their brows, nod, and even gesticulate, not in a random manner but in co-occurrence with their speech. Results from research in human-human communication are applied to human-ECA communication, or ECA-ECA communication. The creation of such agents requires several steps ranging from the creation of the geometry of the body and facial models to the modeling of their mind, emotion, and personality, but also to the computation of the facial expression, body gesture, gaze that accompany their speech. In this chapter we will present our work toward the computation of nonverbal behaviors accompanying speech.

1 Introduction

We convey our thoughts through our (conscious or unconscious) choice of words, facial expressions, body postures, gestures... Faces are an important mean of communication and may have several communicative functions. They are used to control the flow of conversation; that is they help in regulating the exchange of speaking turns, keeping the floor or asking for it. Actions such as smiling, raising the eyebrows, and wrinkling the nose often co-occur with a verbal message. Some facial expressions accompany the flow of speech and are synchronized at the verbal level, punctuating accented phonemic segments and pauses. Other facial expressions may substitute for a word or string of words, or emphasize what is being said. They can also express attitude toward one own speech (such as irony) or toward the interlocutor (like showing submission). They are the primary channels to express emotion. Facial expressions do not occur randomly, but rather are synchronized to one's own speech, or to the speech of others [9,16,30].

M.-P. Huget (Ed.): Communications in Multiagent Systems, LNAI 2650, pp. 300–317, 2003.
© Springer-Verlag Berlin Heidelberg 2003

Faces exhibit not only expressions of emotions but also a large variety of communicative functions that are essential to a conversation. To control the agent 'Greta' we are using the taxonomy of communicative behavior as proposed by Poggi [26]. This taxonomy is based on the type of information a behavior displayed by a speaker communicates to conversants, each class may be composed of several functions:

Information on the Speaker's belief: this cluster includes expressions that provide information on different types of speaker's beliefs:
  - certainty functions: the speaker may be certain or uncertain of what she is saying; she may respectively frown or raise her eyebrows to mark her attitude.
  - belief-relation functions: the speaker may contrast several elements in her speech by raising her eyebrows.
  - adjectival functions: the speaker may mimic the property of abstract entity ('great idea') or object ('small box') by opening wide or squeezing the eyes respectively.
  - deictic functions: the speaker may gaze at a point in space to direct the conversant's attention.

Information on the Speaker's intention: this cluster gathers expressions used to underline the particular intention of a speaker:
  - performative function: the speaker may request (say by an order, a suggest or an implore), ask (interrogate), inform (by warning). In previous work we have exposed the link existing between performative and facial expressions [27].
  - topic-comment function: the topic is the background information the speaker is taking for granted as being shared with the conversant, and the comment is the new information the speaker considers relevant and worth to communicate. The speaker may mark this new information by raised eyebrows and/or head nod.
  - turn-taking function: this function refers to how people negotiate speaking turns in a conversation. Gaze plays a large role in the negotiation.

Information on the Speaker's affective: this cluster represents the expressions of emotions felt or referred to by the speaker.

Information on the Speaker's meta-cognitive: the expressions correspond to a particular thinking activity of the speaker (breaking the gaze while remembering a fact or planning what to say).

A communicative function is made of two components: a signal and a meaning. Signal may be a facial expression, a gaze/ head direction, or a head movement; while meaning corresponds to the communicative value of a signal [27]. We have decided to cluster communicative functions not from the signals involved in the expression (e.g. raising eyebrows) but from their meanings. Indeed the same expression may change meaning depending on its place and time of occurrence in the conversation. Raising eyebrows signal surprise but also emphasis of what is being said; they signal question mark, specially in the case of non-syntactically questions but they are also part of the expression used when suggesting something to someone. A smile may be a sign of happiness but it may also be used as a greeting or a back-channel sign. Moreover not everybody uses the same expression to carry a given function. Some people mark accented words with, for example, eye flashes, other will raise their eyebrows, or nod their head. We believed one has to consider this variety of behaviors in the creation of believable ECAs.

The work presented in this chapter is part of a larger system developed within a European project, MagiCster[1]. The project aims at building a new type of human-computer interface, based on a Conversational Embodied Agent. It wishes to make this Agent 'believable and expressive': that is, able to communicate complex information through the combination and the tight synchronization of verbal and nonverbal signals. As application, the agent is embedded in user interface where it may dialog with a user [25] or with other agents [29].

In the remaining of this chapter we describe how, given a text to be output by the agent (this text may have been generated by a dialog system [25]) and a set of communicative functions, to compute the corresponding animation of the agent. We present our system architecture as well as each of its components in the next sections. In section 8 we describe in detail how we solve conflict at the facial expression levels while in section 10 we present a description language for facial expressions.

2   Representation Language, APML

To ensure its portability, the facial model is compliant with MPEG-4 standards. To ensure the portability of the system as well as to ensure independence between the specification of the facial expressions and the facial models (that is we wish to be able to define facial expressions to be applied to any type of facial models) we are using an XML language, called Affective Presentation Markup Language (APML) [10]. The types of the tags represents the communicative functions as defined above. XML offers also a synchronisation scheme between the verbal and the nonverbal channels as it delineates the action of signals over text spans. An example of annotated text is:

3   Architecture

Our system takes as input a text marked with tags denoting the communicative functions. The tags are part of the APML representation language. The system interprets the input text by instantiating the communicative function into their corresponding facial expressions. The output of the system is a facial animation

---

[1] IST project IST-1999-29078, partners: University of Edinburgh, Division of Informatics; DFKI, Intelligent User Interfaces Department; Swedish Institute of Computer Science; University of Bari, Dipartimento di Informatica; University of Rome, Dipartimento di Informatica e Sistemistica; AvartarME

```
<APML>
<turn-allocation type="take turn">
<performative type="greet">
Good Morning, Angela.
</performative>
</turn-allocation>
<affective type="happy">
It is so <topic-comment type="comment">wonderful</topic-comment> to see
you again.
</affective>
<certainty type="certain"> I was <topic-comment type="comment">sure</topic-
comment> we would do so, one day! </certainty>
</APML>
```

Fig. 1. Example of XML input

file and an audio file. Figure 2 illustrates the detailed architecture of our system, the *Greta* agent system, composed of several modules whose main functions are:

- **APML Parser**: XML parser that validates the input format as specified by the APML language.
- **Expr2Signal Converter**: given a communicative function and its meaning, this module returns the list of facial signals to activate for the realization of the facial expression.
- **TTS Festival**: manages the speech synthesis and give us the information needed for the synchronisation of the facial expressions to the speech (i.e. list of phonemes and phonemes duration) [4].
- **Conflicts Resolver**: resolves the conflicts that may happened when more than one facial signals should be activated on the same facial parts (example: the co-occurring signals should be "eyebrow raising" and "frown" on the eyebrow region).
- **Face Generator**: converts the facial signals into MPEG-4 Facial Animation Parameters (FAPs) needed to animate the 3D facial model.
- **Viseme Generator**: converts each phoneme, given by Festival [4], into a set of FAP values needed for the lips animation.
- **MPEG4 FAP Decoder**: is an MPEG-4 compliant Facial Animation Engine.

4   APML Parser

The input to the agent engine in an XML string which contains the text to be pronounced by the agent enriched with XML-tags indicating the communicative functions that are attached to the text. The APML parser takes such an input and validates it with the corresponding DTD (Document Type Definition). The elements of the DTD correspond to the communicative functions described in

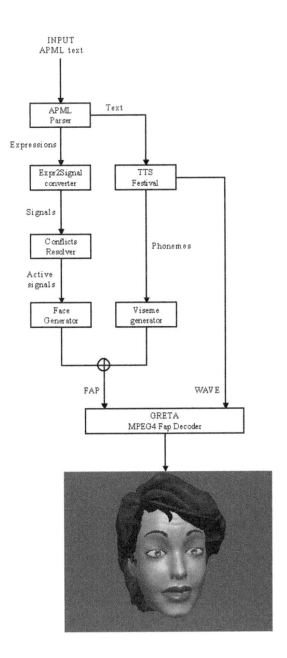

Fig. 2. Agent Architecture

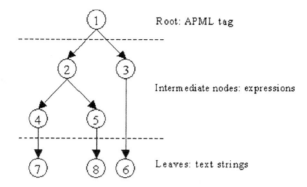

Fig. 3. Tree structure from XML input

section 1 [10]. The next step is to pass the text to be said (specified in bold in figure 1) to the speech synthesiser Festival [4] while the information contained in the markers are stored in a structure that will be used subsequently.

5   Speech Synthesizer - Festival

In the current version of the system we are using Festival as speech synthesizer [4]. Festival returns a list of couples (*phoneme, duration*) for each phrase of APML tagged text. These information are then used to compute the lip movement and to synchronise the facial expression with speech.

6   Synchronisation of the Facial Expressions

Facial expressions and speech are tightly synchronised. In our system the synchronisation is implemented at the word level, that is, the timing of the facial expressions is connected to the text embedded between the markers. The XML parser returns a tree structure from which we calculate, using the list of the phonemes returned by Festival, the timings of each individual expression. The leaves of the tree correspond to the text while the intermediary nodes correspond to facial expressions except for the root that corresponds to the APML marker (see Figure 3).

6.1   Temporal Course of an Expression

Knowing the starting time and duration of an expression, the next step is to calculate the course of the expression intensity. The intensity of the expression is viewed as the amplitude of the facial movements, variable in the time, that composes the expression.

Each expression is characterised by three temporal parameters [12]:

– **onset**: is the time that, starting from the neutral face, the expression takes to reach its maximal intensity.
– **apex**: is the time during which the expression maintains its maximal intensity.
– **offset**: is the time that, starting from the maximal intensity, the expression takes to return to the neutral expression.

Such parameters are different from expression to expression. For example the "sadness" expression is characterised by a long *offset* (the expression takes more time to disappear), while the "surprise" expression has a short *onset*.

The values used for these parameters, have been taken from researches based on the analysis of facial expressions [14,3].

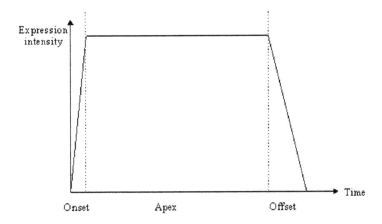

Fig. 4. Temporal course of the expression " surprise" with its respective parameters *onset, apex* and *offset*

It has been showed experimentally that the amplitude of a facial movement is much more complex [14] than a simple decomposition in three linear parameters but for sake of simplicity and for lack of data, we use such trapezoidal functions to represent the temporal aspects of facial expressions.

7   Instantiation of the APML Tags - Expr2Signal Converter

The APML tags correspond to the meaning of a given communicative function. Thus, the next step is to convert the markers of an input text into their corresponding facial signals. The conversion is done by looking up the definition of each tag into the library that contained the pairs of the type (meaning, signals).

Let us consider the following example:

<affective type="satisfaction">
I was sure we will arrive to an agreement.
</affective>

This text contains one communicative function represented by the marker *affective* which value is *satisfaction* as specified by the field *type*. The list of signals for this communicative function is:

$$affective(satisfaction) = \{raised\ eyebrows,\ smile,\ head\ nod\}$$

Figure 5 illustrates the corresponding expression.

Fig. 5. 'Satisfaction' expression

Now, let us consider the following example:

<certainty type="certain">
I was sure we will arrive to an agreement.
</certainty>

Here, the communicative function is given by the marker *certainty* with *certain* as a value. The list of signals for this function is:

$$certainty(certain) = \{frown\}$$

Figure 6 illustrates the expression of *certain*.

In these two examples we have seen two "different" communicative functions that activate "different" signals on the same facial part (eyebrow).

Let us consider the following example:

<affective type="satisfaction">
<certainty type="certain">

Fig. 6. 'Certain' expression

I was sure we will arrive to an agreement.
</certainty>
</affective>

We have two communicative functions that activate in the same time interval two different signals (*frown* and *raised eyebrow*) on the same facial region (*eyebrow*). So we have a conflict that must be solved before visualising the animation. When a conflict at the level of facial signals is detected, the system calls up a special module for the resolution of conflicts, the "conlict resolver" in figure 2 (described in details in the section 8). Such a module determines which signal, between those that should be active on the same facial region, must prevail on the others. If we go back to our previous example, *Conflicts Resolver* returns:

$$\text{resolve\_conflict}(affective(satisfaction), certainty(certain)) = \\ \{frown, smile, head\ nod\}$$

The resulting expression is shown in Figure 7. As we can see the *Conflicts Resolver* has decided that the signal *frown* prevails over the signal *raised eyebrows*.

8   Conflicts Resolver

Few attempts have been made to combine co-occurring expressions. Often additive rules are applied [6,24] that is all signals corresponding to the co-occurring communicative functions are added to each other. Lately, Cassell et al [8] have proposed a hierarchical distinctions of the signal: only the signal with the highest priority rule will be displayed. These last two methods do not allow combination of several communicative functions to create a complex expression. Our proposal is to apply *Belief Networks* (BN) to the management of this problem. Our BN includes the following types of nodes (see figure 8):

Fig. 7. Expression of 'satisfaction', 'certain' and combination of both expressions after conflict resolution

communicative functions: nodes correspond to the communicative functions: performative, certainty, belief-relation, emotion, topic-comment, turn-taking, meta-cognitive.

facial parts: nodes are the eyes, eyebrows, mouth shape, head movement and head direction. For example, the values we count for the eyebrows are: raised, frown, oblique, and neutral. The values we consider for the mouth are: lip tense, lip corner up, lip corner down, and neutral.

performative dimensions: Performatives may be described along a small set of dimensions which are 'power-relationship', 'in whose interest is the requested action', 'degree of certainty', 'type of social encounter', 'affective state' [27]. We have singled out two dimensions among the five ones that are relevant in the characterisation of performatives [27]: 'power relationship' and 'in which interest is the requested action', that are called, respectively, in the BN 'dominance' (whose values are submissive, neutral, dominant) and 'orientation' (whose values are self-oriented, neutral, other-oriented). These dimensions allow us to differentiate performatives not as for their meaning (which requires strictly five dimensions) but as for the facial parts that are used to express the performative, and in which conflict may arise (see figure 9). Indeed, a common feature of the performatives whose value along the orientation dimension is 'other-oriented' is a 'head nod': performatives of this category are, for example, 'praise', 'approve', 'confirm', 'agree'. On the other hand, 'Submissive' and 'self-oriented' performatives (e.g. 'implore') show inner eyebrow raising, while 'self-oriented', and 'dominant/neutral' performatives (such as 'order', 'criticise', 'disagree', 'refuse') have a frown in common. In our BN, the two dimensions are represented as intermediary nodes (thus simplifying the construction of the BN), which are linked to the leaf (signal) nodes. For example the performative 'implore' is characterised as being 'submissive' and in 'self-oriented', 'advice' as being 'neutral' and 'other-oriented', 'order' as being 'dominant' and 'self-oriented'. On one hand this allows us to study how common features of performatives prevail in the final facial expressions; on the other hand, it also helps us in reducing the number of entry nodes of our BN.

emotion dimensions: Using the same reasoning as for the performatives, we define emotion along few dimensions. These dimensions are 'valence' (positive or negative) and 'time' (past, current and future) [20]. Valence is commonly used to differentiate emotions. Examples of positive emotions are 'joy', 'happy-for', 'satisfaction', 'like') while examples of negative emotions are 'anger', 'sadness', 'fear', 'dislike', 'reproach'. The dimension 'time' refers to the time at which the event that triggers the emotion is happening [20]. 'Fear' or 'distress' refer to an event that might happen in the future, while 'sadness' or 'resentment' are due to events happened in the 'past'. 'Disgust' is due to an event happening at the 'current' time. Furthermore this representation allows one to characterise emotions based on their facial expressions. 'Tense lips' are common to the negative emotions (envy, jealousy, anger, fear); a 'frown' will characterise negative emotions happened at the 'current time' (for example anger). 'Positive' emotions are often distinguished by a 'smile' (e.g. 'joy', 'happy-for', 'satisfaction', 'gratitude').

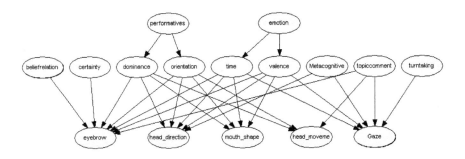

Fig. 8. Belief Network linking facial communicative functions and facial signals

When a conflict is encountered, the BN initialised the concerned communicative function at 100. The BN delivers the probabilities that each signal (involved in both communicative functions) has to be selected to form the new expression. For instance going back to the previous example, the emotion 'satisfaction' and the certainty 'certain' are initialised at 100 by the BN. Knowing which emotion has been selected, the values of the intermediary nodes 'valence' and 'time' are computed (the values are shown in the figure). The value of the eyebrows for resolution of the signal conflicts is then output by the BN: 'frown' receives the higher probability. Thus, the expression resulting from the combination of the affective function 'satisfaction' ('raised eyebrow' + 'smile' + 'head nod') with the certainty function 'certain' (frown) will simply be 'frown' + 'smile' + 'head nod'; that is, it cuts off the 'satisfaction' signal at the eyebrow level (See Figure 7). This method allows us to combine expressions at a fine level and to resolve the possible conflicts at the signal level.

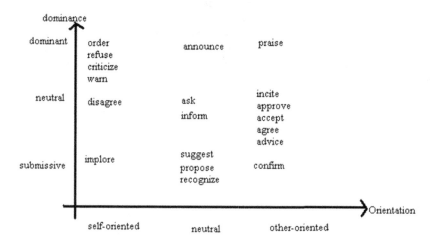

Fig. 9. Cluster of performatives along the dimensions 'dominance' and 'orientation'

9   Generation of the Facial Animation

After resolving the potential conflicts between the facial signals, we proceed with the generation of the animation for the agent. Lip shapes are computed based on a computation model described in [23]. The animation is obtained by conversing each facial signal in their corresponding facial parameters. Our facial model is compliant with MPEG-4 standard [11,21]. The facial model is the core of an MPEG-4 decoder and is based on the specifications for "Simple Facial Animation Object Profile" [23]. Two sets of parameters describe and animate the 3D facial model: facial animation parameter set (FAPs) and facial definition parameter (FDP). The FDPs define the shape of the model while FAPs define the facial actions. FAPs correspond to the displacements of facial features. When the model has been characterized with FDP, the animation is obtained by specifying for each frame the values of FAPs. So we represent each signal as a set of FAPs. For instance: a raising eyebrow that marks uncertainty is generated by the FAPs 31, 32, 33 for the left eyebrow and the FAPs 34, 35, 35 for the right eyebrow. A facial expression is characterized not only by the muscular contraction that gives rise to it, but also by an intensity factor and a duration. The intensity factor is rendered by specifying a given intensity for every FAP. The temporal factor is modeled by three parameters: onset, apex and offset [12] (as explained in section 6.1). Thus, in our system, every facial signal is characterized by a set of FAPs to define its corresponding facial expression as well as by an onset and offset. Moreover, our model includes wrinkles and folds to ensure more realism.

10   The Facial Display Definition Language

Humans are very good at showing a large spectrum of facial expressions; but at the same time, humans may display facial expressions varying by very subtle differences, but whose differences are still perceivable. We have developed a language to describe facial expressions as (meaning, signal) pairs. These expressions are stored in a library. Defining facial expressions using keyword such as 'happiness, raised eyebrow, surprise' does not capture these slight variations. In our language, an expression may be defined at a high level (a facial expression is a combination of other facial expressions already pre-defined) or at a low level (a facial expression is a combination of facial parameters). The low level facial parameters correspond to the MPEG-4 Facial Animation Parameters (FAPs) [23]. The language allows one to create a large variety of facial expressions for any communicative functions as well as the subtleties that distinguish facial expressions. It allows also us to create a "facial display dictionary" which can easily be expanded. When a text marked with communicative function tags is given in input, the 'Greta' system looks in the library to which signals corresponds each meaning specified by the APML tag; These tags gets then instantiated by the corresponding signals values.

Paradiso et al [22] have established an algebra to create facial expressions. The authors have elaborated operators that combine and manipulate facial expressions. Our language has the only purpose to create facial expressions that are associated to a given communicative function.

In the next sections we describe the language we have developed to define and to store facial expressions.

10.1   Facial Basis

In our system we distinguish "facial basis" (FB) from "facial display" (FD). An FB involves one facial part such as the eyebrow, mouth, jaw, eyelid. FB includes also facial movements such as nodding, shaking, turning the head and movement of the eyes. Each FB is defined as a set of MPEG-4 compliant FAP parameters:

$$FB = \{fap3 = v_1, \ldots\ldots\ldots, fap69 = v_k\};$$

where $v_1, \ldots, v_k$ specify the FAPs intensity value. An FB can also be defined as a combination of FB's by using the '+' operator in this way:

$$FB' = FB_1 + FB_2;$$

where FB_1 and FB_2 can be:

- Previously defined FB's
- an FB of the form: $\{fap3 = v_1, \ldots\ldots\ldots, fap69 = v_k\}$

Let us consider the *raising eyebrows* movement. We can define this movement as a combination of the *left* and *right* raising eyebrow. Thus, in our language, we have:

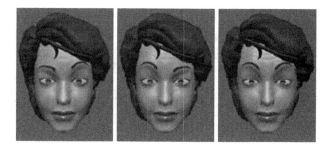

Fig. 10. The combination of "raise_left" FB (left) and "raise_right" FB (centre) produces "raise_eyebrows" FB (right)

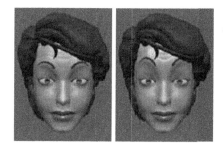

Fig. 11. The "raise_eyebrows" FB (left) and the "large_raise_eyebrows" FB (right)

$raise\_eyebrows = raise\_left + raise\_right;$

where *raise_left* and *raise_right* are defined, respectively, as:

$raise\_left = \{fap31 = 50, fap33 = 100, fap35 = 50\}; raise\_right = \{fap32 = 50, fap34 = 100, fap36 = 50\};$

Figure 10 illustrates the resulting *raise_eyebrows* FB.
We can also increase or decrease the intensity of a single FB by using the operator '*':

$$FB' = FB * c = \{fap3 = v_1 * c, \ldots\ldots\ldots, fap69 = v_k * c\};$$

Where FB is a "facial basis" and 'c' a constant. The operator '*' multiplies each of the FAPS constituting the FB by the constant 'c'. For example if we want a raised eyebrow with greater intensity (Figure 11):

$large\_raise\_eyebrows = raise\_eyebrows * 2;$

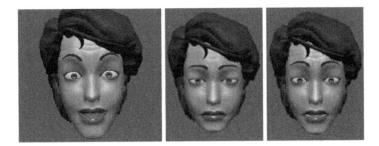

Fig. 12. The combination of "surprise" FD (left) and "sadness" FD (centre) produces the "worried" facial display (right)

10.2 Facial Displays

A facial display (FD) corresponds to a facial expression. Every FD is made up of one or more FB's:

$$FD = FB_1 + FB_2 + FB_3 + \ldots\ldots + FB_n;$$

We can define the 'surprise' facial display in this way:

$surprise = raise\_eyebrows + raise\_lids + open\_mouth;$

We can also define an FD as a linear combination of two or more (already) defined facial displays using the '+' and '*' operators. For example we can define the "worried" facial display as a combination of "surprise" (slightly decreased) and "sadness" facial displays (Figure 12):

$worried = (surprise * 0.7) + sadness;$

11   State of the Art

In the construction of embodied agents capable of expressive and communicative behaviors, an important step is to reproduce affective and conversational facial expressions on synthetic faces [2,6,5,17,18,28,15]. For example, REA, the real estate agent [5], is an interactive agent able to converse with a user in real-time. REA exhibits refined interactional behaviors such as gestures for feedback or turn-taking functions. Cassell and Stone [7] designed a multi-modal manager whose role is to supervise the distribution of behaviors across the several channels (verbal, head, hand, face, body and gaze). BEAT [8] is a toolkit to synchronize verbal and nonverbal behaviors. Cosmo [17] is a pedagogical agent particularly keen on space deixis and on emotional behavior: a mapping between pedagogical speech acts and emotional behavior is created by applying Elliott's theory [13]. Ball and Breese [2] apply bayesian networks to link emotions and personality to (verbal and non-verbal) behaviors of their agents. André et al. [1] developed a rule-based system implementing dialogs between lifelike characters with different personality traits (extroversion and agreableness). Marsella et al. [19] developed an interactive drama generator, in which the behaviors of the characters are consistent with their emotional state and individuality.

12 Conclusion

In this chapter we have presented our work toward the creation of ECAs. We have integrated in our system some aspects of non-verbal communication. The set of communicative functions we are considering are clustered depending on the type of information they provide: information on the speaker's belief, intention, affect and also on the speaker's cognitive state. To each of these functions corresponds a signal in the form of facial expression, gaze behavior, head movement. Working at the level of communicative function rather than at the signal level allows us to concentrate on the type of information a face would communicate as well as to be independent of the way a communicative function gets instantiated as a signal.

A language has been established to define these signals. In this current work we are concentrating only on "prototype" communicative functions in the sense that we have defined a correspondence between the meaning and the signal associated to a communicative function without any information regarding the speaker's identity. Identity is the aggregation of several components such as culture, gender, age, profession, physical state, personality. These aspects intervene in the selection of appropriate signals to display the information to convey and their expressivity. Indeed culture could vary the allowed amount of gaze toward our interlocutor, the display or not of a given emotion; age is a determinant for the selection of gesture; a young child do not have a large variety of communicative gesture; gender may affect the amount of gaze toward our conversation partner... Thus, we need to define a formalism that would integrate identity aspects into the creation of ECAs. This is left for future research.

13 Acknowledgement

We are grateful to Isabella Poggi and Fiorella de Rosis for their valuable help. We greatly thank Elisabetta Bevacqua for developing the lip shape model for speech.

References

1. E. Andre, T. Rist, S. van Mulken, M. Klesen, and S. Baldes. The automated design of believable dialogues for animated presentation teams. In S. Prevost J. Cassell, J. Sullivan and E. Churchill, editors, *Embodied Conversational Characters*. MIT-press, Cambridge, MA, 2000. 315

2. G. Ball and J. Breese. Emotion and personality in a conversational agent. In S. Prevost J. Cassell, J. Sullivan and E. Churchill, editors, *Embodied Conversational Characters*. MITpress, Cambridge, MA, 2000. 314, 314

3. M.S. Bartlett, J.C. Hager, P. Ekman, and T.J. Sejnowski. Measuring facial expressions by computer image analysis. *Psychophysiology*, 36(2):253–263, 1999. 306

4. A.W. Black, P. Taylor, R. Caley, and R. Clark. Festival. http://www.cstr.ed.ac.uk/projects/festival/. 303, 303, 305, 305

5. J. Cassell, J. Bickmore, M. Billinghurst, L. Campbell, K. Chang, H. Vilhjálmsson, and H. Yan. Embodiment in conversational interfaces: Rea. In *CHI'99*, pages 520–527, Pittsburgh, PA, 1999. 314, 314

6. J. Cassell, C. Pelachaud, N.I. Badler, M. Steedman, B. Achorn, T. Becket, B. Douville, S. Prevost, and M. Stone. Animated conversation: Rule-based generation of facial expression, gesture and spoken intonation for multiple conversational agents. In *Computer Graphics Proceedings, Annual Conference Series*, pages 413–420. ACM SIGGRAPH, 1994. 308, 314

7. J. Cassell and M. Stone. Living hand and mouth. Psychological theories about speech and gestures in interactive dialogue systems. In *AAAI99 Fall Symposium on Psychological Models of Communication in Collaborative Systems*, 1999. 314

8. J. Cassell, H. Vilhjálmsson, and T. Bickmore. BEAT : the Behavior Expression Animation Toolkit. In *Computer Graphics Proceedings, Annual Conference Series*. ACM SIGGRAPH, 2001. 308, 314

9. W.S. Condon and W.D. Osgton. Speech and body motion synchrony of the speaker-hearer. In D.H. Horton and J.J. Jenkins, editors, *The Perception of Language*, pages 150–184. Academic Press, 1971. 300

10. N. DeCarolis, V. Carofiglio, and C. Pelachaud. From discourse plans to believable behavior generation. In *International Natural Language Generation Conference*, New-York, 1-3 July 2002. 302, 305

11. P. Doenges, T.K Capin, F. Lavagetto, J. Ostermann, I.S. Pandzic, and E. Petajan. MPEG-4: Audio/video and synthetic graphics/audio for real-time, interactive media delivery, signal processing. *Image Communications Journal*, 9(4):433–463, 1997. 311

12. P. Ekman. About brows: Emotional and conversational signals. In M. von Cranach, K. Foppa, W. Lepenies, and D. Ploog, editors, *Human ethology: Claims and limits of a new discipline: contributions to the Colloquium*, pages 169–248. Cambridge University Press, Cambridge, England; New-York, 1979. 305, 311

13. C. Elliott. *An Affective Reasoner: A process model of emotions in a multiagent system*. PhD thesis, Northwestern University, The Institute for the Learning Sciences, 1992. Technical Report No. 32. 314

14. I.A. Essa and A. Pentland. A vision system for observing and extracting facial action parameters. *Proceedings of Computer Vision and Pattern Recognition (CVPR 94)*, pages 76–83, 1994. 306, 306

15. W.L. Johnson, J.W. Rickel, and J.C. Lester. Animated pedagogical agents: Face-to-face interaction in interactive learning environments. *To appear in International Journal of Artificial Intelligence in Education*, 2000. 314

16. A. Kendon. Movement coordination in social interaction: Some examples described. In S. Weitz, editor, *Nonverbal Communication*. Oxford University Press, 1974. 300

17. J.C. Lester, S.G. Stuart, C.B. Callaway, J.L. Voerman, and P.J. Fitzgerald. Deictic and emotive communication in animated pedagogical agents. In S. Prevost J. Cassell, J. Sullivan and E. Churchill, editors, *Embodied Conversational Characters*. MITpress, Cambridge, MA, 2000. 314, 314

18. M. Lundeberg and J. Beskow. Developing a 3D-agent for the August dialogue system. In *Proceedings of the ESCA Workshop on Audio-Visual Speech Processing*, Santa Cruz, USA, 1999. 314

19. S. Marsella, W.L. Johnson, and K. LaBore. Interactive pedagogical drama. In *Proceedings of the 4th International Conference on Autonomous Agents*, pages 301–308, Barcelona, Spain, June 2000. 315

20. A. Ortony. On making believable emotional agents believable. In R. Trappl and P. Petta, editors, *Emotions in humans and artifacts*. MIT Press, Cambridge, MA, in press. 310, 310

21. J. Ostermann. Animation of synthetic faces in MPEG-4. In *Computer Animation'98*, pages 49–51, Philadelphia, USA, June 1998. 311

22. A. Paradiso and M. L'Abbate. A model for the generation and combination of emotional expressions. In *Multimodal Communication and Context in Embodied Agents, Proceedings of the AA'01 workshop*, Montreal, Canada, May 2001. 312

23. C. Pelachaud. Visual text-to-speech. In Igor S. Pandzic and Robert Forchheimer, editors, *MPEG4 Facial Animation - The standard, implementations and applications*. John Wiley & Sons, to appear. 311, 311, 312

24. C. Pelachaud, N.I. Badler, and M. Steedman. Generating facial expressions for speech. *Cognitive Science*, 20(1):1–46, January-March 1996. 308

25. C. Pelachaud, V. Carofiglio, B. De Carolis, F. de Rosis, and I. Poggi. Embodied contextual agent in information delivering application. In *First International Joint Conference on Autonomous Agents & Multi-Agent Systems (AAMAS)*, Bologna, Italy, July 2002. 302, 302

26. I. Poggi. Mind markers. In N. Trigo M. Rector, I. Poggi, editor, *Gestures. Meaning and use*. University Fernando Pessoa Press, Oporto, Portugal, 2002. 301

27. I. Poggi and C. Pelachaud. Facial performative in a conversational system. In S. Prevost J. Cassell, J. Sullivan and E. Churchill, editors, *Embodied Conversational Characters*. MITpress, Cambridge, MA, 2000. 301, 301, 309, 309

28. I. Poggi, C. Pelachaud, and F. de Rosis. Eye communication in a conversational 3D synthetic agent. *AI Communications*, 13(3):169–181, 2000. 314

29. T. Rist and M. Schmitt. Applying socio-psychological concepts of cognitive consistency to negotiation dialog scenarios with embodied conversational characters. In R. Aylett and D. Canamero, editors, *Animating Expressive Characters for Social Interactions*, Advances in Consciousness Research Series. John Benjamins, London, Avril 2002. 302

30. A.E. Scheflen. The significance of posture in communication systems. *Psychiatry*, 27, 1964. 300

The Future of Agent Communication*

Munindar P. Singh

Department of Computer Science
North Carolina State University
Raleigh, NC 27695-7535, USA

singh@ncsu.edu

Abstract. This short note discusses trends in computing environments where agent communication will have the most value. The main emerging trend in computing is toward openness, that is, toward large systems with dynamically changing, autonomous, heterogeneous components. This trend speaks the end of architecture in the traditional sense. More importantly, it emphasizes on declaratively specified interactions, that is, arms-length relationships, among independent components. Agents and multiagent systems provide key abstractions for computing in open settings. In particular, agent communications will be a key means for structuring distributed computations.

1 Open Environments

Modern information systems can be large and open. The term *open* implies that the components involved are autonomous and heterogeneous, and system configurations change dynamically.

Often, we would not be interested in building an information system that was open *per se*, because often the member components of a system might be constrained in various ways. However, this system would still have to deal with the rest of the world, which would remain open. For example, a company might develop an enterprise integration system that is wholly within the enterprise. Yet, this system would have to deal with external parties, for example, to handle supply and production chains. In other words, the system would still need to function in an open environment. For this reason, it is helpful to think in terms of such environments. We now review some of the key characteristics of open information environments.

Let's begin with a review of the concepts of autonomy, heterogeneity, and dynamism as they relate to open information environments. A simple way to understand and distinguish these concepts is to associate them with the independence of users, designers, and administrators, respectively.

1.1 Autonomy

Autonomy means that the components in an environment function solely under their own control. Imagine dealing with an e-commerce site. It may or may not add or remove

---

* This work was supported by the National Science Foundation under grant DST-0139037.

M.-P. Huget (Ed.): Communications in Multiagent Systems, LNAI 2650, pp. 318–322, 2003.

some items from its catalog. It may or may not even deliver the goods it promised. Of course, one might seek legal recourse if a contract is violated. In fact, the autonomy of the components is the reason that contracts and compliance are so important for open environments.

Simply put, components are autonomous because they reflect the autonomy of the human and corporate interests that they represent. In other words, there are sociopolitical reasons for autonomy. Resources are owned and controlled by autonomous entities and that is why they behave autonomously.

There are also technical reasons for autonomy. The simplest one is that a component that behaves unexpectedly may be doing so because of error, that is, a mistaken requirement or a faulty implementation. A more subtle reason is that sometimes components are designed so as to be externally opaque in certain respects. For example, a well-encapsulated data structure would often not expose its internal structures. To someone who cannot see the internal structures, the behavior will be uncontrollable. A major practical example of this occurs in legacy enterprise systems wherein its database systems might be designed to unilaterally (based on internal considerations) decide whether to allow a transaction to complete. To other components, their decision on whether a transaction may complete or not is purely autonomous. Lastly, certain instances of autonomy reflect the possibility of errors. For example, if a file system can fail, a Web site on which you submit a form may fail to record your changes, thus appearing to have unilaterally decided to discard your completed form.

A consequence of autonomy is that updates can occur only under local control. In other words, you can request another party to do something, but you cannot force them to do it. This simple point illustrates a limitation of object-oriented computing. We can invoke methods on objects and if we have the handle for an object, the object performs the method so invoked. By contrast, for open environments, we need another layer of reasoning so that a component that is requested to perform a method may decide whether or not to accept the request.

1.2 Heterogeneity

Heterogeneity means that the various components of a given system are different in their design and construction. Just as for autonomy, there are both sociopolitical and technical reasons for heterogeneity. Component designers and architects might wish to construct their components in different ways, for example, to satisfy different performance requirements. Often, the causes can be historical: components fielded today may have arisen out of legacy systems that were initially constructed for different narrow uses, but eventually expanded in their scopes to participate in the same system.

Heterogeneity can cause complications for the functioning of a component, because it means that less can be assumed about the other components with which it interacts. However, there is an excellent reason why heterogeneity emerges and should be allowed to persist. To remove heterogeneity would involve redesigning and reimplementing the various components to an integrated standard. Even if the different designers are willing to bear the associated costs, removing heterogeneity is difficult, because doing so assumes that we can come up with a conceptually integrated design. However, integration is not easy to achieve and, when achieved, is fragile. A conceptually integrated system will tend to be unreliable. Most importantly, as the components evolve because of changing local requirements, we would have to keep reintegrating them.

Therefore, it is practically more reasonable to let the components be heterogeneous, but to impose various kinds of weak requirements on their interactions. After all, this is the reason why we have standardized protocols, such as TCP/IP and HTTP, at the lower layers of distributed systems.

1.3 Dynamism

Components change dynamically in their architecture and implementation, behavior, and interactions. Autonomy and heterogeneity mean that there are few constraints on the behavior and architecture of the participants of open environments. However, open environments are also dynamic in another main respect. Their components may change their behavior because of how they happen to be configured. They may also join or leave an open environment at whim.

Moreover, an open environment need not be all amorphous and would contain additional structures, which can be thought of as communities. A large-scale open system would of necessity be designed so as to accommodate the arrival, departure, and the temporary or permanent absence of its components. So would the communities that mark out parts of it.

It is convenient to think of dynamism as a reflection of the independence of the administrators of the given component as well the administrators of the components and the communities in which they participate. However, in general, human administrators may be involved only indirectly, for example, when some components elect a leader in a distributed community or jointly decide to introduce or remove a member.

2 Agents

Open environments pose significant technical challenges. In particular, we must develop approaches that can cope with the scale of the number of participants, respect their autonomy and accommodate their heterogeneity, while maintaining coordination. Specifically, because of the scale, we cannot count on knowing all the available resources in terms of their functionality, reliability, trustworthiness, and so on.

2.1 Locality

As a consequence of their autonomy and heterogeneity, the components must be treated in a *local* manner. In other words, each component must locally decide how to proceed in its interactions with others. This means that components that are able to function in open environments are ideally modeled as agents.

The challenges of open environments described above entail that significant technical obstacles must be overcome in discovering the required components, deciding how to engage them in meaningful interactions, monitoring the interactions, and checking their compliance with any contracts. Clearly, some level of global information is essential for ensuring that the different parties are able to resolve the above challenges.

Notice that global information does not mean that it is gathered and managed centrally, just that one party may need to assemble information about others and about events it cannot directly observe. Still, locality is in tension with assembling global information.

2.2   Interactions

Global information may be required for overcoming the above obstacles. But it comes at a price. The presence of global information creates the possibilities of inconsistencies and causes potential difficulty for maintenance. Consequently, the practical way to resolve this tension is to ensure that, whereas the components in an open environment may have some interdependencies, such interdependencies would be few and minimal—at least that is what a good design would require.

In other words, we would create "arms-length relationships" between the various parties consisting of simple or narrow interaction protocols, thereby eliminating any unnecessary dependencies. Indeed, eliminating extraneous dependencies and minimizing them in general is a major architectural principle for open environments. It is a powerful argument to design for and preserve the autonomy and heterogeneity of the various components—that is, for promoting interoperation and avoiding integration.

2.3   Consistency

Whereas consistency is desirable, in practical settings, it is often appropriate to relax the constraints among the various components. Thus, global information is obtained or aggregated only when needed. More importantly, it is often acceptable to allow inconsistencies to emerge provided they can be corrected quickly enough (depending, of course, on the specific application at hand). The corrective actions in many cases will have a global basis but can be applied locally. For example, an e-commerce transaction may complete correctly only if the goods are received by the purchaser and the payment is received by the vendor. It would be nearly impossible to synchronize these events perfectly in a distributed system, but it is possible to use a reliable payment mechanism such as a credit card and a reliable delivery service. If the vendor fails to ship because of an unexpected shortfall, it can cancel the debit to the credit card.

3   Communications

The foregoing discussion did not refer to communications. Parties who live and function in a shared environment will of necessity interact. However, all interactions are not communications, although they may be interpreted communicatively. I define communications as those interactions that preserve the autonomy and heterogeneity of the parties involved. For example, if I delete your file or push you, we interact, but possibly in a forced manner—you (and possibly I) may have no options but to interact. However, if I tell you that it is rainy, you have an option to interpret it as you please. The latter is then a communication. Communications enable the local control and perspective of the participants, emphasize their voluntary interactions, and provide a means for them to negotiate, for example, the flexible requirements of consistency.

Because of the above properties, agent communications provide the correct means to ensure interoperation in an open environment. Communicating agents can be naturally autonomous and heterogeneous, and can dynamically alter their involvement in various conversations. Traditional approaches to communication fail to accommodate the openness of such systems. Even as flexibility is being improved at some levels, rigidity still dominates. For example, the move to XML for information exchange in business applications and processes has liberated the syntax of communications from ad hoc proprietary notations. However, current architectures remain over-constrained in terms of the semantics and pragmatics (roughly, meaning and usage) of the information exchanged. Agent communications avoid the above problems and provide a natural locus for flexible interaction.

The biggest challenge for research into agent communications is how to combine rigor with meaning. The obvious semantics for agent communication languages from an artificial intelligence perspective involve unverifiable constructs such as beliefs and intentions. The obvious semantics from a distributed computing perspective involve stimuli and responses defined in terms of meaningless tokens. The correct approach would be define meanings that respects the social structure of multiagent systems. Recent work by agent theorists, for example, as described in several chapters in this volume, seems to finally have cracked this problem, at least at a conceptual level.

We are seeing a greater level of technical rigor and robustness while enriched semantics are being developed. This work includes work on flexible protocol specification and execution. Specific techniques include formal methods extending those used for traditional network and distributed computing protocols, techniques geared toward new multiagent applications such as Web service composition and enactment, and decidedly multiagent approaches based on commitments, for example, argumentation and dialogue games.

4   Conclusions

We motivated communication based on the expansion of openness in information environments. However, this expansion applies up and down the entire protocol stack. At each layer, there is value by increasing the flexibility of designs by making the architecture less restrictive. For this reason, I believe the metaphor of agents will find value elsewhere in distributed systems besides just at the application layer where most current work is concentrated. Indeed, this is already happening. More importantly, agent communications will influence the design of loosely coupled architectures in those settings, leading to richer varieties of protocols than presently considered.

As agents expand further into information applications and make inroads into other layers of distributed systems, their strength derives from their ability to interact flexibly, to engage each other meaningfully, to monitor compliance, and to engender trust. The agents community has only to be careful not to attempt to impose some of the ad hoc architectural restrictions that have plagued some traditional work on agents and agent communications. If we do so, the future for agents and agent communications in computing is rosy indeed.

Author Index

Lecture Notes in Artificial Intelligence (LNAI)

Lecture Notes in Computer Science